SIR ROBERT WALPOLE

By The Same Author

ROBERT WALPOLE AS SECRETARY-AT-WAR

SIR ROBERT WALPOLE

THE MAKING OF A STATESMAN

———

BY J. H. PLUMB

LONDON

THE CRESSET PRESS

1956

First published in March 1956 by the Cresset Press
11 Fitzroy Square, London, W1
2nd Impression May 1957
Printed in Great Britain by the Shenval Press Ltd
London, Hertford and Harlow

TO

THE MARQUESS AND MARCHIONESS OF CHOLMONDELEY

IN GRATITUDE

CONTENTS

ILLUSTRATIONS

A NOTE ON DATES

Unless otherwise stated all dates in this book are Old Style, except that 1 January, not 25 March, is taken as the beginning of the new year.

INTRODUCTION

THERE HAS been no full detailed life of Sir Robert Walpole since Archdeacon Coxe published in 1798 his *Memoirs of the Life and Administration of Sir Robert Walpole, Earl of Orford*. It is an excellent book by a long neglected historian of real distinction. In those spacious days historians could publish in full the documentary evidence upon which their work was based. In the case of Coxe this has proved of inestimable value for many of the collections to which he had access have been dispersed and can no longer be traced. Fortunately much remains. As I went from country house to country house, following in Coxe's footsteps, I found his neat grey cardboard folders, often untouched since he first sorted the papers, and my admiration for his scholarly care steadily increased. There was little he missed of value within the limits of his own inquiry. But naturally enough he did not ask questions about Sir Robert and his contemporaries that a modern historian would ask and in consequence he neglected, as irrelevant, material of absorbing interest. To the owners of those manuscripts I am deeply indebted both for access to their papers and for much kindness and hospitality.

My greatest debt is to the Marquess and Marchioness of Cholmondeley. They deposited Sir Robert Walpole's papers for me at the University Library of Cambridge. The Provost and Fellows of King's College, by providing funds which enabled Mr A. G. Chinnery to sort and index the collection, shortened my labours by years. This deposit was one of many kindnesses which Lord and Lady Cholmondeley have shown me in the writing of this book. I could never have appreciated fully the outstanding quality of Sir Robert's artistic judgment had I not paid many visits to Houghton which they preserve with such loving care.

INTRODUCTION

I met with similar generosity in many places. I am particularly indebted to the Duke of Portland, the Duke of Marlborough, the Dowager Marchioness of Bristol, the Marquess Townshend, the Earl Stanhope, the Earl of Harrowby, the Earl of Lovelace, Viscount Sandon, Lady Salmond, Lord Walpole, Lord Sandys, Lord Brabourne, Sir Charles Howard, Sir Hughe Knatchbull-Hugessen, Mr R. W. Ketton-Cremer, Mr W. S. Lewis and the Trustees of the Chatsworth Settlement for giving me access to their papers and permission to quote from them. Professor Robert Halsband has kindly drawn my attention to a number of references. Mr Ketton-Cremer has put his immense knowledge of Norfolk history at my disposal and saved me from many errors. The advice of Sir Lewis Namier, Mr John Hayward and Dr J. P. Kenyon has been invaluable. Mr Frank Fenton has assisted me with the index for which I am most grateful. I am indebted, too, to the patience and kindness of many librarians and archivists, particularly those at the University Library, Cambridge, the British Museum and the Record Offices of Berkshire, Essex, Hertfordshire, Northamptonshire, Staffordshire and West Suffolk.

Even so my list of obligations is not complete. The Master and Fellows of Christ's College and the Leverhulme Trustees made it possible for me to take a year's leave of absence without which this life of Walpole could not have been written. I am very grateful.

2

MY INTEREST in Sir Robert Walpole was first roused by sitting beneath his picture, which hangs over the High Table at King's, during many silent dinners as a junior Fellow. I began to read about him and, as I read, the inadequacy of what had been written about him was painfully apparent. Both the man and his works had been forced into the pattern of constitutional development which nineteenth-century historians imposed on the seventeenth and eighteenth centuries. So in the two volumes of this work I have attempted to reconstruct

both Sir Robert's character and his politics as he and his contemporaries viewed them. The more I have come to know
this great man, the stronger has my admiration grown. His
imperfections were many and glaring. He loved money; he
loved power; he enjoyed adulation and hated criticism. But
in everything that he did he was richly varied and intensely
human. And he was given less to humbug than the majority
of this country's statesmen. Vulgar, coarse, ostentatious he
might be, yet his aesthetic judgment remains incomparably
good—unrivalled, indeed, amongst prime ministers. Only
Gladstone or Burleigh have equalled his capacity for the
steady, implacable dispatch of vast quantities of highly technical business. Even at the height of the Excise Crisis he
found time to copy out a number of medieval charters that
related to the Customs, but unlike Gladstone and Burleigh he
never enjoyed good health; throughout his career he suffered
constant and severe attacks of gravel, stone and fever.

His powers of concentration were of the highest, and they
were backed by an obstinate will, soaring ambition, a greedy
love of power, for he was a man utterly confident of his
capacity to rule.

Yet he had one rarer, and, perhaps, more important gift.
He had a heightened awareness both of the world and of
men. From this sprang both his exquisite taste and his finesse
in human relations. He could live outside his own character.
He possessed *empathy*, the quality to get, as it were, into the
skin of other human beings, to feel with them; an intuitive
quality which, of course, could err, but more often brilliantly
clarified a complex human situation. His power over Queen
Caroline and George II was derived from his capacity to interpret correctly their true feeling for each other; he was
never deceived by the outward vagaries of their behaviour.
A man with less insight into the human heart would have
failed to understand that strange and tortured relationship.
It was this same awareness, this outward-going quality of his
temperament, that brought out his love of the visible world,
his life-long delight in painting, in fine furniture and buildings,

in all that art or craft could render beautiful. Houghton, his great Norfolk house, with its furniture and pictures, was one of the supreme artistic creations of the eighteenth century. There was no arid aestheticism about him; his taste glowed with warmth. Vigorous and grand it was an expression of his own rich personality: his eye for proportion in a building or a chair was complementary to his certainty of judgment in affairs.

Yet he was a coarse man. All of his contemporaries, friends as well as enemies, stress the coarseness of his manners and language. 'Inelegant in his manners, loose in his morals,' wrote Chesterfield, 'he had a coarse, strong wit, which he was too free of for a man in his station.' He was frequently regarded as obscene in an age when men and women were not prudes. Although less of a handicap, perhaps, in the Augustan age than it might have been in later times, such grossness of language and manner must have been as much a hindrance in his youth as it was an advantage when he had achieved eminence. Then, it added to his humanity, gave him an air of ease and approachability and so soothed the irritations which the possession of power engenders in subordinate men.

As a young man coarseness of manner was not his only disadvantage. The late seventeenth century was somewhat less rigid in its social distinctions than the eighteenth century was to become, but it was rigid enough. Walpole lacked important connections; apart from Townshend he was not related, except distantly, to any member of the aristocracy.[1] His lack of influence doubtless underlined the roughness of his manner and conversation. His rise to power was due entirely to his own exceptional abilities; but without a doubt it was a more arduous struggle than it would have been had he been born in the heart of aristocratic society.

[1] His uncle, Horatio the elder, was married to the daughter of Thomas Osborne, Duke of Leeds (Danby), but this was little help as Walpole and his uncle differed about politics (and in any case Danby was a spent force in politics). On the other hand Townshend's first wife was the daughter of Lord Pelham, a most valuable connection.

Yet these difficulties of temperament and birth were never considerable obstacles to success. If on both counts he was much more fortunate than he might have been, the real luck of his destiny was to have been born when he was. It was a world fitting to his genius. Either through a lack of interest or through downright inability, Walpole was incapable of making sound political judgments about widespread public reactions. His career is a record of ineptitude in this respect—Wood's Halfpence, the Excise Scheme, the Porteous Riots, the Spanish War. Time and time again he misjudged public opinion to an extent that would have been fatal to a nineteenth- or twentieth-century prime minister. Also he had no intuitive sense of dynamic political forces, for he held obstinately to a static view of society. His policy was never creative in the sense that Chatham's or Lloyd George's policies were creative, concerned as they were with the urgencies and aspirations of whole classes of men. Nor did he represent a moral force in politics as Gladstone did. Essentially he was an administrator, interested in order and efficiency. Fortunately, it was a time for these virtues to flourish. The early eighteenth century in England was one of those rare epochs in modern history when the attitude of classes to each other was static. There was class hatred, class envy, class fear, which would subtly influence political attitudes, but there was little or no conception that the role of classes could be altered. The strains natural to capitalist society were eased; the rhythm of rapid historical change was momentarily in suspense. It was a time when a total lack of political imagination was no handicap to the King's first minister.

On the other hand the ruling class was very small, using institutions which were exceptionally limited, both in scope and application; in consequence the whole of the political structure of England was littered with personal relationships. Nine times out of ten in all political action, human considerations loomed far larger than policy; indeed parties and political programmes are so obscured that some historians have almost denied their existence in the early eighteenth century.

Although Walpole lacked political imagination he had no rival when it came to an intuitive appreciation of particular men, and he moved with consummate ease through the tangle of loyalties, envies and frustrations of Hanoverian politics.

Singularly fortunate as he was both in his abilities and his epoch, yet these factors were not alone sufficient to secure his remarkable success. Many great and gifted statesmen, lucky too in their times, have not had the confidence, the absolute certainty of their ability to rule, without which achievement is corrupted by doubt. From the time he entered politics Walpole was grandiosely and obstinately assured that he, and he alone, was fitted to be the first servant of the King. In all ages such massive confidence is a vital factor, but in Walpole's time the more so, because, once again, of the personal nature of political society. Without the strong ties of party to bind men together, the power to dominate, to create trust, even the capacity bluntly to assume the right to rule, first drew men to him and then held them in subjection. It was as important for his triumph as his command of patronage and as instrumental in securing his majorities, for there are men, lacking it themselves, who seek the certainty of will in action.

Walpole was of his time in a deeper sense than many great men are said to be; that perhaps is why he has been so generally misunderstood; seen, outlined against his background, across the vista of time, he has appeared as the first prime minister, the founder of cabinet government, the innovator of ministerial responsibility. In such a guise he has acquired the quality of a myth. What little effect Walpole had on the development of these institutions was unpremeditated, accidental, for formalized institutions appeal mostly to men who are inept in personal relations. This distorted view of Walpole, so deeply embedded in all historical teaching and writing, makes it essential to describe the nature of the institutions through which he worked. This need is reinforced by the tact that Walpole himself belonged so completely to his age that misinterpretation of his career is almost inevitable without a knowledge of the world in which he lived. In consequence, the first chapters of this book are devoted to Walpole's time rather than to Walpole himself; but wherever possible he is kept to the fore and his attitude to his age illustrated as fully as possible from his own letters and papers.

For a somewhat similar reason this volume is devoted to the neglected part of his career—his rise to power from 1700 to 1722. Many of Walpole's attitudes both to institutions and to politics were formed in the years of bitter party strife which marked the reign of Queen Anne; others were confirmed by the grave instability to which the Hanoverian succession gave rise. These formative years have been ignored by historians, including Coxe. Most biographers present him riding to power on the crest of public demand, as the one man who could save his country from ruin after the disasters of the South Sea Bubble. How false that picture is this book, I hope, will show. Walpole became prime minister on the death of his great rival Sunderland in April 1722, not before, and in their titanic struggle for power, in which the South Sea crisis was but an incident, were forged those qualities of statesmanship which have given Robert Walpole an enduring place in English history.

BOOK ONE

ROBERT WALPOLE'S WORLD

CHAPTER ONE

THE CLASSES OF MEN

IN THE early eighteenth century English politics were influenced by the smallness of the population, by the difficulty of communication and by the prevalence of disease. People were sparsely spread over the land: outside London, which contained perhaps an eighth of the population, the majority lived in tiny hamlets and small country towns no bigger than present-day villages. The squires, yeomen and the few professional men of the neighbourhood—attorneys, stewards, doctors—came together at the markets and fairs to gossip and grumble. They saw events in personal terms; supported or opposed the election of a mayor or Member of Parliament because they supported or opposed his family. Ancient wrongs and ancient loyalties as much as conviction often led men to adopt the opprobrious title of whig or tory. Sometimes even the hatred of one part of a county for another—East and West Sussex, for example—could result in a bitter conflict of opinion. The number of men in any county with political influence being very small, they all knew each other intimately and in consequence the personal factor in politics was strengthened. Often there was a little oligarchy of power rooted in a provincial town and its neighbouring countryside, but such a group was often isolated and this consequently led to the fragmentation of politics and inhibited the effectiveness of propaganda, confining it to race meetings and quarter sessions.

These neighbourhoods—that admirable eighteenth-century term which describes exactly the basic unit of society and politics—were joined together by wide green roads which sometimes followed the straight line of an old Roman road or prehistoric trackway, but more often meandered haphazardly up hill and down dale, threading their way through the

3

great open fields. Along them lumbered coaches, waggons and strings of pack-horses; in summer movement was easy, but for the rest of the year always difficult and often dangerous. At St Ives, wrote Celia Fiennes, 'the road was so full of holes and quick sands I durst not venture' and later in her journey, on the way to Leicester, she found 'very good land but very deep bad roads . . . being full of sloughs, clay deep way, that I was neer 11 hours going but 25 mile.'[1] Twice she was nearly drowned, a fate which Wesley only just escaped on the Great North Road. Travel was so difficult that business as well as social and political life was circumscribed; within a limited area there was great activity, but men hesitated to leave their 'country' unless necessity impelled them. This did much to prevent the formation of closely-knit political parties at a time when the governing classes of the nation were strongly divided on fundamental principles and particular issues. The absence of parties organized on a national basis consolidated political power in the hands of those actively engaged at the centre and enabled them to take decisions without over-much consideration of public opinion. The effect was to give greater pliability to political leadership often at the expense of principle. The smallness of the population and its isolation had much to do with the intensely personal nature of English politics in the Augustan age; this is well known and hardly needs stressing, but the prevalence of disease is a factor more generally ignored or misunderstood.

The placid exteriors of Georgian houses, the well-kept lawns, the restfully contrived vistas, the distant folly and unruffled lake breed of themselves a sense of expansive well being, of *luxe, calme et volupté*. The hacking coughs, the violent fevers, bloody remedies and desperate deaths are banished and forgotten. Forgotten, too, that longing for the summer and that fear of winter which haunted men and women of those days.

'Since I wrote last to your Lordship I have been under a

[1] C. Morris (ed.), *The Journeys of Celia Fiennes*, 159, 162.

little severe discipline of blisters behind my ears, and other medicinal applications for a swell'd face, attended with a slight fever', wrote Sir Thomas Cave to his brother-in-law Earl Verney. 'Could I but perswade the weather to be a little on the summer establishment, I am hopes my cough would also leave me which is near of kin to the weather glass . . . Poor Peggy too has frequent returns of her illness . . . she would receive benefit too, if the old fashioned thing called summer would make its appearance.'[1]

Sir Thomas Cave's longing for the warmth of the sun is echoed in writer after writer, year in year out, for sickness had a greater hold on life than now. Walpole was frequently and violently ill and at times his career was nearly jeopardized by his prostration. Lord Egmont in 1732 thought that it was amazing that Walpole could undertake the burden of his office, considering his poor state of health throughout his life.[2] As with illness, so with death; suddenly it would strike; every family, rich or poor, was used to its visitation. But for the death of his brother, struck down in his prime, Walpole would have entered either the Church or the Army. Within eighteen months of each other Walpole's greatest rivals— Stanhope and Sunderland—dropped dead, thereby clearing his way to power. The grip of influence, the strength of a faction could suddenly be weakened by unexpected death. As kings and ministers aged, politicians were led to gamble on their futures; speculations in mortality were made by whigs and tories, by men in and out of office, for death was a lottery, breeding anxiety, but giving an edge to appetite, heightening the light and darkening the shade of the passing years.

These are general factors touching all classes and all politicians great and small. They influenced little the distribution of political power which was controlled by wealth and birth.

[1] Margaret Maria Lady Verney (ed.), *The Verney Letters of the Eighteenth Century*, 1717 to 1799, II, 193.
[2] BM *Add MSS* 47117 fo. 333.

SOCIAL AND POLITICAL life was dominated by the aristocracy. It was a small caste, closely inter-related and very conscious of its special privileges, but freer in its composition
than most of the nobilities of Europe. It was saved from rigid-
ity by two factors. The sons of peers became commoners and
there were no social barriers to their economic activities in
the earlier years of the century. Lord Townshend's uncle,
Horatio, for example, was a City merchant. And no stigma
was attached to a nobleman's marrying the wealthy daughter
of a merchant; indeed such heiresses were much sought after.
The great wealth of the Dukes of Bedford came in part from
the wise marriage arranged for the young Marquess of Tavistock in 1695 to Elizabeth Howland, a London merchant's
daughter, and granddaughter of Sir Josiah Child, the merchant, and Chairman of the East India Company. By Anne's
reign the Bedfords had developed wet and dry docks at Rother-
hithe and the *Streatham* was trading for them with the Indies.[1]

The broad base of the nobility's power rested on their
estates which varied greatly but were mostly large. The
Dukes of Newcastle owned considerable lands in thirteen
counties and enjoyed a rent-roll of over thirty thousand a
year. The Dukes of Bedford were equally rich; there were few
acres of the Vale of Berkeley which did not belong to its Earl.
Those disasters of human life to which the eighteenth century
was so prone—early death and failure of heirs—tended
through the close intermarriage of noble families to make
these estates ever larger. But land had ceased to be the sole
source of their wealth for they were quick to seize the opportunities which the growing commercial prosperity of the
country afforded.

They invested in Government securities; they dabbled in
the East India Companies, in building projects, in mines, in
real estate, in water works, in shipping and shipbuilding. In

[1] A. Goodwin (ed.), *The European Nobility in the Eighteenth Century:* Gladys
Scott Thomson, *Life in a Noble Household,* 391–5.

that bustling world of aggressive commercial enterprise their money was everywhere to be found. When the Earl of Sunderland dropped dead in 1722 he had about seventy-five thousand invested in stocks and shares.[1] Harley Street, Wimpole Street and Mortimer Street are witnesses of the land speculation and building promotion of Robert Harley, Earl of Oxford. Cavendish Square was a joint venture of Lords Dartmouth, Carnarvon, Harcourt, Bingley, Bathhurst and Castleton.[2] The Dukes of Chandos and Devonshire with the Earl of Nottingham supported the York Building Waterworks Company against the New River Company in which the 'proud' Duke of Somerset, Queen Anne's Master of the Horse, was heavily engaged.[3] The speculations of the Duke of Chandos were astonishingly varied. He undertook large building projects in London, Bath and Bridgwater; he invested in oyster fishery, pipe clay, coal, copper and alum mines; he dabbled in land in New York State; he promoted a glass works, a soap factory and a distillery; he speculated in diamonds and silver; he invested in every stock and share that was quoted on the Exchange. He admitted having lost £700,000 of his profits in the South Sea Bubble and £125,000 in the Africa Company: his unit of investment in stocks at times was the princely sum of £50,000.[4] True enough Chandos was something of a portent to his own generation—'a bubble to every project' as Onslow called him, but he was symptomatic of the way the aristocracy were using their wealth, and also of the methods many of them were using to make money.

Chandos had become a rich man through office; he was Paymaster-General during Marlborough's wars. This was the most lucrative place which could fall to a politician's lot, but there were many others which brought enduring wealth to their holders. Daniel Finch, second Earl of Nottingham, was

[1] *Blenheim MSS.* D. II. 3.
[2] C. H. Collins Baker and Muriel I. Baker, *The Life and Circumstances of James Brydges, First Duke of Chandos*, 265 *et seq.*
[3] *Ibid.*, 291.
[4] *Ibid.*, 206-13; 337-64.

Secretary of State for just over six years (March 1689–November 1693: May 1702–May 1704) and he made a clear profit of over £50,000 on the office.[1] Smaller places brought in less but in 1726 a quarter of the active peerage held offices of administrative importance either in the Government or about the Court; most of the rest were in the hands of their dependants or relations. Land, speculation, place, these were the sources of the nobility's wealth; the variety of their economic enterprise aroused a keen interest in many aristocrats in the commercial destiny of their country and lifted their eyes beyond the confines of their own broad acres. In a similar way the active pursuit of office, both for gain and for glory, led them into the hard routine of administration as well as politics, which in its turn gave this sheltered and privileged class of men a core of social purpose.

There were very few aristocrats—perhaps never more than about a hundred and fifty really active ones, including the few Scottish noblemen who played a part in English political and social life. They were rich, and getting in general richer; they dominated the Court and the social life of London. They were educated to consider themselves a separate order of society. Such wealth, security and privilege could lead to excess, amounting at times to an open disregard for the law. In 1692 Lord Lincoln's servants battered to death a young man named Webb because he had the impertinence to laugh at his Lordship's belly. Lord Mohun made short work of a brace of men who insulted him, only to die himself in a duel with the Duke of Hamilton. Most, however, confined their excesses to the bottle, the bed and the gaming board.[2] And, of course, there were many who lived peaceful, orderly and sober lives, devoting themselves to the business of their estates and the welfare of their dependants. Yet there were few who did not enter eagerly into the ostentatious display which had

---

[1] H. J. Habakkuk, 'Daniel Finch 2nd Earl of Nottingham: his house and estate' in *Studies in Social History* (ed. J. H. Plumb), 145 *et seq*.

[2] The footnotes of the *Complete Peerage* by Vicary Gibbs treat fully the exuberance and excess of the Augustan aristocracy.

come to be regarded as a necessary aspect of aristocratic life. This usually took the form of building country palaces and adorning them with magnificent collections of furniture and pictures. The great efflorescence of aristocratic building activity in the late seventeenth and early eighteenth centuries was due, however, to deeper motives than mere display. The country house was a symbol of greatness: not only of a man but of a family and of the social and political power which it could exercise both in the neighbourhood and in the nation at large. It was also something more—the administrative centre of a large and complex economic enterprise. The thousands of acres which were farmed or let, the minerals and mines, the vast complexity of property rights, demanded a considerable staff of bailiffs, stewards and clerks. Large houses were necessary, but these were far larger than necessity demanded. It was natural that pride should breed a competitive spirit and that the nobility's growing wealth should lead to an exuberant display. Houses became ever larger; decoration richer and more ornate; furniture more expensive; pictures more costly. Millions of pounds were poured into stone and plaster to give England a magnificent architectural heritage. The old Elizabethan manor houses were torn down and replaced by the Palladian palaces which Burlington and Kent made fashionable. They needed a setting appropriate to their splendour, and the surrounding countryside was remodelled; woods, vast lakes, artificial ruins were created by men who were building not only for themselves but for eternity. At Woburn the Duke of Bedford, confident of the destiny of his house, began plantations which could only reach maturity in the days of his great-grandchildren. And George Dodington bequeathed a handsome slice of his fortune not to his heir, George Bubb, but to the house which he was building at Eastbury; his trustees were to use £1,800 per annum from his estate until this grandiose Vanbrugh palace was completed.[1] On 6 June 1734, Sir Thomas Robinson, the garrulous son-in-law of the Earl of Carlisle, found

[1] J. Carswell, *The Old Cause*, 151.

Lord Malton busily at work building a new home at Wentworth Woodhouse.

'If in some things Lord Strafford's fell short of what I was told of it, I was very agreeably surprised in finding this place improved in all respects since I was last here infinitely beyond my expectations. What may properly be called the house is about the same length in front as Lord Tilney's (260 feet); that front towards the garden is entirely finished, being partly patch-work of the old house and partly a new building, and excepting a very fine library, little can be said in its praise, but when you come to the court front, amends will be sufficiently made to all lovers of architecture, and when finished 'twill be a stupendous fabric, infinitely superior to anything we have now in England; the front of the house and offices (exclusive of the stables) being a line of 606 feet built of the most beautiful hewn stone and the best masonry I ever saw; these offices on each side the house are entirely finished. The upright of the house will be in the same style as Lord Tilney's, only this portico will have 8 columns in front.

The hall will be 64 feet by 53 deep and 48 high, a prodigious room; on each side of it are three rooms, all six 24 high; two of them will be 36 feet square, two 26 in front and 38 deep, and two 24 in front and 36 deep. This whole front will contain 21 windows, 5 of which are now just covered in. The whole finishing will be entirely submitted to Lord Burlington, and I know of no subject's house in Europe [which] will have 7 such magnificent rooms so finely proportioned as these will be. This part of the house will be built entirely new from the foundations, and very conveniently disposed to lay it to the old house; and as Lord Tilney's has hitherto been thought so fine [a] house, as some people imagined would never have been excelled, I am very glad for the honour of Yorkshire to see a pile going forward here that will in every respect infinitely exceed it. The outworks are also large, and my Lord has a very fine command of wood and water; but none of the finishing strokes which give the beauty to the whole are yet completed.'[1]

[1] HMC, *Carlisle MSS*, 136–7.

The rivalry, the sense of competition, is implicit in every line of Robinson's letter. Yorkshire was to have the greatest private house in the land, perhaps the finest in Western Europe! It was an achievement and so it remains.

Such grandiose palaces demanded a style of living which the sovereign princes of Germany and Italy might have envied. Europe was ransacked for pictures and statuary; manuscripts, books, medals, exotic plants and birds, all that could give distinction or singularity were collected assiduously and regardless of expense. The extravagant Chandos maintained a superb collection of exotic birds. In his aviaries were 'whistling owls and flamingos from Antigua . . . blue macaws and geese; Muscovy ducks, Virginia fowls and song-birds; a Gold Coast redbird of peculiar prettiness; Barbadoes "Powises" and parakeets, an eagle and a crown bird'.[1] A large private orchestra, under Pepusch, provided him with music; his personal wants and those of his Duchess and children were attended by ninety-three household servants; the gardens of one of his houses, Cannons, employed nineteen gardeners.[2] A regiment of foreign correspondents strove to meet his needs or excite his curiosity.

'. . . From Captain Massey in Carolina came rice, kidney beans (said to grow prodigiously, like hops or vines), ananas (or pine-apples), and pickles, not to mention certain fauna—a Mexican squash, "which we take to be a little beaver", rough coated, very tame and entertaining, and flamingos. From Major Gordon in Pennsylvania came singing-birds as well as wax; a bill for £84, and hams, unfortunately full of maggots. Mr Chiswell of Virginia sent mocking-birds; Mr Stephens, of Cape Coast, a "tiger" that nearly killed one of the servants who provoked it; and Mr Ashley of the Barbados, pine-apples, cinnamon, coffee trees and berries, and "Avigator Pears". . . . Messrs Harriman of Leghorn supplied broccoli seed and fennel, "agri di cedro" . . . orange-flower water, capers, *muscatello di Castello* vinegar, preserved citron, anchovies, Lucca oil and

[1] Collins Baker and Muriel I. Baker. *Chandos*, 128.
[2] *Ibid.*, 161, 176.

olives, and evergreen-oak acorns. While from Oporto the Duke procured Lamiego hams, more appetizing, let us hope, than those from Pennsylvania, and, from Lisbon, sugar, raisins of the sun, Malagar raisins, currants, lemons, oranges, musk and water-melon seeds.' [1]

The princely Chandos may have had a little more flamboyance than his contemporaries, but he was not singular in his expensive tastes. When Walpole won his way to aristocratic power and wealth he lived with the same opulent disregard of cost; his childhood and youth, however, were spent in far bleaker circumstances.

There was one other aspect of this expensive display in which the aristocracy indulged. Younger sons could be fobbed off with a career in the Army, the Church, or even in trade, but daughters had to be married high. This could not be done cheaply. His daughters' portions cost Daniel Nottingham £52,000, as much as he spent buying his estate in Rutlandshire and nearly twice as much as he spent on his house.[2] Only the very wealthiest merchants could attempt to endow their daughters so handsomely. The effect, of course, was to bind aristocratic families in a close union of blood relationship which gave rise to a heightened sense of caste and privilege. George I's advisers wished to close the ranks of the peerage by Act of Parliament and although Walpole secured the bill's rejection the upshot was roughly the same. The Act would have allowed creations of nobility to replace extinction of title. As it happened George I and George II were so determined to protect the peerage from dilution that they ennobled very few men and the aristocracy hardly increased at all during their reigns. A highly successful lawyer, soldier or sailor might win a peerage; the politically active son of a nobleman was likely to obtain a seat in the Lords to strengthen the government, but there was little hope for anyone else unless they were prepared to spend a lifetime in politics and often a fortune as well.

[1] Collins Baker and Muriel I. Baker. *Chandos*, 185.
[2] H. J. Habakkuk, *op. cit.*

This was all a part of that general hardening of caste which took place during Walpole's lifetime. The aristocracy became increasingly aware of its special privileges and powers. In 1744 the Duke of Richmond was outraged when his daughter eloped with Henry Fox, although Fox's father had been the servant of Charles II throughout his life and died immensely rich. The letters of Chesterfield and Horace Walpole create the same impression of a deepening sense of caste, isolated by its conventions from the rest of society. These attitudes were protective devices used to secure the world of privilege, both social and political, which it enjoyed. The basis of that privilege was landed wealth and the nobility were fully conscious that this was so; by devising very strict settlements they attempted to preserve their great estates from the damage which a feckless and extravagant heir could do. These settlements were hedged about with thickets of legal restrictions and by turning the head of a great estate into a tenant for life they helped to keep intact the conglomerations of wealth which the aristocracy had amassed.[1]

And finally the aristocracy monopolized the Court. It had, of course, always done so, though in earlier centuries there were few to envy their privileged station. But riches were spreading. There were many merchants as affluent as the greatest noblemen: scores of families who had left trade for the land. Their eyes turned enviously towards the privileged world of society which Hervey and Horace Walpole have so brilliantly depicted. Few, however, were bidden into that charmed circle. And, of course, there were not many who could live as the aristocracy lived even if the privileges of birth were ignored. An outstandingly rich merchant or an occasional country gentleman of great estate might vie with the nobility's way of life but no one else. Their world became a world to adore or to hate, to emulate or to despise. This ambivalence of attitude is clearly marked in the class most

[1] H. J. Habakkuk, 'Marriage Settlements in the Eighteenth Century', *Trans. R. Hist. Soc.*, 4th Series, XXXII (1950), 15–30.

closely associated with the aristocracy in their provincial domains—the gentry.

3

'Every man now, be his fortune what it will, is to be doing something at his place, as the fashionable phrase is, and you hardly meet with anybody who, after the first compliments, does not inform you that he is in mortar and heaving of earth, the modest terms for building and gardening. One large room, a serpentine river, and a wood are become the absolute necessities of life, without which a gentleman of the smallest fortune thinks he makes no figure in his country.'[1]

Long before these words were written in the days of Walpole's father, the country gentleman had grown tired of his ancient rambling manor house. The local masons had been called in to give it a classical façade; here and there a rich squire like Sir William Fermor of Easton Neston in Northamptonshire could afford to emulate the aristocracy, demolish his old family house, and employ the most fashionable architects for his new mansion. In each county there were gentle families of ancient lineage—Rolles of Devon, Cartwrights of Northamptonshire, Musgraves of Cumberland, Napiers of Dorset, who were as rich and powerful in their neighbourhoods as many a nobleman; at times they even intermarried. The wife of Sir Roger Mostyn of Mostyn was the only daughter of the second Earl of Nottingham allowed to marry outside the peerage. On the other hand, according to family tradition, Colonel Walpole would not permit his daughter Dorothy to marry Charles, Viscount Townshend, but then the Walpoles hardly belonged to the highest circles of the country gentry.

The lesser gentry lived on a more modest scale and confined their building activities to adding a wing to the old

[1] Quoted by Dorothy Stroud, *Catalogue of the Exhibition of English Landscape Gardening*, 1951.

house, putting in new sash windows, sticking on a portico—jobs done with the aid of the local stonemason, the estate carpenter and a handbook of architectural designs. In the same way their style of life was more modest. Instead of a private orchestra Walpole's father depended on the waits from King's Lynn or the wandering fiddlers from Swaffham and Thetford. His luxuries were confined to an occasional barrel of oysters, a lobster or two, a pot of coffee or dish of tea; these and the strong red Portuguese wine, were the only extravagances which distinguished his table from that of his tenant farmers. For these homespun squires visits outside their counties were rare. They were associated in their daily life with the merchants, attorneys and prosperous yeomen. With them they gathered together over their pots of ale and pipes at the fairs and markets of the little country towns. There was far less distinction of class between these groups than between the aristocracy and the squirearchy. Country gentlemen of the middling sort were prepared to marry their daughters to local families in trade or land, and even their younger sons if an heiress was available, although they would rarely consent to the eldest sons going outside their own class. Until Robert Walpole married Catherine Shorter in 1700 most male Walpoles for well over a hundred years had married into an East Anglian family of equal standing. There was hardly a squire of any importance in Norfolk to whom the Walpoles were not distantly related. As the cousinage of the aristocracy covered the whole of England in a network of blood-relationship so the counties and neighbourhoods were covered with a similar network by the squirearchy.

The gentry's wealth was based on the land. Some of their estates they farmed for themselves; the rest was let to tenants. A thrifty squire would buy a mortgage or add to his lands by direct purchase. He might spread himself in a few luxuries as did Walpole's uncle, James Hoste of Sandringham, whose wife bullied him into buying a coach, gorgeously painted with his coat of arms, with the seats especially constructed to fit her short and dumpy person. Fine clothes, London wigs and new silver plate soon followed. Or they might buy a few tenements in the nearest town. But opportunities for investing money were very limited. The major source of their income remained the land, and was subject to the vagaries which beset it—bad harvests, plagues and equally disastrous bumper crops.

Lord Stanhope of Shelford, the father of the great Earl of Chesterfield, wrote to his cousin, James Stanhope, on 17 February 1702, from Lichfield:

'As I had no occasion for the hundred pounds when some months ago you offered to pay it me back, so I now do freely tell you that at this time necessity obliges me to ask you for it. Since my Tenants never paid my rents so ill as this last half year which puts me in a streight for money to pay off my tradesmen in this little dirty town.'

Later, still desperately short of money, Stanhope tried sterner measures.

'I have sent an attorney among my tenants,' he told his cousin when he wrote on 10 March 1702, to thank him for sending the hundred pounds, 'to force them to pay me my rents, but he finds that all their corn lyes dead upon their hands so that to seize their persons when they have no money among them will do no good.'[1]

As the eldest son of a peer, Lord Stanhope had fine prospects which were ample security to see him through his troubles. Squires of small degree were not so lucky. In January 1700, Sir William Chaytor was forced to quit his ancestral home for the Fleet, the debtors' prison, where he lived until he died seventeen years later. He found plenty of good company there. The gentry had fallen on difficult days. 'Many ancient families,' writes Professor Hughes, 'the Blenkinsops of Bellister, the Radcliffes of Redheugh, the Riddells of Shipcote, to mention only a few, mortgaged and later sold piecemeal their ancestral lands.' And behind the Jacobite re-

---

[1] *Chevening MSS*, V. 6, ff. 21–2. Norfolk gentry were experiencing the same troubles. 'The farmers begin to break hourly round us.' *C(H) MSS*, James Hoste, 22 February 1702.

bellion of 1715 he discerns the discontented gentry poised on the precipice of bankruptcy.[1]

Nor was this situation peculiar to Northern England. In 1736 the Rev Patrick St Clair wrote to his patron, Ashe Windham of Felbrigg: 'Your old neighbour Mr Paston went off in his coach and four, on Sunday last, and absconds ever since . . . they say if he should pay all his debts honestly, he would not have above one hundred a year left, so he is not like to be able to show his head any more.'[2] St Clair's prognostication proved accurate; never again did a male Paston live in Norfolk. They were not the only ancient family to vanish. Le Gros, Palgrave, Heydon, Potts, Spelman, Gleane, ancient families all, who had lived generation after generation on their modest estates, sank into oblivion. This was not a new process; throughout the centuries, since that first great agrarian expansion of the thirteenth, landed families had risen only to fall again. For one that survived a score were destroyed, overtaken by those natural disasters which beset families—failure of heirs, wanton extravagance, reckless loyalty, sheer bad luck. But debt, the crushing, inexorable burden of debt, extinguished most. As it pressed them down, the needy gentlemen viewed with hatred the wanton luxury of the well-to-do, and envied jealously the manna which fell from the Court into favoured laps. It is not an accident that Norfolk's few Jacobites should be found amongst the needy small squires; nor that the crusted and embittered tories were to be found amongst the ranks of those whom life was dispossessing. The failure to succeed had always been hard to bear; the rebellions, revolutions and plots, which make up the narrative of seventeenth-century history, were fed by the gentry's hopeless plight.[3] William's and Marlborough's wars

[1] E. Hughes, *North Country Life in the Eighteenth Century*, 1–5.

[2] R. W. Ketton-Cremer, *Norfolk Portraits*, 56.

[3] And, perhaps, equally true of earlier centuries; a successful baronial revolt meant affluence for the rebels, cf. D. Hay, 'The Division of the Spoils of War in Fourteenth-Century England', *Trans. R. Hist. Soc.*, 5th Series, IV (1954), 91–109. The pattern of English society from 1200–1750 is more consistent than historians have allowed.

piled the heavy burden of taxation on to the squires' shoulders, and men who had reviled James soon learned to hate their Protestant King. The flamboyance of the rich, merchant or nobleman, did not make the gentry's lot easier to bear. It became doubly difficult to accept the frugal life which prudence demanded if bad years were to be lived through without disaster. Nothing, however, was easier to turn into coin than land and the squires found attorneys and scriveners eager to offer mortgages, for the hunger for land of the moneyed classes was not easily assuaged.[1]

Sir Thomas Cave of Stanford Hall in Leicestershire was very typical of country gentlemen of his day. He loved racing his horses almost as much as hunting the fox over the shires. His hospitality was open-handed and generous. He hated taxes, wars, Dutchmen, placemen, courtiers and London money-lenders. Man of action that he was he did not like to hate to little purpose; so he stood for Parliament for his county, raising the money as best he might. At thirty-nine, in 1719, Sir Thomas Cave dropped dead, leaving four young children and an estate vastly encumbered with debt. His wife had to sell everything—plate, coach-horses, hounds, her own jewels, even the one hogshead of red wine in the cellar. Most of the servants were dismissed; the great deer park was turned back into a farm; only after years of the strictest economy was the estate saved.[2] This story could be repeated for every county in the land except that the endings might not be so happy.

The bulk of the gentry were faced with a most difficult problem. Only a lavish expenditure could bring them the style of life which they felt, rightly or wrongly, was due to their station. Only the very wealthiest of them could afford

[1] Although much detailed work remains to be done the evidence of the two counties that I know best—Leicestershire and Norfolk—helps to substantiate Mr H. Trevor Roper's thesis that social disturbance in the seventeenth century was due not so much to the rise as to the plight of the gentry. They supported the politics of discontent whether whig or tory.

[2] *Verney Letters of the Eighteenth Century*, I, 214–56; II, 62–8. *VCH Leicestershire*, II, 123–4.

it without risking mortgage and debt. It was a dilemma from which there were few methods of escape. The most favoured was marriage to an heiress, but even this was not without its dangers. An heiress's conceptions of the appropriate style of life necessary for herself and family could fly very high; her dower was, more often than not, difficult to turn into liquid assets without mortgage, and once mortgage was incurred the old familiar story tended to be repeated again. More satisfactory was a place at Court or in the government, but a small squire had little chance of obtaining a place unless he had suitable connections. Marriage might do this for him, as it did for the Custs of Stamford who had beggared themselves trying to maintain their parliamentary influence there against the inroads of the great house of Bertie. They were saved by a stroke of luck; Sir Richard Cust married a Brownlow of Belton whose family was closely allied with the Dukes of Rutland. They were gradually weaned from their old-fashioned tory prejudices against courtiers; seats in Parliament and a steady flow of perquisites, culminating in the Speakership of the House of Commons, illustrate the wisdom of their decision, as they moved from obscurity and debt into favour and affluence.[1]

Alliance with a great family offered the best insurance to a country gentleman. That was why the powerful Court aristocracy found it so easy to dominate their own localities, or (perhaps more accurately) so relatively easy, for there was not room for all. There were not enough scraps of patronage to go round. Men who were politically astute found little difficulty in assessing the political, social and personal value of any squire; unless he had something to offer and was willing to give unquestioning loyalty he would find entry into the caucus difficult and exclusion easy. If he happened to be related to the dominant family he might have to be accepted, but even the ties of blood were likely to prove very thin in the world of political patronage.

The whig leaders preferred to ally with the more aggres-

[1] Lady Elizabeth Cust, *Records of the Cust Family*, I, 338–84.

sive sections of local society, with attorneys and merchants, or newly-landed families who still retained such interests,[1] otherwise they kept close to the great landowners to whom they were related by marriage.

The small squires tended therefore to drift into the politics of resentment. Some called themselves old whig, others tory. They had their moments of hope in the reign of Queen Anne. At times they could win an election by sheer force of numbers, particularly in the county constituencies. They remained disgruntled, crotchety, drawing consolation from the vituperation which the *Craftsman* poured on Walpole and his government. They developed a venomous hatred of placeholders, pensioners and the aristocratic world of London. They looked back with longing affection to the Stuarts, and sometimes played the Jacobite, under the extravagant delusion that their plight had been better, forgetting that many of their grandfathers had talked treason with Shaftesbury and trundled James II out of the land.

The ambivalence of attitude between the aristocracy and the smaller gentry gives an edge to local politics in the early eighteenth century which otherwise they might lack. It kept alive the old struggle of whig and tory in the constituencies long after the conflict between them had become meaningless at the centre of politics. And this too must be remembered—they were far more numerous than the whig oligarchs who ruled their lives. After Walpole had brought peace to the land, the growing prosperity of the country in which they shared, tended as year followed year, to soften their asperity and bring them to a grumbling indifference. But they could never be ignored. Their representatives in

[1] An admirable illustration of this is the rise of the Banks family of Revesby, Lincolnshire. Joseph Banks began life as an attorney in Sheffield; through mortgage speculations he made money, bought Revesby where he established his son, acquired a seat in Parliament, and the friendship of the Duke of Ancaster and Sir Robert Walpole, who in 1727 found him a Treasury seat at Totnes. His daughter at the cost of £10,000 portion married Sir Francis Whichcote, Bt. J. W. F. Hill, *The Letters and Papers of the Banks Family of Revesby Abbey*. Lincoln Record Society (1952).

Parliament, the independent country gentlemen, could act decisively in a conflict between factions. When roused to violent opposition, as they were by Excise, they could still play an effective part in general elections. In the political struggles with which this volume deals they were of far greater influence. It was on their fears and jealousies that Robert Harley played so dexterously. By their help he was able to climb to power, by their folly Bolingbroke was able to betray him. This conflict within the landowning classes sharpened the struggle for power at Westminster.

Before we leave the gentry to examine other and equally important strata in society it is necessary to dispel a myth—the attractive myth of Squire Western, that boorish, stupid, unlettered, drink-sodden oaf of good heart and no wit. A literary caricature was given historical reality by Macaulay in his Third Chapter and the country gentleman of Stuart or Hanoverian days has been a figure of fun ever since. Often, however, these small squires were men of culture and learning. There were sots among them but sots could be found at Court, in the Army, on the Bench, or in the Church. There were lechers, too, and men crazed with horses and gaming. The rest of society, high or low, were not ignorant of such vices. But the bulk were well educated. Their libraries, like Sir Pury Cust's or Walpole's father's, contained the classics—Homer, Thucydides, Plutarch, Livy, Cicero, Seneca, Virgil, Ovid, Lucretius, Pliny; plenty of history; Dugdale, Brady, Holinshed, Daniel, Raleigh; some French books, perhaps, usually Bossuet, Corneille, Racine, and Bayle's Dictionary; a book or two on architecture; a great number of law books; a little poetry, Spenser and Milton, occasionally Dryden; a shelf of sermons and theology; a few pursued the new rationalism and purchased Bacon, Hobbes and Locke.[1]

At every fair in East Anglia there were bookstalls, and it was not only the local parson who bought there. Political problems were then couched in historical terms. Men believed that by studying the country's past, especially its law, they

[1] Cust, *op. cit.*, I, 382, and see below, Chapter II.

could unravel those mysteries of authority and obligation which so baffled them. As the strong red wine circulated round the oaken tables the talk ran on statute law, on Norman despotism, on Witanagemot, on Adam and patriarchy. Sometimes the deeper problems of man's destiny troubled them, for the old biblical certainties were crumbling. Yet squires were not always solemn; they had their lighter side. They loved music—every village had its waits and fiddlers who wandered from country house to country house certain of a warm welcome and modest tip. They were passionately devoted to architecture and knew something of painting; most of them spent more time and money than they could afford on their gardens and trees. They studied intelligently the new forms of husbandry and made their own modest experiments. There were mindless ones amongst them who thought of nothing but horses, hounds and gun: others were equally obsessed by their pursuit of learning; but most combined a little of both, happy with a good day's hunting in the crisp autumn air but just as content to spend a raw day indoors by the huge log fire in the panelled library, reading of the iniquities of Dudley and Empson and thinking darkly of Walpole and Townshend.

4

THERE WERE other strains in society in the early eighteenth century which helped to sharpen political differences. The merchant class was no more harmonious than the landowners. Throughout the seventeenth century the number of merchants had been growing and so, too, had their wealth and power. The long wars with France, which had been a consequence of the revolution of 1689, had given the wealthier merchants a chance to make large fortunes and to consolidate their economic position. By the time Walpole entered politics the commercial life of London was dominated by a small group of financiers of immense wealth. These men were not only directors of the Bank of England but were also the controllers of the East India Company, the Africa Company and Levant Company. They owned blocks of London property; they dabbled in mortgages; they spread their money in land; wherever there was gain or security for money, they were investors and buyers. The extent of their wealth is undiscoverable. Sir James Bateman, one-time Governor of the Bank of England, Sub-Governor of the South Sea Company, director of the East India Company, gave his daughters £10,000 each for their portions. He bequeathed his eldest son an estate in Herefordshire, his second an estate in Kent and his youngest an estate in Essex. They were all given houses and property in London. The grandchildren were not forgotten, careful provision being made to permit them to use free of charge the slate and stone from his quarries in Durham in addition to their legacies in estates. Largesse was scattered to the poor of half-a-dozen parishes and Sir James was wise enough to make provision in his will for his executors to have a book-keeper at £50 per annum.[1] His son acquired the social distinction which his wealth commanded. He married the daughter of Charles, Earl of Sunderland, and in 1725 became the first Viscount Bateman; true, the viscounty was only of Ireland, for George I had strong prejudices about birth, but it was sufficient to obliterate the stigma of trade. Nor was Sir James Bateman's reputation for wealth confined to London; his name was good security in Antwerp, Holland and Germany.[2] Bateman was an extremely rich man but he was not unique. Sir Josiah Child held over £50,000 India stock in 1691, and India was only one of his many interests.[3] Or there was Sir Robert Clayton, the scrivener, who held mortgages on the estates of half the nobility of Surrey and Sussex. He was rich enough to buy the manor of Bletchingley and with it the right to return two members of Parliament, and so rich that, although

[1] PCC Tenison 109. Bateman died 10 November 1718. *GEC.*
[2] HMC, *Portland MSS*, IV, 559, 560, 583.
[3] K. G. Davies, 'Joint Stock Investment in the Late Seventeenth Century', *Ec. Hist. Rev.* (1952), IV, II Series, 297.

he was an intolerable nuisance as a Commissioner of Customs, he was too powerful to be dismissed.

'Besides these imputations of corruption and partiality to his old fellow servants, however unfit and disaffected they are,' wrote Sir John Somers bitterly in 1694, 'he does continually insist so stiffly and unreasonably against reforming any errors or abuses that are practised in the office, that it is sufficient to say a thing is an ancient custom, to ingage him blindly to espouse it, so that while he remains no reformation can be hoped for in that office.'[1]

Shrewsbury, Sunderland, Godolphin and Trenchard, in fact all of King William's leading ministers, agreed with Somers, yet much as they hated the obstinate and cantankerous old man, they dared not recommend his dismissal. They left the decision to the King. Clayton, however, had lent William III £30,000. He remained in office for a further three years, until, goaded beyond endurance, the ministers secured his dismissal. These merchants were comparable to the Carnegies, Huntingtons and Mellons of the great age of American capitalism. Like them they had their favoured charities. Edward Colston, a Bristol slave trader, besides making vast and generous endowments for schools and almshouses in his native town also left legacies to augment thirty parishes and nineteen charity schools elsewhere, but he hedged about his charities with the utmost care to prevent the possibility of any of his benevolence reaching a dissenter.[2]

---

[1] *Cal. S.P. Dom.*, 1694–5, 244, cf. also *DNB* and D. C. Coleman, 'London Scriveners and the Estate Market in the Late Seventeenth Century', *Ec. Hist. Rev.*, IV, II Series (1952), 221. All directors of companies and fellows of colleges will sympathise with Somers's exasperation and recognize the note of helpless frustration to which he had been reduced by obstinacy, pedantry and the authority of age, at once self-righteous and corrupt. Clayton raised to himself, wife and dead child one of the most beautiful of the sepulchral monuments of the Augustan age. It is at Bletchingley, cf. K. A. Esdaile, *English Church Monuments*, 28. He was also a generous benefactor of St Thomas's Hospital. Earlier in life he had received a royal pardon for extorting more than six per cent interest on loans.

[2] PCC Buckingham 236, pr. 18 December 1721. His will runs to thirty-three pages; he insisted on being escorted to his grave by the old men and women from his almshouses and by the boys from his charity school.

Such merchants could live on a scale comparable to that of the richest members of the aristocracy. Sir Josiah Child built Wanstead House, the largest residence in England until Vanbrugh completed Castle Howard. 'Some merchants', wrote César de Saussure in 1727, 'are certainly far wealthier than many sovereign princes of Germany and Italy. They live in great state; their houses are richly furnished, their tables spread with delicacies.' [1] They formed an aristocracy of wealth, in many ways as narrow and as exclusive as the aristocracy of birth into which their daughters so frequently married. [2] They were drawn to the government rather than the Court. They were willing to forgo the passions of party strife and throw in their lot with any group of politicians who could give security to an administration. Their natural allies were the courtiers who, like them, preferred to avoid extremes for the sake of stable government. They looked to Godolphin or Harley rather than to Bolingbroke or Wharton, and in Walpole they found a man entirely after their own heart—compliant, unadventurous, careful of the pence—at least in public policy if not in pursuit of his own career. England was prosperous; they were rich; plots, riots, rebellions, and in Walpole's day, even wars, were to be deplored. There was a rich cake and few of them to eat it.

Just as this great but narrow aristocracy of wealth dominated London, so smaller oligarchies dominated the commercial cities of the provinces. Bristol was controlled by its sugar and tobacco magnates and the princes of the slave trade—the Colstons, Days, Yates and Youngs. Hull was firmly in the hands of the Baltic and Dutch merchants, the Maisters, Ramsdens and St Quintins; Newcastle in the hands of the Blacketts, Liddells and Ridleys, the lords of the coal trade. King's Lynn was just as firmly under the sway of Walpole's relatives, the Turners.

King's Lynn thrived in the late seventeenth century. The

---

[1] César de Saussure, *A Foreign View of England in the Reigns of George I and George II*, 217.

[2] Two of Sir Josiah Child's granddaughters became duchesses.

draining of the fens opened up new, rich farming land whose products found their way down the Ouse. The improvements in its navigation—by 1700 barges could reach Bedford and Cambridge—made the port a convenient entry for much trade to the East Midlands. Until the 1730s when the silting of the harbour led to a sharp decline in its prosperity, King's Lynn enjoyed boom conditions in which many families made their fortunes. Coal, wine, consumption goods of all kinds were shipped through Lynn, and in exchange corn, hides, hay and some woollen goods were exported to home and foreign markets. It was in wine that the Turners had first made their money.[1] John Turner, the son of a Norfolk attorney of modest means, founded his fortune in story-book fashion. Apprenticed to a Cambridge vintner, he married his master's widow and immediately moved to Lynn. There his brother, Charles, was already well established as an attorney. They prospered, indeed they prospered exceedingly. They became aldermen, and were mayors not once but several times. They built splendidly, fine houses for themselves and costly public buildings for the town's comfort and embellishment. In politics they were all discretion. John Turner shared the representation of Lynn with his friend, Samuel Tayler, another vintner; discreetly they avoided the perils of Exclusion politics. Together on their knees they surrendered their town's charter to James II and in return received the accolade. But this did not prevent Sir John from promptly deserting his King for William of Orange in 1689, thereby keeping his seat in Parliament and his control of the borough. As became men of wealth, the Turners planted themselves out in the country, buying estates at Warham, taking others on lease or mortgage at Crostwight and Great Dunham. Sir John, too, had the pleasure of seeing his nephew marry into one of the most important Norfolk families, the Walpoles. It

[1] For Lynn and its merchants cf. H. L. Bradfer-Lawrence, 'The Merchants of Lynn', *Supplement to Blomefield's Norfolk*, ed. C. Ingleby, and B. Mackerell, *The History and Antiquities of King's Lynn* (1736). For Newcastle and Durham cf. E. Hughes, *North Country Life in the Eighteenth Century*, 151–257.

was natural that so distinguished a nephew should join him in the representation of Lynn and add to the family honours by becoming a baronet. By the time he was seventy, Sir John had the satisfaction of knowing that his family had no rival in Lynn; feeling his age and knowing his place, he readily resigned his seat, as soon as it was demanded of him, to Walpole; without the Turner influence Walpole would never have enjoyed the complete security of tenure of his seat in parliament. By wealth and by persistent attention to local politics, the Turners, in alliance with families into which they married, became as powerful and as unassailable as the Childs or Batemans in London.

'The vested interests of these families,' writes their historian, 'stretched like the tentacles of an octopus in, over and around the entire life of the borough in all its aspects—commerce, politics, customs, law, all fell within their compass.'[1]

These great merchants, metropolitan and provincial, acquired so much power and so much wealth, that it induced in them great caution, a desire to avoid change, and a passionate adherence to any administration which avoided risk. Subservient to authority they deplored the buccaneering spirit which had created, and was creating, that vast revolution in trade in which the strength and greatness of England lay.

Broadly speaking, these men lacked passion in politics, they were close kin to the Vicar of Bray and moved from discreet toryism to discreet whiggery as occasion demanded. For them Walpole's ministry, once established, was all excellence. It offered years of untroubled security and peace. Their contentment was disturbed only by their own colleagues.

Some merchants, some of the very richest, were not content with Walpole's world. They were restless for greater power and greater wealth. They were happy in Marlborough's war, distressed by Utrecht, and in the 'twenties and 'thirties bewildered by Walpole's forbearance to France and Spain.

[1] H. L. Bradfer-Lawrence, *op. cit.*, 155.

They were alive to the opportunities of their age. Many were truculent, courageous, aggressive men like 'Diamond' Pitt, Chatham's grandfather, who defied the East India Company, damned its monopoly of trade, and made a couple of fortunes before he was thirty.[1] The early eighteenth century offered glorious opportunities for quick wealth. England's trade had expanded with great rapidity towards the end of the seventeenth century; not only was it brisk in exports, but the favourable trade balance stimulated the home market and home industries. There were insufficient outlets for capital investment and this gave rise to extravagant projects long before the South Sea Bubble.[2] In consequence there was money, and money to spare, for exotics, and the consumption of tea, coffee, chocolate, new muslins and calicoes from the East rose quickly. Men in commerce or industry profited most and the gentry with high taxes and insecure rents least; and it was natural that the appetite of traders and manufacturers should be whetted. The expansion of English wealth could not proceed too rapidly for them. They were impatient of any foreign policy which curbed their aggressive spirit; they hated the great chartered companies from which they were excluded; they undermined the Elizabethan legislation which protected their journeymen from exploitation. They were impatient of authority, hence their natural sympathies were whig, although they were opposed to Walpole who, they felt, betrayed their interests by the appeasement of Spain and friendship with France. Many of them, particularly provincial merchants, were drawn to those forms of protestantism which encouraged individual judgment. And amongst them, too, lingered the puritan attitude to life with its stress on plain living, thrift and hard work, for the most aggressive merchants were of the middling sort. And, as is natural with men, they were not above denouncing the morals and fashions of those from whom their wealth was derived.

'We are fond of French clergymen, French goods and

[1] Cf. J. H. Plumb, *Chatham*, 1–3.
[2] K. G. Davies, *op. cit.*

28

French fashions though mere trifles, shittlecocks and gew-gaws. No inventions please us unless they be French-made, and, like their apes, we imitate their garb and their house-keeping. Their toothdrawers and their barbers are our admired surgeons. We are mad upon French music, French players, French misses, French danceing-masters, French language, French airs, French legs, French hats, French grimaces and compliments.'[1]

Barnes and his kind hated the luxury of the Court and the corruption of government, for they deplored its sophistica-tion. They busied themselves with the morals of the poor whose discipline and capacity for honest toil meant so much to them. They concerned themselves with the social content of religion, giving warm support to all religious societies bent on the reformation of manners. Some extended their bene-volence to include the support of charity schools where small boys were taught the elements of book-keeping and girls those of domestic service. Aggressive, suspicious, hard-fisted, relentless in the pursuit of wealth, they were the sinews of England's trade.

They were, of course, a large and amorphous class, lacking the unity and self-consciousness of the aristocracies of birth or wealth, or even of the gentry; thus their attitude to politics, although coherent on the broad issues, became less predict-able on specific questions. As most of them were freeholders, they created the factor of uncertainty in those parliamentary elections which could not be controlled by patronage. Be-cause they were literate and had leisure to read, they were the target for the stream of political propaganda which poured from the Press. As far as there was a public opinion, they, with the gentry, formed it. Because of the fascination of the art of patronage and political management, their sig-nificance for eighteenth-century politics has been overlooked by recent historians. Yet the struggle for their support gives life, vitality and meaning to political history of the eighteenth century.

[1] Cf. *The Memoirs of Ambrose Barnes, Late Merchant and Sometime Alderman of Newcastle-on-Tyne*, Surtees Soc. (1866), 225.

STILL NOTHING has been said of the mass of the population. Here again there were fine gradations of wealth and rank from the prosperous shopkeepers and craftsmen to the day labourer, from the upper servants to the casual weeders in the garden. But their lives are submerged and must be reconstructed indirectly from newspapers, police and poor-law records, wage assessments, wills and inventories, an occasional letter and even more rarely a diary or autobiography. More vividly their lean faces and hollow eyes stare at us from the savage satires of Hogarth. It was a life of great insecurity and only those who were hardworking, thrifty, cunning and lucky survived. The ease and wellbeing of the majority of working men varied in direct relation to the fluctuations of harvest and trade. Hours were long, wages far from high but food in good years was plentiful and cheap; more often than not there was an abundance of work. Even so men and women could starve to death in the very heart of London. Disease flourished in the overcrowded and insanitary conditions in which they lived; death was frequent and sudden, a common visitor to youth as well as age, and a lover of children. And yet there was an atmosphere of prosperity.

'They eat well,' Defoe wrote of the mass of the population in 1728, 'and they drink well; for their eating (*viz.*) of flesh meat, such as beef, mutton, bacon, etc., in proportion to their circumstances, 'tis to a fault, nay, even to profusion; as to their drink, 'tis generally stout strong beer, not to take notice of the quantity which is sometimes a little too much, or good table beer for their ordinary diet; for the rest, we see their houses and lodgings tolerably furnished, at least stuffed well with useful and necessary household goods: Even those we call poor people, journeymen, working and pains-taking people do thus; they lye warm, live in plenty, work hard, and (need) know no want.'[1]

[1] D. Defoe, *A Plan of the English Commerce* (Oxford 1927), 76. Defoe was writing on behalf of Walpole's ministry to boost English prosperity and this

Furthermore in London, and perhaps in Bristol and Norwich, they were exceptionally free from restraint. There was no police force in the modern sense, the power of the Church to enforce social discipline was greatly decayed. In the rural communities the authority of squire and parson was more effective. The drift to the towns was partly due to the lack of economic opportunity in the villages but it was also the air of freedom and opportunity and prosperity which lured many a young countryman to London.

Broadly speaking, the bulk of the working population was tory and was to be opposed to Walpole's government. Furthermore they were passionately interested in politics and devoured the newspapers avidly.[1] They were tory because, although there was an opportunity to make money, the conditions of labour were hardening. Their masters, who wanted more and more goods, insisted on longer hours and did whatever they could to destroy what remained of the protective legislation and guild organization of the Tudors and Stuarts. It was natural that the journey-men, like the gentry, should look back to a world in which their position had been more secure. But some of their toryism was due to a hatred of government and authority, a dislike of restraint, and a healthy contempt for an institution which they were convinced was corrupt to the core. They relished the savage attacks on Walpole and the lampoons on the Court. It was their animosity which was to breed in Walpole a hatred of

panegyric may be somewhat over-sanguine, but foreign travellers made much the same observation, cf. De Saussure, *op. cit.* The same air of modest prosperity amongst the shopkeepers and craftsmen, but not amongst the labourers, is conveyed by their inventories, cf. F. W. Steer, *Farm and Cottage Inventories of Mid-Essex*, Essex Record Society, No. 8.

[1] Literacy was very widespread, especially in London; de Saussure comments on the passionate interest of working men in politics and foreign affairs, *op. cit.*, 162. There was an extremely extensive elementary education throughout England run mainly by private enterprise; both grammar schools and charity schools constituted only a small fraction of the total number of schools. More than 100 educational establishments were advertised in the *Northampton Mercury* between 1720 and 1760; sixty-seven in the *Norwich Mercury* from 1749 to 1756. G. A. Cranfield, *The Development of the Provincial Newspaper, 1700–60*, unpublished thesis. Cam. Univ. Lib.

London and brought him to the decision to curb its powers. Yet, though the bulk of the population was tory, it was an old-fashioned, naïve toryism, and not in the least Jacobite.

But there was a part of the working class which was more volatile and dangerous. There was always a large number of men and women in Hanoverian England who lived on the verge of starvation, to whom unemployment meant absolute personal disaster. Their attitude to the government moved directly with the index of prices. Dear corn meant violence and rioting in which plunder was as important as their impotent protest against the hostile world. The rabble in action was a terror to all governments, and yet politicians in opposition never hesitated to provoke them. Their prejudices were deliberately exploited by Bolingbroke and others who were opposed to Walpole. But it was a dangerous weapon and on occasion the cynical use of the mob rallied responsible men to the government's support; a factor, indeed, which was to help Walpole through the dangers of many a crisis. In the countryside the abject poor could for the most part be more easily controlled. They were herded into workhouses or kept alive on a pittance from the parish rates. At times their despair drove them to riot, and mobs gathered in the countryside almost as frequently as they did in towns. On 7 June 1696, Abraham de la Pryme wrote in his diary:

'This day I heard of one that is come from Lincoln, that the country people had been up about Stamford, and marched in a great company, very lively, to the house of Sir John Brownley. They brought their officers, constables, and churchwardens amongst them, and as they went along they cryd, "God bless King William, God bless King William" etc. When they were come to Sir John's, he sent his man down to see what their will was, who all answered: "God bless King William, God bless the Church of England, God bless the Parliament, and the Lords Justices, and Sir John Brownley! We are King William's true servants, God forbid that we should rebel against him, or that anything that we now do should be construed ill. We come only to his worship to bisieech him to be merciful to the poor; we and our familys being all fit to starve, not having one penny that will go," etc. Sir John hearing all this (as soon as his man) at a window where he was viewing them, sent them a bagg with fifteen pound in it of old milled money, which they received exceeding thankfully, but sayd the sum was so little, and their number and necessitys so great, that they feared it would not last long, therefore must be forced out of their necessity to come see him again, to keep themselves and their familys from starving. Then they desired a drink, and Sir John caused his doors to be set open and let them go to the cellar, where they drank God bless King William, the Church of England, and all the loyal healths that they could think on, and so went their ways.' [1]

No doubt they hoped to get more money and more drink from the neighbouring landowners. This was an astutely led mob which made full economic advantage of its implied threat of violence. Fears of destruction of their wealth often caused landowners, merchants and manufacturers to adjust wages rapidly or to display a hasty benevolence. Such victories kept alive the rural mobs and in Walpole's old age they were as common as in his youth. In the summer of 1735 the poor of Gloucestershire and Herefordshire revolted, tore down turnpikes, and threatened the countryside. The gentry assembled and made what was called 'a becoming opposition', but they were too weak to win a victory and troops had to be dispatched before the countryside was pacified. [2] Violent mobs, urban as well as rural, induced a sense of apprehension in the upper classes; the fear of anarchy put a high premium on authority and made the longing for political stability more intense. The main political effect of the restlessness of the poor was to help take off the edge of controversy amongst the property-owning classes. There were squires of Bray as well as vicars who were just as willing to

---

[1] Charles Jackson (ed.), *The Diary of Abraham de la Pryme*, Surtees Society (1869), 95–6. 'Sir John Brownley' was Sir John Brownlow of Belton, Lincs. The re-coinage was largely responsible for the difficulties of the poor at this time, cf. Max Beloff, *Public Order and Popular Disturbances*, 1660–1714, 92–106.

[2] BM *Add MSS*, 32,690, ff.73,83.

C

give their allegiance to any power which could prove itself strong enough to maintain its authority. Fear of the consequences had a tonic effect on the national genius of compromise.

6

FROM THE thousands of letters, pamphlets and newspapers which Walpole's contemporaries left behind as a testimony of their age, there is one abiding impression that, rich or poor, they were willing to accept society as they found it. Naturally men satirized their institutions, lampooned their politicians, idealized the past, but scarcely ever did they question the foundations of their society—its ranks, its institutions, the distribution of its wealth. This acceptance was allied with a bounding self-confidence which was vociferously asserted by all classes of society but the highest.

'I do not think,' wrote de Saussure, 'there is a people more prejudiced in its own favour than the British people, and they allow this to appear in their talk and manners. They look on foreigners in general with contempt and think nothing is as well done elsewhere as in their own country.'[1]

It was during the early years of the eighteenth century that the symbolic figure of John Bull emerges. His gross, overfed face is typical in its frankness and coarseness of the age; and there is no doubt that the ebullience and self-confidence which he represents sprang from the prosperity of the land. In the race to make money many were crushed and defeated, but a surprising number survived and all Englishmen, rich or poor, were convinced that the pursuit of wealth was the one desirable end in life. Bristol shopkeepers risked their entire capital in slaving voyages, and the smallest shares were eagerly sought by men with a few pounds to risk.

Typical of his age was John Russell, sometime consul in Spain and Italy. Wherever he went, he searched out 'curiosities' which he hawked round his aristocratic friends in Eng-

[1] *Op. cit.*, 177.

34

land. It was a profitable sideline which eked out his slender fortune, but his exuberance outran his judgment.

'I am much obliged to you, for the goats,' wrote the Duke of Bedford, one of his more reluctant customers, in August 1736, 'but I really find them so mischevous in barking the trees, that I do not care to keep them.'

Already the Duke had expressed a strong dislike of 'Black boys and monkeys', but, nothing daunted, Russell tried again. The Duke's reply was brief.

'I return you many thanks for the offer of the Tiger, but do not care to concern myself with any of these sort of animals.'

But Russell triumphed, for within a year the Duke's steward was writing:

'I received the Turtle and well in health. His Grace was afraid it would not come. His Grace had about twelve ladies and gentlemen at the eating of it. We dressed it after the West India manner and the Duke said he never eat a better in his life. His Grace said he hoped he should get another this year, but could not tell. He should be glad if he could, for he loves them exceedingly. The goose and cocoa nuts I shall have tonight. . . .'[1]

7

THE DUKE OF CHANDOS, Sir Thomas Cave, Bateman and Clayton, the Turners of Lynn and the irrepressible John Russell were typical of the nation which Walpole was to rule; a nation in which there were violent contrasts between riches and poverty, elegance and squalor. The squires and many merchants felt for different reasons a deep sense of frustration which was mirrored in the unrestrained acerbity of political debate. The past was venerated for virtues which it had never possessed; the future feared for dangers which it was to avoid. Knowledge of the course of events leads us to belittle that deep sense of insecurity which a century's turbulence had created. In Walpole's boyhood men had taken down their armour and gone out to fight for liberties whose

[1] M. E. Matcham, *A Forgotten John Russell*, 106–7.

preservation was a necessity if they were to retain their traditional position in society. No one could foresee that 1688 would be the last time the country would be plunged into fierce civil strife. Even so, the expulsion of the Stuarts left an aftermath of danger to the stability of the nation, which we tend to underrate. It was prosperity, which mounted steadily year after year, that weakened controversy and nourished an indifference to political debate. Envy was soothed in the general gain and men found it easier to accept authority. Violent constitutional experiments gave way to a settled pattern of politics which Walpole was to foster. The institutions which he used were those by which earlier generations had been governed, but they suffered a transformation; ceasing to be a safeguard of liberty, they became the bulwarks of oligarchy.

CHAPTER TWO

THE STRUCTURE OF GOVERNMENT

WALPOLE GREW up in a world of political instability in which the Revolution of 1689 seemed to his contemporaries to be but a phase, lacking finality, in the struggle which had lasted for generations between Crown and Parliament. Men of property, great or small, squire or merchant, farmer or shopkeeper, longed for a settled government. The vast majority believed without question that the King should rule, for the disasters of the Commonwealth experiment had made republicanism distasteful to most Englishmen. But the authority of kings varied from the absolute authority wielded by Louis XIV to the very limited powers exercised by the Dutch Stadtholder. On the question of which type of kingship was best for them, Englishmen had been very much divided. Neither experience nor tradition was a great help although both were endlessly debated. Both sides appealed to history and as was only to be expected found complete documentary evidence for their opposing views. Dr Brady, the formidable Master of Caius College, a friend, oddly enough, of Walpole's father, who was to save young Walpole's life when he was sick of smallpox at Cambridge, maintained that all authority was in the King—Parliaments existed only by his grace. This William Petyt flatly denied; Parliaments were as old as the nation, contemporaneous with its King, for *Parlement* was merely the Norman name for the Saxon Witanagemot. To strengthen his case he had Dr Brady excluded from the Tower records after the Revolution, but posterity has acknowledged Brady's accuracy and scholarship. As with historical scholarship so with political philosophy, though here perhaps the victory was reversed. The authoritarians were convinced by the theocratic arguments of Filmer and Bossuet. The King was the nation's father as

Adam was the father of creation. The family was divine in origin and the father's authority over his children absolute and sanctioned by God. This was not an absurd argument but an extremely forceful and cogent one to the thousands of men who believed explicitly in the truth of the Old Testament. Locke recognized its power when he devoted the first treatise of his book on civil government to its refutation. To men imbued with the new learning, who had read Harrington and Wharton or listened to Locke, such theories were nonsense; institutions, including kingship, were devices of men to secure their own happiness; if that happiness were to be threatened then the institutions would have to be changed. The basis of all human happiness was, they argued, the free enjoyment of property which was not merely lands or money, goods or chattels. Property for them had a more mystical significance. Property could exist in a man's status or in the free exercise of his professional privileges. When James II dismissed Dr Hough, the President of Magdalen, from his office, even that crusted tory declared that he had lost his freehold.[1] This was no figure of speech; his contemporaries knew exactly what he meant. And many of them regarded these rights as both natural and inalienable. When authority in the State threatened the free enjoyment of such rights then resistance became a duty.

The patriarchal theory of Filmer and Bossuet was held very strongly by Charles II and James II and their courtiers, who believed not only in the divine nature of kingship but also that monarchical authority had achieved the perfection of form in France. Furthermore, a few, particularly James II and his closest friends, sincerely believed that their own religion—Roman Catholicism—not only sanctioned and blessed royal authority but also provided a stronger means for securing social discipline and that proper sense of subordination which was an essential part of their social ethic. But the diffi-

[1] F. C. Turner, *James II*, 344. The idea that a man's office was a freehold had a long history and was no innovation; it was stated more emphatically at this time.

culty of the full royal creed of Charles II and James II for most Englishmen was twofold. First, it would lead to the destruction of the Church of England which men loved, not perhaps so much for its doctrine, but because it was a symbol of national independence. And secondly, the royal policy was bound to lead to subservience to France, England's most dangerous commercial rival. Yet men were extremely reluctant to believe that this must be so. Shaftesbury thought that he could steer Charles II clear of the tentacles of Louis XIV. He failed. Halifax, frightened by the implications of the Exclusion crisis, thought likewise. He too failed. After him the most conservative statesmen were brought only reluctantly to the same view. And it was with the utmost hesitation that men of great power and wealth, merchants as well as aristocrats, brought themselves to reject the attitude to monarchy which these two Stuart brothers had nourished.

Some men, however, had consistently opposed all attempts to extend royal authority. They had supported Shaftesbury in his attempt to exclude James and to strengthen the authority of Parliament. They wished to see the country ruled as the United Provinces were ruled. These men, though not republicans, held that monarchy should be strictly limited; both royal servants and royal policy were to be controlled by Parliament, the representative assembly of England's propertied interests. They hated France and they hated popery, for both were symbols of arbitrary government. And they saw the gravest danger to the wealth of England in the French leanings of the Stuarts. Many of these men had dabbled in treason; others had gone into discreet exile in Holland; the majority, like Walpole's father, tended their estates and bided their time, waiting for the folly of James to accomplish its own ruin.

They had not long to wait. The acts by which James II brought about his downfall need not be recounted here. There is, however, one aspect of his foolishness which receives too little notice. This was his attack on local government. Charles II had been disturbed by the violence of the House of Commons during the Exclusion crisis and by the utter inability of his ministers to keep it under effective control. He went to the root of the matter. Borough after borough was forced to surrender its town charter and then it was graciously granted a new one. The new charters reserved more often than not the privilege of electing a member of Parliament to the chief officials of the town and the King himself either appointed these officials or controlled their appointments.[1] By this means the royal control of the composition of Parliament was to be steadily extended. James II pursued the same policy but with more thoroughness; age-old alliances between great local families and the boroughs which they had patronized were broken. Corporations were bullied and cajoled into pledging their support in future elections to men lacking in property or distinction but willing to acquiesce in James's policy. Worse followed. Even after a most thorough remodelling of the parliamentary boroughs James felt far from secure. He was frightened of the unspoken but massive opposition of the country gentry who, as justices of the peace and deputy-lieutenants, ruled their neighbourhoods as of natural right. He decided to displace them unless they pledged themselves to support him.[2] Commissioners were dispatched to all counties. Their investigations were thorough and very distasteful to the gentry, who refused as tactfully as they could to acquiesce in James's policy. In county after county men who had been loyal to James hitherto were discovered to be as adamant as their whig neighbours, but whig or tory, they were turned off the bench and cleared from the militia. They were infuriated when they learnt that they were being replaced by men of no property, by obscure Catholics and dissenters; sometimes even by bailiffs and servants. Sir

---

[1] The King's own keen interest in the process is illustrated by A. Browning (ed.), *The Memoirs of Sir John Reresby*, 321. There are some very peremptory letters from the Earl of Dover to the Mayor of Bury St Edmunds about the King's wishes and the composition of the corporation in the *West Suffolk Records* at Bury.

[2] James's investigations into the loyalty of the gentry are to be found in Sir G. Duckett, *Penal Laws and Test Act*.

John Reresby worshipped the Crown as the symbol of God's authority. His whole life had been spent in unswerving devotion to Charles II and James II. For their sakes he had helped to humble the proud corporation of York by securing the surrender of its ancient charters. For years he never questioned the wisdom of James's measures but even his eyes were opened in 1688 and he sat down on 14 November with foreboding in his heart to write to the Duke of Newcastle.

'. . . in the afternoon we was all surprized by the clerke of the peace comming to supersede Sir Henry Goodrick, Mr Tankard, Sir John Kaye, Sir Michael Wentworth, Sir Thomas Yarburgh, and above twenty more principall gentlemen of this rideing (the most eminent for quality and estates) from being justices of the peace, bringing at the same time another commission wherein severall new ones are put in, and amongst others John Eyre of Sheffield Parke, Mr Ratcliff, &c. The first can neither write nor read, the second is a bailiff to the Duchesse Dowagere of Norfolk's rents, and neither of them have one foot off freehould land in England. My Lord, I fear this matter being unseasonably notified at such a time may change the good measures we were upon and divide the country. . . .'[1]

A few were not disturbed by these proceedings, but for the majority they violated nature and implied a social revolution which could not be tolerated. Such an attack on the gentry's vested interest made the country almost unanimous in its rejection of James.

The Revolution brought a restoration of the borough charters and new commissions were issued, appointing justices of the peace; the old familiar names, a Knatchbull for Kent, Onslow for Surrey, Rolle for Devon, Walpole for Norfolk, Strangways for Dorset, Stanley for Lancashire, indicated to all that the natural order of society had been restored. Moreover, this restoration came to be regarded as sacrosanct. Generation followed generation and still the Onslows, the Knatchbulls, the Walpoles ruled their neighbourhoods as their fathers and grandfathers and great-grand-

[1] A. Browning (ed.), *Memoirs of Sir John Reresby*, 584.

fathers had done before them; and not only ruled, but ruled in the same way, using the same unchanging machinery of local government, no matter how inadequate it was for the problems of a changing society. The Revolution confirmed the right of the gentry to rule by its old traditional methods. In the same way, it confirmed the old corporations. Small, self-electing bodies of men, wielding great wealth, yet divorced from all but the most ancient of social obligations, and frequently even these, they came to be regarded as a part of the divine order of things. From the point of view of the structure of political society, the Revolution had been thoroughly conservative, a rejection of the revolutionary designs of Charles II and James II.

2

IT IS NECESSARY to understand the structure of local government because it was the basis of all political power in the eighteenth century. The source of Walpole's massive strength was the institutions by which the English countryside was governed. The Lord Lieutenant was the greatest of all local officials. He was the King's representative, particularly in military affairs, and with his deputies he was responsible for the county militia. In times of war and rebellion, the office could be onerous, but more frequently duties were formal if important. Nevertheless it was a key position and eagerly sought after.[1] On the death of the Duke of Norfolk in 1701, Walpole's friends were extremely agitated in case Lord Townshend might fail to succeed him, for they realized that their position in the county would be weakened if they failed to capture this office.

The great importance of the Lord Lieutenancy was that it gave local friends and clients of the Lord Lieutenant a spokesman at Court, at the centre of patronage. And he himself was able to keep an eye on all appointments, including

[1] Spencer Compton urged the Earl of Dorset, only 16, to apply at once for the Lord Lieutenancy of Sussex in 1706, on the death of his father. Charles J. Phillips, *History of the Sackville Family*, II, 3.

those of justice of the peace, sheriff and the like which might be to the advantage of his local faction to hold. The vital nature of this office can be seen from the type of men who held it. The Duke of Newcastle was Lord Lieutenant, throughout most of his life, of no less than three counties—Sussex, Nottingham and Middlesex—the spheres of his greatest influence. The Duke of Bolton held Hampshire, Dorset and, because his wife was a Vaughan, Carmarthenshire, but the moment he quarrelled with the government in 1733 he was dismissed from all three. The government knew the power which the Lord Lieutenant wielded and insisted on reliability. On the accession of Anne, rumours spread through Norfolk that Townshend might lose this office because the Queen was determined to weed out the extreme whigs. Such news, fortunately untrue, caused great consternation since the loss of a Lord Lieutenancy might be the reversal of fortune for hundreds of lesser men; no longer would they become the cynosure of sycophantic friends at Quarter Sessions or at the convivial evenings when the corporation met in the local tavern. Instead they would know the gnawing envy of those who stand and watch whilst their rivals, self-satisfied and self-important, contentedly savour the sweet delights of power.

It was not wholly a question of influence; the Lord Lieutenant also controlled a few highly desirable and very profitable sinecures.

'The Clerk of the Peace of Oxfordshire is dead' Lady Cowper wrote to Mrs Clayton, the Mistress of the Robes (to the Princess of Wales), 'and the place is in the gift of Lord Godolphin (Ld. Lieut. Oxon) who I believe would willingly put my brother Edward in, if Mr Clayton would be so kind as to name him to my Lord Godolphin. It would strengthen the King's and the Woodstock interest . . . we are sure he is a zealous whig.'[1]

Edward, of course, had no intention of *acting* as Clerk of the Peace, an office worth about £400 per annum. A deputy,

[1] A. T. Thomson, *Memoirs of Viscountess Sundon*, I, 329–30. The letter is undated, but *c.* 1717.

a local attorney and of course an ardent whig, would willingly undertake the work for £50 per annum for there would be plenty of opportunity to help both himself and his friends equally zealous for the King and the Cowpers. Just as important as £350 per annum for nothing was the status. Edward's appointment would demonstrate to the world that he was 'in', a recipient of Court favour. A prosperous marriage became more probable and certainly debts would be far easier to float. By such means the Lord Lieutenants kept their adherents in devoted subjection.

3

IF THE Lord Lieutenancy was the loom upon which the pattern of local patronage was woven, the justices of the peace were its restless shuttles. The nature and functions of this peculiar English institution are as intricate as they are extensive. The justice was expected to supervise, administer and judge every aspect of life of his neighbourhood. Not only did he deal with petty crime but he controlled the poor rates, the repairs of highways, the licensing of alehouses; he fixed wages, apprenticeships, settlements; he made affiliation orders; disposed of orphans; supervised gaols and workhouses. All persons of inferior status were in his power, and he had a strong temptation to become a rural tyrant. Petty offences could be dealt with in his own parlour; more serious cases demanded the presence of a neighbouring justice; four times a year all the justices met at quarter sessions when they settled the major problems of law and administration for the county.

Any man of great estate could expect to be a justice almost as of right, whether he supported the government or not. Sometimes the Lord Lieutenant could secure the exclusion of his rabid opponents but it was extremely difficult if they belonged to a long-established wealthy family. The control of the bench had to be secured amongst the smaller fry; dependable clergymen or stewards gave the Lord Lieutenant his majority. The fact that the bench always comprised men

of opposite factions and attitudes led to considerable excitement and intrigue at quarter sessions when the county expressed its views on current affairs by sending up a loyal
address either to the Sovereign or to Parliament. The phras-
ing of such addresses could lead to bitter wrangling and the
final wording was a clear indication to the politically astute
of the shifting emphasis of political opinion on the bench.
But the sense of the county could also be taken at the Assizes
where the Grand Jury, composed as it was of all the leading
county figures, had the traditional right to address. In 1706
the tories in Norfolk were stronger on the Grand Jury than
at the sessions, and they resolved to address the Queen
separately on the success of her arms at Ramillies. Townshend, infuriated and somewhat alarmed at this manoeuvre,
wrote agitatedly to Walpole:

'By a letter I received from my brother yesterday I find
an Address was to be presented to the Queen on Wednesday last; I heartily wish Sir Jacob Astley had signed it.
The Grand Jury have resolved to send up theirs by Mr
Cook who is to go for London on Monday next. Your
uncle was with me yesterday to know whither I would join
with them in it, but did not bring me the Address (however I have seen a copy of it), I told him I had sent up the
Address which was made at the sessions, which in my
opinion was a very good one, that for the Grand Jury to
make another was in my opinion very irregular, and
tended to create divisions and therefore I would not join
in it. It has been the constant practise of the country when
ever there has been any occasion for Addressing to draw
the Address at the first publick meeting either sessions or
assizes and I am sure it would have been thought the
deputy lieutenants and justices of peace had shewed very
little zeal for the Queen and her Government if, after the
wonderfull success of her arms, they had omitted making
an Address at the sessions. I suppose the cheif reason the
Grand Jury had for refusing the session's Address, was,
that they might have an opportunity of sending one up by
Mr Cook, his party is extremely pleased with these proceedings, and think it will be a great step towards carrying

the next election. I have sent you a list of the Grand
Jury who signed their Address, I think the session Address
has many and as considerable hands to it, and if this
method of proceeding is countenanced above, I suppose
the next victory we shall have four or five Addresses from
the county.'[1]

The danger, of course, lay in the loss of face; for a separate,
tory-inspired address to be made to the Queen indicated to
all that Townshend's hold on his county was not secure.

The core of a justice's strength lay in his own neighbourhood, frequently one of the old county hundreds. There his
preserves were jealously guarded.

'That yo are sworne justice of peace,' John Wrott wrote
to Walpole on February 11, 1702, 'I think is very good
news. My old master[2] always acted for the hundreds of
Galloe, Smythdon and Brother Cross and Coll Browne
mett him in Galloe hundred, and Sir Charles Turner sometimes and Mr Dunsgate at Bircham for Smythdon and
Brother Cross hundreds. Now there being no other justice
of peace in Galloe hundred but yourself, I presume you
may take who you will to meet you there and I think that
Sir Charles Turner have a better pretence of coming into
that hundred then either the Coll. at Holkham[3] or Capt.
at Sandringham.[4] And for Bircham if you take Capt.
Hoste to meet you there, I thinke you have a good claim
for meeting him in his hundred of Freebridge citra Lynn.'[5]

In this way the tentacles of the Walpoles' power spread
over the whole of this corner of North-West Norfolk. And it
was so important to control the life of his neighbourhood that
Walpole remained a justice of the peace throughout his life
and took his place on the bench whenever he was in Norfolk.
With his strong political realism he knew well enough that
the strength of his party rested on the loyalty of his brother
justices. Without their tacit consent no political structure

[1] C(H) MSS, Townshend, August 1706.
[2] Walpole's father.
[3] Walpole's uncle, Horatio, a difficult volcanic character and a tory.
[4] The captain was James Hoste, an uncle of Walpole's by marriage. He was
to prove very unreliable.
[5] C(H) MSS, John Wrott, 11 February 1702.

46

could last for long. They were the most vital part of local government.

4

THERE WAS only one other office of any distinction in the county and that was the office of sheriff, but oddly enough political power was measured, in this case, by the ability to guard one's friends from being chosen for it, because the duties of a sheriff were both onerous and expensive and at the same time the office lacked authority and controlled little patronage. It had one further disadvantage; no sheriff could be elected to Parliament. So at times it became necessary, vitally necessary, to prevent the appointment of a friend; yet it might be highly desirable to secure the appointment of an enemy. This could involve risk in an election year for the sheriff controlled the place and time of polling. Consequently the office was often wished on to young men eager to work their way into the party caucus. During the early years of their alliance Townshend's correspondence with Walpole is filled with alarms and excursions about shrieval appointments. On 6 November 1704, he wrote agitatedly from Raynham to Walpole who was in London.

'I am very heartily concerned to find three of my particular friends named in the list for Sheriff and am in such perplexity that I know not what to do, however I have by this post, I hope, secured my Cosin Windham, as to the two others, I have not done anything, though I must confess I do not think making Sir Edward sherriff is the best way to prevent his standing, for he will think he is made upon that account only, and consequently he and his friends, amongst whom I reckon Mr Harvey, will be very much disobliged, and if there is any division on that side of the country, I believe it will be difficult to propose anything in matters of election with any success. Whereas I believe it will not be very difficult to prevail with him not to stand, especially if he is excused being sheriff by my interest for this year, and you know his name brought into Exchequer the next. As to Hoste you can best judge of the

inconveniences that will attend his being made sheriff, I
should be glad to hear from you as soon as you can.'[1]

Townshend's surmise about Sir Edward Ward was correct.
Almost as soon as he had written to Walpole, a servant of
Ward's arrived at Raynham with a letter from Sir Edward,
complaining that he was put into the sheriff's list to prevent
his election to Parliament. Townshend, realizing that such a
rumour would badly damage his influence in Norfolk, at
once approached the Dukes of Somerset and Newcastle as
well as Robert Harley in order to make certain that neither
Ward nor Windham would be pricked. He was successful, but
only at the price of sacrificing Walpole's uncle Hoste of
Sandringham. Immediately he heard of his danger, Hoste
had ridden over to Raynham to see Townshend in person.
It was a saddening interview, for Townshend told him bluntly
that he was apprehensive that he would be the sovereign's
choice and that he could do nothing to help him as he was
engaged to extricate Ward and his own cousin, Ashe Windham of Felbrigg.[2]

Hoste was a choleric man, full of *amour propre*; and he was
always overplaying his part as a leader of the county. He
irritated Walpole by giving heavy-handed advice. Furthermore their relations were somewhat soured by Walpole's
failure to repay a large loan, or even to pay the interest on
it. During his first years in London, Walpole had been full
of little attentions to the Hostes; supervising the construction
and finishing of his uncle's new coach and even buying his
wigs for him. But as he became absorbed in affairs, Walpole
found Hoste increasingly tedious and no doubt the sense of an
obligation which he could not discharge also made Walpole
neglectful of him. His failure to help over Hoste's appointment as sheriff made matters worse, but Hoste was even more

[1] C(H) MSS, Townshend, 6 November 1704.
[2] *Ibid.* Townshend, 6 November 1704; 8 November 1704. As a further
illustration of the importance of the sheriff's appointment, Townshend recommended a Mr Rogers as sheriff in 1707 'because I thought it might be of service
to have one of our friends sheriff next year upon the account of the election',
ibid., 8 November 1707.

infuriated when Walpole made a complete hash of his orders
for a High Sheriff's livery. For Hoste this was the last straw—
the unmistakable display of a total lack of respect in a
nephew who thought too much of himself. He became
clamorous for his money, spread rumours of Walpole's extravagant living, stirred up strife with the hot-tempered
Colonel Horatio Walpole of Beckhall and intrigued against
Walpole in his pocket borough of Castle Rising, not once but
at every general election until his death. Even in 1722, at
one of the most difficult moments of Walpole's career, he was
distracted by Hoste's attempt to seduce his voters.[1]

Hoste, however, suffered for the luxury of his opposition.
Turners, Holleys, Allens, Cremers, all enjoyed tit-bits of
patronage as Walpole rose in the world. Although his benevolence responded quickly to loyalty, his hostility was as
quickly aroused by aggressive independence. The Hostes
failed to prosper. This was the danger of a world of politics
in which personal attitudes were more important than any
principle. The total lack of any sort of party organization,
local or national, the absence of any but the vaguest political
dogmas to which men could subscribe, meant that political
alliances were at the mercy of the human temperament in
all its vagaries. Such a system gave Townshend and Walpole
a heightened sensitivity to personal problems; and it made it
necessary for them to assess every action in human terms.
The reason why such detailed attention was given to the
appointment of local officers was because one man's sense of
disappointment might change the delicate political balance
of a neighbourhood with, perhaps, dangerous consequences
for parliamentary representation. The composition of Parliament was, of course, the governing factor of local politics,
the end for which all the arts of personal management were
designed and the reason why Walpole devoted the most de-

---

[1] C(H) MSS, various letters of Hoste; also references to him particularly in
the letters of John and Charles Turner. The intrigues of Hoste in 1722 are in a
letter of Jonas Rolfe, 19 August 1721. Further correspondence of Hoste is to
be found in the *Chicago (Walpole) MSS*.

tailed attention not only to Norfolk affairs but also to those of all the counties of the land and of all the boroughs, great or small.

5

IN 1726 Thomas Madox published his *Firma Burgi*, a fascinating panorama of the wide variety of communities enjoying special franchises in Hanoverian England. There was extravagant diversity. Beccles in Suffolk was ruled by the owners of its fen; Newport in Northumberland by the owners of its quay. Haverfordwest, a tiny hamlet, was the only town to enjoy the same privileges as the City of London, proudly boasting a Lord Lieutenant and Custos Rotulorum of its own. Or there was Durham where the Bishop exercised privileges more akin to those of a Prince-Bishop of the Holy Roman Empire than those of an English prelate. Franchises had nothing to do with the size of urban communities.[1] Birmingham and Manchester, both large and growing towns, were administratively speaking, only parishes. Fortunately for Walpole in this bewildering variety there was a dominant type in which significant changes were taking place which were to make for the ease of his government. Corporations whose privileges were based on royal charters, had developed, and were developing, in similar ways. They were governed by a mayor, aldermen and common-councilmen, the latter were frequently elected by the freemen of the borough, that is those who by birth, by marriage, by servitude of apprenticeship or admission by the corporation were free to exercise their trade within the corporation's jurisdiction without the payment of a fine.

Theoretically, a qualified democracy, in practice, except in London, it was nothing of the sort. During the seventeenth century certain changes had taken place which brought about a concentration of power into the hands of oligarchies as narrow as those which dominated rural society. No one

[1] For boroughs and borough franchises, see S. and B. Webb, *English Local Government*, II.

very much cared. Most human beings are prepared to be ruled; their energies are absorbed by their pursuit of wealth and by humanity's deepest needs—daily bread and family life. Only bodies of politically active and politically astute freemen could have preserved their privileges against the steady and insidious attack of the aldermen. To these men who aspired to dominate their communities the freemen were a hindrance, so their power was curtailed in a variety of ways. At Boston, the fine for admission was raised from £5 to £50 between 1689 and 1719, thus effectively reducing their number to a manageable proportion. The Corporation of Retford ceased to admit any freemen at all, so did Plympton. At Hastings two were admitted yearly, friends always of the Duke of Newcastle, more often than not men of great substance, who paid for the honour by providing the Corporation with a sumptuous banquet, and then never troubled it again—except to appear and vote for the Duke's parliamentary candidates. Other corporations failed to summon their freemen except for formal and unimportant business meetings, which most freemen were too bored to attend.

It was not long before the common-council went the way of the freemen; instead of an organ of government it became a sort of antechamber where friends and relations of the aldermen who became the real rulers of the towns waited for them to die and make a place. The aldermen were, by virtue of their position, justices of the peace, which armed them with the authority of law. They had at their disposal great wealth, accumulated by the corporation during the centuries of its existence. They controlled important charitable trusts. Yet it was exceedingly rare for any of this wealth to be ploughed back into social services[1]; usually it was spent on feasts and plate, frittered away into each other's pockets in a thousand and one forms of petty corruption. Only the children and dependants of their sycophants found their way

---

[1] Liverpool was a notable exception, cf. Webb, *op. cit.*, II, pt. 2, 481–91. An excellent study of an eighteenth-century corporation is by R. W. Greaves, *The Corporation of Leicester*, 1689–1832.

into the schools and almshouses. These aldermen were the tradesmen and merchants of the town, long practised in the amiable art of feathering each other's nests. Naturally they married into each other's families, creating neat conglomerations of wealth and interest until a few, self-perpetuating families controlled the life of a town for a century.

This concentration of power into the hands of a small number of men was to be advantageous to Walpole in many ways. The fewer the men, the easier it was for him to have a sound working knowledge of the pattern of personality and influence in all boroughs that were politically important. The patronage and honours which he controlled were limited, so the fewer pockets to fill the better—a point quickly appreciated by the recipients.

There was, however, a more subtle aspect of this change. Oligarchs quickly learn to know their place. They saw no value likely to accrue to them from sending up two merchants of the town to represent them in Parliament as their fathers had so often done. A member of a great landed family in Walpole's world would prove far more influential; the son of a peer or a well-established placeman would be better still, and a much stronger link in the great chain of patronage.

This is exactly what had happened at King's Lynn. For most of the seventeenth century Lynn had been represented by merchants who dwelt and traded in the town, but in the early eighteenth century both Walpole and Sir Charles Turner belonged to the neighbouring gentry, Sir Charles being the first of the Turners to leave trade and lead the life of a gentleman. And this was true of many towns like Lynn. Hence the astonishing homogeneity of the House of Commons in which the vast majority of members were country gentlemen, although technically speaking most of them were there as burgesses. Of course, not all the town oligarchies favoured Walpole. Often they took the colour of their politics from the neighbouring gentry or aristocracy. Sometimes there were special interests, as at Bristol and Liverpool, which dominated; and there were also a few towns where this slide into oligarchy was not taking place. The greatest of these was London.

6

THE CONSTITUTION of London was a complex qualified democracy. There were so many advantages associated with the freedom of the City of London that it was always keenly sought after even when the admission fine was abruptly raised from £2 6s. 8d. to £25. The freemen participated in the administration of their wards; they elected both the aldermen and the common-councilmen who represented their ward in the government of the city. About half of these freemen belonged to the livery of the great City Companies, membership of which had brought them their freedom. Those who were of the livery took part in the yearly election of sheriff, an office of considerable importance in the judicial and administrative life of the City. The vital components of the City's government were the twenty-six aldermen and the two hundred and thirty-four common-councilmen. During the Commonwealth the Common Council had improved its position in relation to the aldermen. The point at issue was the right of the aldermen to veto the acts of the Common Council. The remodelled charter of Charles II had restored to the aldermen what was probably their ancient right, but the Revolution had witnessed a new confirmation of the independence of the Common Council.[1] This was far more than a constitutional issue, for the Common Council was more radical in its approach to political problems than the aldermanic bench, which was full of directors of the Bank and the great chartered companies who naturally tended to favour the government. But Walpole was to find that he could not be certain of controlling the aldermanic bench, for aldermen were elected and tories or critics of his administration were frequently to be chosen. By tradition the office of Lord Mayor rotated in strict seniority. An unhappy consequence of this

[1] For a more detailed description of the City constitution, cf. Webb, *op. cit.* II, pt. 2, 574–81.

for Walpole was that during the most critical years of his life he was faced with a tory Lord Mayor. London was the one great institution in which the arts of management were hamstrung. There was a vociferous and literate public opinion, well catered for by newspaper, pamphlet and ballad, an opinion which could in a limited way make its voice heard in the deliberations of the nation either by using its ancient right to petition the King or by creating such uneasiness in commercial and financial circles that the ministry was forced to take notice. But its independence was aided by its institutions which no minister, not even Walpole, much as he hated the City, dared bring into final subjection. The key to a great deal of the politics of Walpole's day and of the rest of the century lies in the City's continued independence.

7

IN THE interplay of local government, the decisive factor was the effect any action might have on parliamentary elections, for the final assessment of any man's power lay in his ability to influence voters. Also, from the time of the Revolution, the desire to get into Parliament became more intense and a tremendous battle for power flared up, which lasted well into the eighteenth century. Before 1689 the existence of Parliaments had depended on the King's will. They might last two months or seventeen years; at times men doubted whether Parliaments would be called again. This factor of uncertainty made many men reluctant to invest their time, energy and money in pursuit of the doubtful privilege of sitting at Westminster. Also the lack of frequent elections presented Parliamentary candidates with completely changed conditions in their constituencies; and, in order to flourish, influence and patronage need constant use. But after 1689 men realized that Parliament was to be a perpetual feature of constitutional life, that it would meet every year. In 1694 the Triennial Bill made a general election certain once in three years, unless the sovereign thought fit to dissolve Parliament earlier. The Revolution Settlement had, however, ignored the need of

Parliamentary reform, so strongly stressed by Shaftesbury. A few pious platitudes were written into the Bill of Rights on the need for freedom and purity of elections.[1] Subsequently one or two Acts were passed, half-hearted attempts to stop the racketeering which the parliamentary franchise invited; they had no effect. Frequent elections, a feverish desire to get into Parliament or to control elections, the extraordinary franchise—these conditions caused a violent struggle for political power in the parliamentary constituencies, which in its turn influenced the whole structure of politics in the early eighteenth century. Fully to understand the significance of these changes, something must be said of the nature of Parliamentary franchise.

Before the Union with Scotland, the House of Commons was composed of 513 members. There were twenty-four Welsh members; eighty Knights of the Shire for English counties; four University members; the rest, the overwhelming majority, were returned by boroughs. The distribution of parliamentary seats was remarkably uneven. At the time of Elizabeth and the early Stuarts a considerable increase in parliamentary boroughs had taken place, particularly in the south-west.[2] The upshot was that twenty-five per cent of all members came from the five south-western counties, Cornwall, Devon, Dorset, Somerset and Wiltshire, which between them returned 142 members, Cornwall leading with forty-four. Such a distribution bore little relation either to population or wealth but it was not so outrageous, judged by these yardsticks, as it was to become by the early nineteenth century. The bulk of the population lived south of the Trent and there, too, was to be found most of the nation's wealth,

[1] For Shaftesbury cf. D. Ogg, *England in the Reign of Charles II*, II, 482–3. *Report of the Deputy Keeper of the Public Records*, XXXIII, 229–30; also Locke, *Two Treatises on Civil Government* (Everyman ed.), 197.

[2] Cf. J. E. Neale, *The Elizabethan House of Commons* in which he demonstrates that the extension was due not to a desire to increase royal authority but to a demand on the part of her privy councillors who desired clients. For this section in general cf. A. E. Porritt, *The Unreformed House of Commons*, and Sir Lewis Namier, *The Structure of Politics at the Accession of George III*, particularly Vol. I.

industry and commerce. Even so there was no rhyme or reason about representation. East and West Looe, two halves of a tiny Cornish fishing village, returned as many members as the City of London. Old Sarum had long ceased to have any inhabitants except the sheep which grazed its iron-age ramparts, yet its representation equalled Bristol's, the second city of the land. The accidents of history had brought these boroughs into being; and their diversity of franchise was due to the same cause. The right to vote differed from borough to borough, but the variety can be reduced to five main types.

There was a small group in which there was universal male suffrage; three groups, much larger, in which the right to vote was confined either to the corporation, or to those who paid the poor rates, or to the owners of specific pieces of property, usually houses.[1] Finally, there was the largest group, of about eighty boroughs, where the right to vote was enjoyed by the freemen of the town. None of these franchises gives an accurate idea of the size of the electorate, except in the roughest fashion. All male inhabitants of Gatton in Surrey had the right to vote, but with a population of less than a dozen such a generous suffrage meant little. Nor did it necessarily follow that the fewer the number of voters, the easier the borough was to control. It was generally true but not always so. Nottingham and Bedford docilely obeyed the dictates of the Dukes of Newcastle and Bedford, although they each possessed over a thousand voters, whereas the obdurate independence of the thirty-two electors of Bath was notorious. They would brook no patron and scorned influence. If allowance is made for the vagaries of human nature, then it is generally true that the fewer the voters, the easier the borough was to control. On the other hand absolute ownership of a borough was very rare. The most complete control was achieved in burgage boroughs where the vote was attached to property. Patrons purchased the houses,

[1] At Droitwich the franchise belonged to those who possessed shares in the salt mine.

temporarily conveying the ownership to a relative or a menial servant. But even in burgage boroughs there were rivalries and difficulties, and it was quite rare in the early eighteenth century for a family to have absolute control.

Castle Rising was a burgage borough where most of the property was owned by the Duke of Norfolk. After the Revolution, in 1695, he sold most of his property there to his relative Thomas Howard of Ashstead in Surrey. The Duke's ownership of the burgages, however, had never been quite complete; a few belonged to the Walpoles, some to merchants in Lynn; Hoste of Sandringham also possessed a few, so that the Howards thought it politic to allow Walpole's father to sit for one of the seats.[1] Colonel Walpole, realizing the insecurity of his position, rallied his forces, the Turners and Hostes who had just married into his family and the Hamonds of Wootton who were also close friends. They were persuaded to split their burgages, thus bringing dependable extra voters into being.[2] His brother Horatio of Beckhall purchased a few cottages and did likewise. The Howards recognized the threat to their hold on the borough and fought back; the price of a burgage cottage soared from £30 to £300. The election of the mayor of the borough was a vital factor in the control of its parliamentary elections. In 1695, Colonel Walpole took advantage of the recent change of ownership between the Duke of Norfolk and Thomas Howard, using all his influence to get his nominee appointed. Bailiffs moved in on the parson, a strong Howard supporter, who hid from them in the church steeple, a cunning ruse as the mayor was elected in church. Other voters were conveniently arrested for debt and the tiny town was in an uproar. Peace was saved by the arrival of a letter from the Howards accepting Walpole's right to a seat and to the privilege, implicitly rather

[1] Thomas Howard was the son of Sir Robert Howard, KB, MP, the dramatist who was a great-grandson of the Duke of Norfolk and a grandson of the Earl of Suffolk. Thomas's only daughter and heiress, Diana, married the Hon William Feilding, son of the Earl of Denbigh, a staunch tory family. Feilding sat for Castle Rising in his wife's right.

[2] This practice was stopped in 1697 by Act of Parliament.

57

than explicitly stated, of appointing his nominee to be mayor in alternate years. Colonel Walpole was overjoyed by this recognition of his influence in the borough on equal terms, although he possessed less of the property than the Howards. The latter, however, acknowledged that his proximity to, and their distance from, the borough cancelled that advantage. Secure in his triumph he graciously allowed the parson to leave his steeple and not only take part in the election of Howard's candidate as mayor but also in the great feast which Colonel Walpole ordered afterwards. He 'sent in 4 stone of beef and 2 dozen double bottles of his hogan to the Mayors, and after invited us to the Mayor Elect and treated us with several bottles of wine there. He was very generous and brisk'. But several of Colonel Walpole's party were less happy at the compromise, particularly his brother Horatio, who had spent considerably. He had hoped to occupy the second seat, if the Howards had been ejected, and it was said that he 'could not recover himself of his dump all day'.[1] For the rest of his life, this affair of Castle Rising rankled; in politics he was tory which made his family reluctant to see him represent the family borough. But the compromise with the Howards proved very uneasy. Colonel Walpole was deeply disturbed in 1696 on his return from London where he had been for the parliamentary session. He was told in Rising 'that noe Burgher that was a freind of mine should rent any of your [i.e. Howard] lands as they have constantly done'. And to make matters worse Howard expressed displeasure with Walpole's favourite mayor. An uneasy truce was patched up. Grave difficulties recurred in 1699, which were only resolved by a visit of the Howards to Houghton.[2] When Walpole succeeded his father, the affairs at Rising continued to tax his ingenuity.

The expense of Rising was not confined to the purchase of

[1] Bradfer-Lawrence, 'Castle Rising and the Walpoles', *Supplement to Blomefield*, ed. C. Ingleby.

[2] *Howard MSS*, Castle Rising. Colonel Walpole to Thomas Howard, [Aug.?] 1696; 11 September 1696; 15 September 1699.

the burgages. When the cottagers were assembled they had to be royally entertained. In 1701, the voters dined at three tables, according to their social status, and their fare varied accordingly; the first table had such luxuries as dried ham with pigeons, green geese, and the fore-quarters of house-fed lamb; the second table had to be content with a buttock of beef and a shoulder of mutton, while the third was given but a large leg of pork and the hind quarters of lamb; but drink was common to all tables, and the amount was prodigious, about thirty gallons of port being drunk by the forty-seven voters; this in addition to 'beer and cyder in plenty'. And expense did not stop with election feasts. There were a few independent burgage owners at Rising and they had to be treated with extravagant generosity.[1]

And yet by any standards, the Walpoles were very secure at Rising, far securer than the majority of patrons who possessed nothing so concrete as a piece of property which carried a vote, and naturally such patrons were forced into greater expense with far less certainty of success. As general election followed general election after 1689 the owner of a vote became adept at trading it. Costs of election rocketed as families fought to secure control of boroughs with small electorates. It cost Samuel Pepys just over £8 to lose his election at Harwich in 1689; in 1727 the same number of electors, thirty-two, drew nearly £1,000 from the Earl of Egmont's pocket.[2] A contest at Weobley cost a candidate £70 in 1690; in 1717 he laid out £722.[3] The costs of entertainment were frequently prodigious. At Clitheroe Guicciardini Wentworth intended to spend £200–£300 on a tiny electorate.[4] Nor did costs stop at elections, for the insecure loyalty of voters demanded constant attention. Lawrence Carter provided Leicester with a piped water supply. Sir Cloudesley Shovel and Sir Joseph Williamson built Rochester

[1] For Castle Rising cf. Bradfer-Lawrence, *op. cit.*, and a great deal of correspondence in *C(H) MSS*.

[2] Bodleian, *Rawlinson MSS*, A. 174, fo. 177; HMC, *Egmont Diary*, I, 293.

[3] BM *Add MSS*, 34,518, fo. 57.

[4] HMC, *Kenyon MSS*, 275.

a town hall and Sir Joseph threw in a grammar school for good measure.[1] And there were other costs; the clerk of the poll, the carpenters who built the booths; the town-criers and bell-ringers; the scores of officials who sprouted like mushrooms on election day, all these had to be paid for by the candidate. It was rare, too, for an election to be finally decided at the poll. There were always votes of doubtful legality, and frequently actions more dubious—bribery, kidnapping of voters, polling of dead men; no candidate ever lacked grounds to petition Parliament against the return of his rival though he might, like Sir Pury Cust, lack the money to do so. In 1690, Robert Harley had to transport witnesses from Radnorshire to London, which could only be done by hiring a coach at Oxford for the purpose. He supported them in London at his own expense, paid their wages, and of course made it worth their while to be his witnesses. It is not surprising that when his brother heard of the success of the petition he fell on his knees and offered his humble thanks to God.[2]

Only the wealthy could stand such a vast expense; many families beggared themselves trying to maintain an old family interest which had cost their forefathers little more than a glass of beer and a side of beef. The small squires and merchants tended to be forced out of electioneering, and by and large, the electorates did not want them, for they quickly learnt that there was more to a good patron than mere money. Influence was even more valuable, as Walpole was quickly to learn:

'The bearer hereof,' wrote Charles Turner to Walpole on February 21, 1704, 'Mr Benjamin Holly is the nephew of Mr Alderman Holly of our Towne, and haveing through excess and the follys of youth reduced his estate would gladly if possible assume a career in the forces now to be raised. His unckle will advance forty guyneys but if noe such imployment cann be gotten then that you would

<hr>

[1] HMC, *Bath MSS*, II, 176.
[2] *Ibid*. *Portland MSS*, III, 451.

please to procure him to be admitted a Midshippman in one of the Majesties shipps of warr.'[1]

Alderman Holley, a power in Lynn, had been reluctant to accept Walpole as burgess, but his reluctance had been overcome. Now the price was to be paid. Walpole lost no time and secured for him the post of ensign in Wightman's Regiment of Foot.[2] Another wastrel, Daniel Goodwyn, had to be found a place in the Customs. Lynn's bankrupt teacher of arithmetic was 'forced from the theory to the practick part of navigation', so Walpole got him a berth on the *Cumberland*, bound for Smyrna. It was this capacity to please all and sundry which endeared a member to his constituents, and made constituents seek men who were well placed to dispense patronage.[3]

The growing cost of elections, the need to dispose of influence, made a place in the government or an alliance with a minister of state exceptionally desirable to many members of Parliament; and so places and pensions came to be as eagerly sought as seats in Parliament. Administrations were quite eager to provide them in return for loyalty, expressed by regular attendance in the Commons and an appearance in the government lobby at critical divisions. Governments, whether whig or tory, desired security and an easy passage for the annual budget; without any strong party discipline, a majority tied by self-interest to the administration was the soundest form of government. Hume saw with exceptional clarity that the exclusion of pensioners and placemen would lead to administrative anarchy, just as he also realized that the deliberate exploitation of places and pensions must lead to the weakening of political principle. But, like most of his contemporaries, he could see no way out of this dilemma; to him as to them a reform of Parliament could not be contemplated; yet without a reform of the franchise the growth of patronage, influence and oligarchy was inescapable, which

[1] *C(H) MSS*, Charles Turner, 21 February 1704.
[2] C. Dalton, *English Army Lists*, VI, 92, 274. Holley had risen to be a lieutenant by 1710.
[3] *C(H) MSS*, John Turner, 3 October 1705.

was bound to lead to a destruction of political parties or inhibit their growth.[1]

In Walpole's early years, the party names, whig and tory, were still something more than labels; so to describe a man was the conventional method by which men defined their political attitudes. On the very broadest issues there was a clear distinction between whigs and tories. A man who detested the war against France, who would brook no toleration of dissenters, such a man was clearly a tory; just as an out-and-out supporter of the war and of religious toleration could with justice be called a whig. In parliamentary politics, these attitudes came into conflict in boroughs with large electorates, whereas in towns with few voters a candidate's political opinions were not of much moment. It was in the counties, however, that party strife became most intense, because whig and tory were names about which factions could crystallize their natural hatred for each other, a hatred which had in some cases lasted for centuries. In Leicestershire, long before the Wars of the Roses, the Hastingses and the Greys had hated each other; one family became Lancastrian, the other Yorkist; the Hastingses supported Mary Tudor against the Grey's own pretensions; in the Civil War the Hastingses ruined themselves in the King's service, the Greys fought for Parliament. After the Restoration the Hastingses were tory, the Greys whig. From time out of mind the lesser gentry had linked their destiny with one of these families; the strife of these factions was timeless although the names under which they fought each other changed with the centuries.[2] The same is true of Norfolk. The animosity between the Pastons and the Townshends was deep and bitter before the Exclusion crisis enabled them to hurl the epithet of whig and tory at each other. Elsewhere party

[1] Hume, *Essays Moral, Political, Literary* (1742), especially 'of Parties in General' and 'of the Coalition of Parties'. Also, Sir Lewis Namier, *Monarchy and the Party System* (Romanes Lecture, 1952).

[2] For the influence of the Hastings-Grey struggle on Leicestershire politics cf. J. H. Plumb, 'Political History of Leicestershire', *VCH Leicestershire*, II, 102–21.

strife was due to age-old conflicts between the north and south or east and west of counties. But the fact that such terms as whig and tory existed gave a focus to factional strife, and a justification for its continuance. And in the immediate post-revolution period added force was given to this division by a very real fissure in society; the smaller gentry found the land tax a crippling burden; and this gave an added bite to their toryism.

But all the facts of political life were destructive of party warfare. Contest followed contest in county after county from 1689 to 1714; Essex, for example, went to the poll no fewer than eleven times, as rival factions tried to secure control of its political life. The excessive expense of county elections in the end forced men to adopt a variety of compromises; once the compromise was achieved, the party conflict withered through lack of use.[1] Party labels, however, must quickly lose their meaning in the heart of politics. Although Godolphin and Marlborough passed as tories, they were Walpole's close friends and patrons, and so was Orford who called himself a whig. Newcastle and Somerset, both whigs, threw in their lot with Harley in 1710, because they thought he was more likely to follow a middle course rather than with the Junto whigs with whom they had previously associated. Tory groups split as easily as whig. Harley deserted Nottingham over the Tack; Rochester was at loggerheads with Nottingham; Bolingbroke worked for the ruin of Harley. This created a bewildering world of intrigue where party attitudes could suddenly acquire importance and then cease to have meaning just as quickly. They were picked up or laid aside according to the politician's need as he fought for power or clung to office. As the years passed men recognized the danger of excess in political life. Too much money, too much

---

[1] In 1715 it cost Walpole £110 13s. 7d. to take his freeholders with a county vote to Norwich for the election; one wagon load consumed four gallons of brandy on the journey. C(H) MSS, 'Account of the Disbursements of Mr John Turner, Jnr, for the County Election, 1 February 1715'. His father on 2 February 1679 spent £1 8s. 6d. 'att the election att Norwich'. C(H) MSS, Account Books, 15(1).

time and energy were consumed in getting into Parliament for men to wish to see their capital dissipated. Patrons of boroughs naturally preferred long-continuing, stable administrations with which the complicated process of influence could be evolved in a mutual security. Party fervour became a menace to all governments, although it remained the wine of life to oppositions—a lesson Walpole was quick to learn from Harley.

A further twist was given to the complications of party by the resentments which arose from the increasing cost of elections and by the blatant exploitation of patronage which, more and more, was becoming the decisive factor in political life. These things did not pass unnoticed.

'I believe Sir Pury Cust', Peregrine Bertie wrote to his brother, the Earl of Lindsey, 'will not be very willing to enter into battle with so great a family (i.e. the Berties) for I told him he must expect, if he stood, to spend £500 or £600.'[1]

Naturally, such an attitude caused envy to flare up, stimulating men to take counsel as to how best to protect their interests. They put their faith in strange cures—frequent Parliaments, preferably annual; the total exclusion of all office-holders from the Commons; a high qualification in land for all members; the prevention of aristocratic influence in elections; severe penalties against bribery; entertainment to be stopped once the writ has been received. Bills on such topics were perennial; some became law; others were modified until they were meaningless; standing orders were framed against the interference of the peerage. Yet none of these things had the least effect. All that they achieved was the creation of a few traditional war-cries which could always be relied upon to rouse that corner in the Commons where the knights of the shire and a few independent members clustered together. For a time in the reigns of William and of Anne, the

[1] HMC, *Ancaster MSS*, 250. Lady Elizabeth Cust, *The Records of the Cust Family*, 250-1. The income of Sir Pury Cust at this time amounted to £656 per annum, derived from rents, but he was over five thousand pounds in debt; the Berties were immensely rich.

attempt to stop the glissade into corruption was a vital concern of many members, sufficiently vital for it to be worth Harley's while to adopt many of these measures as his own, and to incorporate them into the official tory programme although they sprang from the resentments and jealousies of that self-same country party which had been one of the strongest allies of Shaftesbury. Harley's solicitude for the purity of elections needs little explanation; the country gentlemen who supported such a measure numbered nearly two hundred. The spread of corruption and the growth of oligarchy steadily diminished this number until it reached about one hundred, a figure at which it remained for the rest of the eighteenth century. But for the early years of Walpole's career these independent country-gentlemen remained a vital factor in politics. Their existence forced politicians to clothe their actions in the respectable garb of party principle and to justify themselves in the same terms. Their presence greatly complicates the politics of the period and makes the Augustan age one of the most difficult in English history. The nature of Parliament, the needs of government, the instinct of politicians were all opposed to any system of party politics. But a complex web of patronage could not be spun in a decade. The parliamentary franchise being what it was there could only be one end—oligarchy; events being what they were, the oligarchy had to be whig. But until the battle for power had been fought out in the counties and little boroughs and until Harley and Bolingbroke had proved their folly, party slogans and party issues had their role in politics.[1]

8

THE CLERGY as well as the laity were under no misapprehensions about the political role of the Church. In spite of infinite provocation the Church had followed the Stuarts

[1] Cf. R. R. Walcott, 'English Party Politics (1688–1714)' in *Essays in Modern History in Honor of W. C. Abbott* (Harvard, 1941). Although I am in substantial agreement with Professor Walcott, I think that he allows too little significance to conceptions of party, particularly amongst the whigs.

D

with unswerving loyalty and it was not until the bishops were clearly faced with the probable destruction of the Church's privileged position that they could bring themselves to a protest. The Revolution endangered the Church only momentarily. Few of the bishops and fewer of the clergy had any difficulty in repudiating their belief in the divine hereditary right of Kings or the doctrine of passive obedience. The minority who followed Sancroft were ineffective and the non-jurors remained a small eccentric sect of no political importance. Indeed their greatest value was to empty a number of bishoprics which William proceeded to fill, naturally enough, with men like Gilbert Burnet—a sound whig and a low churchman, who believed in toleration for dissenters. Whenever opportunity offered William strengthened the bench of bishops with men of similar views; during his reign the ladder of preferment was closed to all passionate high-churchmen. The accession of Anne called a halt to this process. There were many men in the Church who had found it possible to square their consciences in order to take the oath of loyalty to William and Mary but, once done, they shut their eyes to the logical consequences of their act and maintained the same stiff-necked high Anglican principles which had dominated the Church since the Restoration.

The major point of contention arose from the problem of toleration. In order to avoid toleration the High Church party under the Earl of Nottingham had tried to bring in a measure of comprehension: they were prepared to make a few meaningless modifications in the liturgy in order to draw off the right wing presbyterians, so that they could happily deny toleration to the rest. This project failed and toleration of a sort was granted in 1689. The dissenters, however, were still denied full civic rights, which they failed to obtain for another century. Many of them got round their legal difficulties by taking communion in their parish church once a year, a practice which infuriated the high-churchmen, who were so shocked by such a cynical treatment of the Sacrament that they demanded the suppression of occasional conformity. They harboured another grievance for they strongly disapproved of the rapid growth of dissenting academies after the Revolution. These schools were so excellent both in what was taught and in how it was taught that they were patronized not only by dissenters but also by Anglicans. Naturally, the high-churchmen wished to close these schools; they were a danger to the Church's monopoly of education and an insidious threat to Anglican doctrine.

Some high-churchmen felt also a prick of conscience about the future succession. They argued that Mary and Anne were both true Stuarts whereas the Hanoverians represented a complete break with the sacred line of direct inheritance. So they dreamed of a Jacobite future and this helped to soothe their resentment towards a world which was rapidly becoming alien to them. In their hearts they probably knew that the tide of life was setting against them. But for the twelve years of Anne's reign these crypto-Jacobites prospered; the Queen was moved by their profound veneration for the Stuarts and her dislike of dissenters was as ardent as their own. For better or for worse, it was impossible to remove a bishop, which limited the opportunities of these high-churchmen for advancement. Also for many years, Anne's advisers were moderate men who hated religious fanatics of any variety. Nevertheless the High Church party obtained sufficient places of importance for them to become a formidable force in politics. Bishops had seats in the House of Lords and perhaps more important—votes. They could strongly influence the attitude of their chapter which, as in York, Winchester, Salisbury, Durham and elsewhere, played a vital part in the local parliamentary elections. Many of the higher clergy were gifted writers with a natural love of polemics, so that much political propaganda came to be written by the clergy. Perhaps the deepest divisions of opinion in Anne's reign were caused by the struggle within the Church between Erastians and high-churchmen, but the accession of the Hanoverians soon put an end to it, for a determined government could very easily secure a complacent

Church; the system of preferment made it a relatively easy task.

Bishoprics varied in value, some such as Winchester, Salisbury, London, Durham, and of course Canterbury and York, were exceedingly valuable, possessing incomes of five to seven thousand pounds a year, a princely salary for the early eighteenth century, enabling these prelates to live in the greatest magnificence. Other dioceses carried only a moderate salary; some, mainly the Welsh, were quite poor, bringing the bishop but a moderate stipend of three or four hundred pounds a year. But bishops could climb; they were never doomed to Welsh obscurity if they studied to please, for a bishop could be translated—at the sovereign's pleasure.

The career of Bishop Hoadly is a perfect illustration of method. All that Hoadly had to recommend him was wit, force of character, bold ambition and a tireless pen. He was severely handicapped in more than one way, for he was so badly deformed, he could only preach on his knees and as the son of a Norwich schoolmaster, he lacked all aristocratic influence. He adopted the Low Church attitude and until the Hanoverian succession slowly struggled up the ladder of preferment. After 1714, he never looked back. His support of the government was undeviating. He could be relied on in the House of Lords, even for the most disagreeable of tasks such as denouncing Place Bills. His pen was always at Walpole's service not only on ecclesiastical matters but also for foreign affairs and general ministerial propaganda. His political tasks were so onerous that he was unable to visit his diocese during his six years as Bishop of Bangor. But a man like Hoadly did not remain a Welsh bishop for long; the fruits of his loyalty were large and juicy. He was translated first to Hereford, then to Salisbury, and afterwards to Winchester—the fourth richest bishopric, worth five thousand pounds a year. Naturally the High Church party did not relish this rise to greatness; but there was nothing they could do about it except vent their rage on Hoadly with biblical fury, denouncing him as a 'Deist Egyptian! A rebel against the Church! A vile republican! An apostate of his own order! The scorn and ridicule of the whole kingdom!' But it was Hoadly's world.[1]

Gibson, Bishop of London and for sixteen years Walpole's lieutenant for Church affairs, was determined that promotion should be given only to men who were absolutely devoted to the administration. Every bishop's appointment was so closely scrutinized that Walpole could rely on twenty-four of the twenty-six bishops' votes in the House of Lords, usually sufficient to ensure him a majority; wherever possible the same discipline was imposed on the lower clergy. A number of fat benefices attached to cathedrals and collegiate churches could be used to reward the faithful. The Rev. James Baker acted as an election agent for the Duke of Newcastle in Sussex. An active man, he rushed round the county from horse races at Steyning to a cricket match at Lewes, proselytizing the reluctant tories. Indeed he so irritated the spectators at Lewes that he was nearly mobbed for his pains. A part of his ardour may have been due to the fact that already, through the Duke's influence, he enjoyed the comforts of plurality. But his rewards more than outweighed the danger of a martyrdom, for his political loyalty secured him the Archdeaconery of Chichester, and afterwards a most lucrative prebend's stall at St Paul's. Thoroughly and systematically the patronage of the Church was used to reward clergymen or their relatives for services rendered to the State.[2]

Townshend and Walpole learned to weigh the appointments of all Norfolk clergymen with the same care and attention that they were to devote to the selection of justices of the peace. On 23 September 1706 Townshend wrote urgently to Walpole: 'Mr Crispe, Minister of Ellingham being either dead or dying, I must beg assistance on behalf of one Mr Baron who is a very honest man and a near neighbour of Sir Charles Turner. Ellingham lyes not far from Kirby and the

[1] For Hoadly, cf. *DNB* and N. Sykes, *Church and State in the Eighteenth Century;* Hervey, *Memoirs.*
[2] Sykes, *op. cit.*, 81 *et seq.*

living is worth between £60 and £70 p.an. It is in my Lord Walden's gift. If you could either yourself or by any friend prevail with my Lord to give Mr Baron this living it would be of very good service to our interest in that part of the country. Pray take all the care you can in this matter and above all things be sure to loose no time, that my Lord may not be engaged before you apply to him.'[1]

Sir Charles Turner wrote by the same post and he was more urgent and more specific:

'I should not have troubled you again so soon but on a matter of very great consequence which in short is this. Mr Crispe a notorious Jacobite parson in my neighbourhood of Kirby is a-dyeing if not dead. . . .[2] This is the first opportunity I have had towards enabling myself to be a checkmate to my loving friend and neighbour, Sir Edmund Bacon.[3] There are ten or twelve freeholders in Ellingham and as it joins to Kirby so as to be almost the same town (being generally wrote Kirby-cum-Ellingham) could I but get an honest parson in I should not much question but with his assistance to strike a good stroke towards bringing these poor deluded people to their senses again . . . therefore beg of you for the sake of the publick more than upon my own account that you would leave no stone unturned to obtain it and set about it the moment you have read my letter. . . . For God's sake do not neglect this affair.'[4]

Townshend's and Turner's agitations were in vain. The living of Ellingham was in the hands of Lord Suffolk who was unsympathetic to the whig cause and Sir Charles had to wait for another opportunity before he could deliver his neighbour a checkmate.

There were of course patrons who were largely indifferent to politics, and who refused to be dragooned by the politically minded into making a political appointment. Many parsons

[1] *C(H) MSS*, Townshend, 23 September [1706].

[2] Samuel Crispe was presented to Ellingham by James, Earl of Suffolk, in 1670, Blomefield, *Norfolk* (ed. 1775), IV, 233.

[3] Sir Charles Turner had married for a second time Mary, daughter of Sir William Blois and widow of Sir Nevil Catelyn of Kirby Cane, GEC, *Barts,* V, 66.

[4] *C(H) MSS*. Sir Charles Turner, 23 September 1706.

lived out their lives unconcerned with either great men or great affairs. For the most part they were steady commonplace men, inclined to toryism, strongly distrustful of all change or innovation, unmoved by the deeper problems of religious faith, who nevertheless tended their flocks with care and with charity. Often they acted as physician and lawyer as well as parson, for it was natural that their parishioners should bring to them all problems which required skill in book-learning. About most of their lives there was a steady, self-indulgent benevolence which comes to men locked in a narrow world of easy circumstances.[1] But for the ambitious clergyman there was but one way of advancement: a well-placed patron and unwavering devotion to politics.

9

LOCAL GOVERNMENT, Parliament, the Church were the three bases upon which the pyramid of government rested. Their management and control absorbed most of the time and a great deal of the energy of all the ministers of state, yet without the forceful backing of the Crown, their time and energy would have been wasted. The position of the Crown in the late Stuart and early Hanoverian times has been constantly misunderstood. Anne could on occasion be overborne, particularly by the resourceful and vigorous Duchess of Marlborough, but she could be extremely obstinate and her views on policy as well as on appointments had to be respected. Nor were the Georges mere cyphers. George I possessed more than a smattering of English, and all his ministers, including Walpole, had a fair or fluent knowledge of French, the language used naturally by the King.[2] Both George I and his mistresses had a keen interest in domestic politics, whilst George II's and Caroline's was avid; no promotion was too small to escape their attention and they insisted on

[1] An excellent illustration of a typical eighteenth century parson's life is to be found in C. D. Linnell (ed.), *The Diary of the Rev. Samuel Rogers*. Bedfordshire Historical Society, XXX (1950).

[2] The myth that Walpole could only converse with the King in dog Latin is based on a legend started by Horace Walpole in his reminiscences, written in

listening to lengthy and detailed reports of the debates in Parliament. Lord Hervey's *Memoirs* would make this clear enough even if we did not possess many of Walpole's memoranda, listing matters which he wished to discuss with the King, ranging from ambassadorial appointments to the rules of the college which Bishop Butler wished to establish in Bermuda. The Court was the heart of political life and without the entire and loyal support of George I or George II Walpole could not have lasted a month; it was as vital to his power as was his majority in the Commons, indeed more so, because had he not possessed the royal good-will his majority in the Commons would not have been secured. It is necessary to look more closely at the machinery of government to appreciate the power of the Court in eighteenth-century politics. Parliamentary sessions were short and mainly concerned with the passage of financial bills. Legislation as we know it was quite rare, with the consequence that the actions of the executive became the main target of criticism in debates; foreign affairs and the cost of the armed forces took up most of Parliament's time. The King's ministers were not, however, usually troubled with Parliament for more than four or five months of the year and for the rest they could devote themselves to diplomacy, patronage and administration, of which patronage and diplomacy were the most important.

The King controlled an immense field of patronage. Every civil servant was the King's *own* servant, appointed by him and paid out of the royal pocket. The entire administration of the country was carried out by the Royal Household, which, like the constitution, had grown up haphazardly over the centuries; when new problems had arisen they had been met either by increasing the duties of a minor official or by the creation of a new office. Old ones were never abolished.

advanced old-age for the Misses Berry. Cf. Paget Toynbee (ed.), *The Reminiscences Written by Horace Walpole* in 1788, 14–15. All foreign dispatches were duplicated in French for the King's benefit. Cf, Townshend's diplomatic correspondence at Raynham and Horatio Walpole's at Wolterton Hall. Walpole when Secretary-at-War had the French gazettes sent over to him.

Many offices became sinecures with no duties; if the office had duties, more often than not (unless they were great offices of State) they could be easily discharged by a deputy, so that the Household became the haven for the needy place-hunter. Walpole's strength as a minister arose from the fact that nine times out of ten the King accepted his advice on appointments. Naturally Walpole used this power to secure himself in the Commons, and all places great or small were made to pay political dividends. This was a wasteful policy financially, for the abolition of such offices as the Taster of the King's Wines in Dublin, useless and absurd as it was, could never be entertained; its bestowal on a member of Parliament or his relatives would keep him in dependence on the Court. So the resources of the Household came to be ruthlessly exploited by place-seekers and politicians, with the result that historians have come to overstress the corruption of eighteenth-century politics. Sinecures might be without duties, but they were rarely without obligations, and often entailed hard work.

In 1726, the Board of the Green Cloth had become an archaic survival of the Middle Ages. Its function was to settle disputes arising amongst the King's servants. By 1726 it had long ceased to have much business, yet there were four clerks—Richard Sutton, Sir Robert Corbet, Gyles Earle, Robert Bristow—all drawing £500 per annum.[1] Naturally they were to be found in the government lobby in all critical divisions. They could be mistaken for typical placeholders selling their vote for the sake of a sinecure. This, however, is a distortion, for these men played the part of junior ministers. They attended debates with great assiduity, served on count-less committees, and helped with energetic skill to pilot government measures through the Commons. Although they lacked administrative responsibility in a narrow sense, in all other ways they may be regarded as hard-working members of the government, fully deserving their £500 per annum. Many sinecures were so filled, and a great deal of the jockey-

[1] Chamberlayne, *Magnae Britanniae Notitia* (ed. 1726), Pt. II, Bk. III, 106.

ing and intrigue which went on to obtain a place at Court was as much for the sake of cutting a figure in government as for the money it brought. These places possessed one other attraction; they conferred distinction. The whole of London's social life revolved around the Court; its gaiety, wit and malice were inbred; it was a closed yet glittering world which dazzled all who did not belong to it by birth. This mixture of luxury and power intoxicated the ambitious, and its compulsive quality only weakened as the monarch aged. Then, as his hold on the future loosened, the young and the discontented drew closer about his heir, and spent happy days sharing the spoils of future office as they awaited the King's death. At such times cautious men found in an independent attitude the way of virtue and profit, and ministries encountered difficulties in securing their majorities. For many years of Walpole's ministry both he and the King were in the prime of life, and age and death did not cast their disturbing shadows across the political scene.

Naturally there were gradations of power within the Court. The great officers of State were of two kinds, those with and those without departmental duties. As Chancellor of the Exchequer and First Lord of the Treasury, Walpole was to be burdened with exceptionally heavy day-to-day business, whereas the Duke of Montagu, as Master of the Great Wardrobe, had nothing more than a few traditional duties to perform for the King personally. These offices of great honour and small duties were usually bestowed on loyal noblemen of great wealth and territorial power—the Dorsets, Graftons, Richmonds and their like, whereas the offices with administrative duties went to the active politicians, the men who ran the Lords and Commons on behalf of the Crown.

Traditionally both types of official were the King's advisers on questions of policy; and there were times when they all met together as a cabinet. But these large cabinets were not loved by the politicians. Walpole came to distrust them, and avoided them when he could, for in such a large body it was easy for disagreement on points of policy to fester and to create factions competing for the King's approval.[1] Also there was a great deal of business, particularly foreign affairs, where detailed knowledge was essential and could only be acquired by close application to ambassadorial reports.

Naturally the politicians preferred to decide such questions in close conclave. In time of war, the need for secrecy became more critical, and as carelessness was more likely to arise from a large cabinet, so smaller ones were favoured. And lastly, there was the undeniable fact that many holders of great household offices were not clever men, and their opinions were more likely to befog than clarify business. These factors resulted in the early development of a small inner cabinet which met frequently and consisted almost entirely of the political officers of the Household—the Lord President, the Privy Seal, the First Lord of the Treasury, the two Secretaries, and the Lord Chancellor—the men who bore the burden of government. They met informally wherever it suited them best, sometimes at the Cockpit, which housed the Treasury and the Secretaries, but frequently in their own homes; sometimes one of the Secretaries jotted down their decisions or made a few notes, but many meetings have gone unrecorded.[2] Once this inner ring, or 'efficient cabinet' as it is called, had determined its policy, it had little difficulty in imposing its views on the large cabinet which from time to time was required to meet to give a more formal sanction to certain acts of State. This system did not develop during the early years of Walpole's career when the formal cabinet with the Sovereign present discharged a great deal of business, but under the Georges the formal cabinet suffered an eclipse. George II maintained that no good ever came from it, an

[1] Professor A. Aspinall in his Raleigh Lecture, *The Cabinet Council*, 1783–1835, quotes a number of remarkable instances of cabinet quarrels. Although of a much later date, they reflect a situation which was common in Walpole's day.

[2] The cabinet notes of Harley, Sunderland, Townshend and Dartmouth survive. Harley's notes are amongst the documents deposited by the present Duke of Portland in the British Museum, the Sunderland notes are at Blenheim, the Townshend notes at Raynham, and the Dartmouth notes at the William Salt Library, Stafford.

opinion which Walpole encouraged. When the King was in Hanover the meeting of a more formal body could not be avoided and then policy was considered by the Lord Justices, a body which was almost identical with the large cabinet, but not, of course, before the vital decisions had been decided by the efficient cabinet.

We have a very clear picture of how this system worked from the diary of Lord King who was Lord Chancellor from 1725 to 1733.[1] Walpole, naturally, took the initiative. Technically he was often invading territory which by right belonged to others. Foreign affairs, strictly speaking, were the concern of the Secretary of State and none of his business. He had to find the money for subsidies or to pay for war, if war ensued, and this was sufficient excuse, if excuse were needed, for his interference. When a treaty or a negotiation was on foot, Walpole would dine with each of the chief ministers or spend a night with them in their country houses. In the benevolent and easy atmosphere induced by good food and better wines, Walpole would air his views, counter criticism, and plant his suggestions. The ground prepared, the efficient cabinet meeting would be called. Unanimity, in the heyday of his power, did not take long to achieve. Once the inner ring was certain of its line, the Lords Justices or the formal cabinet would be summoned and, with alacrity and little discussion, formalized the decisions previously taken. Then, of course, came the struggle to persuade the King to accept the proffered advice. The Hanoverians were deeply interested in foreign affairs and often held to their views with great obstinacy. The Secretaries did not present the King with a decision but with an advice, and it is essential to remember this, for it explains why Walpole, Townshend or Newcastle were forced to spend so long at Court cajoling and persuading the Monarch to go the way they wanted him to go; why it was necessary for them to have Court

[1] Lord King's diary is printed in volume two of King, *Life and Correspondence of Locke* (ed. 1830). I have compared this with the original in the possession of the Earl of Lovelace; the transcript is accurate. Cf. also Hervey, *Memoirs*, I, 121-131.

spies, such as Hervey, who could report at once the purveyors of counter-advice, men who were hunted remorselessly by Walpole until he secured their destruction.[1] And, of course, the jealousies and envies of those who were excluded from this inner ring were always at work. Because the King was head of the executive, policy-making demanded extreme care and dexterity; and a fluid, semi-formalized system was much easier to manage than a rigid constitution.

But policy was largely a matter of foreign affairs. A great deal which nowadays would demand the attention of the cabinet was settled out of hand by Walpole himself. In 1731 the Earl of Egmont wanted to secure an easing of the trading conditions between Ireland, Great Britain and the Colonies. To strengthen his case he secured the support of most of the Irish peers and members of the Commons with Irish interests, who held formal meetings at the Thatched House Club and passed resolutions in favour of his policy. A situation of great complexity arose which entailed decisions involving relations with Ireland and America. On this matter Walpole consulted no one but his brother Horace, whose office as Cofferer of the Household lacked the remotest connection with Ireland; yet he was present at meetings called by Egmont in order to put forward his brother's views. When at last Egmont brought the matter before the House he was dexterously outmanoeuvred by Walpole, who from start to finish seems not to have consulted any other minister, so that Egmont wrote bitterly and with a certain justice in his diary:[2] 'Thus we see how the welfare of that poor Kingdom (Ireland) lies in the breath of one Minister's nostrils.' Rarely has a minister wielded such independent authority.

There is one further point about the central government at this time that needs to be stressed. There was less, infinitely less, administration. There was only one really large Department and that was the Treasury. A series of reorganizations

[1] At Raynham there is a large file of Townshend's correspondence with George II. Each letter was carefully annotated by the King, no matter how trivial. Coxe printed some of his correspondence, *op. cit.*, II, 520–43.

[2] HMC, Egmont, *Diary*, I, 173–5.

undertaken at the end of the seventeenth century had greatly increased the number of its employees, both in London and the provinces, for it controlled both the Customs and Excise. But even here methods were primitive by modern standards and business was small. Other Departments were tiny. Matters which required the attention of the Secretaries of State were extremely varied—all foreign dispatches, which involved ciphering and deciphering, passed through their office; at the same time they were responsible for law and order, for the Colonies, for Scotland; all final decisions about the Army and Navy were their concern. In fact, all that touched the King's affairs, except finance, had to be dealt with by them. Even when a child was eaten by a tiger, they needed to be consulted. Was the tiger forfeit to the King? If so, could it be destroyed? Only a Secretary could decide.[1] But such oddities seldom strayed into the Secretaries' office, for the people at large ignored the official world and made their own decisions. The Secretaries' minute staff—twenty-six including the caretaker—devoted themselves mostly to ambassadorial dispatches and agents' reports, leaving the country to govern itself as well as it could. Without protection the poor, the weak and the sick went under; the rich and the strong prospered. But few cared, and any increase in the government's power, any extension of its activity, was bitterly resented.

This was to be Walpole's world—a small prosperous nation which had thrown off the shackles of monarchial despotism and created the undefined compromise of a parliamentary monarchy. So long as the King remained head of the executive, the Court was bound to be the focus of political power and this in turn weakened the party basis of politics. Patronage, in all its complexity, became the dominant theme in political life. At such a time force of personality and skill in human relations were more than ever desirable in a statesman. Walpole had both in good measure and it is time to turn to the story of his life.

[1] Mark Thomson, *Secretaries of State*, 1681–1782, 111.

BOOK TWO

THE YOUNG STATESMAN

CHAPTER THREE

EARLY YEARS, 1676-1708

ROBERT WALPOLE was born on 26 August 1676 in the old manor house at Houghton in Norfolk, the younger son of a prosperous, well-established county family whose fortunes had been founded in the thirteenth century. Apart from Ralph de Walpole, a Bishop of Ely who died in 1302, the family had produced few men of distinction, only the Jesuit martyr, Henry Walpole, executed at York in 1596, and the Jesuit apologists, Richard and Michael Walpole. Fortunately for the family their sufferings did not weld them to the old faith, and Walpole's father was out with his brother squires hunting down recusants during the scare of the Popish Plot. Although Walpole's ancestors lacked distinction, they were shrewd men of business, steadily increasing their patrimony by judicious marriage and careful husbandry.[1]

His grandfather, Sir Edward, Member of Parliament for King's Lynn, had sufficient social standing and political influence to obtain a Knighthood of the Bath, an order which his grandson was to revive in 1726. For the first years after the Restoration, Sir Edward's prospects were very bright for he quickly made his mark in Parliament.[2] But death struck first his wife and then himself. In 1667, at the age of seventeen, Walpole's father was left alone to look after a large estate with a nursery full of young brothers and sisters. Fortunately he was built on a heroic scale, possessing sufficient strength of will and acuteness of intelligence to carry him easily through the difficulties which beset him. The foundations of the family's future greatness were laid by this Robert

---

[1] *DNB;* A. L. Rowse, *The England of Elizabeth,* 455-6; Jessop, *One Generation of a Norfolk House* (3rd ed., 1913); J. H. Round, *Family Origins and Other Studies; Cal. Treas. Bks.,* 1672-5, 698.

[2] H. Walpole, *Aedes Walpolianae* (2nd ed., 1752), 38-9.

Walpole, known to his friends as Colonel Walpole from his rank in the Norfolk militia.

His abilities have been overshadowed by the greatness of his son, but he cannot be dismissed as a simple Norfolk squire. When his father died, he was at Trinity College, Cambridge, where he had already acquired the reputation 'for study and learning extraordinary'.[1] His scholarly habits persisted throughout his life and he rarely came back from the great East Anglian fairs without a parcel of books strapped behind his man's saddle. They remain at Houghton; good editions of the classics, Latin rather than Greek, imported from Holland; weighty folios of history, European as well as English; some theology and a little law; Spenser's *Fairie Queene* and a few other volumes of poetry; most significantly there are copies of almost everything Francis Bacon wrote. Colonel Walpole admired him deeply and gave a copy of *Sylva Sylvarum* to his son almost as soon as he could read. His library was full of heavy, dullish books with a bias towards knowledge, to the factual life of the past rather than to theory or speculation. His reading was deep and rather sombre, as one might expect of a serious, weighty man, old beyond his years. His account books tell the same story. Every penny that he spent was carefully entered, even a screw of black buttons for twopence, or the first shilling's pocket-money which he gave to the young Robert at the age of six. And he never changed; the meticulous record goes on year in, year out, decade after decade. Long after his death, when Sir Robert was packing up to leave 10 Downing Street, he turned up one of his father's old account books, which highly amused his young son Horace, who wrote to his friend Mann at Florence:

'In three months and ten days that he was in London one winter as member of Parliament, he spent—what do you think? Sixty four pounds seven shillings and five pence. There are many articles of Nottingham ale, eighteen-pences for dinners, five shillings to Bob (now Earl of

[1] *Lives of the Norths* (1826), III, 304.

Mary Beale

I. COLONEL ROBERT WALPOLE

Orford) and one memorandum of six shillings given in exchange to Mr Wilkins for his wig. . . . He little thought that what maintained him for a whole sessions would scarce serve one of his younger grandsons to buy Japan and fans for princesses at Florence.' [1]

His frugality was needful. His father had left in his care four sisters and three brothers, to be provided for out of an estate of little more than eight hundred a year, and as he married very young, his own children were soon playing with their aunts and uncles in his nursery. His bride was Mary Burwell, a girl of sixteen, whose father, Sir Jeffrey Burwell, possessed lands close by Walpole's Suffolk property. [2] He was a lawyer, a bookish man too, but given more to theology than his son-in-law. His present to his daughter on her tenth birthday consisted of three fat folios, the collected works of that rabid puritan, William Perkins, Fellow of Christ's College. At least she started to study them for on the title page is a brief index, written in a girlish hand. The last entry reads 'on how to dye, 474'. [3]

Sermons were not her only reading; someone, perhaps her future husband, gave her a translation of Ovid's *Metamorphoses*. Maybe she was something of a bluestocking for her surviving letters show a consistency of orthography rare amongst seventeenth-century gentlewomen. She seems to have taken no interest in housekeeping and needlework. Colonel Walpole himself searched the stalls in Lynn market for hats, shoes and neckerchiefs. Mrs Cremer and Lady

---

[1] W. S. Lewis (ed.), *Horace Walpole's Correspondence with Sir Horace Mann* (Yale, 1955), I, 505–6. This account book is now in the possession of Lord Walpole: I am grateful to Mr R. W. Ketton-Cremer for drawing my attenion to its existence. Horace Walpole made a slip, however, for his grandfather's stay was just over two, not three months, from 22 October to 30 December 1690. He went up early for the session in order to take his son, Robert, to Eton. Frugal as he was he found 13*s*. 6*d*. for Samuel Pepys's recently published book on the Navy.

[2] J. Foster, *Chester's London Marriage Licenses* (1887), 1406. They were married at Rougham about 22 February 1671.

[3] These books, with others equally solemn given to her by her father, are still at Houghton, together with those collected by him and her husband.

Barkham of South Acre made the children's shirts and Colonel Walpole's cravats. Colonel Walpole also supervised the purchase of food, the payment of nurses; indeed he seems to have controlled the entire expenditure of the household. Mrs Walpole's letters give some insight into her character; their tone is forceful yet petulant; certainly there is a curious absence of any expression of affection. Although she lived until 1711, and scores of her letters survive, she never displays the slightest interest in her son's career; other members of the family congratulate him warmly on his early successes, she remains silent. She never enjoyed good health; many difficult labours undermined her strength and the frequent purchase of 'hysterical cordeall water' may imply nervous instability. Unlike her husband she was given to bursts of extravagance; once she laid her hands on any money she spent wildly, but her husband, and afterwards her son, saw to it that her opportunities for indulgence were rare. The character which emerges is of a woman cool in affection, intelligent, strong-willed, querulous and occasionally rash.

Life at Houghton might be frugal and sombre, but Colonel Walpole demonstrated clearly enough to the growing boy that ambition steadily pursued could lead to success and success to a certain opulence and grandeur. Notwithstanding his meanness, Colonel Walpole was aware that his position as a leader of the county required a display of grandeur as soon as he could afford it. After his sisters married, he began to spread himself a little, buying a new coach and refurnishing his hall with Dutch chairs. He started to entertain more extensively and increased his popularity by setting up a pack of hounds, a judicious investment, as his neighbours loved nothing more than hunting the hare over his wide-skied lands, ending the day in his parlour drinking down the famous Houghton *hogan* and noisily arguing the problems of the day. No doubt they talked bitterly of Jesuits, railed at the Court's Romish and lecherous ways, cursed France and Spain for their tyranny and their riches. But these hard-drinking, hard-hunting squires were not mindless, thoughtless

men; dangerous and tumultuous days had driven them to
ponder on the nature of governments and the principles of
power; to read deeply in English history and English law
which seemed to contain the key to the problems besetting
them. Dugdale, Tyrell, Petyt, Brady lined their shelves as
well as Colonel Walpole's. But at times the talk turned to the
land, for the traditional methods by which it had been cul-
tivated from time out of mind were being discarded and
Colonel Walpole was an ardent champion of this remarkable
revolution.

Nothing illustrates so well either his intelligence or strength
of purpose as the way he managed his estates. He had adopted
as soon as he could the Dutch methods which were just beginning to take root in this corner of Norfolk where the soil
was very similar to that of the barren coast lands of Holland.
By 1673 he was growing considerable quantities of turnips.
When they were a success, he increased his acreage to forty
and more, and encouraged his tenants to grow them too.
Clover and ray grasses followed shortly afterwards. He ex-
perimented with wheat and again succeeded. Naturally he
enclosed land whenever he could and extended the marling
process by which his ancestors had strengthened these light
sandy soils. He began to rotate his crops to avoid leaving the
soil fallow. These were all points of Norfolk husbandry which
Arthur Young was to single out for special praise a hundred
years later. 'Turnip' Townshend and Coke of Holkham were
mere publicists of a system of agriculture, already well established in Norfolk. Colonel Walpole was not a lonely pioneer,
for he obtained his clover seed from many neighbours, some
—like the Rudkins—barely more than yeomen farmers. His
large-scale turnip cultivation could be paralleled at Raynham and Holkham. His enterprise, however, brought a
handsome return and enabled him to pay off debts, find
without overmuch difficulty his sisters' portions, educate his
brothers and his own children, without incurring debt. Indeed he had saved enough by 1697 to buy the Pells' estates
at Dersingham and West Winch, a valuable property, worth

nearly five hundred per annum. This very considerable purchase did strain his resources and forced him to take out several mortgages which would not have taken him long to discharge. His son, incapable of frugal living, found them a sorry burden.[1]

Slowly but surely Colonel Walpole made his way in the world. His prudence and capacity for steady, dependable friendships brought him the leadership of the whigs in his neighbourhood. Indeed, Dean Prideaux thought that there was not a man in the whole whig party who could compare with him, and he thought that the only way to heal the violent divisions in the county would be for his protégé, Lord Townshend, to succeed the Duke of Norfolk whose health in 1700 was such that his early death (which occurred in January 1701) was confidently predicted.[2] Although Townshend became Lord Lieutenant, the divisions were not healed. Colonel Walpole's great reputation was based not only on the soundness of his judgment but also on his capacity for business. He was most painstaking in everything he undertook. Amongst the few papers which he left behind are a mass of legal arguments and counsel's opinions on the complicated and entangled affairs of Sir Thomas Hare of Stow Bardolph of whose children he had become a trustee. He devoted hours to this complex and tiresome case, soothed the vexed and vexatious widow, and finally secured a private Act of Parliament to put the estate on a sound footing.[3] Quite obviously he had a capacity to move adroitly through thickets of detail, a faculty which his son inherited in full measure.

A clear picture of Walpole's father and mother emerges

[1] Details of Colonel Walpole's expenditure are derived from *C(H) MSS*, Account Books; in addition there is the book at Wolterton. A more detailed study of them is to be found in my 'The Walpoles: Father and Son', *Studies in Social History* (1955). For his agricultural methods cf. J. H. Plumb, 'Sir Robert Walpole and Norfolk Husbandry', *Ec. Hist. Rev.* (1952), II series, V, 86-9.

[2] E. M. Thompson (ed.), *Letters of Humphrey Prideaux to John Ellis*, 1674-1732, 195.

[3] *C(H) MSS*, various letters to Colonel Walpole. HMC, *House of Lords MSS* (N.S.), I, 429.

from the few trivial memorials which they left behind them. His father was intelligent, ambitious, prudent and industrious, capable of leadership, knowledgeable in the exercise of authority, yet avaricious and ruthless. His mother neither inspired nor sought affection. A clever, taut, imperious woman, she possessed qualities which are often found in the mothers of great men. Both were built on a heroic scale. Uneasy to live with, perhaps, they endowed their children with sanguine, forceful and ambitious temperaments.

2

ROBERT WALPOLE makes only a few fleeting appearances in his father's account books and consequently all too little is known of his childhood and early education. His mother had a difficult labour; a nurse took up her residence in the house about a fortnight before he was born. The family doctor, Dr Richard Short, a crotchety, violent tory, rode over from Bury St Edmunds. He remained at Houghton for four days, receiving three guineas for his trouble. He was a great friend of the Walpoles, and the entire family remained in his charge until he died; later in life Walpole sent his own young children to live with him at Bury in spite of his Jacobite leanings. In accordance with family custom a wet-nurse was brought from Syderstone for the baby.

He belonged to a large and growing family for his mother gave birth to a child almost every year. Many of them died in infancy, for they were a sickly brood, prone to rickets and fever. When he reached the age of six, he was sent with his brothers to Great Dunham where the Rev Richard Ransome kept a small school. He received a thorough elementary education in which holidays played little part. He returned to Houghton only two or three times a year for a week or two. His strong attachment to his young brother, Horace, most probably developed during these lonely years away from home. He enjoyed little luxury and his clothes were plain, picked up by his father at local fairs or from wandering tinkers; once he had a coat made for him by a neigh-bouring gentlewoman. As a younger son he was intended for the Church and Colonel Walpole decided to send him to Eton, where he was entered in 1690 under a false age, twelve instead of thirteen, in order that he could qualify as a King's Scholar. [1]

The collegers in Walpole's day lived roughly. Bullying of the fiercest kind was rife and discipline was achieved through brutal flogging. The boys, nevertheless, were at least well taught in the classics. The life of a colleger contrasted sharply with that of the rest of the school. Colonel Walpole's young ward, Viscount Townshend, enjoyed much greater comfort. The oppidans lived in private houses; they furnished their own rooms, and studied a far wider range of subjects in which French and history were given almost as great a pro-minence as the classics. Throughout his schooldays Walpole experienced the same sense of constraint and frugality which had marked his childhood. Nevertheless he developed an abiding affection for Eton and for the friends he made there. When he grew rich and powerful he did not forget them. Henry Bland, his closest friend, flourished under his patronage, becoming first Headmaster, then Provost, of Eton. [2]

After six years of Eton, Walpole went up to King's College, Cambridge. He had been in residence for only two years when his eldest brother, Edward, died. On returning to Houghton he found that his father intended to cut short his academic career. His help was needed on the estate and it was desirable that he should learn as quickly as possible about turnips, sheep and clover. He tried unavailingly to persuade his father to allow him to continue at King's, and on 19 May 1698 wrote to the Provost:

'The days of my leave of absence from the college being

[1] Sir Wasey Sterry, *Eton College Register*, 1441–1698, 348.

[2] *Ibid.*, 37–8. Walpole also provided Bland with two of his own livings—Great Bircham and Harpley—and made him Chaplain of Chelsea Hospital in 1714.

near expired, and my father holding his resolution that I shall not any more reside here [*sic*], I do hereby resign my schollarship of Kings College in Cambridge. Witness my hand the day and the year above written.

Signed in the presence of   Robert Walpole.
Hen. Hare.'[1]

Colonel Walpole, who loved learning too dearly to interrupt his son's career needlessly, had cogent reasons for wanting Robert to learn the business of the estate as quickly as possible. His own health was very bad, and showed no signs of improving. He was finding his parliamentary duties so exhausting that he needed several weeks at Tunbridge Wells, when the session ended, before he had the strength to return to Norfolk. Once disease had taken a firm hold on a man in the seventeenth century, he could only view the future with apprehension. Less and less of Colonel Walpole's time was being spent on his estate and although he had an admirable steward in John Wrott he appreciated the value of that careful supervision and attention to detail he had himself given to his farms.[2]

In 1699, wishing to see his son well established before he died, he began negotiations to find him a wife. Sir John Mordaunt helped him find a suitable heiress and finally they settled on Catherine Shorter, the daughter of John Shorter, a Baltic timber merchant of Bybrook, Kent, and granddaughter of a former Lord Mayor of London. The bride brought a dowry of £7,000, but £4,500 of this was to be paid to Colonel Walpole; the remaining £2,500, secured on lands in Warwickshire and Derbyshire, belonging to Catherine Shorter's grandmother, Lady Philipps, was to go to Robert on condition that it was used to discharge the mortgage on the Dersingham property which Colonel Walpole

---

[1] *King's College MSS*. Mr A. N. L. Munby very kindly drew my attention to this letter—the first of Walpole's extant. Coxe, I, 5, and *DNB*, following Coxe, misdate Walpole's resignation by six days (25 May 1698).

[2] *C(H) MSS*. Letters to Colonel Robert Walpole contain many references to his illness: in the vouchers are many bills from apothecaries.

settled on him.[1] They were married at Knightsbridge on 30 July 1700.[2]

Catherine Shorter, a slender round-faced girl with large full lips and luminous eyes which seem in her portrait almost too large for their heavy lids, quickly stirred Robert Walpole's ardent nature. She lacked self-control and luxuriated in the riot of sensation and passion; but jealousy and rage would possess her as easily as love and desire, and Walpole lived an unquiet life as his one remaining love letter betrays.

'My dearest dear,

For I will still use the same language to you, although you can soe easily change your style. I will not say what might be said upon this occasion, but had I given you any provocation, any the least occasion for two soe very unkind letters, it must have been some satisfaction to me to have deserved it and would have been a great [——?][3] to me to know how to account for soe great an alteration. But what can I say? What can I think? Am I to judge by my self? May I measure your heart by my own? O there I find that love, that tendernesse, for you, that are there any failings in you they are still perfections to me and doth my Dearest doe or omitt any thing that might seem better otherwise, I am blind, cannot, would not see any thing in my dearer self but what is most agreeable. Why then this difference betwixt us? Why soe hard to believe what I am fond of and most happy in thinking? Why soe easy to entertain thoughts to me so distracting? I could have found a thousand excuses for you rather than have arraigned you of coldnesse, indifferency, neglect or want of love. Is this then the prologue to that delightful scene that I have been framing to myself? Are the pleasures of promised joy and rapture to be clouded over with jealous and uneasy thoughts? Doe you thus prepare yourself for those dear embraces the

---

[1] *Walpole MSS.* Marriage Settlement, dated 25 May 1700. Lady Philipps, daughter of Edward D'Arcy and granddaughter of the first Earl of Chesterfield, married Sir Erasmus Philipps of Picton Castle; their daughter married John Shorter but they soon parted, and Catherine, their daughter, lived with Lady Philipps at her house in Berkeley Street.

[2] Coxe, I, 5.

[3] MS illegible.

Sir Godfrey Kneller

II. CATHERINE WALPOLE

hopes of which have been my only support for your absence? Are we then to meet with cold faint hearts and chideing complaining eyes? Noe, my dearest soul, think again, examine the life of him you so severely censure and you'll find cause enough to believe that the greatest surprise and concern I ever mett is your unexpected and unjust complaints, and reason enough to convince you that my obedient wife and humble servant has a most tenderly affectionate, and passionately loving husband, whom nothing, not your own unkindn[esse] can alter from being my dearest creature

most sincerely your

R. Walpole'[1]

Unfortunately, too, Catherine proved extravagant. Her grandmother had been a burden to her husband and to her sons-in-law, and foolishly she encouraged the girl's delight in the vivid luxury of fashionable life.[2] In the early years of his marriage Walpole loved his wife deeply. He indulged her whims, quite reckless of the consequences, so long as she quieted the needs of his passionate heart.

They had not been married many months before Colonel Walpole became gravely ill. He took to his bed yet could not believe that he was dying. He loved life and clung desperately to it. At fifty years of age he stood on the threshold of achievement. He had built up his estates; at first honoured and respected in his county, he was now enjoying the same honour and respect in Parliament. Indomitable in his optimism he dictated a letter to his son for Lord Townshend, telling him that he would soon be on the road to London to take up his duties at Westminster, refusing to accept what must have been so clear to his family. The end came quickly and he

[1] *W. S. Lewis MSS*, 10 July 1702.

[2] *Chevening MSS*. G. S. Steinman in letters to the 5th Earl Stanhope, 4 December 1869 and 27 January 1870, describes a MS which he had seen, written by Sir John Philipps of Picton Castle, Lady Philipps's son, in the possession of Mr John Pain Philipps of Haverfordwest, which contained notes on the financial and marital difficulties of Lady Philipps, the Shorters and the newly-married Walpoles. According to Steinman, Lady Philipps was 'giddy and extravagant, fond of town life, and hating the country'. I have failed to trace this document.

died on his fiftieth birthday, 18 November 1700. He was buried as simply as he lived under a plain stone in the chancel of his parish church.

He left his son a difficult inheritance—a prosperous estate and an established position certainly, but there were heavy burdens. In addition to his mother, Walpole had to support two sisters and two young brothers: his wife was already three months gone with child; Lady Philipps was as extravagant as her granddaughter and neither had any intention of living in Norfolk. And again, he was a young man, lacking his father's experience and authority, both of which were badly needed to control the hot-tempered and vigorous Walpole brood whose power in Norfolk depended considerably upon their harmony. Yet as head of the family he was expected to be both arbiter and friend. A cautious or timid man might have moved slowly after his father's death, but Walpole rushed at the opportunity to play a more effective role in social and political life. Perhaps he had been waiting impatiently to move into a wider world. For a man of his aching ambition the long winter months in Norfolk must have dragged interminably, for all his fondness for hunting and the deep drinking of the Norfolk squires. Before his father was buried he had written off to Thomas Howard of Ashstead to secure his support at Castle Rising where he intended to succeed his father.[1]

The funeral over, Walpole dashed to London, probably to see Lady Philipps and arranged to live at her house in Berkeley Street. He returned for a few days in January 1701 to appear at Castle Rising for his own election and to collect his tenants for the county election at Norwich. In this whirl of activity he found time to give extensive orders for altera-

[1] *Howard MSS.* Robert Walpole to Thomas Howard, 20 November 1700: 2 December 1700. *C(H) MSS.* Thomas Howard, 25 November 1700. Howard informed Walpole that the Parliament was likely to be dissolved. This took place on 19 December 1700, before a writ could be issued. Howard and Walpole were returned at the general election on 11 January 1701. But Howard's approval of his candidature on 25 November 1700 made Walpole's election certain.

tions to the plain rambling Elizabethan house which he had inherited. Colonel Walpole had spent little money on it and Walpole's wife must have viewed it with horror. She hated country life. The ancient mullioned windows, open fireplaces and plastered walls hung with old tapestry presented a violent contrast to the sophisticated splendours to which she was accustomed. John Wrott, the fat, kindly, utterly devoted steward, whose life was to be harassed by his young master's extravagance, was bewildered by the spate of instructions he received. Walpole's chamber was to be gutted and refitted with new sash windows, a marble fireplace, new doors and the whole room panelled in deal. That done, the parlour and other rooms were to follow. As well as alterations to the house, Walpole ordered the construction of a vast new barn, to be built from timber brought from his Suffolk estate, and roofed with expensive pantiles, imported from Holland. Yet Walpole scarcely had a guinea to his name, and within a few months of succeeding his father he had opened negotiations for the sale of two small estates at Mildenhall and Cavendish in Suffolk.

Once the Walpoles were established in London, the prudent Wrott tried to keep down housekeeping costs by sending up a regular supply of turkeys, geese, collars of brawn and sides of bacon from Houghton.[1] But Walpole wanted power and his wife social distinction; both were costly, and soon Walpole began to sink steadily into debt. Yet the extravagance and the rapidity with which Walpole moved alike argue an elation, an excitement at the prospect opened up for him by his father's death. By that event he was released from years of drudgery as his father's estate agent and given the chance to test his powers which he knew to be exceptional.

3

THE POLITICAL world which Walpole was about to enter was full of confusion, treachery and divided counsel, at a

[1] C(H) MSS. John Wrott, various letters, 1701–7.

time when there was an overwhelming need for national unity. In 1700 there had been two disastrous deaths. The only surviving son of Princess Anne, the Duke of Gloucester, had died suddenly of fever and by his death the problem of the succession to the English throne became once more acute. Anne was past childbearing and William III knew himself to be too ill to face another marriage. A strengthening of Jacobite intrigue was an inevitable consequence; and this danger was made more real by the death of Charles II of Spain who left his vast dominions to a grandson of Louis XIV. For years the consequences of Charles II's death had been the earnest concern of diplomacy. William III's life work had been to contain the ambition of Louis XIV, and by his dexterous coalitions and the folly of James II he had succeeded in thwarting the French King. Knowing the dangers of the Spanish succession, he had spent three years in negotiating an agreement with Louis about the division of the Spanish kingdoms. In February 1700, they had signed the second Partition Treaty, the first having been rendered void by the death of the heir whom they had agreed to accept. But, as so often happens, diplomacy availed nothing. The Emperor could not be brought to accept the solution offered by William and Louis; neither could Charles II who refused to divide his inheritance nor the Spanish grandees who welcomed a Bourbon King. And naturally Louis, although fearful of war, could not bring himself to ignore the dynastic principles in which he had been brought up. France was the greatest industrial and commercial nation of Europe; the Spanish Empire presented the largest market; interlocked they might become the most formidable power on earth.[1] This William III had long foreseen and sought to check, for such a combination must mean the end of English and Dutch prosperity. But his fierce anti-French attitude was not strongly supported by Parliament. The long war which had

[1] For an admirable discussion of the causes of this war, cf. M. A. Thomson, 'Louis XIV and the Origins of the War of the Spanish Succession', *Trans. R. Hist. Soc.*, 5th Series, IV (1954), 111–34.

lasted from the Revolution to 1697 had saddled the country with debt. Increased taxation had fallen heavily on the gentry. They smelt corruption in high places; their suspicious isolationist minds imagined that the war had been fought for the Dutch. They wanted no repetition. So far as the majority of the back benchers was concerned Louis's grandson was welcome to the Spanish inheritance. This mood had led the Commons to attack fiercely the King's ministers—Somers, Portland, Halifax, Orford. From 1698 to 1700 they used every political art to secure their continuance in power. The end, however, came in the summer of 1700. The country gentry were jubilant but their managers, of whom Harley was the most important, found it difficult to secure both a ministry which would command respect and a stable majority to back it in the Commons. It was for this reason that a general election was held from December 1700 to January 1701.

William parted with his old advisers only on terms and the settlement of the succession in the Hanoverian line had been the chief of these. Although the Act of Settlement, passed in 1701, named Sophia, Electress of Hanover, as heir to Princess Anne, this Act was as much concerned with establishing constitutional principles, dear to the squirearchy, as settling the succession. Placemen were to be excluded from the Commons; judges were to be controlled by Parliament; ministers were no longer to avoid impeachment by pleading the King's pardon; the privy council was to accept full responsibility for its acts; no war was to be waged for any territories which did not belong to the Crown of England; the sovereign was not to leave the Kingdom without the consent of Parliament. Here were enshrined the prejudices and fears of the gentry; fears of courtiers, fears of ministerial power; fears of war and foreign alliances. In these demands of the tories there were distant echoes of Pym and Shaftesbury. It was the high-water mark of isolationist, anti-ministerial feeling, but it proved a dead letter. None of these clauses was to be operative until Anne's death; by then, how-

ever, the control of the legislature by the Court had proceeded too far to permit the subordination of the administration which the Act of Settlement demanded.[1] Yet in 1700
it was so necessary to commit the tories to anti-Jacobite
measures that William had no alternative but to accept
clauses which, if carried, would have made a chaos of
government.

The Act of Settlement, however, proved to be the most
moderate act of this wild Parliament.[2] It is true that the
threatening attitude of France forced them to approve in the
most lukewarm terms the King's diplomacy, which was concerned to build up anew an alliance against Louis. For the
rest, the Commons attacked ferociously the King's late
ministers and the petitioners of Kent.

On 12 May 1701 Walpole received his first letter from a
constituent, Benjamin Rudkin, a farmer of some substance,
who, though he handled a pen with less skill than the plough,
felt impelled in the circumstances to write to Walpole and
inform him of the feeling in Norfolk. 'Our people . . . seem
pleased,' he wrote in his large and crabbed hand, 'with the
sentiments of the Grand Jury of Kent, though not propper to
direct a Parliament, but think this time ought not to be neglected to make hast to secure ourselves and allyes which, Sir,
I assure you is the opinnion of all those that loves the present
government'.[3] Throughout the country many held to a
similar attitude—the realization of danger and of the need
for unity. But unity was not forthcoming. The attacks on the
late ministers were bitter and protracted; their impeach-
ments, narrowly carried in the Commons, were defeated in

[1] For the text of the Act of Settlement cf. W. C. Costin and S. Watson, *The
Law and Working of the Constitution*, 92–6.

[2] Even Uncle Horace Walpole, an ardent tory, was disturbed by their proceedings. 'Had my inclinations been much stronger to the honour of a Senator
it would not have prevailed with me att this junction to come amongst you till
you have gotten a bigger house to cool your hott heads for I must needs say
I thinke ye are a parcell of very familiar fellows and I am informed some
peoples tongues go before their witts.' *Chicago (Walpole) MSS*, Horatio Walpole,
20 April 1701.

[3] *C(H) MSS*. Benjamin Rudkin, 12 May 1701.

the Lords; after heated debates the five gentlemen of Kent who had presented the petition, urging action against France, were thrown into jail. Political feeling had not run so high since the days of Exclusion.

Although it was a time for a young politician to walk warily, Walpole seems never to have hesitated for a moment in throwing in his lot with the confirmed whigs, in sharp contrast with Henry St John, afterwards Viscount Bolingbroke, Walpole's most relentless enemy. St John, while supporting with fiery eloquence the most extravagant tory attitudes, contemplated going over to Hanover 'and laying the foundation of a future fortune to myself'.[1] Bolingbroke's tragedy was to spring from his inability to root himself into a consistent attitude to his age. Why Walpole supported the cause of the impeached ministers without hesitation can only be surmised, but almost certainly it was due to his friendship with Lord Orford, the victor of La Hogue, and one of the accused ministers. Until Orford died in 1727, Walpole remained his close friend, staying often at his house at Chippenham, near Newmarket, on his way to London. It was, of course, a friendship of moment for Walpole. His only connection of importance in London was Lord Townshend, who had yet to make his mark; indeed his first speech in Parliament was not made until May 1701. On the other hand Orford, an intimate friend of Halifax, Sunderland, Marlborough and Godolphin, had been First Lord of the Admiralty and a Lord Justice. If the impeached ministers recovered their power, Orford would dispose of considerable patronage from which Walpole might reasonably expect a reward for his loyalty. That they might recover power must have seemed almost certain to a man of Walpole's political judgment and optimism. In spite of the high tory antics in Parliament, the tide was setting so strongly for war that moderate tory after moderate tory began to trim his sails in

---

[1] HMC, *Downshire MSS*, I, 805. Cf. also letter from brother Horace, 5 April 1701, *Chicago* (*Walpole*) *MSS*. 'I fancy the parliament business in some measure run counter to your opinion when I see that Ld S(omers?) so narrowly escape.'

the hope of avoiding shipwreck. Neither Marlborough nor
Godolphin wished to see an intensification of party strife.
Although they were tories by name they were courtiers in
action and appreciated the King's need to secure a firm
authoritative ministry in full control of the Commons. He
demanded not only approval of his foreign alliances but a
generous supply if he was to succeed in his struggle with
Louis XIV. When William III dissolved Parliament on
11 November 1701, many tories were doomed. The dis-
possessed ministers had spent months cultivating the constituencies where they or their friends had influence; and they
did not hesitate to use their great wealth. The Court and
many members of the administration were concerned to
secure moderate men. Public opinion in so far as it had influence was at this time predominantly whig; the fear of
Jacobitism, France and loss of trade had swung the country
more in favour of William's policy.

4

WALPOLE EXERTED himself wherever he had political influence. In April 1701, Wrott received peremptory orders to
discover the names and estates of all the freeholders in Freebridge Hundred, which surrounded Lynn, so that Walpole
could use his influence for the election which was expected
in the summer. He kept up his father's friendship with Sir
John Holland and Sir Edward Ward, two exceptionally influential Norfolk squires. In the first Parliament in which he
sat, he was given through unexpected, though tragic, circumstances a chance to show his capacity for business. Sir
John Turner, the senior burgess of King's Lynn, was beginning to find his parliamentary duties onerous at seventy
years of age and he encouraged his nephew, Sir Charles, to
take the initiative in business which concerned the town. In
April 1701, Sir Charles's wife, Walpole's eldest sister, died,
and he was forced to return at once to Norfolk. Thus, the
piloting of a Bill to enable Lynn to erect workhouses for the
poor devolved on Walpole. Such local measures were very

frequently lost in the hurry of business created by the brief parliamentary session. Walpole was both assiduous and forceful. He took the chair in the committee stage and hurried the Bill through its third reading in time for it to pass the Lords before the session closed. Sir Charles, who had been most anxious about the Bill, was very impressed and wrote on 8 June 1701: 'I heartily thank you for your care in our Lynn Bill. It cannot surely but please the towne when no other bill of that nature but theirs hath been able to get through this sessions.'[1] He busied himself too with the appointment of the land tax commission for Norfolk, a vital matter to his friends and supporters as they assessed the taxes; a resolute and intrepid commission could work wondrous changes in political opinion and the profits which they themselves made in tax collection gave rise to an almost amorous regard for their patrons. So Walpole exerted himself whenever there was Norfolk business.[2]

But unfortunately he was unable to use to the full the little influence he possessed in the frequent parliamentary elections that took place at this time. His own seat was safe at Castle Rising so long as he remained on good terms with Thomas Howard. In spite of frequent quarrels and misunderstandings the Walpoles and Howards had avoided a contested election. When, however, Thomas Howard died in April 1701, Walpole, knowing that he would increase his political influence if he could control another parliamentary seat, toyed with the idea of putting up a candidate of his own at Castle Rising. This alarmed his friends and old Edmund Hamond wrote firmly to dissuade him on 7 April 1701. Although the Turners offered to help him, the tone of their letters was very lukewarm.[3] Lady Diana Feilding, Howard's daughter and heiress, quickly learned of Walpole's intentions; she sent him a peremptory note.

'I have received a letter from Mr Dilman, my steward

[1] *C(H) MSS.* Sir Charles Turner, 15, 22 May, 8 June 1701; *CJ*, XIII, 409, 426, 449, 518, 561, 592.
[2] *Ibid.* Sir Charles Turner, 15 May 1701.
[3] *Ibid.* Edm. Hamond, 7 April 1701. Charles Turner, 9 April 1701.

at Riseing who intimates as if a new interest was setting up against mine. You was pleased in yours[1] to tell me you would readily agree with any whom I should recomend, therefore I desire the favour of yo to satisfye your friends by the first post that I have recomended a relation of Mr Howard's[2] and a fit person to serve the burrough, least any opposition should be made, and you will oblige.'[3] Walpole capitulated, writing to assure Lady Diana of his utmost loyalty, but she, cautious woman that she was, sent down fourteen voters from Surrey under the charge of her bailiff, a show of strength which infuriated Walpole's supporters.[4] For the next two elections Walpole accepted Lady Diana's nominees without question. In January 1702, much to his chagrin, she put up the Earl of Ranelagh, a courtier and placeman who had recently been harried by the Commons for peculation in the office of Paymaster-General. To the relief of the Walpoles and Turners, Ranelagh decided to sit for West Looe, where he had also been elected and Lady Diana's second choice, the Marquess of Hartington, the Duke of Devonshire's eldest son, who had failed in Derbyshire, thoroughly delighted them. Walpole struck up an immediate friendship with Hartington which lasted throughout their lives; it was to prove a great source of strength.[5]

Although in these two elections Walpole used his influence on behalf of Lady Diana Feilding's candidates, he did so with the knowledge that his own supporters were becoming restive. The cause of the trouble was the rivalry between his two uncles, Captain James Hoste of Sandringham and Colonel Horatio Walpole of Beckhall, his father's brother. Something has already been said of Hoste's truculence and self-regard. He possessed burgages at Castle Rising and his manor of Sandringham lay close to the town. In his emphatic forthright way he made it quite clear that he regarded

[1] Not in *Howard MSS*.
[2] This was the Hon. Robert Cecil, younger son of the 3rd Earl of Salisbury.
[3] *C(H) MSS*. Lady Diana Feilding, 17 April 1701.
[4] *Ibid*. Edm. Hamond, 21 April 1701.
[5] *Howard MSS*. Walpole to Lady Diana Howard, 11 January 1702, and 3 June 1702. Also *Devonshire MSS*, Walpole to Hartington, 22 September 1705.

himself as an admirable candidate for the seat. And so did
Colonel Horatio. Horatio had married well—the daughter
of the Duke of Leeds and the widow of Coke of Holkham;
this distinction gave him a claim, he felt, to national honours.
He liked to think of himself sitting with the droves of his
Bertie relatives in the Commons. He was an exuberant man
who always spoke before he thought, who enjoyed a quarrel,
and whose temper was exceedingly quick. When he caught
a young farmer poaching, he at once hamstrung his grey-
hounds and gave him a severe thrashing. On the receipt of a
couple of dozen bottles of wine from his nephew, he drank one
bottle straight off as a bumper to toast him. No man hunted
harder; no man drank deeper. The whole of Norfolk did not
contain a more choleric or more uninhibited character. He
loathed Hoste, despised the Turners, and felt that he could
jockey his nephew into playing his game.[1]

Walpole tried to placate both, as well he might, for not
only did they threaten his position at Castle Rising but he
also owed them money, for Walpole had started his married
life too extravagantly. Tilers, joiners, carpenters had to be
paid; so had the silversmith who had recently supplied a new
service of plate.[2] In consequence he ran about London getting new glass for Hoste's coach which had been recently
overturned, buying his wigs for him, sending him the votes
and newsletters and writing long gossipy letters, unfortunately
lost, in the hope of keeping him happy and contented.[3]
Uncle Horatio proved more difficult to handle, for he held
trump cards. As trustee to Walpole's mother, sisters and
brothers, hardly an acre of land could be sold or mortgaged
without his consent. Hoste might lend two or three hundreds
but Uncle Horatio could release thousands. He agreed to the

---

[1] C(H) MSS. John Wrott, 1 May 1701. Edm. Hamond, 21 April 1701.
James Hoste, 2 February 1702. There are many letters in C(H) MSS and
Chicago (Walpole) MSS upon which I have drawn for my view of Hoste's and
Horatio Walpole's characters. Hoste was willing to stand down at Rising so
long as Uncle Horatio did the same.

[2] Chicago (Walpole) MSS, Horatio Walpole, 5 April 1701.

[3] C(H) MSS and Chicago (Walpole) MSS, letters of James Hoste.

sale of Cavendish and Mildenhall and talked more loudly of his intentions of getting into Parliament. Walpole lent him Houghton and Uncle Horace had a glorious binge lasting three weeks in which he and his friends drained a butt of hogan. He talked more wildly than ever and his very pronounced tory opinions irritated Hoste and the Turners excessively. But Walpole had to capitulate. He was so desperately short of money that he had decided to mortgage or sell Hessett, a large Suffolk property which had been in his family since the Commonwealth.[1] He could not open negotiations without Uncle Horace's consent and although no threats were made, Walpole realized that he would have to be found a seat in Parliament. An attack on the Howard interest at Castle Rising was certain to fail; the only solution was to allow Uncle Horace to have his seat and find another for himself. Two possibilities existed—Lynn and the County. At a meeting of the gentry at Norwich Quarter Sessions on 7 May 1702, Sir Charles Turner reported to Walpole that 'you were named too by a great many who very briskly offered to engage for you'. Wisely Sir Charles declined on Walpole's behalf, for a most complex situation had arisen. Townshend's uncle, another Horace, a very prosperous London merchant who was known to be a very strong candidate for Lynn, was being canvassed. Sir John Holland, Sir Jacob Astley, Colonel Harbord, Sir Edward Ward and two violent tories, Sir Roger Potts and Richard Hare, all commanded such support that a contested election could scarcely be avoided, and the cost of fighting a county constituency was quite beyond Walpole's means, much as he would have liked the honour of being Knight of the Shire at this time.[2]

So he turned to Lynn where he stood a greater chance of

[1] C(H) MSS. Letters from 15 April 1701–7 June 1702. First mention of raising money on Hessett is on 13 December 1701. For the violent quarrels between Uncle Horatio and the Turners, cf. Horatio Walpole, 14 February 1702. Walpole had decided that his uncle must have a seat by 8 May 1702, John Turner, 8 May 1702. Hesset was finally sold to Captain Aubrie Porter, MP for Bury St Edmunds and son-in-law of the Earl of Bristol. Cf. W. A. Copinger, The Manors of Suffolk, VI, 297.

[2] Ibid. Sir Charles Turner, 7 May 1702.

winning a seat without a contest. Sir John Turner, the head
of the Turner clan, had represented the town in Parliament
since 1678. His nephew, another John Turner, did not think
it 'advisable for Sir John (upon whom old age and infirmitys
begin to grow) to putt himself upon the inconvenyency and
fatigue of a winter's campaign, ill dyett, and worse lodging'.
But others had noticed Sir John's ageing as well as his family,
and he had not been very circumspect about his intention to
retire; consequently speculation, gossip and tentative suggestions about his successor had started before Walpole indicated his intention of standing. There were three possible
claimants to Sir John's seat apart from Walpole. 'Our dissenting brethren are generally for Capt. Host,' John Turner
informed Walpole on 8 May 1702, 'but they know their interest too weake to undertake it without us.' So Hoste could
not be regarded as a serious danger, though his dissatisfaction, inflamed by Uncle Horace's triumph at Castle Rising,
might create difficulties. Horatio Townshend, Lord Townshend's merchant uncle, was a far more formidable candidate.
John Turner thought that he would be unanimously chosen
if he stood, 'for my Lord Townshend's quality and the good
will they beare him outweighted all other considerations, and
wee could better offer arguments for him, as if the reason of
the thing and the interest of the town had swayed us without any private concern or ambition of our family, for I must
fairly lay there are a great many that grudge and repine at
our governing here (as they are pleased to call it) and want
onely an opportunity to show a dislike'. Fortunately Townshend was undecided whether to stand and Walpole's influence with Lord Townshend was considerable enough to
clear away that obstacle. The third candidate raised a more
delicate problem. He was Alderman Henry Bell, the architect, a very close friend of the Turners who had employed
him to build their own houses and the Customs House which
they gave to the town.[1] Furthermore, several influential
members of the Turner caucus had given public approval of

[1] H. M. Colvin, *Dictionary of English Architects*, 1660–1840, 70–1.

Bell's aspiration to sit in Parliament, including John Turner himself. Bell was a serious obstacle. Many freeholders felt that one of their members should be a townsman; the animosity towards the Turners could be used effectively to arouse support; and John Turner bluntly told Walpole that the arrangement at Castle Rising might have serious repercussions. As he pointed out, 'turning with the wind', *i.e.* supporting a tory for the sake of family convenience, contrasted ill with their previous whig declarations.[1]

Old Charles Turner, the attorney of Lynn, did not make much of these difficulties, which were due rather, he thought, to Cousin John's passion for politics.[2] In his strong room he had locked away piles of mortgages and bonds which were a better guarantee of how the voting would go than Turner's ale-house gossip. And so it proved. Bell withdrew as soon as he heard that Walpole had entered the field. He stood no chance against the Townshend-Walpole-Turner combination; had it come to a contest the expense would have been beyond his pocket. Also Walpole had demonstrated his capacity for business over Lynn's Poor Bill; such quick prompt action impressed the merchants, and Walpole's friends made considerable capital from it as they gathered at the Customs House or in the Duke's Head. But Bell did not go unrewarded. In January 1703, Walpole obtained a Captain's commission for him in the Marshland Company of the Norfolk militia, and two other commissions for his relations.[3]

As Member of Lynn instead of Castle Rising, Walpole's political status was increased, for Lynn was still one of England's great ports as Norfolk was still one of her most highly populated and highly industrialized regions. It is absurd to regard Walpole as a mere Norfolk squire; from his

---

[1] *C(H) MSS*. John Turner, 8 May 1702.

[2] *Ibid*. Charles Turner, 17 May 1702.

[3] *Ibid*. John Turner, 18 May 1702, 1 January 1703; Henry Bell, 25 January 1703 (Bell wrote a most beautiful script). Bell's commission incensed Hoste. 'I wish you much joy of your new Capt. Bell,' he wrote to Walpole, 18 January 1703. 'I heard of it long agoe but did not believe it.' *Ibid*.

earliest days he was involved in questions of trade and industry upon which the wealth of many of his family was
based. His importance in political circles was enhanced by
his local connections, not diminished. It was as if in the nineteenth century an extremely able member of a county family,
but with close connections in commerce, had appeared in
Lancashire and, after sitting for a few months for the family
borough, had been adopted by Liverpool.

5

WITHIN TWO years Walpole had succeeded in establishing
himself as a leader of his county in spite of the obstacles
which his hot-tempered family placed in his way. Norfolk
affairs, however, absorbed only a little of his time and
energy. His heart and his ambition made London the centre
of his interest. Although for economy's sake the young Walpoles made their home with Lady Philipps, they had no intention of living a frugal life. A young forceful politician
needed patrons who were unlikely to be impressed by rustic
habits. Neither Mrs Walpole nor her grandmother had ever
flinched at the consequences of their extravagance. Jewels
could be pledged; bonds were easy to sign and money not
hard to come by. Walpole loved his wife deeply and enjoyed
indulging her whims as much as he did his own. After a childhood and youth of frugality and provincial isolation, the
riches and extravagance of London society intoxicated him.
He determined to live as if money were of no importance to
him—open-handed, generous, extravagant, he pinned his
hopes on the future for an office of profit could quickly reduce a mountain of debt. Each month the demands for payment became louder and more insistent.

At this time Walpole's income was derived entirely from
his estates. When his father died, he inherited about £2,000
per annum gross. The estates at Dersingham, however,
carried two life annuities; and his mother's jointure, the
maintenance of his sisters and brothers, and land tax at four
shillings in the pound made large inroads into his income.

Walpole, moreover, was unlucky. The great expense which necessarily arose from his recent marriage and entry into politics took place at a bad time for farming. On 7 December 1702, John Wrott wrote to his master:

'However pressing my Lady[1] may be for money, I am sure she cannot be paid till moneys come in. I have been with most of the tenants since you went from home and have not received five pounds of them. They promise to gitt what they can up against Christmas, but I fear then not so much as wee expect. Their great complaint is (and not without reason) the want of a price for their corne....'[2]

Three years later, on 10 December 1705, Wrott was still complaining:

'I cannot possible tell how to answer these demands for money which your last mentioned so soon as Xmas. The tenants are slack and make great complaints and I am satisfied not without reason for the crop this year is mean and prices low, and if these times hold, I fear some of your tenants the more they runn in, the worse.'[3]

Indeed, the winter of 1705 was a terrible time; shortage of money was so acute at Houghton that Wrott could not find the cash to pay the smuggler.[4]

Until the correspondence ends in 1706, Wrott's constant complaint is the failure of the tenants to pay, either because their crops failed or were so abundant that prices dropped too low. In the few years covered by the correspondence several tenants went bankrupt; others had to give up their farms; on other occasions Wrott was forced to reduce rents in order to attract farmers.[5] In the last three months of 1704, a year when Wrott's complaints are less insistent than usual, he was able to send Walpole only £40 out of the Norfolk rents; wages and tradesmens' bills had absorbed the rest (£260).[6]

Apart from rents, Walpole's only income at this time was

[1] Walpole's mother.
[2] C(H) MSS. John Wrott, 7 December 1702.
[3] Ibid. John Wrott, 10 December 1705.
[4] Ibid. John Wrott, 23 November 1705: 'I have not forty shillings in the house.'
[5] Ibid. John Wrott, 1702–6, various dates.
[6] Ibid. John Wrott, 29 January 1705.

the money raised by his steward's farming in which he himself naturally took a very close interest. Almost the earliest scrap of Walpole's own handwriting is a few scribbled notes on a letter to Wrott, memoranda for his next letter. They run:

'What deer are dead
To put off buying of sheep
What fall of lambs'

and Wrott's correspondence is principally about this farming, full of details about Walpole's crops and cattle.[1] Yet it was not easy to get rid of either at reasonable prices, and Walpole's brother, Horatio, an undergraduate at King's College, was sent round the Cambridge butchers to see if he could get rid of a parcel of wethers. He was unsuccessful.[2]

Walpole was forced to raise money. He sold what he could, including his Suffolk property (a process which took two years to accomplish owing to the complexity of the title and the number of Walpole's relatives whose consent was necessary because of their interests in the estate). But neither sales nor mortgages were sufficient to meet his needs. So he borrowed. In 1702 he owed James Hoste £400; by 1705 this had increased to £1,000, but Hoste was only one of a score of creditors. Walpole evaded payment wherever he could. Mistress Pell's attorney repeatedly threatened him with distraint before he obtained her tiny annuity from him.[3] Walpole's post-bag speaks for itself.

'Deare son,' wrote his mother on 29 April 1702, 'it is with no small conserne that I torment you thus for money, but I am now put to those straights as I can no longer make shift.'[4]

---

[1] *C(H) MSS.* John Wrott, 14 March 1701. Walpole, through Wrott, farmed about 150 acres of arable. In 1701, it was sown 70 acres barley, 40 acres of turnips, 12–14 acres of oats; 'as to other grains, as pease etc. 'tis little or nothing'. 8 acres were to be marled, less than was customary owing to the bad winter. The extent of the pasturage or size of the herds of sheep or Scotch bullocks are not known with certainty for these early years.

[2] *Ibid.* Horatio Walpole, 14 January 1701.

[3] *Ibid. Chicago (Walpole) MSS.* Various letters of Hoste, Craste and Charles Turner between 1701–7.

[4] *Ibid.* Mary Walpole, 29 April 1702.

'I writt to you before which I supposed you reseived before you went into Suffolk and I hoped I should have had your answer for I depended so much upon your promas that I should have money at Xmas that I did not writt for any till necesity made me. Therefore pray doe not faille of takeing care I may have it in a weeke.' (4 January [? 1704].)[1]

'My necesity of present money makes me trouble you thus soone but your promas that I should have twenty pounds the beginning of this weeke, and Wrott not having brought me any, have bine a great disointment to me. I desire you would not faile to order me at least that sum as soune as your reseive yours and hope, according to your promas shall have more soune after.' (6 May 1706.)[2]

There is scarcely a letter in the seven years' correspondence from his mother that does not contain complaints about his failure to pay her jointure. In 1706 she grew so desperate that she went to North, her attorney, for advice and threatened to take her son to law, an action which naturally put him in a great rage. Mrs Walpole was not alone in her exasperation with his dilatory habits. The small shopkeepers and merchants of King's Lynn who made him loans through Charles Turner, the attorney, were constantly in the latter's office with their complaints. 'Your creditors tire my heart out,' he wrote to Walpole on 3 November 1704. 'Mr Hoste was this day with me and rages like a madd man. Mr Garrett and Mr Stafford have been with me severall tymes and make great complaint; Mr Pepys was alsoe with me and I conceive I have quietted him untill Christmas. The rest of the people are very urguent for their interest, particulerly Tho. Browne, Mistress Peatfoote, Mistress Wardell whoe is now at Lynn, and Mistress Buckenham sent yesterday for her £50. It will take £560 to answer them and Mr Host. I shall have noe rest unless care be taken. I need not enlarge to know the noyse they make.'[3]

[1] *Chicago (Walpole) MSS*. Mary Walpole, 4 January [? 1704].
[2] *Ibid*. Mary Walpole, 6 May 1706.
[3] *Ibid*. Charles Turner, 3 November 1704.

Two years later, they were still complaining. 'They make me uneasy and clamour me because I lent the money.'[1]

In 1702 Roger Pepys of Impington had married one of Walpole's Turner cousins; almost immediately after the wedding Walpole had touched him for £100. Time and time again he wrote to Walpole, at first demanding the interest but in the end, frightened that all might be lost, urging Walpole to repay the principal as well. Uncle Charles Turner was quite mistaken when he thought that he had put Pepys off till Christmas, for ten days after his uncle's letter, Walpole received a sharp reminder from Pepys.

'I am sorry,' he wrote, 'that you should give yourself and me so often the trouble to write about paying the principall and interests which I have so long since desired: indeed I did not think to have mett with such putt offs and delays from a person of your rank and figure, but was in hopes at least at Michaelmas past that you would have paid it.'[2]

Walpole, however, quickly became an expert at 'putt offs' as all who lent him money learned to their cost, and much of his creditors' fury was due to their sense of impotence in face of his magnificent effrontery. He refused to be harassed by his debts and cheerfully ignored the clamour. Only his brother Horace seems to have discovered the art of extracting money from him at this time. His youngest brother, Galfridus, could go without shirts, the girls without new dresses; Mrs Walpole could be left high and dry at Warham lacking the means to move; his own children might want clothes but Horace could always wheedle a guinea or two out of him, and his letters are little masterpieces of diplomatic tact. Horace neither grumbled nor nagged at his brother. He rejoiced at every success that Robert enjoyed; confided his own hopes; stressed his dependent status; amused him with a richly bawdy sense of fun; mocked at his own poverty; responded, in fact, to life as Walpole himself responded. At the same time Horace's letters subtly conveyed an ardent belief in

[1] *Chicago (Walpole) MSS.* Charles Turner, 7 August 1706.
[2] *Ibid.* 14 November 1704.

his brother's powers and in the prospect of their future success.[1]

Although Walpole remained desperately short of money throughout his early years in Parliament, he never permitted his debts to influence his way of life. He accepted them cheerfully, and gave full rein to his ebullient delight in extravagant living, picking up ready cash anyhow on any terms, completely untroubled by the fierce criticism circulating in Norfolk.[2] He loved life: few young politicians were gayer or happier than this 'Walpole who will always be laughing and talking'.[3]

Yet there must have been days when Walpole himself despaired; when the laughter died and the talk gave way to a brooding silence. At times his straits were desperate: on one occasion his London tradesmen cut off supplies; on another he was saved from the Fleet only by the prompt and generous loan of £1,500 by Thomas Gibson, his scrivener.[4] The temptation to adjust his political principles to further his immediate ambition can only have been strengthened by experiences such as these; Walpole, however, did not succumb. He avowed himself a whig in the very first Parliaments in which he sat, although the future prospects of his party were dimmed by the sudden death of William III.

6

THERE WERE no doubts of Queen Anne's sentiments. 'My own principles,' she told William's last Parliament as she dismissed it, 'must always keep me entirely firm to the interests and religion of the Church of England, and will incline me to countenance those who have the truest zeal to support it'.[5] Her uncle, Rochester, was an ardent tory and Nottingham, whom she immediately appointed Secretary of State, was devoted to High Anglican principles. So long as she ruled, the

---

[1] C(H) MSS and Chicago (Walpole) MSS, various letters, 1701–7.

[2] Ibid. Charles Turner, 7 August 1706. 'Here are some reports spread about your extravagant way of liveing very much to your prejudice.'

[3] HMC, Lonsdale MSS, 118, 29 November 1705.

[4] Chevening MSS. G. S. Steinman, quoting Sir John Philipps' memorandum.

[5] K. Feiling, History of the Tory Party, 1640–1714, 362–3.

natural tendency of her administration would be to associate with tory factions; the bias of Court life was against Walpole, though the tide of events was initially, at least, with him. England was involved in war. Louis XIV's opening of the Scheldt and his acknowledgment of the Prince of Wales as James III had at last swung public opinion into line with the ministry's realization of the necessity of a full-scale war against France. War strengthened the City as well as Marlborough who, as Commander-in-Chief, was more concerned with a united nation and full supplies than with the animosities of factions. His wife, whose volcanic personality held the Queen in subjection, was more preoccupied with the glory of her husband than with questions of party principles. These combined needs of the Marlboroughs, money for war and personal ambition, were a strong force for moderate councils and for ministries which provided refuge for the heads of all accommodating factions. The war, in fact, played into the hands of those men of both parties who regarded administration as the first end of good government. Amongst these Walpole could certainly be counted.

In the reorganization of the ministry which took place on Anne's accession Walpole's friends had lost rather than gained, for none of the Junto Whigs were taken into office and Orford, his chief patron, was left out of the Privy Council. Yet it might have been worse; his friend, Hartington, became Lord Steward and neither Marlborough nor Godolphin, now firmly in power, viewed him with distaste. In most counties there was a vigorous purge of whiggish justices of the peace; but Norfolk, and particularly Walpole's corner, was spared and his friends left in office. The survival of Townshend as Lord Lieutenant would indicate that the ministry did not regard them entirely with disfavour.[1] Yet, when Anne's first Parliament met, Walpole adopted a vigorous whig attitude and showed himself to be thoroughly loyal to his Junto friends.

[1] G. M. Trevelyan, *Blenheim*, 199–200. HMC, *Portland*, IV, 122; 269–71. *C(H) MSS*, John Turner, 3 June 1702.

Whereas in his previous Parliament Walpole had confined himself almost entirely to local affairs, he now began to intervene in party conflicts. Sir Edward Seymour, an ardent high-church tory who was embittered by sickness, thwarted ambition, and the moderation of the administration, proposed that the Crown should resume all grants made in William's reign; Walpole quickly countered by proposing the like motion for the reign of James II, a proposal which was overwhelmingly rejected.[1] Nevertheless the Commons took no further action on Seymour's motion. He adopted the same strong whig line in the case of *Ashby v. White*, and opposed forcibly the introduction of a Bill to stop occasional conformity, a practice by which dissenters avoided the consequences of the Test Act.[2] In both debates he acted in concert with Hartington; together they were acquiring a position of leadership and authority amongst the younger whigs in the Commons.

At the same time business from Lynn brought him into close contact with members of the administration. The Dunkirk privateers were active off the Norfolk coast and Lynn merchants were anxious for protection. Prompt news of convoy sailings helped them to plan the loading of their corn which deteriorated quickly if kept too long in the dark holds of their ships. Rumours of a malt tax disturbed their markets and they demanded quick and reliable news. The war was also a handy way of getting rid of undesirables—the disreputable nephew of Alderman Holley, and the bankrupt arithmetic master; the army or the navy was the place for them and Walpole the man to place them. As solicitations were urgent and to neglect them was foolish, Walpole had to learn to cajole patronage from the reluctant great, learning the tricks of the pursuer and the pursued, an art which was to become second nature with him.[3]

---

[1] Chandler, III, 245.

[2] Coxe, I, 19, and *Commons' Journal* there quoted; also Chandler, III, 383–4.

[3] *C(H) MSS*, various, 1702–5; also *Chicago(Walpole) MSS*, letters of James Hoste and Horatio Walpole (the elder).

III. CHARLES, 2ND VISCOUNT TOWNSHEND

When Walpole first entered Parliament, he had few friends in London except Lord Townshend with whom he had spent much of his boyhood when the latter had been his father's ward. For thirty years they remained close friends and ardent colleagues and their names are forever linked in the political history of their country. During his early years Townshend acted as his guide and sponsor and it was through him and Lady Philipps, who was related to the Stanhopes, that Walpole was introduced into the brilliant social life of the young aristocratic whigs. Townshend, however, did not belong naturally to this world. His manners 'were coarse, rustic, seemingly brutal', defects, however, which the sweetness of his disposition quickly glossed. He believed in hard work and remorseless application to business. A poor speaker, he forced himself to overcome this defect by constant participation in debates. Like Walpole, he loved and hated quickly, and rarely changed his mind. Unlike Walpole, he possessed a more conventional respect for morality. He was faithful to his wife, and he was one of the few early eighteenth-century statesmen who refused to make a penny out of the offices he held. His ambition equalled Walpole's, and he came to rely on his friend's shrewd appraisal of affairs and his remarkable capacity for decisive action; yet at no time did he consider himself to be other than Walpole's leader. It was this attitude that finally broke their friendship. [1]

James Stanhope was one of the first friends whom Walpole made amongst the younger whigs. Slightly older than Walpole, he had been bred to the army by his father who was Ambassador at The Hague, but he had already begun to display exceptional political and administrative ability. A scholar and fine linguist he possessed far higher intellectual qualities than the majority of his colleagues. [2] His good looks, quick wit and obvious charm made him the centre of the

[1] J. Bradshaw, *Letters of Philip, Earl of Chesterfield* (3rd ed., 1926), III, 1408-9. J. Macky, *Characters*, 89.
[2] He built up a remarkable library, exceptionally rich in Spanish books (he spoke the language perfectly), which remains at Chevening. His father had been ambassador at Madrid from 1689-99.

social life of the younger whigs—Spencer Compton, Henry Boyle, Hartington and Charles, Earl of Sunderland. Of these Sunderland was the most remarkable. He inherited a complex personality from his father who survived the disasters of James II's friendship to become the closest confidant of William III—a feat of political dexterity and resilience scarcely equalled in modern times. The son, a man of large ambitions, craved power and found it difficult to dissimulate his need. He relished intrigue and remained cool in his political friendships; yet he was far from being devoid of passion. He could rarely view with detachment any question of political principle. He found compromise difficult and flew all too quickly into a rage against those who crossed his path. He was more highly intellectual than the majority of politicians and in consequence could not accommodate himself so easily to their self-deceiving manoeuvres. From his earliest years his father had intended him for the service of the state and Sunderland confidently expected the highest honours. Expected them, perhaps, too confidently for his contemporaries regarded him with distrust. Although willing to patronize an able man, Sunderland could not bring himself to consider that Walpole's or Townshend's merits might equal his own. By marrying Marlborough's daughter, whom he loved intensely, he had greatly strengthened his lien on the future.[1]

These men readily accepted Walpole. His lively spirits stimulated their own and in a curious way he possessed great charm. His physique bordered on the absurd, for he was short and plump; but his lively brown eye and clear pink skin, set off by a neat wig, saved him from the grossness which overcame him later in life. His slightly comical figure

[1] After her death he married Judith, daughter of Benjamin Tichbourne; his letters to her, *Blenheim MSS*, D.II, 1, are full of the same passionate adoration that he felt for his first two wives. He became almost frantic with despair when he thought that there might be an obstacle to his marriage with Lady Anne Churchill and he was rendered desolate by her death. Whenever he was parted from his wife, he wrote an ardent letter by each post—no matter how busy he might be.

seemed an appropriate vehicle for his irrepressible gaiety. His sharp appetite for all that life could offer endeared him to his friends, and once he had settled down in London he began to move with great confidence in ever widening social circles. Some time in 1703 he became a member of the Kit-Cat, the most fashionable of all whig clubs, devoted to politics, letters, wine and women, and he was thus brought for the first time into frequent contact with the most influential whig leaders—Somers, Halifax, Wharton and Somerset—and with the liveliest members of London's literary life—Addison, Steele, Congreve and Vanbrugh.[1] Significantly enough, Sunderland had never been elected a member.

It was at these weekly meetings of the Kit-Cat that Walpole learned the arts of convivial politics—if he needed to learn, for no man's temperament was more fitted to take advantage of all the opportunities presented by characters and wills enfeebled by drink. Yet, with these men he had no natural advantage, neither birth nor riches. To achieve his mastery of them he had to learn to bridle his too obvious ambition; to check the merited rebuke; to suppress the biting witticism; to learn, in fact, to subjugate his temperament. His obvious ability and his appetite for power could not fail to arouse the envy and malice of his feebler contemporaries. To placate, if not entirely to please, became his endeavour and he hid the uncommon man in the commoner pursuits of drink and bawdy talk. But these riotous, extravagant evenings, with their abundance of rare food and costly wine, were as valuable to Walpole as the long days spent in the Commons, listening with attentive care to the tedious eloquence of lawyers. For here in the guttering candlelight, amidst the litter of toasting-glasses, as dawn lifted over a sleeping London, drink and fatigue broke down reserves, showing him the true nature of these men, at once his friends and rivals, with whom his

[1] The Kit-Cat at the time of Walpole's election had just moved into its new room at Barn Elms, Ranelagh, the home of Jacob Tonson, the publisher, who acted as its secretary. The walls were hung with portraits of the members by Kneller, cf. J. Caulfield, *Memoirs of the Kit-Cat Club*. The Kit-Cat portraits are now in the National Portrait Gallery.

ambition was interlocked. Here was the raw material which his sensitivity to personality could transmute into knowledge, judgment and action.

Even to belong to the Kit-Cat was a sign that he was regarded not only as a promising young politician but also as a leader of the Junto constellation. It was a remarkable achievement in three short years for a young Norfolk squire. He had become a most popular social figure and was sadly missed when his affairs forced him to visit Norfolk. James Stanhope wrote to him on 28 October 1703, to express the sense of loss which his friends felt at his absence:

'Several of your friends having heard that you doe not design to come up till Christmas, I am commissioned by a full committee of them to expostulate with you if it be so. My Lord Hartington, Lord Halifax, Mr Smith, and Lord Sunderland, are particularly solicitous about it, and doe think that for what concerns the publick, you had as good not come at all. Having thus told you their opinions, I do not suppose anything I can say from myself will be of any weight; but you will easily believe that I should be very gladd both on the publick and my own account, to have your good company for the little time I shall have to be amongst you, and I fancy we shall have some sport before the King of Spain can sail. My Lord Cornwallis has promised us to use his interest to send you to us.' [1]

to which Walpole replied from Houghton on 12 November 1703:

'I received yours and am heartily concerned my friends should think I want any arguments to engage me to attend the publick. You, I am sure, cannot think that any alteration in my opinion makes me absent myself. But if publick considerations were not enough you may easily believe I want noe inclinations to kisse your hand before you goe. But the only reason, noe reason perhaps to you, of my stay, is, I am now clearing off being a farmer and clearing

---

[1] Coxe, II, 4, and C(H) MSS. James Stanhope, 28 October 1703. Stanhope was about to leave for Spain to take up his military appointment there. The King of Spain was the Archduke Charles of Austria who was on his way to claim his throne.

my hands of county businesse which ten days will give a dispatch to, and then I shall think myself inexcusable to my country and to you if I do not in person assure you how much I am etc.'[1]

He was as good as his word for by 26 November he was back in London with his wife, having left his son and the new baby girl, Catherine, with his mother.[2] He cannot have felt much regret at leaving Norfolk with its angry creditors and bickering relations. In London his cares quickly vanished for there the swift-moving days were full of hope and life's small disasters could more easily be borne, so much more easily because life was bearing Walpole and his friends towards office and power. There are few sensations so gratifying to a young politician as that of moving speedily from opposition to office.

7

THE WAR was proving whiggish, in spite of the ministry. Nottingham and Rochester wanted a sea war. 'We shall never have any decisive success nor be able to hold out a war against France but by making it a sea war as accompanies and supports attempts on land.'[3] This attitude naturally infuriated Marlborough's wife who feared for her husband's loss of influence if any such policy were adopted: in consequence the tired and wretched Queen was subjected to remorseless pressure by the virulent Sarah, who wanted her to get rid of the High-Church faction of tories. For better or for worse they played right into Sarah's hands. Their trivial envy

[1] *Chevening MSS.*

[2] *C(H) MSS*, John Wrott, 26 November 1703. *Chicago (Walpole) MSS.* Mary Walpole, 3 June [1703]. *Chevening MSS*, Lady Katherine Philipps to Hon. Alexander Stanhope, 23 February 1703. Walpole's son, Robert, was born in March 1701; his wife miscarried in 1702; a further disaster nearly overtook them in February 1703 when his wife, five months pregnant, was knocked over in her chair by a drunken coachman.

[3] *Cal. S.P. Dom*, 1702–3, 698; quot. K. Feiling, *op. cit.*, 368. This conception of British strategy was held by many eighteenth-century politicians and its efficacy was amply demonstrated by Chatham. Because Marlborough won many victories, the attitude of Nottingham and Rochester is dismissed as purely factious; their case on military grounds was a strong one.

in trying to prevent Anne from lavishing honours and gifts upon her favourite, Marlborough, embittered the Queen. They showed a lack of judgment in allowing the Bill against Occasional Conformity to be tacked on to a Money Bill, a most dangerous precedent which threatened the balance of the Constitution. This alienated many moderate tories. What was worse, they were not united in their opposition to Marlborough, for if Rochester blew hot, Nottingham blew cold and vice versa.[1] Divided, their destruction proved easy, though the great victory of Blenheim must in any case have swept them from office. This daring and brilliant achievement quelled all doubts. A costly land war was to be fought and the City was ready to back it. Criticism, even criticism of the Marlboroughs, lacked patriotism. The Court, tired of the endless factional strife of the tories, decided that the war could best be fought by allying itself with the whigs and with the moderate Harley tories. To this the Queen consented. From 1704–5 there was a steady purge of High-Church tories; in the reconstruction which followed, Walpole secured his first office. In June 1705 he was appointed a member of Prince George's Council. Prince George of Denmark, the stupid, drink-sodden husband of the Queen, was Lord High Admiral.[2] It was almost certainly due to the Earl of Orford that Walpole's first office was naval. His ability had already been noticed by Lord Treasurer Godolphin, though his influence in Walpole's appointment has been greatly exaggerated; the solid backing for it came from Orford and his friends in the Kit-Cat.[3]

[1] Cf. R. R. Walcott, 'English Party Politics (1688–1714)', *Essays in Modern History* (Cambridge, Mass.), 108.

[2] *C(H) MSS*, Henry Boyle (April–May 1705).

[3] *Ibid.* Henry Boyle, Chancellor of the Exchequer, n.d. (but March–May 1705). 'I am very unwilling for my own sake to send you any encouragement to stay longer in the country, but I thinke you have a very good reason for it: I have acquainted my Lord Treasurer with the business who is very well satisfied that you stay 'til the county election is over, especially since the new commission of the Prince's Councell is not yet passed . . . there are orders given for yours which I suppose will be passed by that time you come to Towne.' That Godolphin had already developed a keen admiration for Walpole's

Walpole's clients and relations in Norfolk were jubilant. 'I presumed to give you the trouble of a line by way of congratulation to lett you know how great a satisfaction it is to me to find what we so rarely meet with in this age, viz.: desert and reward accompanying each other,' wrote Captain Aldred of the *Sole Bay* which was lying in Yarmouth Roads. He had been drinking bumpers to Walpole's health with John Turner, the choleric mayor of Lynn, who was not slow to take full advantage of Walpole's new influence. 'I wrote to you two posts since to which refer. I write this post to Captain Charles Carter, Commander of the *Barretta* sloop (now in Harwich, as I am informed), having here severall ships corne laden, bound for London, I desired he would repair hither and take them along with him, if not interrupted by his Wells orders, as they always take care to furnish him with before wee have any notice where he is. If you please to second this desire to him at the very first, it will be an obligation (and give me an answer).' Turner's brother was less masterful and more courteous in his demands.

'I am very sensible,' he wrote, 'what trouble you meet with in your post from sollicitations on all sides and therefore would not have added to it but upon this occasion. It is at the request of Mr Henry Parr that I write this who is one deserves to be obliged (if it can be with any conveniency) being a brisk active man, hearty in any thing he undertakes and he liveing at Salthouse in Holt hundred, where the strength of Sir Jacob's interest lay, did not a little contribute towards it so that if by any obligation or kindness he can be brought off, it would be a very great service to the publick in improveing that interest in the countrey which wisheth best to it, and which, as matters now are with us, I am sure you know ought not to be neglected. He requests your favour towards his brother,

business acumen is based on the unreliable testimony of his chaplain, Etough, made long after Walpole was dead. Coxe, I, 21. It was known as early as 9 April 1705 that Walpole was to be given this office. *C(H) MSS*, Galfridus Walpole, 9 April 1705. He had, however, been sending out orders on behalf of the Council as early as 14 February 1705. *Chevening MSS*, Walpole to Philip Stanhope, 14 February 1705.

Mr John Parr who hath been in the service ever since before the Revolution and a Lieutenant thirteen years and for ought I have heard hath always behaved himself well in his office. He was Captain Lieutenant on board Admiral Hobson (*sic*) at Vigo and was the onely officer that staid on board that ship when she was on fire there, but upon that Admiral's quitting the service, the Marquis of Carmarthen's haveing that ship brought all his own officers on board with him so this poor gentleman was outed and hath not been able to get into the service again but in a lower post than his former which he thinks very hard to submit to as every one (you know) is unwilling to go backwards especially in these cases. I beg for the reasons above that you would use your endeavours to do him right and justice and besides I shall own it as a great favour.' [1]

Such letters were a welcome change from the complaints of his mother, his steward and his attorney about shortage of money which had hitherto filled his post-bag. And as the months passed the stream of demands for help and patronage broadened and deepened. By judicious use of his influence he was able to strengthen greatly his position in Norfolk. His services to Lynn were considerable, for he was able to provide early notice about convoy arrangements. To make certain that their interests were well looked after, his brother, Galfridus, was promoted and put in charge of the east coast convoys—an act which gratified his friends and his family. [2]

Moreover Walpole did not neglect the small perquisites which he could extract from his office. John Wrott was puzzled by the appearance at the back door at Houghton of

[1] *C(H) MSS*, Aldred, 8 June 1705; John Turner, 18 June 1705; Sir Charles Turner, 29 June 1705. Sir Jacob Astley, a moderate tory, had been elected for Norfolk in 1702. Ultimately he became a firm adherent of Walpole's. The Marquis of Carmarthen was the eldest son of the Duke of Leeds (Danby). Thirteen years as a lieutenant was not uncommon for sailors without influence.

[2] *Ibid.*, various, 1705–6. Galfridus was made Captain of the *Sole Bay*, the Lynn convoy in December 1705—Walpole had been prompt in finding promotion so quickly for Galfridus only joined the navy in 1703. The correspondence between Walpole and his Norfolk friends between 1705–6 deserves publication for it illustrates better than any other correspondence that I know the very considerable volume of local business carried out by a member of Parliament in the early eighteenth century.

a rough sea-captain who demanded twenty-three pounds for fine Holland linen. He refused to accept it and waited Walpole's instructions; all, however, was in order and Swanton, the smuggler captain of Wells-on-Sea, became a familiar figure, for smugglers as well as tradesmen had to wait at Houghton for settlement of their bills. A year later Walpole was personally engaged in a smuggling transaction of greater magnitude. His partner in the venture was none other than Josiah Burchett, Secretary of the Admiralty, and the object was to smuggle through the customs a large quantity of claret, burgundy and champagne from Holland. Philip Stanhope, the brother of James, who was shortly afterwards killed at the taking of Minorca, negotiated the shipment. The wine reached the Pool of London easily enough but Burchett had great difficulties in slipping it past the customs. Eventually he overcame them by boldly using an Admiralty launch. Walpole was less successful when he tried to run his wines through the Lynn customs. They were impounded by Kent, the customs' officer, owing to the slackness of Charles Turner's son-in-law, Thomas Archdale. On another occasion he evaded customs by the prompt action of a man he had befriended. 'Heareing last night,' wrote his mother, 'the Holand shipes where come home—they being so stricht beleved the least would be to pay the Custom: Dan Gooden being heare I tould him you had some things and he went and with the help of brandy securyed all the offisers till he and Swanton to gether gott them of and brought them heather; there is 2 peces of Holand and a littell lase. I desire you to send me word if I should sent them to Wrott for Dan does not think it safe to send them by the wagon unles you send a man to take them ten milles out of towne.'[1] Walpole, Burchett, the Stanhopes and the Turners wrote absolutely

---

[1] *Chicago (Walpole) MSS*, Mary Walpole, 6 November (? 1705). This was the Goodwin whom Walpole had found a post; he died in 1740 as Land Surveyor for the port of Lynn. Bradfer-Lawrence, *op. cit.*, 173. Swanton was the owner of a small ship, trading with Holland. His home port was Wells-on-Sea, two miles from Warham, where Mrs Walpole lived with her two unmarried daughters at the house of her son-in-law, Sir Charles Turner. The house at

frankly and without the slightest compunction about these ventures.[1] To them there was nothing in the least abnormal or immoral about cheating the government which they served. Long afterwards, when Walpole was Chancellor of the Exchequer, he was still buying contraband lace from Holland. In this he was not alone; many great men did likewise. Did they perhaps feel a twitch of conscience as their coaches lumbered by a gibbet, creaking with a smuggler's corpse?

Walpole's first office was not so important as he may have wished, and he may even have felt some disappointment as all men of exceptional abilities do when passed over for less able men; but he made the most of what he had. He was able to secure promotion for Galfridus but better still he obtained a place for his favourite brother, Horatio. Early in 1706 he was appointed secretary to General James Stanhope at Barcelona—the first step in Horatio's diplomatic career.[2] Later in life Horatio Walpole became a butt for Grub Street wits. His coarse features, his dirty clothes, his broad Norfolk accent, the homely habits of his wife 'Pug', were all mercilessly lampooned. Hervey belittled his ability and deplored his character.

'He loved business, had great application, and was indefatigable, but, from having a most unclear head, no genius, no method, and a most loose inconclusive manner of reasoning, he was absolutely useless to his brother. . . . He was a very disagreeable man in company, noisy, overbearing, affecting to be always jocose, and thoroughly the *mauvais plaisant*; as unbred in his dialect as in his apparel ,

---

Warham was pulled down in the nineteenth century. The Turners' tattered hatchments still hang in their private chapel in St Mary's Warham, built by Walpole's sister, Sir Charles' first wife.

[1] *C(H) MSS*, John Wrott, 23 November and 27 December 1705; P. Stanhope, 4 February 1706; A. Stanhope, 5/16 March 1706; J. Burchett, 4, 9, 16 April 1706; Tho. Archdale, 14 November 1705; Robert Mann, 16 April 1706. Other French wines, sent by the Stanhopes, were disguised as port so that they only paid the lower duty.

[2] Horatio, with Stanhope, reached Plymouth on 15 February 1706, where they were held up for some days owing to foul weather. They reached Lisbon on 11 March; the expedition helped to take Barcelona on 11 May. *Walpole MSS*, 15, 19 February, 11 March, 16 May 1706 all to Robert.

and as ill bred in his discourse as in his behaviour and gestures; with no more of the look than the habits of a gentleman. . . . Horace was envious, revengeful, inveterate and implacable.'[1]

Horatio's nephew and namesake, who quarrelled with him, has also been responsible for confirming this unflattering portrait of Hervey's.[2] Yet it was far from deserved. He may have been mean, his features coarse, his clothes dirty, his wife a slut, but he had qualities of mind and character which far outweighed these disadvantages. He was intelligent, gay, loyal; his letters to his brother, about whose greatness he had not the slightest doubt, are full of devotion. They sparkle with life; sometimes coarse, obscene and lecherous, but always witty and vivacious. No doubt this gaiety endeared him both to Queen Caroline and to her daughters, particularly Princess Amelia.[3] He had many of the social qualities of his brother, much of his capacity for work, but lacked both the finesse and strength of his temperament. Throughout his life Robert depended heavily on Horace and perhaps his brother's unwavering devotion caused him to overvalue his qualities as a diplomat, for although Horace was quick, observant and shrewd, his affections were too readily engaged and once engaged his loyalty clouded his perception.

In 1705 Walpole decided to make a move which his new political standing rendered imperative. From his first arrival in London he had continued to live with his wife's grandmother, Lady Philipps, in Berkeley Street. But lodgings were

[1] *Hervey*, I, 285. Hervey is more severe on Horatio's wife, 'a tailor's daughter whom he had married for interest, with a form scarce human, as offensive to the nose and the ears as to the eye, and one to whom he was kind not from any principle of gratitude, but from the bestiality of his inclination', *ibid.*, 284-s. She was Mary, daughter of Peter Lombard of London. Her sister married Isaac Leheup who later acquired Walpole's property at Hessett, Suffolk, from Aubrie Porter.

[2] R. W. Ketton-Cremer, *Horace Walpole*, 133–4.

[3] *Walpole MSS*. There are two volumes of Royal Correspondence at Wolterton; both the Queen and the Princess wrote to him with great frankness; they both wrote affectionately of Mrs Walpole. 'Come back pray soon,' wrote Princess Amelia on 15 November 1736, 'for Horace is allwaies the same *mignon* amongst us all.'

no longer commensurate with his dignity and he took a house on the east side of Dover Street, where he continued to live until he moved to Arlington Street in 1715.[1] The removal took place during his absence in Norfolk for the general election of 1705, but no sooner was he in his new home than he went down with fever. His illness was partly nervous exhaustion, a release from tension after a period of fierce concentration. Strangely enough, Walpole's career is studded with such feverish illnesses, which always tended to occur after a period of anxious waiting had been eased by success.[2] On his recovery the Walpoles gave a ball in January 1706, which was attended by the Duke of Grafton and other whig aristocrats. A house of his own also enabled him to entertain his favourite sister, Dolly, for his mother was getting too old to make the winter journey to London for her daughter's sake. Dolly was twenty years of age, 'a beautiful, innocent, well-meaning girl', according to Lady Mary Wortley Montagu, 'but endowed with only a moderate portion of sense; giddy, thoughtless, vain, open to flattery, utterly ignorant of the world; in short, though not capable of acting designedly, just the person, if we may use the vulgar tongue, *to get often into scrapes*.'[3] She had already caught the eye of Lord Wharton, one of the more alarming rakes, and this tempted her into an act of folly.[4] She and Walpole's wife quarrelled. That was natural enough, seeing that Catherine Walpole's beauty,

[1] *Rate Books*, Westminster Public Library. No more exact position can be traced.

[2] *C(H) MSS*, Sir Charles Turner, 2 July 1705. 'I am very glad to hear by my mother that you are recovered of your late fever, you will never leave till you have ruined that constitution of yours as good as it is.'

[3] Wharncliffe, *The Letters and Works of Lady Mary Wortley Montagu* (2nd ed. 1837), I, 28–9.

[4] Sheffield Central Library, *Wharncliffe MSS*, 439. Lady Louisa Stuart to Lord Wharncliffe, *c.* 1838:
'In the memoir of Dolly Walpole, Lady Mary mentioned that once Dolly came to spend a day with her at Acton, where her father was giving a great men-dinner. After tea, the two girls, thinking his company engaged with their wine, strolled into the garden; but Lord Wharton and Lord Carlisle, spying them from the dining-room windows, agreed to steal out and surprise them: which they did; and a noble game of high romps followed. . . .'
I am indebted for this reference to Professor Robert Halsband.

if not her appetite for admiration, was fading, and she grew exceedingly jealous of Dolly's success. True to the family temperament, Dolly translated her rage into action; packing her bags and without thinking twice she took refuge with Lady Wharton, who was known to be sympathetic to her husband's gallantries.

As soon as Walpole heard the disastrous news he went straight to Wharton and, according to Lady Louisa Stuart, ordered his sister out of the house and expressed his opinion of Lady Wharton in a few plain but explicit phrases. As it was impossible for Dolly to return home with him, the Townshends came to his aid. Dolly stayed with them until he could make arrangements for her to return to Norfolk, a step of singular consequence, for Townshend quickly succumbed to her charms. Within a few months he was paying her marked attentions and as soon as his wife died he married her.[1]

London and Norfolk rang with the scandal. Walpole was to enjoy a thoroughly bad press most of his life. His character aroused controversy and his enemies, who were always numerous, thoroughly enjoyed anything to his discredit. And gossip about him was rarely allowed to die, with the result that when Dolly married Townshend in 1713, this episode was used to blacken his character, and Lady Strafford asserted confidently that she had been Wharton's mistress. The Grub Street writers hinted that Walpole had furthered Wharton's designs on his sister for the sake of office.[2] Damaging as this incident was, Walpole's affection for his sister never wavered, and even his mother, not normally a responsive woman, was moved by the tenderness he showed at this difficult time.[3] He knew the difficulties which his wife created; each year their own life together became more intolerable, and although

[1] *Chicago (Walpole) MSS*, Mary Walpole, 20 and 23 June 1706. *C(H) MSS*, Horatio Walpole (Uncle), 18 September 1707. Townshend was at Beckhall teaching Dolly how to play the spinet.

[2] J. J. Cartwright, *The Wentworth Papers*, 1705–39, 321, also *The Testimonials of Several Citizens of Fickleborough in the Kingdom of Fairyland concerning the Life and Character of Robert Hush, commonly called Bob* (1712).

[3] *Chicago (Walpole) MSS, loc. cit.*

he could not condone Dolly's action, his sympathies were with his sister to whom he was deeply attached. Nevertheless such a scandal was an unfortunate blow to a young politician just beginning to make his name at Court.

Although not very important, Walpole's new office brought him into the centre of affairs and to the notice of the country's leading statesmen. The Prince's Council met each Sunday with the Cabinet in the Queen's presence to give its report on the state of the Fleet, a privilege granted to no other subordinate council.[1] This provided Walpole with an excellent opportunity to show his skill in business. He rapidly mastered the confused muddle into which naval supply and finance had fallen. They were subjected to his ruthless efficiency, thereby earning him the respect of the Cabinet, which began to regard him as the chief of the Prince's Council. He ingratiated himself further with Godolphin and Marlborough by a vigorous and able defence in the Commons of Marlborough's wayward brother, George, whose incompetence as the Prince's Commissioner of Revenue was largely responsible for the chaos which Walpole discovered in his affairs.[2] Above all, this defence demonstrated to Godolphin and Marlborough that Walpole was prepared to put the claims of the administration before the rancour of party prejudice. Events were steadily driving them to a closer alliance with the whigs of the Junto and the moderation of Walpole was an attractive contrast to the violent and ill-concealed animosity of those young tories who had never been reconciled to Marlborough's strategy.

The folly of his sister must have seemed but a trivial incident in these exciting months of his entrance into government when, for the first time, he could match his exceptional abilities against men who already held office. Although his place brought him great opportunities it furnished him with little reward. His frequent attendance at Court, his growing

[1] BM, *Portland MSS*. List 4. 29/9. Harley's Cabinet minutes.
[2] Coxe, I, 21–2. George Churchill, an ardent tory, was a constant worry to Marlborough. Cf. Coxe, *Marlborough*, II, 285, and below.

need for extensive hospitality, strained his insecure finances still further. Fortunately two events in 1707 somewhat eased the situation. The death of his father-in-law, John Shorter, increased his fortune; and his sister Susan was married advantageously and cheaply to Anthony Hamond of Wootton. Neither, of course, radically altered Walpole's position, which could only be changed by his obtaining a lucrative place; events in the world and at Court, however, made this happy solution to his difficulties increasingly likely.

The administration, which Walpole had joined in 1705, enjoyed two years of success for, in addition to the great victory of Marlborough at Ramillies, the successful achievement of the Union with Scotland helped to make the government popular in the City. To this was added the sweeping success of Peterborough in Spain and the triumph of Eugène before Turin. These were years of incomparable victories in which criticism was stilled, and for a time the grievous burdens of war were lightly borne. But not for long. In 1707 the Austrians did a deal with the French over Italy, thereby freeing two French armies for Flanders; Peterborough was checked in Spain; the Dutch viewed with apprehension the opening of Spanish trade to British commerce which enabled their own peace party to argue that Dutch money and Dutch men were fighting England's commercial war. In England, too, taxes were heavy and the pressing of men to fill the empty regiments caused growing dissatisfaction. Yet none of these things could in itself have provoked a political crisis. Discontent at home or trouble with allies abroad did not unseat governments in the eighteenth century. The real crisis had occurred much earlier at Court. In the winter of 1706, at the height of Marlborough's triumph, the ambition of the Junto had been provoked by the swing of the administration in their direction. The employment of their junior allies such as Walpole and Smith did not greatly satisfy them. Their loyalty to the régime demanded a greater prize. The decision was taken to demand that the young Earl of Sunderland be made Secretary of State. He was Marlborough's son-in-law, which excited the ambition of Sarah, stilled the criticism of Godolphin, even if it irritated the Queen immeasurably, because she hated this young man for his violent opposition to the financial provision made by Parliament for her husband. For a time she would have none of him. Both Marlborough and Godolphin feared for the safety of the administration. Neither of them trusted Harley and they dreaded an alliance by him with the high tories before they themselves had cemented their partnership with the Junto. Added to this was Marlborough's belief that only the whigs would be willing to accept the financial burdens he thought necessary to win the war. Anne, however, was obdurate. The Duchess became livid with fury, the Duke bitter and angry, Godolphin anxious. They all assailed the Queen day after day until resentfully she gave way.[1] But the Marlboroughs had overreached themselves; the Queen's profound humiliation snapped the strange bond of affection which had held her for so long in subjection to the tempestuous Duchess. She began to look elsewhere for the solace which her nature craved. For a time the whigs won in spite of the urgent pleas with which Harley assailed the Queen.[2] His days were numbered, neither Godolphin nor Marlborough trusted him; he was also disliked and feared by the Junto. The discovery that his secretary was in treasonable correspondence with the Pretender finished him and by February 1708, he was once more in opposition. The administration entered into a closer alliance with the Junto whigs. In the reconstruction which took place Walpole succeeded Henry St John as Secretary at War. His career as a statesman had begun.

[1] *Blenheim MSS*, A.I., 37; E.III, 18, 20; G.I., 4. These letters are extensively quoted in Tresham Lever, *Godolphin*, 156–8. Also Coxe, *Marlborough*, II, 1–18, and Sir Winston Churchill, *Marlborough*. Harley tried his utmost to persuade the Queen not to give way about Sunderland, for he realized that if she complied with this request nothing could stop them. 'Can you stop the whigs that they will not possess themselves (as a faction) of your Authority. If you stand not here?' Harley's notes for a conversation with the Queen, 25 September 1706. BM, *Portland MSS*, List 4, 29/9. Walpole was too junior a minister to play a part in these negotiations.

[2] BM, *Portland MSS*, List 4, 29/9.

CHAPTER FOUR

SECRETARY-AT-WAR, 1708-1710

WHEN WALPOLE left his house in Dover Street on 25
February 1708 to receive his commission as Secretary-
at-War, he must have felt a smug satisfaction.[1] It was just
eight years since he had set out from his lodgings in Berkeley
Street for his first Parliament. Possessing few friends, and
these mainly in disgrace, he had discovered a political world
which offered him little prospect of advancement so long as
he clung to his inherited attitudes. But neither heavy family
burdens nor growing debt deterred him. Circumspect he
might be, but he was also doggedly obstinate in his belief
that the war should be fought as it was being fought; that
Marlborough deserved the unreserved support of the Court,
the Commons and the City—a unity which could best be
achieved by an alliance between the administration and the
whig Junto. The war favoured him, and so did his abilities.
Both in politics and society he had steadily increased his
stature. Before he was appointed to the most important of all
junior offices, he was being regarded as the leader of the
young whigs. On the surface it looks a simple enough story:
success achieved by sound judgment, hard work and a capacity to please. But these early years had their darker side.
There was not only the endless burden of debt and family
responsibility but also the anxieties caused by his wife's extravagance and wantonness. Then, too, there had been the
first ominous beginnings of those fevers and nervous prostra-
tions which were so often to jeopardize his career. Yet he had
triumphed. Both power and affluence were now within his
grasp. No longer the junior member of a subordinate council,
he was at last in the very heart of politics.

[1] Walpole's commission is dated 25 February 1708. PRO, *SP*, 44/172,
fo. 150.

His satisfaction, too, must have been spiced with malicious delight at having ousted his rival, Henry St John. St John and Walpole had been at Eton together and from that time their lives were entwined in rivalry. Temperamentally they were thoroughly uncongenial. St John, known better to posterity as Bolingbroke, was a mercurial character, intelligent, witty, ingenious in argument. Both in speech and in writing he commanded a gracious style. He could shine in any company with far greater brilliance than Walpole. He was quicker-witted and a far better dialectician. Physically he was thin, taut, nervous, but very handsome. He was insatiably amorous, drank far harder than Walpole, but his dissipation never destroyed his capacity for work. Amongst the younger generation, he was Walpole's most formidable rival. His capacities had early brought him to the attention of the Marlboroughs, particularly the Duke, who enjoyed his wit and admired his efficiency at business. Sarah's intuition may have sensed the great weakness of Bolingbroke—the rootless nature of his temperament, for he lacked loyalty and could not arouse it in others. Wherever he went he created mistrust and suspicion. No amount of philosophical rationalization could dispel his air of duplicity and hypocrisy. For a politician, there was a fatal lack of integration between his personal life and his political attitude. That such a lecher should be the apologist of High Anglican principles was bound to give rise to damaging ribaldry. Certainly Sarah distrusted him and was glad to see him go.[1] For the time being she regarded Walpole with a warmth that he was not slow to exploit.

Yet he had reason to be grateful to St John. During the late seventeenth century the office of Secretary-at-War had steadily grown in importance, absorbing duties, responsibilities and powers which had previously been exercised by the

---

[1] The fullest life of Bolingbroke is by W. Sichel (2 vols., 1902). It is excessively adulatory and a re-assessment of Bolingbroke's career is long overdue. His letters to Marlborough are at Blenheim; some are printed in Coxe, *Marlborough*, II, 195–495; III, 1–97.

Commander himself.[1] Marlborough's absence abroad, combined with the vast extension of military activity, which his wars had created, had multiplied St John's work greatly, a process which he had done everything to encourage, for he was an astute enough politician to know that work meant power. Walpole inherited from him an office of complex administrative functions; all aspects of military life in England and Scotland were under his control. Some idea of the scope of his work can be derived from the letter-book which he started on 2 April 1708.[2] The first letter is addressed to Adam Cardonnel, the Duke's Secretary:

'I herewith send you an extract made out of all the memorials that have been given in by the several officers setting forth their pretensions; be pleased to lay it before my Lord Duke for his perusal, and if his Grace has any commands for me upon this occasion, you'll be so kind as to lett me know his pleasure. There are a great many pretensions and more, I presume, than will receive satisfaction but I thought it proper to lay all before his Grace that have come to my hands to do as he pleases.

Lord Stair has applyd here for levy money for himself and Lt. General Rosse for the additionall men added to their regiments. They have allready had £15 for each horse but desire now to have 40/- a head for every man which, they say, my Lord Duke did consent to upon this augmentation. Pray receive my Lord Duke's commands about it.

I have received the Queens orders to march the Forces that were gone northward back again and to quarter them about Hampshire and in the neighbourhood of Portsmouth. The Foot and Dragoons are to halt at Nottingham where the Prince has ordered Lt. General Erle to take a review of them all. Before I had received these

[1] Hon J. W. Fortescue, *History of the British Army*, I, 583–6, also G. A. Jacobsen, *William Blathwayt* (Yale, 1932).

[2] The material for Walpole's work at the War Office is to be found in the *C(H) MSS*, particularly his out letter-book from 2 April 1708 to 30 June 1710. His *Common Letter Books* are also to be found in PRO, WO, 1/7. His correspondence with Marlborough is at Blenheim, B. I, II, III. Other letters to Marlborough are at Wolterton. *Walpole MSS.* 'Letters to Sir Robert Walpole in 1710.'

orders from Her Majesty I was preparing by an intima-
tion from Mr Erle routs for his own regiment and the
Bataillon of Guards to march and quarter in the neighbourhood of Harwich, expecting my Lord Duke's commands for them and one regiment more that his Grace
should pitch upon to be embarked for Flanders. If his
Grace has still any such designs it were convenient I might
know it as soon as possible that such bataillons might go no
further out of their way than to Nottingham. But I ought
to submit it to his Grace whither, if any service is designed
for the bataillons now in England, it will not be a great
weakening to them to take away the three best bataillons
for I am afraid the seven Almanza regiments will scarce
be fitt for any service this year. [1]

On Weddnesday the House of Commons went upon the
recruits and though they were so very defective came to
no resolution but an address to the Queen to issue out a
proclamation to enforce the former Act which was doing
nothing at all.

I received this day letters from Lt.-General Wood and
the Commissioners of Transports at Harwich who give
me an account that one of their convoys being but just
come the horses suffer'd very much by being so long on
board, and the wind then just come easterly. If it did not
change suddenly they were afraid they must land their
horses again. [2]

My Lord Duke had me inquire after Ensign English
who I understand is in Walkin's Regiment and a stop put
to his pay.' [3]

Promotions, troop movements, convoys, recruitment, army
business in the Commons, [4] these matters formed the bulk of

---

[1] Almanza, fought 25 April 1707 (N.S.). Galway was decisively beaten by
Berwick and the British regiments suffered very great losses in officers and
men. Fortescue, *op. cit.*, I, 488–9.

[2] The east coast was the favourite hunting ground of Dunkirk privateers
who were extremely audacious for on one occasion they destroyed a vessel in
Lynn Deeps, *C(H) MSS*, Sir Charles Turner, 19 September 1705. Wood had
constant trouble. No sooner had he put to sea than he was caught in a gale and
forced to return. There were great losses in horses, which Marlborough needed.

[3] *C(H) MSS*, 6.

[4] St John was the first Secretary to take complete control of army business
in the Commons. Cf. Fortescue, *op. cit.*, 584.

Walpole's work though by no means all of it. A great deal of his time was taken up with the problems of supply—money, armament, horses, clothing and forage, but he was even involved in questions which would now be regarded as questions of discipline and quite improper for a civilian. He obtained the pardon of a deserter and drafted him to a new regiment, ignoring the advice of the man's senior officer. He saved a captain from being cashiered for fraud. He even threatened a junior officer with disciplinary action for a minor offence and summoned another to his presence at Whitehall. Indeed there was no aspect of military affairs which escaped his vigilance; but the most ticklish problems were promotion, recruitment and supply.[1]

And his new post brought him much closer both to the Court and the cabinet. When Marlborough was abroad, he acted as chief spokesman to the Queen on questions relating to promotions. Although he was not a member of the cabinet, he was in constant consultation with the Lords of the Committee at the Cockpit, and he was responsible for drawing up for them logistic proposals for the projected attack on Quebec in 1709. His work also made him a familiar figure at the Board of Trade and he frequently sat with the Commissioners of Transport, of Sick and Wounded, and with the Board of Ordnance. During these years Walpole proved himself to be one of the most energetic and hardworking members of the government.[2]

It did not take him long to master the work of his office, which had been reduced to an admirable order by one of the ablest civil servants, William Blathwayt, a man whose genius for organization far outweighed, in William III's view, both

---

[1] *C(H) MSS*, 6, various dates; also PRO, WO, 1/7, Secretary's Common Letter Book, ff. 58, 71, 76, 144, 266, 283.

[2] Walpole's proposals concerning Quebec are to be found in the *Blenheim MSS*, C.I. 16, which also contain many references to Walpole being called in to the Cockpit meetings. For the involved political manoeuvres on the Quebec project in 1709 and 1711, cf. G. S. Graham, *The Walker Expedition to Quebec*, 1711 (Navy Records Soc.), xciv, 9-11; he underestimates the whig interest in Quebec.

the pedestrian quality of his mind and his admiration for James II. Nevertheless even Blathwayt had failed to obtain a satisfactory number of clerks and the Secretary was forced to undertake a great deal of clerical drudgery. Walpole's letters to the majority of his correspondents, wherever the originals can be traced, are in his own hand, a practice in marked contrast to the general officers in the field who almost invariably used a clerk. But Walpole was always a wolf for work. Even in his busiest days he was never daunted by the prospect of a dozen lengthy letters or the necessity of starting them at six in the morning.[1]

The work was not all drudgery. He was no sooner in office than he was involved in the scare of a Jacobite invasion. He took office on 23 February and on 6 March the Pretender sailed from Dunkirk. The splendid fast-sailing French privateers had twelve hours' start on Sir George Byng's squadron, but this fine sailor, by taking his ships along the treacherous shallows of the east coast, managed to keep within distance. In such a race a day was vital, and Byng got to Leith Roads in time to prevent a landing. After the French fleet had escaped, he sent an account to Horace Walpole who was acting as secretary to the indolent Henry Boyle, Secretary of State.

'*On board the Medway in Lieth road the* 25*th of March* 1708
My friend Walpole's letter of the 9th came to me by the *Worcester* yesterday, I know I'm obliged to you for your friendly good wishes, and were there any thing to be said for an luckie fellow, know you would say as much for me as any frind. I expect a parcell of knaves and rogues that are in your Towne will ever censure all my actions. Especially if ever I shall have the fortune to do any service to my countrie. Know thay will not forgive me for it, but I'l tell you a secret, I will dispise them, knowing I have no other aim in serveing then to endeavour to do good, and to serve my countrie faithfully and that's more than many of them can or dare do. I promise you as my frind I will not move one step to gaine any popular

[1] HMC, *Carlisle MSS*, 156.

applause but will go on to do every thing I think is right, if it succeeds it's well, if it does not, let them find somebody else that will serve better, & I'l to my dogs againe, but a pox of those sons of whores, to our business.[1]

You are acquainted wee met the young Gentleman at an anchor at the mouth of the firth of Edenborough; had wee been three houers sooner, or six houers latter wee had caught him in a net. It was night when wee anchord, and, when the day opend, found him with his fleet getting under sail (for he was at anchor too). Neither of us thinking wee were so near each other goeing up the river. Had wee been some houers later wee had shoved him up before us and distroyd them all. Non coud have escaped. But so it is, he had room and distance from us to stretch into the Sea, all his ships clean tallowed, no lugage, and wee a parcell of foul ships, but one clean sayler amongst us, and that was Mathews in the *Dover* who got up to stop two or three of them in hopes more coud have got up to his relief, but by the favour of a very dark night lost sight of all but one, and that is the *Salisbury* in which were some men of note (the list I sent by last express).[2] This I think is a misfortune that coud not be helped in the condition our ships were in. This I will venter to say, my predecessor him self had he been at the head of us coud neither have councilled or contrived how to have worked fowl shipps better. If he thinks he can, let him be sent to sea and I have leave to go to the Bath. I am all over sore, disabled, unfit for service in these damned northern climes, so hope my friends will contrive to be better served and give ease to

Your faithfull humble
Servant

Jennings is your servant   G. Byng

My very humble service to Mr Boyle and to our late Admirall your Brother who I truelie am pleased is no more so.

---

[1] There was considerable criticism in London about Byng's failure to stop the Pretender leaving Dunkirk or to destroy him in the Firth of Forth. Cf. *Byng Papers*, II, ed. B. Tunstall (Navy Records Soc.), lxviii, xi–xiv.

[2] The *Salisbury* was an English ship, captured by the French; on board were the Jacobites, Lord Griffin, Col Warcope and two sons of the Earl of Middleton. Coxe, *Marlborough*, II, 201.

Wee have had damned weather these three daies but with the first wind shall move southward again.'[1]

Walpole could take pride in the efficiency with which the naval precautions had worked, for much of the criticism levelled against Byng was factious. As a member of the Prince's Council, Walpole had been largely responsible for what had been done. But he must have been appalled by what he found at the War Office. The troops in Scotland were in a wretched condition. As Lord Leven, the commander, wrote: 'Here I am. Not one farthing of money to provide provisions. . . . Few troops and naked. It vexes me sadly to think I must retire to Berwick if the French land on this side of the coast.'[2] Immediately the scare was over, Walpole set about repairing the deficiencies in the army in North Britain, a difficult task, due to the remorseless demands of the armies in Flanders and Catalonia.

2

THE GOVERNMENT might have planned James's invasion, so exceptionally opportune was it for a general election in the early summer. Throughout 1707 there had been growing criticism of the length of the war and of the waste and incompetence of so much of the naval and military administration. But the Pretender in the Firth of Forth had rallied opinion to the government, and Walpole set out from London on 28 April, confident that the elections in Norfolk would give him and Townshend little trouble. As it turned out they swept the board: only at Yarmouth did the obstinate, anti-Townshend tory faction win a seat. But a greater triumph was in the county where Townshend's whig cousin, Ashe Windham, was returned with that loyal Walpolian, Sir John Holland. This victory deeply impressed the discerning, and the crotchety old Dean of Norwich, Humphrey Prideaux, wrote

[1] *C(H) MSS*, also there is an account by Walpole of military precautions which he took, *ibid.*, 6, 8 April 1708, to Lord Galway.
[2] Quot. Trevelyan, *Ramillies*, 343; also S. F. H. Johnston, 'The Scots Army in the Reign of Anne', *Trans. R. Hist. Soc.*, 5th Series, III (1953), 12–21.

to his crony, John Ellis, the Under-Secretary of State, on 13 September 1708:

'But the Lord Townshend flourisheth much among us, for the whole countey is absolutely at his beck, and he hath got such an ascendant here over everybody by his courteous carriage that he may doe anything among us what he will, and that not only in the countey, but alsoe in all the corporations, except at Thetford, where all is sould.' [1]

The lack of any mention of Walpole is an interesting comment on how difficult it was for a gentleman to create a great interest and how easy for an aristocrat. Nevertheless Walpole and his supporters had played their part.

Before Walpole arrived at Houghton, his friends and steward had been preparing the ground for him at Lynn. In March his cousin Turner and John Wrott had given six parsons a handsome dinner and regaled them with music as well as port. The pace quickened in April and the wine began to flow by the gallon. On 8 May, Walpole celebrated the election in person with a handsome feast—fifty gallons of port helped out with thirteen gallons of Rhenish, Bliark, Lisbon and Viana. Once more the clergymen were much in evidence, and again there were musicians and songs to keep the thirst going. [2] Walpole's hospitality tended to be excessive and grandiose, so much so indeed that it must have sprung from some deep necessity rather than policy; out-vaunting the aristocracy to which he did not belong; deadening the anxiety of his debts by a challenging extravagance; obliterating the memories of his penurious childhood; one or all of these things may have provoked his unbalanced attitude to money. [3]

---

[1] E. M. Thompson (ed.), *Letters of Humphrey Prideaux to John Ellis*, 1674–1722 (Camden Soc., 1875), 200.

[2] *C(H) MSS*. Vouchers. The major celebration took place at the Duke's Head, but subsidiary feasts were held at the Hound and the Rose.

[3] No Walpole seems to have enjoyed a balanced attitude to money. His father's account books, as we have seen, show that he kept a most careful tally of every halfpenny spent. His mother's letters are preoccupied with money to the exclusion of all else. His Uncle Horace was notoriously extravagant, his brother Horace notoriously mean. As this book will amply demonstrate, Walpole himself was an odd mixture of avarice and generosity.

Whatever the reason, the Lynn voters had cause to be grateful that they were served by a Walpole and a minister.

Walpole had planned to hurry back to London but he was detained by the county election which was not settled until 26 May; but immediately it was over, he left for Whitehall and riding fast reached his office on the 28th. He wrote at once to Marlborough, his excitement bubbling up through the rather hushed and formal tones which his respect for the Duke inflicted on his prose. 'The elections are now allmost over in England where the whigs have had the advantage very much. I believe by the most modest computation there are near thirty more whigs chosen in the room of toryes than toryes in the room of whigs, which makes them in Parliament stronger by double that number . . . I wish Your Grace all the successe, glory and happyness that is due to your matchless virtue.'[1] But his gaiety was soon checked by the realities of the political game. He had hardly got back into harness when he found himself the victim of an ugly trap.

Marlborough's brother, George Churchill, was confidently asserting that Walpole had secured a regiment for Colonel Jones at the request of Harley and without Marlborough's knowledge. This damaging rumour created immense excitement in the coffee-houses. Harley was under eclipse owing to the conviction of his secretary, Greg, for treasonable correspondence with the Pretender, so the gossips at once concluded from this story that his favour at Court was as strong as ever. Others were naturally fortified in their belief that the Queen's real sympathies were for her half-brother. As the rumour spread, the reputation of the ministry and of Walpole was steadily damaged. Walpole, alarmed and infuriated, acted at once and took the risk of offending the Marlboroughs by exposing their brother. He went immediately to Churchill's house and demanded an explanation. Churchill prevaricated and blamed another junior minister, named Hopkins, whom Walpole immediately fetched with witnesses. Hopkins denied all knowledge. Having proved Churchill a

[1] *Blenheim MSS*, B.I.2. A copy is in *C(H) MSS*.

malicious liar, Walpole went post-haste to Kensington where
he found the Queen and the Prince incensed at the rumour.
By producing evidence of Churchill's duplicity and his own
file of correspondence with Marlborough, Walpole was able
to clear himself. To protect himself against damage with the
Duke he sent a long dignified account of the fracas but laid
the blame squarely where it was due—on the shoulders of the
hot-headed, irresponsible, treacherous George Churchill, who
constantly fretted the adamantine patience of his brother.
Naturally the Duke was annoyed, for he had a high regard
for Walpole. 'The business of Mr Walpole has very much
vexed me,' he wrote to his wife, 'for by what he writes me
my brother George has been much to blame. I wish with all
my heart he would retire.' Nevertheless the mild reproachful
manner of the Duke seems to have satisfied neither Walpole
nor the Duchess, who continued to nag her husband long
after the gossip had died; but this was a fateful summer for
Sarah, and the apprehension that she was losing the affection
of the Queen tore her nerves to shreds.[1]

Yet this seemingly trivial incident has a curious importance. The avidity with which the social world seized
upon it demonstrated a lack of confidence in the ministry.
More importantly, it is the first glimpse we have of Walpole
confronted with a complex personal and political crisis.
George Churchill was the boon companion and secretary of
the Queen's husband and therefore a man of great influence
in the closet. Walpole had sat with him on the Prince's
Council and had done much to clear up the mess caused by
Churchill's incompetence, even defending him in the Commons. It was probably envy of Walpole's success and reputation for business which had provoked Churchill, for his own

[1] *Blenheim MSS*, B.I.2. *Walpole MSS*, Robert Walpole, 22 June 1708, printed
Coxe, III, 9–11. Cf. also Coxe, *Marlborough*, II, 285–8; *Private Correspondence
of Sarah Duchess of Marlborough* (1838), I, 146. Even so, the Duke refused to act
in any way likely to cause his brother any trouble, although the Duchess
pleaded for him to do so. J. Macky described him as 'a very honest man,
tho' as rough as the sea bred him; a good, but a severe enemy; a coarse fat
man, much marked with the small pox'. *Characters*, 167.

failure was as clear to himself as it was to the rest of the world—always excepting Prince George. Yet it required great courage and sound political acumen to act as decisively as Walpole did against the Prince's favourite. Every step he took was excellently and wisely judged and, even if his reputation was not enhanced, he had saved himself from damage.

Whether from pique or policy Walpole spent the rest of the summer weeding out some of the adherents of St John from the War Office, and replacing them by his own loyal nominees, an action which embarrassed both the Duke and Cardonnel; and then in the autumn he went off to Norfolk for a month in the country. On his return he plunged into work. It would be his duty to present the army estimates to Parliament when it met and it was essential to eradicate the impression made in the previous year by St John, who had at first given the Commons to understand that increased expenditure had been poured into a diminishing army. In the Commons this naturally caused indignation and dismay, which was not dispelled by his excuses and explanations. Many members of Parliament thought that his mistake was the result of deliberate malice, an attempt to damage the ministry in which his days were numbered. But one result was to create a critical awareness at Westminster of the army's financial arrangements and of its recruiting methods. Already Walpole had seen enough to make him worried about the problem of recruitment. 'I could wish,' he wrote to Cardonnel on 2 November, 'if any officer can be spared from your army they might immediately sett about recruiting. I am afraid that service will go on very slowly and heavily if some new measures cannot be obtained.'[1] Godolphin was equally worried about finance and would not allow Walpole to ask for an increase in the estimates, for he wished to soothe Parliament, not foment the growing criticism on the length of the war and its crippling cost.[2]

Godolphin, perhaps more than any other man in the

[1] *C(H) MSS*, 6, 2 November 1708 to Adam Cardonnel.
[2] *Ibid.*, 6, 26 November 1708 to the same.

country, realized the dangers and difficulties which beset the ministry, yet he lacked the strength of character to force the decisions which might have saved him. Like all politicians losing power he lived from shift to shift, hoping that time would come to his rescue. Nothing could save him. The ministry's position at Court had also been weakened by the death of Prince George on 28 October 1708, a fortnight before the meeting of Parliament. A dull, undistinguished man, George nevertheless had had the wit to realize the worth of both Godolphin and Marlborough, and he had little use for extremists whether whig or tory. In the emotional crisis caused by his death Sarah Churchill proved a hindrance rather than a help to the ministry. Frustrated and lonely, Anne might still have turned to her for the warmth and love which were as much a part of Sarah's tempestuous nature as her anger and violence, but Anne had found another solace. Abigail Hill, Sarah's own protégée, had won her heart. She was both intelligent and serene, a cool, controlled character who by contrast made Sarah's moods more intolerable to her. Furthermore Abigail held, more perhaps through guile than conviction, those High Church and tory sentiments which Anne herself had long cherished. The circle of power—Anne, Marlborough, Godolphin—upon which the most successful ministries of her reign had been based—was broken. It was of too long a standing, however, to be destroyed in a day. And Anne herself had a long memory and an obstinate loyalty to her own past; nor could she easily rid herself of the habit of Sarah. Sarah, too, was prepared to fight every inch of the way. What she could not control by love she was prepared to dominate by rage. But the more violent she became, the more certain was her ultimate disgrace.[1] Her control of the Queen had lasted so long that many, including Walpole, could not believe that she would be defeated. They expected her to weather the storm; even

[1] The considerable correspondence which deals with the break with Sarah is at Blenheim. Most of it has been printed by Coxe, Churchill, Sir Tresham Lever's *Godolphin*, Sarah's *Own Defence* or in *Private Correspondence of Sarah Duchess of Marlborough* (1835).

as late as 18 October 1709, Walpole thought that she was holding her own with Abigail. He wrote her a gay, bantering letter about a man called Barham in whose promotion Sarah was interested:

'I have a very good character of him from his Colonel and was acquainted that he had the happinesse of being under your Grace's protection, which may still be of service to him, in spite of Abigail, if you will behave as you should do; I ask your Grace's pardon for that expression, for Maynwaring saith you do; and if you can hold it, I could say you are very good. I am a very impertinent fellow, but with all imaginable respect and duty.'[1]

Marlborough's continued victories, particularly Oudenarde in 1709, helped to create a deceiving confidence. 'The good the publick and common cause reaps from so glorious an issue . . .', Walpole wrote to him on the capture of Lille, 'fills all true English hearts with joy unspeakable.'[2] But Godolphin had long known that the government was between the devil and the deep blue sea.

The elections of 1708 proved less satisfactory than they might have been. The ministry had won the election— eighteenth-century ministries always won elections—but the margin was narrow. The Commons proved difficult from the first. In passing the estimates in January 1709, they insisted on an Address, demanding that the Queen urge her allies to make their contributions as great in proportion as hers— intended, of course, as a hint to the Dutch that the English were wearying of the war.[3] The test election petition, Sir Simon Harcourt *versus* John Hucks (who disputed the seat at Abingdon), was only won by the government after a heated debate which lasted until two o'clock in the morning.[4] On two clauses of the Scotch Treason Bill the government was defeated by the large majority of 51, and throughout this

---

[1] *Blenheim MSS*, E.43.

[2] *C(H) MSS*, 6, R. W. to Marlborough, 23 November 1708.

[3] Chandler, IV, 106.

[4] The petitions of defeated candidates against the return of the elected member were usually decided on party lines, and, therefore, the first to come before the House, and might be regarded as a test of party strength. Cf. p. 60.

session there is an unmistakably anxious note in Walpole's correspondence to Marlborough. He feared Harley's influence and was particularly disturbed by Harley's remarkably effective speech on the mismanagement of the war in Spain.[1] Aspersions were cast at Stanhope, amongst others, and Walpole resented the unjust insinuations about his closest friend. During the difficult years which followed, he did all that he could in and out of the House to protect his friend's reputation.[2]

The trouble arose from the pressure which the Junto was exerting on Godolphin. Without Harley to balance their influence he was at their mercy and they knew it. He was forced to persuade the Queen to accept Somers and Wharton as ministers. Her reluctance had been overcome only when she was prostrate with grief after the death of her husband. Wharton became Lord Lieutenant of Ireland, Somers President of the Council. This made the Junto easy and increased threefold Harley's capacity to damage the ministry. The Queen listened with sympathy to Abigail Hill's sharp criticisms and the independent members of the Commons felt there was truth in Harley's accusations that the war was being waged for the profit of Marlborough and his friends.

Walpole himself experienced the growing hostility of the Commons when he introduced the army estimates and his new scheme for recruitment. His estimates were accepted but his attempt to put recruiting on a more rational basis was rejected. He hoped to introduce a form of conscription and he prepared a Bill by which each county would be responsible for a fixed quota of recruits. Yet his hopes were quickly dashed. Within a week he wrote to Cardonnel telling him that it was already 'more than I durse engaged for'. On 21 December he fought bitterly for it in committee, but before he left the next day to spend Christmas at Houghton he knew that he had been defeated on this issue. In its place he had agreed to

[1] *C(H) MSS*, 6, Walpole to Marlborough, 14, 21 January; 8 April 1709. Both Trevelyan, *Ramillies*, 392, and Churchill, II, 505–6, state that the Commons proved very tractable in this session; the evidence does not seem to bear this out.

[2] G. M. Trevelyan, *The Peace*, 335–6.

accept the lamentable proposal that a rebate of £4 on the land tax should be allowed every parish producing a recruit. In this form the Bill was quickly passed in the New Year.[1] But the difficulties of recruiting were not resolved and it continued to be not only one of Walpole's greatest problems but also a focus of social resentment.

On 4 January 1709 Walpole had written to Marlborough that he had been driven from Houghton by the 'severest weather and snow that I remember'. This was the beginning of the Great Frost. Not only the Thames but Harwich harbour was frozen over; the channel ports were choked with ice. When the milder weather came in the spring it was accompanied by such prolonged rain that the harvest was utterly ruined. The poor suffered acutely and an uglier note crept into their hatred of press-gangs and high prices. The need for peace was so strong that the government sent Townshend to join Marlborough to take part in negotiations between France and the United Provinces. Many hoped that these limited negotiations would lead to a general settlement. Indeed Marlborough himself had secretly opened talks with his nephew, the Duke of Berwick, during the autumn of 1708.[2] But they came to nothing, for the French hoped to retrieve their desperate position. Also they were aware of the war-weariness of the Dutch, which they hoped to exploit during their discussions on the question of the barrier. Detached from the Dutch, England and the Empire would not be able to demand the concessions which their victories might lead them to expect.

Marlborough, by initiating peace negotiations with the

[1] *C(H) MSS*, 6, Marlborough 21, 22 December 1708; 11, 14 January 1709. *Blenheim MSS*, B.I.2. As he wrote to Marlborough 'it was plain that the House would not come to any such method (i.e. as conscription) which obliged us to take what we could gett rather than goe on the old method'. The £4 for every soldier raised, he thought 'so great an encouragement to the Parish officers that they will bring in all the fellows they can possibly find'. Churchill, *Marlborough*, II, 510, is in error in thinking that the cabinet turned down Walpole's proposal for conscription.

[2] The Duke of Berwick was the illegitimate son of James II by Lady Arabella Churchill, Marlborough's sister; he had become a general in the French army.

French, had hoped to net 2,000,000 *livres* for himself. Mortified by the refusal of the French and indifferent to their abject overtures to which the fall of Lille and their terrible domestic plight soon reduced them, he determined to teach them a further lesson by annihilating what remained of their forces and leading his troops into the heart of France. He was all praise for the slow, obdurate peace negotiations being carried on by Townshend in Holland. The desperate plight of France, ravaged by a famine more severe than England's, created a warm optimism amongst the Allies. But in Villars Marlborough was opposed by an administrator of genius who was also an accomplished general of iron resolve, and popular throughout the length and breadth of France. As summer turned to autumn Marlborough was frustrated, and his career blighted. The massive lines of Villars at La Bassée ended the dream of a rapid march on Paris. Villars watched patiently the slow elaborate siege of Tournai, grateful for time. Mons followed Tournai, but during this siege he was brought to battle at Malplaquet, which Marlborough fought and won with a brilliance of which he alone was master. Villars, great as he was, was quite outmatched. The Dutch losses were very severe; the English moderate; the French heavy but not decisive. And although Villars was defeated he had saved France for the arbitrament of another campaign. No longer need she plead for peace at any price. Malplaquet meant a continuing war and in that fact lay Marlborough's doom.[1]

The rumours of slaughter quickly reached London and were as quickly magnified, for, as Walpole wrote to Cardonnel: 'The malice and ill nature of some people here makes them very industrious to lessen the advantages of the late glorious victory and to magnify the loss on our side which nobody has been able to refute for want of an authentick account of the numbers of our killed and wounded and I'm satisfied it is whispered to be double what it is really because

---

[1] Trevelyan, *Peace*, 1–20; Churchill, II, 558–632. In the flush of victory Marlborough thought that the French would make peace on any terms; he was soon disillusioned.

none of our papers of authority have as yet taken notice of it.'[1] But no authoritative statement, no ringing of Junto bells, could rouse the enthusiasm of the British people for a victory whose consequences they did not relish. The Queen showed her bitter animosity by not mentioning the victory to Sarah or inquiring after Marlborough's health.[2] The government's determination, loudly expressed, to have no peace without Spain, and their continuing failure to achieve it, had spread despondency which was fortified by near starvation and harsh recruitment. The war had never been popular with the poorer classes and they now execrated it. But their tribulations had been ignored in the first flush of Marlborough's early victories.

This no longer availed. The ministry needed a flamboyant disgrace of the war's enemies if victory would not still criticism. Only peace—a resounding, profitable and immediate peace—could have saved them and for that they lacked not only time but also the will. As it was they tried to rally their ebbing fortunes by the impeachment of a high-tory cleric, Dr Henry Sacheverell, for attacking the principles of the Revolution.

3

SIR SAMUEL GARRARD, the tory Lord Mayor of London, invited Dr Henry Sacheverell to preach before him at St Paul's on 5 November 1709.[3] The Fifth of November sermons were a yearly event at which distinguished clerics were expected to discourse on the evils of popery. Sacheverell had already won a reputation as the boldest orator amongst the High-Church party, a man in whom an undertow of hysteria gave a remarkable effectiveness to his eloquence. To choose such a cleric for such an occasion amounted to deliberate

[1] C(H) MSS, 6, Walpole to Cardonnell, 13 September 1709.

[2] Churchill, II, 632–3.

[3] For the Sacheverell case cf. The Tryal of Dr Henry Sacheverell (London, 1710). F. Madan, The Bibliography of Sacheverell (privately printed, 1887), is a guide to the extensive pamphlet literature. A. T. Scudi, The Sacheverell Affair, Columbia Univ. Studies (New York, 1939), provides a useful summary. C(H) MSS, 67, contains Walpole's working papers as a manager of the trial.

provocation. Dr Sacheverell did not disappoint the Lord Mayor.[1] After a few perfunctory phrases on the iniquity of popery in general and the Gunpowder Plot in particular, he warmed to his theme. He turned his attention to the present state of the Church whose 'Holy Communion has been rent and divided by factions and schismatical imposters, her pure Doctrines corrupted and defiled; her primitive worship and discipline profaned and abused; her sacred orders denied and villified; her priests and professors (like St Paul) calumniated; misrepresented and ridiculed, her altars and sacraments prostituted to hypocrites, deists, socinians and atheists'. This promising beginning led on to a thorough castigation of the government, with a particularly vicious jibe at Godolphin, for its tolerant attitude to occasional conformity and to dissenters' schools. After a pious reference to the Royal Martyr he exhorted his congregation 'to an absolute and unconditional obedience to the supreme power in all things lawful' and affirmed 'the utter illegality of resistance upon any pretence whatsoever'.[2] This angry, uncompromising sermon echoed through the land. A seal of authority was attached to it by the flattering attentions of the Lord Mayor who carried the preacher off in his coach.

The government was in a quandary. There had been nothing accidental about Sacheverell's sermon. It was almost impossible to ignore it without a total loss of face. And yet any notice was dangerous. Godolphin was incensed by the scarcely veiled reference to himself but he is unlikely to have acted out of personal pique. There are rumours that he was urged by Wharton to plunge into an impeachment in the hope that he might disgrace himself. Others lay the blame for the trial on the rashness of some of the younger whigs,

[1] Sacheverell had preached for some time at St Saviour's Southwark; his sermon preached at Derby assizes in the summer had already achieved a *succès de scandale*. Garrard must have known that he was playing with fire. Garrard, who was MP for Amersham, had voted tory in 1700, for the Tack in 1704 and naturally he was pro-Sacheverell in 1710. He ceased to be a member in 1710.

[2] *C(H) MSS*, 67. Walpole's copy of the sermon.

particularly Sunderland, who wanted a showdown with the tories.[1] On what little evidence there is it would seem that only Somers and Boyle, the Secretary of State, were reluctant to engage in the trial. The rest of the ministry seem to have entered into the impeachment in the hope that they would dish the tories on an issue which would bring them wide public approval.

The trial aroused passionate interest. Wren was commissioned to design the staging in Westminster Hall. The Queen was provided with a royal box, whilst the public galleries were crowded with the Court. Pamphlets and tracts poured from the Press. Whether this was what the ministry had intended is doubtful. But it was soon clear that they as well as Sacheverell were on trial.[2]

They put forward their most skilled parliamentary debaters to manage the trial, but by February 1710 the signs were so ominous that they decided to reinforce them and Walpole was made an additional manager on the 11th.[3] From the opening of the trial of Sacheverell, Walpole had followed with great attention. He had read and annotated both the Derby and the London sermons, tracked the references to White Kennet's *History* and copied them out assiduously. He attended the preliminary examination of Sacheverell and his bookseller, Clements, by the Commons and took extensive notes. He prepared his speech on the first article of the impeachment with unusual care. Several drafts exist but his final speech was written out in the form in which it was afterwards printed. This ran clean contrary to his usual practice of confining his preparation for speeches to brief headings.[4]

The first article of the impeachment ran as follows:

[1] Swift, *History of the Four Last Years*, 14; G. Burnet, *History of His Own Time* (Oxford, 1833), V, 435 n. HMC, *Portland MSS*, V, 649; *Blenheim MSS*, E.15. Sunderland to Duchess of Marlborough c. February 1710: 'I find by Mr. Boyle's manner of talking this morning about the business of Sacheverell's sermon that Ld. Marlb. and Ld. Treasurer had spoke to him for he talked of it with another sort of warmth than I ever heard him.'

[2] J. J. Cartwright, *Wentworth Papers*, 110–12.

[3] N. Luttrell, *Brief Relation*, VI, 544.

[4] C(H) *MSS*, 67. *Tryal*, 60–3.

'He, the said Henry Sacheverell, in his said sermon preached at St. Paul's, doth suggest and maintain, That the necessary means used to bring about the said Happy Revolution, were odious and unjustifiable; That his late Majesty, in his declaration, disclaimed the least imputation of resistance; and that to impute resistance to the said Revolution, is to cast black and odious colours upon his late Majesty, and the said Revolution.'

Walpole's support of this accusation was short but trenchant, full of power, yet he was careful to avoid exaggeration or excess. He called attention to the violent and licentious nature of the Press—an evil which, however, could be dealt with by the common law[1]; but 'when the trumpet is sounded in Sion, when the pulpit takes up the cudgels, when the cause of the enemies of our government is called the cause of God, and of the church . . . and the people are taught for their souls and consciences sake to swallow these pernicious doctrines' then, felt Walpole, it was time for the Commons to put a stop to such an attack on the Revolution Settlement. Walpole was, however, well aware of the dilemma of his party—that by supporting resistance they encouraged a revolutionary and anti-social attitude which was bound to undermine the security of the nation—and he stated this dilemma boldly and plainly. 'Resistance,' he asserted, 'is no where enacted to be legal but subjected by all the laws now in being to the greatest penalties; tis what is not, cannot, nor ought ever to be described, or affirmed in any positive law, to be excusable. When, and upon what never to be expected occasions, it may be excercised, no man can foresee; and ought never to be thought of but when an utter subversion of the realm threaten the whole frame of a constitution and no redress can otherwise be hoped for.' To deny the existence of this right of resistance was 'a matchless indiscretion' for 'the doctrine of

---

[1] In March 1706, Walpole had drawn the attention of the Commons to two pamphlets which were voted by the House to be a scandalous and malicious libel (Luttrell, VI, 24). Although he was an adroit pamphleteer himself Walpole seems to have harboured a strong dislike of the Press throughout his life.

unlimited, unconditional passive obedience was first invented to support arbitary and despotic power'. Sacheverell's plea that there was no resistance in the Revolution he dismissed as 'rubbage' and a violation of common sense.[1]

This speech was not subtle in argument but it was full of that practical realism which suffused his attitude to politics. What he said related to the way men had behaved, were likely to behave and, Walpole felt as a good whig, ought to behave. For a junior minister it was an excellent, well-judged performance. But it availed little.

In their prosecution of Sacheverell the ministry had over-reached themselves. The wide and general dissatisfaction was fanned into a burning animosity towards the government; then the public outcry was used to draw away its half-hearted supporters at Court and in the Commons. In fact, the ministry only just scraped home on the Sacheverell issue. On 21 March 1710, Walpole wrote gloomily to Cardonnel: 'This day has put an end and a most disagreeable end to Dr Sacheverell's tryal for though he was voted guilty yesterday by a majority of 17 his punishment was reduced very low this day by a majority of one that I think they had as good as acquitted him.'[2] Instead of the severe sentence for which the government had hoped, Sacheverell was merely forbidden to preach for three years and his sermon given to the common hangman to burn. It was, as Walpole feared, equivalent to an acquittal; bonfires and illuminations greeted Sacheverell wherever he went. As the irascible old Dean of Christ Church was quick to observe, in attempting to roast a parson the whigs had scorched themselves.[3]

4

VASTLY IRRITATING as the public clamour for Sacheverell must have been, it was not the sole cause of Walpole's

[1] *Tryal*, 62–3, checked by *C(H) MSS*, 67.
[2] *C(H) MSS*, 6, Walpole to Cardonnel, 21 March 1710.
[2] Burnet, *Own Times*, V, 444–50; HMC, *Portland MSS*, IV, 530. *Blenheim MSS*, C.I.16. Bonfires were made and healths drunk by servants of the Queen within the vicinity of Parliament.

despondency. There were signs—too obvious signs—that the ministry had drifted hard on the rocks. For some months, too, he had been deeply concerned about his own future. His spirits were further weakened by an illness of such severity that his friends were deeply troubled, and it was with the utmost difficulty that he struggled back from Houghton in January to take part in Sacheverell's trial.[1] Personally he was in a most unenviable position. With office his desperate financial position had eased, but not sufficiently for him to view a period in opposition with any relish. The death of Sir Thomas Littleton had enabled him to take out one insurance against the future. He became Treasurer of the Navy in his place. As he wrote to Arthur Maynwaring on 11 January 1710: 'The prospect of a peace, which everybody concludes to be soe near, leaves me noe room to hesitate in this matter, for there is a thousand pounds a year of my present salary that is paid out of Mr Brydges's office, upon consideration of the foreign businesse; which, determineing with the war, will make a very great difference betwixt the two employments, that if I may be pardoned for preferring soe considerable an advantage before the particular honour that my present office entitles me to in receiving my Lord Duke's commands, I must accept of this offer.'[2] And there may have been the further thought in Walpole's mind that it was no bad thing to extricate himself a little from a too close dependence upon the Marlboroughs, whose relations with Anne had deteriorated even further owing to a fracas about the promotion of Abigail's relations in the army. This matter was to harass Walpole throughout the summer, for in spite of his acceptance of the Treasurership of the Navy he was kept on as Secretary-at-War.

When Walpole, sick and weary, reached his office in the middle of January 1710, to take part in Sacheverell's trial,

[1] *Walpole MSS*, Townshend to H. Walpole, 31 January 1710 (N.S.). *Blenheim MSS*, E.43. Walpole to same, 11 January 1710. 'I think of setting out for London tomorrow: tho' indeed, in the condition I find myself, I am afraid I shall be obliged to travel very slowly, if I am able to come forward at all.'

[2] *Blenheim MSS*, E.43. Walpole to Sarah, 11 January 1710.

he found a violent quarrel in progress over Anne's insistence on granting a vacant regiment to Colonel Hill, Abigail's brother. Such a promotion would by-pass many loyal officers of greater seniority, those moreover who had borne the brunt of the war in Flanders or Spain. More seriously for Marlborough it was a test of power and he made it one.[1] The Queen was faced bluntly with this issue. She had to choose Marlborough or Abigail. But Anne was not so easily cornered. After showing great obstinacy, she yielded the point of the regiment for which she expected Marlborough to be humbly grateful, but Abigail still remained unbanished. Yet Marlborough's friends were so terrified of the dangers of an overt crisis that they urged on Marlborough an accommodation, to which he reluctantly consented. Unfortunately the diplomatic situation made Marlborough's presence at The Hague urgently necessary and when he sailed he left behind a defeated ministry.[2]

The signs were clear to those politicians who had disliked the monopoly of power exercised by the Marlboroughs and their friends. And the Sacheverell case had given them their opportunity to show a lack of enthusiasm for the ministry. The Dukes of Shrewsbury and Somerset with their clients had voted the doctor 'not guilty'. The Duke of Argyll for

[1] He retired to Windsor on 14 January 1710 and let it be known that he wished to give up. He wrote as follows to Godolphin on 18 January: 'If her Majesty would be pleased to reflect for some time past she would find that my uneasiness does not proceed only from her intention for Mr Hill, that being but one of many mortifications I have received, it is the Queen's change to me that has brook my sperit, and my silence has been the effect of my great concern and respect for Her Majesty for I cant but think that the nation would be of opinion that I have deserved better then to be made a sacrifice to the unreasonable passion of a bedchamber woman; I hope if Mrs Masham continues to endeavour to make people beleive that I retier because the Queen has a mind to make a Collonel that I may be allowed to tell my reasons, by which the world will see that she is the author of my mortifications which I heartily wish may be the last ill effect of her power.' Godolphin forwarded this letter to Cowper, the Lord Chancellor, and suggested that he should read it to the Queen before the cabinet meeting. Marlborough's letter was unknown to Sir Winston Churchill and has not been printed before. Herts RO, *Panshanger MSS*, C.I.3.

[2] Churchill, II, 662–70. Coxe, *Marlborough*, III, 6–21.

the sake of his Scottish influence had voted *for* the impeachment but *against* the penalties. He followed this up with a
terse note to Marlborough tantamount to a declaration of war,
expressing his disapproval of the treatment of his brother
about the purchase of a regiment.[1] The Duke of Newcastle,
a man of wide parliamentary influence, was known to be in
frequent consultation with Harley and Shrewsbury. These
men commanded sufficient interest, in Harley's eyes, to con-
struct a stable ministry if the government's defeat could be
secured. He knew that his avowed policy of peace would receive popular approval and also the support of the influential
independent members of Parliament. But Robert Harley's
nature compelled him to avoid a dramatic clash with the
Junto; he preferred a more piecemeal destruction in the hope
that as disgrace followed disgrace, the timid might be induced to desert their benefactors.

5

AS SOON as Marlborough was safely in Holland the blows
began to fall. For many months the Queen had been coldly
hostile to Sarah. Her presence alone recalled the obligations
which Anne wished to obliterate; but her vehement demands
for affection and clamorous accusations of neglect bred an
uncontrollable bitterness in the Queen. On 6 April 1710 they
met for the last time, Anne listening in wooden silence to the
angry reproaches of the Duchess, which sprang as much from
the warmth and generosity of Sarah's nature as from thwarted
ambition and the shame of her disgrace. In April, too, the
question of further promotion for Colonel Masham, whom
Abigail had married, was opened and Walpole was insistent
that it could not be withheld. This made the Duchess believe
he was playing a trimming game. But more ominous and
more public was the replacement of the Marquess of Kent by
the Duke of Shrewsbury as Lord Chamberlain. All these

---

[1] *Walpole MSS*, A.1. Argyll to Cardonnel for Marlborough, 24 March 1710;
with Marlborough's reply. Copies sent by Cardonnel to Walpole for information.

events struck a chill in Marlborough's heart and he wrote gloomily to Walpole towards the end of the month: 'I am extreamly obliged to you for the account you give of the Queen's present temper, which I believe to be such, that if I considered onely myself, I would not serve one minut longer.'[1] But worse was to follow.

In the promotion of Masham, Walpole sensed danger. 'If one could be assured that it would end there,' Walpole wrote to Marlborough on 28 April 1710, 'and this honour extend to the service of one family, perhaps it were advisable to be more easy: but if it is to go on, a stop at some time must be put to it.' Of course, it went on, the Duke of Ormonde, as General of the Horse, complained about Walpole. He was never consulted, he said, about routes, marching orders and quarters, and he demanded to control these things himself. This was a dangerous invasion of Walpole's power, which he was quick to counter. 'I told the Queen,' he wrote to Marlborough on 2 May 1710, 'that these affairs were in the same method that they had been for nineteen years, which appears by the office books, and that I did apprehend this would give the Duke of Ormonde a power or command here which would be entirely new, upon which the Queen agreed it should remain upon the old foot. But I am fully satisfied this was an instance of trying their strength.'[2] Another quickly followed. On 11 May the Queen sent for Walpole and told him that she wanted Abigail's brother, Colonel Hill, made a brigadier. The general promotion had stopped short of him by three commissions, a line drawn no doubt quite deliberately by Marlborough to underline his victory on this issue in February. But the Masham faction were restless in

[1] Coxe, II, 12-13. The letter is undated but endorsed 28 April 1710 (O.S.).

[2] Walpole's correspondence with Marlborough for 1710 is printed with Marlborough's replies in Coxe, II, 11–35. The originals of Walpole's letters are at Blenheim; Marlborough's replies, together with Walpole's copies of his own letters, are at Wolterton in a bound volume entitled *Letters of Sir Robert Walpole 1710*. This collection of letters was originally at Houghton but was borrowed in the 1750s by Horatio Walpole who contemplated writing his memoirs. Coxe's transcripts are good but they have in all cases been checked with the originals; references, however, are to the printed version.

defeat for by securing a commission for Hill they could demonstrate to the world the greatness of their power, their
ability to make changes in the heart of Marlborough's own
territory, so they had persuaded the Queen to order Hill's
commission at once without further consultation with Marlborough. 'I represented,' Walpole wrote on 12 May, 'in the
strongest terms I was able, the mortification such a step must
be to your Grace, the unreasonableness of doing any thing
disagreeable to you in the army, and the ill consequences
that must attend the lessening of your creditt or authority in
the army, and said a great deal more than can come within
the compasse of a letter, or is proper for me to repeat, and
did at last, but with the greatest difficulty, prevail with her
not to order those three commissions untill she heard your
grace's opinion.'[1] Walpole moved skilfully to secure a compromise which would save Marlborough's dignity and the
Queen's pleasure. It was not easy. Marlborough wanted to
refuse to sanction the commission: the Queen to issue it in
spite of Marlborough's disapproval. Walpole patiently and
persistently argued with both, and drew to his support
Godolphin, Sunderland and Craggs in his effort to bring
Marlborough to an accommodation. Finally he achieved it.
Hill's commission was signed but sent to Marlborough to
confer at any time during the campaign. To put a stop to
further criticism Marlborough conferred it at once. But, of
course, it was a defeat. Walpole had saved him from a public
disgrace but the whole political world knew that he had been
compelled to act against his own interests.[2]

6

HILL'S COMMISSION was no sooner settled than graver worries
beset the whigs. The Junto had signalized their return to
power by making a point of securing a Secretaryship of State
for Sunderland: Harley decided that their return to the

[1] Coxe, II, 17.

[2] *Ibid.*, 17–24. Naturally the Masham faction became increasingly cock-a-
hoop and in June Abigail went to the opera wearing a miniature of Sacheverell
on her fan. *Chevening MSS*, Sir John Cropley to James Stanhope, 17 June 1710.

wilderness might be marked by his dismissal. Harley, though by nature over-subtle, could at times display a mastery of political dexterity to which the blunter nature of Walpole could never quite attain. The selection of Sunderland as a victim was a brilliant, if malicious, choice. The fact that he was Marlborough's son-in-law gave added edge to his disgrace. Yet he was an easy target, for he had not been successful as Secretary; his uneasy and autocratic temperament had already alienated so many of his colleagues that an attempt to make a last ditch stand failed.[1] With skilful timing the prospect of his removal was allowed to become common knowledge. The uncertainty corroded the whigs' confidence and bred intolerable anxiety about their own futures. Their failure to save Sunderland when they had time to do so, advertised the full measure of their impotence. Walpole saw this situation with clarity. He urged Marlborough to bring home to Godolphin their utmost danger. Godolphin, in fact, acted with resolution if not as promptly as Walpole wished. He let it be known that if Marlborough chose to resign on the issue, he would go with him.[2] He also tackled the Queen, stressing the unhappy effect that Sunderland's dismissal would have on the Allies, an effect which it must be admitted the whigs were trying hard to stimulate. Somers had written to Townshend to urge him to stir up the Dutch and the Emperor in their interest. He was told to drive home the implications of Sunderland's fall. It would mean a new Parliament, and a new Parliament would mean peace—consequences which had already been drawn for them by their

[1] Coxe, II, 25. Walpole to Marlborough, 6 June 1710. 'Sunderland...by none endeavoured to be saved'. Somerset, it is true, was a prime mover in securing Sunderland's disgrace but he was in constant consultation with Harley. The handling of the whole situation betrays a dexterity in politics outside Somerset's class; but, of course, Somerset provided Harley with an admirable cat's-paw. He is reported as being 'entirely out with the whig lords' as early as 15 March 1709. *Chevening MSS*, Sir John Cropley to James Stanhope, 15 March 1709.

[2] The whigs in the cabinet had considered resigning in a body if Sunderland were dismissed. As late as 17 June 1710, Walpole told Sir John Cropley that he 'expected this desperate stroke in a few days'. *Chevening MSS*, Sir John Cropley to James Stanhope, 17 June 1710.

ambassadors in London who were not to be hoodwinked by Anne's assurance that Sunderland's dismissal meant no change of measures. But Sunderland fell on 14 June 1710, and no one resigned. Indeed the Junto met in solemn conclave at the Duke of Devonshire's house and sent Marlborough a round-robin pleading that he should not consider resignation. There was little else that they could do, for their only hope lay in a continuing war and the necessity of Marlborough's leadership. This hope was strengthened by the breakdown of the peace negotiations at Gertruydenburg, due as much to the prevarication of Townshend as to the intransigence of the French.

The prospect of a continuing war might gladden the whigs and the directors of the Bank of England, who had been distressed by Sunderland's fall, but it appalled the country at large. Walpole was not ignorant of the temper of the country. Service in the army was detested; recruitment became difficult and inadequate; desertion was commonplace and impossible to check. In June three regiments mutinied in Yorkshire, including Islay's, the brother of Argyll. As Sir Charles Hotham wrote to Walpole on 26 June 1710, these mutinies were 'of the utmost detriment to the service and has occasioned such a clamour amongst all people in the country that gives our men all imaginable encouragement to desert, finding everywhere protection'.[1] Unrest was not confined to the army; bad harvests and high prices had led as usual to rioting, but the violence and intensity of these outbreaks were exceptional. The militia in many counties had to be called out to suppress them. John Wrott, Walpole's steward, spent the summer under arms, and the last of his letters to survive describes an ugly situation at Oundle, caused by the invasion of common rights. On the 31 May 1710 he wrote hurriedly to Walpole:

---

[1] C(H) MSS, Sir Charles Hotham, 26 June 1710; also Walpole to Cardonnel, 24 June 1710, for elaborate precautions taken at Hull to prevent mutiny and desertion. The garrison at Gibraltar was also mutinous. The direct cause of the mutiny was the very considerable arrears of the soldiers' pay.

'Yesterday I march't my troop to Bedingfeild Common where I mett my Lord Cardigan, the High Sherriff, Sir Caesar Child and some few other gentlemen of Northamptonshire. The mobb begann to gather from all corners, some in disguise with masks, and in women's cloakes, and others with axes, spades, pickaxes etc but how great the number of rioters would have amounted to (had wee not been there) I cant say; for I observed that the very men the sherriff summoned to assist him, I believe but for us, had joyned the mobb, for whatever prisoner was given in to their custody they still suffered, nay assisted in escaping. To prevent and make all sure I kept patroling all night, soe that for this season there is noe more apprehension of them.'[1]

For many years Harley had maintained a nation-wide system of intelligence. And he knew that these mutinies and riots could not be dismissed as isolated acts of desperate men. They sprang from a deep revulsion from the war. Nor was this hatred of the war confined to the politically insignificant. The squires detested the grinding burden of the land tax and their loathing found an echoing response amongst the substantial yeomen and the middle classes of the towns.

The knowledge that he had wide public support made Harley confident that his policy of a new Parliament and a quick peace would succeed, in spite of powerful opposition from the City, if once he could win the Queen's open support. He was also aware of deep divisions in the ministry. Somers and Halifax seemed prepared to negotiate with Shrewsbury, Somerset and himself.[2] They regarded the sacrifice of Godolphin almost with equanimity. This lack of loyalty was, of course, exceedingly welcome to Harley who wanted to avoid depending too exclusively on his rival St

[1] *C(H) MSS*, John Wrott, 31 May 1710.

[2] Shrewsbury and Somerset had grave difficulties in making up their minds which way to go. As late as 23 April 1710, Walpole told Sir John Cropley that Shrewsbury had made an offer of renewed friendship with Godolphin. Somerset, too, was said to be keen on a reconciliation. *Chevening MSS*, Sir John Cropley to James Stanhope, 23 April 1710. Harley exploited these divisions with great dexterity.

John, and the high tories. He knew that without some whig support he would have the utmost difficulty in securing a stable ministry. Steadily and remorselessly the government's lack of the Queen's confidence was brought home to the whigs in office. No sooner had they recovered from the shock of Sunderland's removal than they were plunged into consternation by the white staff being peremptorily taken from Godolphin. As Townshend bewailed to Stanhope: 'God only knows what destruction our new ministry is preparing for us.'[1]

Walpole knew himself to be a marked man. He had risen to office by the patronage of Orford, one of the most intractable members of the Junto, but, more dangerously, he had been the close confidant of Marlborough and Godolphin in office. Yet so long as he remained Secretary-at-War and Marlborough Commander-in-Chief, the influence of Harley in the army (with its important patronage of promotions) was likely to be small and difficult to exert. The struggle for the commissions for Masham and Hill had at least made that obvious. Walpole was aware of his danger. He discovered in the early summer that his correspondence with Marlborough, Townshend, Cardonnel, Stanhope and his brother at the Hague was being opened and examined.[2] Rumours were current in July that he was to be dismissed at once.[3] Yet he survived Godolphin's dismissal by many weeks and until the very last moment seems to have hoped that some arrangement might be made with Harley. But on 19 September 1710 he sat down to write his last letter as Secretary-at-War to James Stanhope in Spain. The latter had just won the battle of Saragossa—a victory which Marlborough and Walpole, with the unflagging hope of the born politician, expected would rally the Queen and the country to their cause. After having congratulated Stanhope, dealt with his recruiting and personal problems, Walpole's reserve broke down and he could not check the despair he felt. 'We are in such a way

[1] Coxe, II, 34. The staff was given to Harley in May 1711.
[2] C(H) MSS, 6, 30 June 1710, to Cardonnel. *Walpole MSS*, **A.1**, Horace Walpole, 23 May 1710 (N.S.).
[3] Luttrell, VI, 604.

here that I cannot describe, but you can imagine nothing worse than you will hear. The Parliament is not yett dissolved but this week will certainly determine it. Dear Stanhope, God prosper you and pray make haste to us that you may see what you will not believe if it were told you.'[1]

The dissolution of Parliament had long been dreaded by Walpole. He and his whig friends had exerted the utmost pressure on Shrewsbury to try to prevent it. They knew well enough that the combination of Treasury hostility and popular animosity would be more than sufficient to destroy their slender parliamentary majority, and give Harley a victory. Walpole's dismissal may have been carefully timed for the election. It showed the world at large, and Norfolk in particular, that he did not enjoy the full confidence of the ministry. Yet Walpole was allowed to retain his Treasurership of the Navy, in the hope, no doubt, of encouraging in him a desire to please. Such action was typical of the involved subtlety of Harley's manoeuvres.

7

FOR ALL Walpole's sanguine temperament, it must have been with a heavy heart that he set out, half disgraced, for the long drive to Houghton. As the coach slowly laboured along the heavy undulating roads, through the wide open fields of golden stubble, he had time enough to cast his accounts and to brood on the dangers that lay ahead. He was no longer a young man or a rich one. His career and his fortune depended upon his judgment of events. If Harley succeeded, and he played no part in his success, his career was over. If Harley failed, but with his support, his career might still be over. Yet surely Harley could not fail! The whole nation, except the bankers and a few trained politicians, was crying out for peace; and Harley was offering peace. But could Harley escape the clutches of the High-Flyers, the rabid

[1] *Walpole MSS*, A.1, copy. The original is at Chevening. The letter is dated 29 September, which must be N.S., as the Parliament was dissolved on 22 September 1710.

tories whose hatred of dissenters, of city merchants, and of placemen was so immoderate that they must ruin any government, particularly as so many of them were tainted with Jacobitism and capable of treason? If not, then association with Harley would be folly. The Queen, never healthy, was also ageing. George of Hanover, her likely successor, was said to dislike Marlborough owing to a slight at Oudenarde. Too much reliance, therefore, could not be placed on the Hanoverian succession bringing back the Junto whigs into office, unless the High-Flyers had sufficient time and opportunity to reveal their Stuart predilections. For Walpole there was no clear course of action which offered an easy solution to his difficulties. The choice between Harley and opposition was not easy to make, and for the moment Walpole deferred the decision. In all anxious temperaments there is inordinate hope.

Walpole, too, desperately needed the emoluments of office. The burdens on his estate had grown no less with the years, for, with office, his own and his wife's extravagance had grown. Their happiness had been brief. Her life was darkened by moods of suspicion, jealousy and hate which alternated with outbursts of reckless gaiety and wantonness. She clutched at fashionable distractions—clothes, jewels, cards, painting, a collection of exotic birds, anything that was gay and *à la mode*. Her need for distraction, the underlying hysteria of her nature, drove her to more dangerous delights until their marriage lay in ruins.[1] But Walpole continued to treat her with tender indulgence, ignoring her follies and paying for the extravagance which he could ill afford.

As his coach reached Norfolk, Walpole had to assume the bold, ebullient manner for which he was already famous. He was soon surrounded with a crowd of relatives and friends, full of schemes and anxieties, for they knew full well that their

[1] It is significant that from their marriage in 1700 to 1706, Catherine had a child or a miscarriage almost every year. After 1706 she did not bear another child until 1717 when Horatio was born. The possibility that he was not Walpole's child cannot be dismissed, cf. below, pp. 257–9.

G

power in Norfolk was in jeopardy. Born politician that he was, the prospect of battle buoyed his spirits, for he lost in the restless energy of electioneering the doubts of a defeated heart. And yet there must have been harsh moments of perception, accompanied by the harrowing fear that the power which he sought might never be his, and by a taste of those frustrations which sear men unreserved in ambition and in love.

CHAPTER FIVE

DEFEAT AND DISGRACE, 1710-14

THE NEXT four years witnessed some of the most difficult and confused periods in Walpole's life and his career was jeopardized by factors over which he could have no control. The longer the Queen lived, the more likely it was that Harley would succeed in establishing himself so firmly in power that he would prove irremovable at her death. Alternatively, Bolingbroke might have time to oust Harley, win over the Pretender to the Anglican Church, secure a Stuart succession and smash the whigs for ever. Nor could the possibility be ruled out that he and his friends might have to fight for the liberties which their fathers had won. Every faction was out to play for the highest stakes, and in this dangerous game it was easier to lose than to win. For the time Harley held the trump cards. The gentry throughout the land were utterly tired of the war, except for those few in each county whose fortunes were intimately tied to the whig cause, but they could no longer maintain their hold over waverers and those inclined to independent views.

Walpole knew that he would find a difficult situation in Norfolk. Both he and Townshend had been in correspondence throughout the summer with their relatives and friends, trying to discover some way by which they could maintain their hold on the county and its boroughs. Their difficulties were increased by Townshend's being in Holland where he was involved in the protracted peace negotiations with the Dutch and French. In his absence his brother deputized for him. He was told to 'goe down to Raynham and kill a sheep or two', but, as Horace Walpole, who was Townshend's secretary at The Hague, reported on 9 September 1710: 'I believe my namesake is nott the best manager in affairs of this nature; but, however, he will take away all pretence from anyone to say that his Lordship (i.e. Townshend) is neuter and, therefore, you must prevail on Mr Horace to go into the country, lay aside the merchant, and spend and speak like a gentleman.'[1]

Horace Townshend was not keen to engage in active electioneering nor was his brother willing to press him so very hard. This reluctance did not escape notice and the rumour grew that Townshend wished to play a neutral part, much to the detriment of the cause of Walpole and the whigs. It is doubtful, however, whether the most vigorous and prolonged campaign could have brought them success. In a desperate effort to hold the county Walpole allowed himself to become a candidate; he came bottom of the poll. In Yarmouth and Norwich the results were equally disastrous to the whigs, whose nominees were rejected. Walpole even had his doubts about the loyalty of King's Lynn, for he took the precaution of getting himself elected for the family pocket borough of Castle Rising. In the event it proved unnecessary, for Lynn remained loyal to the old families, and was rewarded by an election feast at which he and his friends drowned their tribulations in a hundred gallons of port. Yet the whig defeat was overwhelming. Apart from Lynn, every constituency returned tories, even Castle Rising; for when Walpole gave up his seat, he had to hand it over, according to the family arrangement, to his tory uncle who at once became an ardent supporter of Harley.[2]

At the end of November, Walpole returned to London. He was quickly besieged by his friends, who had fared as badly as himself in their own counties. Harley's group, and the associated factions of high tories, had won a resounding success for the government at the polls. The hatred of the war was so intense that even constituencies with tiny electorates deserted

[1] *Walpole MSS*, Horatio Walpole to Walpole, 9 September 1710.
[2] *C(H) MSS*, vouchers, 1710; 432 quarts and 1 pint of port were drunk; the cost, £43 5s. *Returns of MPs*; HMC, *Townshend MSS*, 339-40; HMC, *Portland MSS*, V, 192, 228.

After Sir Godfrey Kneller

IV. ROBERT HARLEY, AFTERWARDS 1ST EARL OF OXFORD
AND MORTIMER

their old whig patrons.[1] Indeed, such success was almost an embarrassment to Harley, for the House of Commons was filled with the strange new faces of modest country squires and small town tories, who were hot not only for peace but also for the damnation of dissenters. Passions of this kind were to prove hard to control if easy to exploit. After such successes Harley had no need of the whig support. In any case Walpole had resolved on outright opposition to the government, an attitude which was quickly endorsed by his close friends. He threw down the challenge to Harley in the first days of the session and by the end of the year it had become pointless for Harley to retain him any longer as Treasurer of the Navy; and his dismissal was conveyed to him by Dartmouth. Walpole replied on 2 January 1711, with great dignity, stressing his devotion to the Queen and his readiness to do her service.[2]

Harley was faced with a great opportunity. He knew that he would have the Court and the country behind him as far as making peace was concerned, so long as it was reasonably just. He was also shrewd enough to realize that his political future could not be based solely upon a successfully negotiated peace. He needed to destroy the power of his enemies as well as to rivet his friends to him both by interest and by policy in order to prevent them from being seduced by St John's rash promises. For the moment the destruction of his enemies absorbed his attention.

[1] HMC, *Townshend MSS*, 75. For the 1710 election cf. Miss Mary Ransome, 'The Press in the Election of 1710', *Cambridge Historical Journal*, VI (1939), 209–21.

[2] *Ibid.*, *Dartmouth MSS*, I, 303. There is no evidence at all that Harley tried to win Walpole's wholehearted support for his government by threatening to expose Walpole's part in the Forage Bill scandal. Coxe, I, 32, asserts this and it has been uncritically repeated by Stirling Taylor, *Walpole*, 111. Coxe based his statement on the pamphlet *Letter to Mr Pulteney in Answer to his Remarks* (1719), 47, but unsubstantiated rumours used in an angry pamphlet battle cannot be relied upon. Twelve months elapsed between Walpole's dismissal and the forage scandal. It is almost certain that this approach (with or without threats) came just before the forage scandal and after Walpole had shown himself to be dangerous in opposition. Harley certainly had a high opinion of Walpole and probably of Townshend too. He also realized that their attitude to administration and government was not far from his own.

Marlborough remained Commander-in-Chief. His reputation in Europe was immense, and the greatness of his victories too recent, for Harley not to fear that by one bold measure Marlborough might bring absolute defeat on France and so revive his waning popularity. And Marlborough was not the man to sacrifice himself readily either for his friends or for his principles; but even he could not disentangle himself from the whigs; nor did he entirely wish to do so, for they were the only party in favour of prolonging the war upon which his pre-eminence was based. If he were to be dismissed, any ensuing defeat, no matter how trivial, would be magnified to terrify the public and inflate the whigs.

Harley's solution to this dilemma was typical of the man. As the Duke of Somerset informed Cowper, the late Lord Chancellor, on 21 December 1710, Marlborough was to be mortified until he threw in his hand and quitted.[1]

Walpole's dismissal in January 1711 was a part of this campaign, for his devotion to Marlborough's interest was public knowledge. After his most intimate junior colleague had been dealt with, Harley turned to his Duchess and Sarah suffered her final disgrace. She was peremptorily dismissed her offices. Considering the vituperation which she had heaped upon the Queen, it speaks eloquently of Anne's patience and underlying obstinacy of heart that her final disgrace should have been so long delayed. Casting all pride aside, Marlborough went down on his knees and begged the Queen to spare his wife. The humiliation was wasted, and the malicious gossip corroded further his tarnished reputation. But still Marlborough did not resign. He baffled Harley and skilfully avoided becoming either the whigs' martyr or the tories' victim, for he was as much at home in the grand strategy of politics as of war. He knew the Queen's life to be a gamble—one—two—three years. And then? If a crisis about succession arose, the commander of the army might settle the issue as Monk had in 1660 and Marlborough himself had in

[1] E. C. Hawtrey (ed.), *The Private Diary of William, First Earl Cowper* (Eton, 1833), 51.

1688. Upon his ability to remain, therefore, in control of the army rested his own and his country's future. So he bore with patience and hope the campaign of humiliation and obloquy by which Harley hoped to break his spirit. Throughout 1711 the disgrace of Marlborough became a major objective of the ministry and in this struggle Walpole was deeply involved.[1]

A quick peace and the humiliation of Marlborough— these were the major political tasks which Harley set himself. Except in the most general sense they did not concern Parliament. It was certain that the majority of the Commons would welcome with delight the accomplishment of both tasks, but Harley had to find other work to keep his supporters contented. This, however, involved danger to his own position and Marlborough was quick to appreciate this. If by joining with the whigs Harley could form (Marlborough told Robethon, the Hanoverian minister) 'a party stronger than that of the tories, he would do it tomorrow.[2] But the tory party (or rather, the Octobrists) is so strong in the Lower House that it is to be feared that Harley, who will always sacrifice everything to his ambition and private interests, will be obliged, if he is to keep his place, to devote himself to them, and to embrace all their schemes.'[3] There was a very personal danger in this for Harley. Henry St John wanted to destroy him. In order to obtain supreme power St John was willing to inflame the hatreds and envies of these rural tories. His reckless disregard of consequence bred a virulence that heightened the danger of these last stormy years of the Queen's reign.

In his first parliamentary session Harley played his hand skilfully, and the Octobrists were satisfied by a wide variety

---

[1] Churchill, 767–801, and more particularly Marlborough's admirably clear-sighted survey of the situation to Robethon in April 1711, *ibid.*, 799–801.

[2] Marlborough almost certainly knew of Harley's desperate attempts in September 1710 to keep Cowper as Lord Chancellor. At one point he threatened suicide unless Cowper promised to stay. Cowper, *Diary*, 45. Cowper was shrewd enough to realize that Harley was afraid of the 'old torys' overrunning him.

[3] Churchill, 799–801.

of legislation which fed and soothed their prejudices. They tried to bolster up the political rights of their class by passing a Land Qualification Bill in 1711, which made it necessary for a member of Parliament to possess freehold land to the value of three hundred pounds a year—a measure which Swift considered the 'greatest security ever contrived for preserving the constitution'.[1] Their piety was gratified by the proposal to build fifty new churches in London and Westminster; their prejudice by an attack on the poor palatines—destitute German protestants—whom the whig government had allowed to flock into the country. High tory traditions were maintained by a demand to reduce the number of office-holders sitting in the Commons and by a proposal to resume those grants of Crown lands by which William III had discharged his obligations to his friends; measures which warmed their blood and kept them on their benches though they sighed for their homes and hounds. All these titbits were intermingled with the great work of destroying the reputation of the last ministry. Its victories could not be turned to defeats, but those victories could be belittled if proof were forthcoming that the war had been prolonged in order to line the pockets of Marlborough and his friends and supporters. The vast taxes were a disagreeable yoke which chafed the nation. If they could be proved to be mis-spent the disgrace of the whigs might be completed.

That Marlborough had been greedy was not difficult to prove. Swift made great play of the contrast between the modest cost of a Roman general's triumph, estimated at a mere thousand pounds, and the half a million which had already been lavished on Marlborough. But to convict him of corruption was a more formal matter. It required investigation and legal proof. For this purpose a committee to investigate public accounts was set up—all tories to a man. Gossip soon magnified into corruption the inconsistencies

[1] The Bill was an utter failure, easily evaded by legal ingenuity. It was aimed at the sons of peers, who rarely possessed land, as well as at merchants and contractors. The October Club consisted of the most confirmed tories.

and delays of the current financial methods. Thirty-five million pounds were confidently asserted to be missing, although the Committee merely reported on 12 April 1711 that they had not been accounted for. The iniquity of the whigs was further exposed by the expulsion from the House of Thomas Ridge, a wealthy Portsmouth brewer, who was rightly charged with swindling the navy.

But Harley realized clearly enough that accusations of corruption did not make a financial policy. Armies and navies still had to be paid for, and this necessitated heavy taxes, but taxes were slow to collect and any ministry had to lean heavily on the Bank—in Harley's opinion, too heavily, for the Bank's directors, largely whigs, had no hesitation in using their power to further their own policies. The new tory Parliament had been faced in the autumn of 1710 with a financial crisis of the first magnitude which the Bank had helped rather than hindered. To prevent such a dependence Harley proposed to create a new company, the South Sea Company, which was to be allowed a monopoly of the South Sea trade in return for taking over the responsibility for a part of the public debt. The South Sea Company's prime function was financial and it was designed as a counterpoise to the power of the Bank. Owing to the disasters which afterwards overwhelmed it, the South Sea Company has come to be regarded as fundamentally unsound from the start. On the contrary it was for many years a reputable and successful enterprise, and one of Harley's most considerable achievements.

Harley's ministry had, therefore, put forward in its first parliamentary session an exceptionally varied programme, designed to undermine still further the strength of the whigs and to establish more firmly the control of his ministry over the Commons and the City. But the harmony of his party was more apparent than real. Harley was an ageing man whose health and stamina were steadily being undermined by excessive drink. The over-conscious subtlety of his political behaviour created suspicion and he seemed almost to take pleasure in his reputation for cunning and secretiveness. He was essentially a politician of the Court whose power had grown out of his flair for intrigue. Yet his very success had taught men to distrust him. The shrewd Chancellor Cowper had immediately grasped the essence of his nature when they had first met in the Cabinet some years previously and Cowper had described in his diary 'that manner of his which was never to deal clearly or openly but always with reserve, if not dissimulation, or rather simulation; and to love tricks even where not necessary but from an inward satisfaction he took in applauding his own cunning. If any man was ever born under a necessity of being a knave, he was.'[1]

This tortuous aspect of Harley's character had come to dominate him so completely that every politician, fearing betrayal, felt uneasy. Such duplicity made a great gulf between him and the rural tories who made up the bulk of his supporters. They admired plain dealing, blunt opinions, decisive action, and these St John, who longed to get rid of Harley, was quite prepared to offer them. He disliked Harley's caution and distrusted his assumed loyalty. St John knew that he himself might be sacrificed at any time by the renewed alliance of Harley with the Court whigs, hence he had to commit himself to the most violent tory measures. His avowed intention became 'to break the body of the whigs, to render their supports useless to them, and to fill the employments of the kingdom, down to the meanest, with tories'.[2] And for this purpose he began as early as February 1711 to form his own party amongst the tories, a party which was intended to destroy Harley as well as the whigs. By chance he suffered a set-back; on 8 March 1711 Harley was stabbed by one Guiscard, whose treasonable correspondence with the French was being examined by the Lords of the Committee at the Cockpit. For the first, and last, time in his life Harley acquired popularity, and in so doing brought the appearance of harmony to his ministry. But a politician as shrewd

[1] Cowper, *Diary*, 45.
[2] Bolingbroke, *Letter to Sir William Wyndham* (1753), 21–2.

as Walpole was unlikely to be deceived by these appearances of unity.

2

THIS FIRST session of the new Parliament made great demands on Walpole. We have little detailed knowledge of his work but it is obvious that he was regarded by his followers as one of the leaders of the opposition to the government and that he devoted himself heart and soul to parliamentary business. We have one glimpse of him in a letter written by the tory Peter Wentworth at the very beginning of the session, during the debate on the Address.

'Mr. Walpool, at the committee that was appointed to draw up their Address of thanks for the Queen's speech, Sir Thomas Hanmore was in the chair, took notes and writ down what he seemed not to like; they there told him 'twas unparliamentary to writ so before the thing was finisht. But he mentained it to be the right of every member to writ what he pleased or why had they pen and ink allowed. After some squabling they yield him the point, but when 'twas finisht they desire to have his notes, but he made no answere but took his paper and lapt it up very deliberately and went away with it into the house, and showed it to Letchmore and some more who sett there heads together how they would desire to have it amended when it came into the house. The tories tell me as they had cookt it they made arrant nonsense on't and there was an hour debate about the words *which* and *and*, who was for the Which and who for the And I know not, after that Mr Walpool would have the Pretender mentioned which accationed some debate, but Mr Harley's speech yeild up that matter.'[1]

These manoeuvres of Walpole's were not, as Wentworth implies, mere tactics of embarrassment. He was to prove resolute in attacking every aspect of tory policy as well as in meeting charges of corruption, yet such actions were largely defensive. He needed to expose the ministry on the most vital question of English political life—the question of a pro-

[1] *Wentworth Papers,* 160.

testant succession, for this, he realized, was their Achilles heel. Naturally, repeated assertions of the desirability of the Hanoverian succession were distasteful to the Queen, underlining as they did her own mortality. Many tories equally loathed these assertions because they still cherished Jacobite principles. The slightest reluctance displayed by Harley, therefore, on the question of the succession was used by Walpole to hammer home his conviction that the tory party was still the party of James II bent on restoring the Stuarts. Walpole put his finger unerringly on the crux of the tories' dilemma: unequivocal support of the Hanoverians would split the party and destroy their precarious majority; unequivocal support of the Stuarts would have the same effect. Whenever he could, he raised this question in the Commons.

Throughout the session Walpole used all his skill in debate to hamper the tory programme, devoting particular care to their financial plans and attacking in particular the foundation of the South Sea Company.[1] But he did not confine his opposition to the House of Commons. He realized the particularly dangerous nature of Harley's accusation of corruption by the Junto to which the tendentious report of the Commissioners of Public Accounts seemed to give substance. In two trenchant pamphlets *The Debts of the Nation Considered* and *A State of the Five and Thirty Millions* Walpole demonstrated forcibly the misrepresentation of the Committee who had used the technical delays of accountancy to try and create an atmosphere of colossal corruption, 'so that here', he wrote, 'are accounts from King Charles's, King James's and King William's reign in the principal branches of expence in all the revenue brought in to make up and swell this general account'.[2] The argument was cogent but there was a

[1] C(H) MSS, 88. There are scraps of notes for a speech on the South Sea Company in Walpole's hand but they are far too disjointed to reconstruct the drift of his argument.

[2] *A State of the Five and Thirty Millions*, 2. These are ascribed to Walpole by his son, H. Walpole, *A Catalogue of Royal and Noble Authors* (1806), IV, 198. Although his attributions are not always certain, style and method of argument make them in this case almost certain.

slight air of self-justification about these pamphlets and occasionally a rapid gloss of awkward facts. There can be little doubt that the accusations of the ministry obtained a wider currency than the excuses of the whigs put forward by Walpole.

In the winter of 1711 Walpole was as ingenious and as restless in opposition as in debate. At this time political battles were fought on the stage as well as in the press; and during this first session he was busy organizing a burlesque of the Italian opera which was supported by the tories to mark their disapproval of the whigs' singer, Pilota, who came from Hanover. He entered into this contest with such gusto that he was to be seen standing at the door of the opera house, scrutinizing the tickets of the audience to prevent entry of any tories who might be bent on wrecking the performance.[1] Anything which irritated the ministry was worth Walpole's while. When the session ended and the summer heat drove Walpole to Houghton he could look back on a successful year of opposition. Marlborough still remained Commander-in-Chief. The City disliked the talk of peace as much as the squires liked it. The jealousy of Harley and St John gave promise of an early break-up of the ministry once peace had been secured. He also had the personal satisfaction of knowing that his opposition had been more constant, more varied and more effective than anyone else's —a fact which Harley brooded on during the summer vacation.

3

IT PROVED to be a bad summer for Walpole. His mother had died on 15 March 1711, and now he had the melancholy task of clearing up her affairs at Warham with his uncle, Horatio, her chief trustee.[2] His sister, Dorothy, needed to be

---

[1] S. H. A. Hervey (ed.), *The Letter-Books of John Hervey* (Wells, 1894), I, 301; HMC, *Clements MSS*, 251.

[2] Collins, *Peerage* (1756), III, 597. She was buried at Houghton on 17 March 1711, *Parish Register*.

settled for, since the trouble with Lord Wharton, she had lived with her mother, making only the briefest visits to London. It was quite impossible for Walpole—much that he loved her—to take her into his own household. For more than ten years Sir Charles Turner had provided a home for both mother and daughter. Although he possessed Kirby Cane as well as Warham, his own son was approaching marriageable age and would soon need a home, so that Dorothy could not without inconvenience go on living at his house. The not very satisfactory solution which Walpole finally adopted was for her to live with his Uncle Horatio. Although he was generous and kind-hearted, the passing years had made him neither wiser nor soberer nor less quarrelsome. No sooner had he taken his niece into his house than he became an ardent devotee of Harley, who plotted to widen the rift in the family.[1]

But that was only one of the many conspiracies which Harley (recently raised to the peerage as Earl of Oxford and Mortimer) was busy manufacturing during the summer of 1711. As so often happened with him, he was also scheming in the opposite direction. He had begun to approach Townshend to see if he and Walpole could be brought back into the ministry—naturally on Oxford's terms, at least as far as his shifty nature and bemused intellect allowed him to formulate them with any clarity.[2] However, in November, Oxford was jolted into action. Rumours reached him of a meeting at Orford's house at Chippenham, next to Newmarket, during the autumn races in which the whig lords had expressed their determination to oppose any peace which left Spain in the hands of the Bourbons. Walpole had been present so that he could concert measures for the Commons. The confidence and excellent spirits of the whigs was due to

[1] Harley appointed Horatio Commissioner for the Revenue of Ireland in 1712, which made him so grateful that he attempted in 1713 to get his nephew defeated at King's Lynn. HMC, *Portland MSS*, IV, 685.

[2] For the inability of Harley at this time to express himself clearly and definitely cf. Cowper, *Diary*, 43-51.

the decision of the Earl of Nottingham to go into opposition with them.[1] Nottingham, an elder statesman of impeccable High Church sentiments, resented his lack of place in the tory government. He distrusted Oxford, disliked Bolingbroke intensely, and feared that they might jeopardize the protestant succession. His defection finally came just after the death of the Queen's uncle, Rochester, another old-fashioned Court tory to whom the Queen had often turned for guidance throughout her life. The loss of these two men distressed the Queen. In any case she was deeply perturbed by the course of events. Her allies, and the Court of Hanover, had expressed themselves unequivocally as supporters of Marlborough. Much as she hated Sarah, she could not forget the glory which Marlborough had brought her country. The Dutch and the Imperial ambassadors warned her that grave disasters would follow any peace which gave Spain to a grandson of Louis XIV. These fears preyed on her mind. Oxford read the signs and acted accordingly. The Queen was not even discouraged by him when her thoughts turned, under the influence of the Duchess of Somerset, to the more complaisant whig leaders—Halifax, Somers and Cowper. He himself spent long hours in conference with Halifax and Somers, allowing himself the luxury which he enjoyed most—fruitless speculation on hypothetical political arrangements.[2] Oxford, too, may have been carrying on a more devious negotiation which would have enraged his devoted admirer, Jonathan Swift, had he known of it. On 26 November 1711, about the time when the discussions with Halifax and Somers were being most frequently held, he wrote, probably to Townshend:

[1] HMC, *Portland MSS*, V, 106, 119. Poulett wrote to Harley in November 1711 that he found Nottingham 'as sour and fiercely wild as you can imagine anything to be that has lived long in the desert'. Nottingham was intensely lobbied by Marlborough, Godolphin and Townshend early in December in order to get him to join with them in demanding 'no peace without Spain'. Townshend negotiated the final agreement with him for the whigs. Cf. Nottingham's letter to his wife 16 December 1711. Northants RO, *Finch-Hatton MSS*, 281, ff. 3–6.

[2] *Ibid. Portland MSS*, V, 115–6, 118, 120, 125, 131–2.

'My Lord,

It has been no small trouble to me that my indisposition has occasion'd any inconvenience to your Lordshipp's affairs, I do assure you that no-one shal study more zealously to serve you in all respects than I wil. I wil wait upon your Lordship in a few days and wil put this affair here after on such a foot as may leave no room for disappointment.

I am with greatest respect, my Lordd,

Your Lordshipp's most humble and most

obedient servant,

Oxford.'[1]

This may, of course, refer to financial business associated with Townshend's ambassadorial expenses—incurred during the negotiations at Gertruydenburg. That is possible, but not very likely, as this letter was discovered in Walpole's papers, possibly passed on to him because it touched his interests. Townshend, recently returned from The Hague, had been far less active in opposition than Walpole and he was therefore the obvious person for Oxford to approach. At the same time Oxford let it be widely known that he had the highest opinion of Walpole's ability.

From the tone of Oxford's letter it would seem that there was no reluctance on Walpole's and Townshend's part to play Oxford's game of politics with him, for in late November and early December 1711, it looked as if the whigs might be able to force a change of ministry. If that should happen, their need for Oxford would be as great as his for them. Without him they had no chance of controlling the Commons; without them his measures would founder in the House of Lords.[2] Yet none of these intrigues may have been more than forlorn hopes on Oxford's part that he might widen rifts amongst the whigs which he knew to exist.

The strength of the whigs lay in the House of Lords. With

[1] C(H) MSS, Oxford to ?, 26 November 1711; also HMC, Portland MSS, V, 110, which may refer to Townshend.

[2] Berks RO, Braybrooke MSS, C. Aldworth to Duke of Northumberland, 18 December 1711, shows that the terms of the alliance between Nottingham and the whigs were widely known.

the addition of Nottingham and his friends they had secured a narrow majority. In order to obtain Nottingham's support they had taken the decision to neglect the interest of the dissenters, agreeing to his demand for a Bill to suppress the practice of occasional conformity by which the dissenters had avoided the penalties and disadvantages of the Test Act. In return he himself proposed an amendment to the Queen's Address on 7 December 1711, which demanded that no peace should be signed which left Spain and the West Indies in the possession of the Bourbons—an attitude which the whigs had long maintained.[1] Much to the distress of the tories the whigs carried Nottingham's motion against the Court. Swift was in despair. He wrote to Stella Johnson the same day: 'It is a mighty blow and loss of reputation to Lord Treasurer, and may end in his ruin.'[2] The next day he concluded that the Queen was false, that the whigs would soon be back in power, and that it was all due to the influence of the Duchess of Somerset who had replaced Sarah as Mistress of the Robes.[3] Swift urged Oxford to get her dismissed. Oxford refused. She was too valuable a channel to the moderate whigs in case he needed to double-cross St John. Oxford, however, took this defeat very lightly. Whether or not he ever seriously considered an alliance with Townshend and Walpole is almost impossible to judge. His approach to them may only have been an attempt to raise their expectations in order to render them cautious about joining forces with Nottingham. If so, the manoeuvre failed. Yet it did no harm, nor could it have injured Oxford even if St John had learnt of it, at least, not after the defeat of the Court in the Lords, for that demonstrated to St John that he could not hope to govern without Oxford.

Although the whigs were jubilant, Oxford took his setback calmly enough. He had thought up a trump card. The de-

---

[1] Walpole proposed a similar amendment in the House of Commons; the tories easily defeated it. Coxe, I, 34.

[2] Sir Harold Williams (ed.), *Journal to Stella*, II, 432.

[3] *Ibid.*, 433–4.

cision had been taken by the ministry to create twelve tory peers, sufficient to give them a majority in the Lords, an act which so decisively scotched the whigs that they never forgave Oxford. They came to regard this act as an abuse of the Queen's prerogative. Time and time again during Walpole's lifetime this trick of Oxford's was to lead to violent recriminations between whigs and tories. In January 1712, however, it resolved the impasse in which the government found itself.

By January 1712, when the new peers began to receive their patents, the real crisis had passed and the tories, confident that both Houses would now accept their measures, went forward bull-headedly for peace. The coffee-house politicians were prepared for the desertion of the Allies by Swift's masterly analysis in *The Conduct of the Allies*, wherein their obvious shortcomings were laid bare with skilful sarcasm and their sacrifices with equal skill ignored. But the Allies could not be deserted so long as Marlborough was Commander-in-Chief, and no provocation was likely to make him resign. Nor could he be disgraced unless the Court securely controlled the House of Lords. That having been achieved, accusations of peculation on the grand scale were brought against him; before he could reply, Parliament was prorogued and during the prorogation he was dismissed his appointments—as adroit a piece of political timing as the country had ever seen. The whigs were aflame at his disgrace; the Allies shocked; the bulk of the nation indifferent. They were heartily sick of the war and longed for its end, and they cared little about Marlborough's fate. Oxford decided to break Walpole at the same time, but to put him on trial first. A successful prosecution would be 'a leading card', wrote Swift, 'to maul the Duke of Marlborough'.

Walpole was accused of corruption as Secretary-at-War. The Commissioners of Publick Accounts maintained that Walpole had declared his intention of reserving a part of the forage contract for the army in Scotland for his friend, Robert Mann. Rather than share the profits with another, the contractors agreed to pay Mann five hundred guineas to stay out, and this had been done for two contracts. Through carelessness the bill for one payment had been made out to Robert Walpole or Order, but it was agreed that the money had been made over to Mann. Others, too, were accused of receiving *douceurs*, including James Taylor, Walpole's clerk, who was to have received £50.[1] These charges were admitted in substance, but Walpole denied that he himself benefited. Robert Mann swore on affidavit that he had received all the money that had been paid. During the debate in the Commons no one pointed out that Mann was Walpole's banker. But years later Mann's son told Lord Hardwicke that his father had said that Walpole obliged him in this way because he had 'advanced money to Sir Robert in his necessities'.[2] Of this there can be no doubt. Amongst Walpole's papers there are a number of vouchers and bills, showing that Mann was handling most of Walpole's investments and accounts; from the interest frequently charged, Walpole was at times considerably in Mann's debt.[3] Besides, Mann had been Walpole's confidential agent since his first settlement in London. His obligation to him must have been very great. It was Mann who provided the mourning clothes when Walpole's father died, who found dress material for his unmarried sisters, who helped him smuggle

[1] Walpole had been extremely obstinate in insisting on Taylor's appointment, his obstinacy had caused some embarrassment to both Cardonnel and Marlborough. Cf. *C(H) MSS*, 6, Cardonnel, 6 July 1708; Marlborough, 20 July; Cardonnel, 20 July; Erle, 10 May. He had also pressed Taylor on Stanhope for post of agent to the British forces in Spain. *Chevening MSS*. There can be no doubt that Walpole quickly realized his danger. He wrote urgently to Col. Douglas to come at once to London from Scotland to help him in his defence. 'I beg once more you will make what haste you possibly can, and as my justification will in a great measure depend upon you, you may be sure the favour and justice you shall doe me upon this occasion will be a very great obligation to me and I shall [study] to acknowledge with all possible returns of gratitude.' Scottish RO Edinburgh, *Morton MSS*, Box 104. I am indebted to Mr. P. W. J. Riley for this reference.

[2] Hardwicke, *Walpoliana*, 6.

[3] *C(H) MSS*, vouchers. Mann also handled victualling bills for the Duchess of Marlborough, *ibid*. Mann's grandmother and Walpole's great-grandmother (Burwell) had been sisters. J. J. Muskett, *Suffolk Manorial Families* (Exeter, 1910–14), III, 807.

his wines through the customs. In a thousand and one different ways Walpole depended on 'Cousin' Mann, so that to oblige him with a cut out of a forage contract was natural enough and not in the least immoral by current standards. That Walpole himself derived some profit from the transaction cannot be proved. The tories would have jumped at the chance to prove it, had they possessed the slightest scrap of evidence. What was withheld from them has been withheld from posterity. There is nothing, absolutely nothing, to show that Walpole himself took any bribes or percentages on contracts. But, as we shall see, his wealth grew immeasurably during these years and just how this happened we do not know. Certainly 'Cousin' Mann knew, for he continued to act as Walpole's banker. After the scandal of the forage contracts he was discretion itself, and his letters acquire a deeper note of humility and submission. Walpole must have made it clear to him that his career had been jeopardized by the carelessness with which the arrangement had been made.[1]

Walpole, of course, was found guilty. After a furious and heated debate on 17 January 1712, he was committed to the Tower and expelled from the Commons, measures which only passed by narrow majorities in this partisan House. A move by his friends to secure the adjournment of the House in order to prevent the motion for expulsion from being put was defeated by only twelve votes.[2] The punishment was out of all relation to the crime, even by the standards of public morality to which lip service was paid, and by the standards of the practice of the age it was ludicrous. But this attack was a party measure. The tories wanted to vilify the men who had of course *conducted* the war and to demonstrate to the country that they had senselessly prolonged it for the sake

[1] Sir John Cropley, a close friend of Walpole's at this time, wrote to Stanhope on 22 March 1712: 'I am very confident he was innocent of takeing the money but must own he made a slip in suffering his name to be used in the matter.' *Chevening MSS.* On the other hand, in September 1710 Brydges (later Chandos) thought that some of his own shady deals would be difficult to manage with Walpole out of office. Collins Baker and Muriel I. Baker, *Chandos*, 57.

[2] *C. J.* xvii, 30; Coxe, I, 35–40.

of private gain. When Walpole surrendered himself at the Tower he was naturally filled with rancour. He wrote at once to Dorothy in Norfolk, for he knew her anxiety for him. Only a few mice-chewed scraps remain, but it is one of the very rare letters that betray his feelings.

'Dear Dolly,

You [MS illegible] hear from me from this place but I am sure it will be a satisfaction to you to know that this barbarious injustice being only the effect of party malice, does not concern me at all and I heartily despise what I shall one day revenge, my innocence was so evident that I am confident that they [that voted me] guilty did not believe me so [the rest illegible].'[1]

'I heartily despise what I shall one day revenge.' These were ominous words, for Walpole had a long memory and an implacable heart, which could not dissemble for long either its hatred or its love. This imprisonment gave an edge to his detestation of St John, a detestation which lasted as long as his life, for he knew that St John was the main instigator of the attack on him and Marlborough.

One speaker in the debate on Walpole's guilt had callously recommended hanging as a fit punishment for the prisoner but, 'there are confident tempers in the world, that, instead of standing corrected, can glory in their punishments be they of what sort they will. . . . I expect to see such a parade made, and such a countenance shewed him in prison, by some sort of persons, who would be glad for their own sakes, to screen the foulness of the crime as well as the person convicted of it, that I am afraid that part of your judgment will not sit so heavy upon him as it ought to do'.[2] And in this the speaker's judgment was fully vindicated. To a man of Walpole's standing, incarceration in the Tower was not very onerous. He had his own servants, his own table, pen and ink to write with, and no friend was ever denied access. In consequence, his imprisonment became a triumph. His noble

[1] *C(H) MSS*. The postmark is 24 January, therefore written after Walpole entered the Tower.
[2] Chandler, IV, 246–7.

whig friends rattled through the City in full panoply of coach and livery so that all could note to whom they did honour—Marlborough with his Duchess, the elder statesmen, Godolphin and Somers, as well as the young whig leaders, Sunderland, Devonshire and Pulteney.[1]

His friends in Norfolk did not lag behind in loyalty and they saw to it that Lynn returned him unopposed at the by-election caused by his expulsion, an action which the Commons denounced as illegal; so in his place they sent a man after his own heart, Jack Turner, the choleric, plain-speaking, rollicking merchant whose own family even found his whig opinions too blunt for its taste. But for the rest of his life Jack Turner regarded this as his greatest distinction, an honour of which he was proud to boast to posterity. In the dank chapel of St Mary's, Warham, where the Turner hatchments hang in tatters, these words are inscribed on his tomb:

ANNO REGINAE ANNAE DECIMO IN EXITIUM RUENTE PATRIA
AD PUBLICA REGNI COMITIA LIBERIES CIVIUM SUFFRAGIIS ELECTUS
LOCO AMICI, QUEM COLEBAT MAXIME, ROBERTI WALPOLE,
QUI PATRIAE LIBERTATEM, REIPUBLICAE MAJESTATEM
SUA ELOQUENTIA FORTITER PROPUGNANS
POTENTIORUM SCELERE, JUDICIO INIQUISSIMO
SENATU EXPULSUS ERAT.

And so the damp chill of decay and neglect is dispelled by the warmth of an ancient friendship. The injustice of Walpole's punishment aroused others, apart from Jack Turner, and the tories were to pay heavily for their temporary advantage of getting Walpole out of the Commons. By the standards of the time, the charge was too trivial to blight Walpole's career and his imprisonment was quickly magnified to a whig martyrdom.

The fall of Walpole and Marlborough was not allowed to

[1] The Duchess of Marlborough took along the first draft of her *Defence*. Walpole strongly advised against publication, which, later in life, she came to regard as a betrayal of her and the Duke's interest. *Blenheim MSS*, G.I.10, G.I.15. His wife visited him more modestly in a Hackney cab, and once had to borrow the fare, 2s. 6d., from her maid, who was repaid eighteen months later. (*C(H) MSS*, vouchers.)

go unsung. Broadsides, ballads and pamphlets tumbled from the Press; *The Jewel in the Tower* was rapidly countered by *As Bob as a Robin*, and *An Account of the Examination of R. W. Esq. for bribery and corruption* drew forth a broadsheet, *Mr Walpole's Case*. Weightier pamphlets followed: *A Letter from a Curate in Suffolk to a High Church Member covering the D. of M. and Mr W . . . . le*[1] presented the whig case in good trenchant prose, but most of the tory pamphlets depended on scurrility for their effects; a typical example is *The Testimonials of Several Citizens of Fickleborough in the Kingdom of Fairyland concerning the Life and Character of Robert Hush, commonly called Bob*, where it is said that 'in his younger days he persuaded his sister to be an whore in order to get preferment', that 'he had been caballing at Taverns, Horse-Races, and such like places how to depose the Queen', and that 'he is continuously bespattering Her Majesty with lyes and calumnies and writing libels upon her administration and in a habit, unbecoming his bulk, has stretched his lungs, thrown his arms akimbo and roared intolerably'. Worthless trash, perhaps, but eagerly devoured by the coffee-house public and important enough for Walpole himself to take notice, for almost immediately there followed *The Present State of Fairyland in severall letters from Esquire Hush*. No doubt readers of the former pamphlet bought this one eagerly, expecting a string of even coarser insults in reply to the virulent nastiness which had been heaped on Walpole; if so, they were disappointed, for the pamphlet contains a brilliantly satirical attack on the ministry's policy towards France. The writing has all the marks of Walpole's own emphatic skill in argument and it would seem that he himself turned the tables with real journalistic flair on the Grub Street hacks.

That he was using his enforced leisure in this way was common knowledge and there can be little doubt about the authorship of *A Short History of Parliament* which Walpole wrote partly to refute Swift's *Conduct of the Allies* and partly to

---

[1] These are all in the BM and will be found catalogued under Sir Robert Walpole. *The Jewel in the Tower* is printed by Coxe, I, 39–40.

strengthen the whig case at the forthcoming election.[1] His imprisonment, which lasted until 8 July 1712, and exclusion from Parliament (until 1713), deprived him of his natural platform for criticism of ministerial policy, but he was able to convey his natural eloquence with equal facility into prose, and this pamphlet will stand comparison with Swift's masterpiece. The Treaty of Utrecht had been signed with France on 11 April 1713 and was naturally the central target for Walpole's invective, for he considered it to be totally destructive of the aims for which the war had been fought, and immensely dangerous because it failed to achieve a proper balance of power in Europe, leaving as it did France in virtual possession of Spain and the Indies. The Treaty scourged, Walpole turned to the accusations of embezzlement and corruption which had been levelled against Godolphin, Marlborough and himself. He exposed the tricks and lies which had been used, showed how this Parliament, so solicitous for the nation's pocket, had increased rather than lowered expenditure, and sarcastically pointed to the true reason for the charges. 'Mr Walpole had often been very troublesome in the House, talked of Publick Accounts which he pretended to understand, and would, upon all occasions, be defending the late ministry, when he thought them clean and innocent; he must therefore be sent to the Tower, and expelled the House to prevent his giving further trouble.'[2] After a sneer at the ministry for raising £50,000 to pay off the debts of the Civil List, he dealt extensively with the proposed Treaty of Commerce with France, which had been narrowly defeated in the Commons by nine votes, 'so narrowly did the Trade of Great Britain and all its manufacturers escape the most fatal blow that ever was attempted to be given them'.[3]

[1] Cf. H. Walpole, *Catalogue of Royal and Noble Authors* (1806), IV, 198. Horace Walpole is not entirely reliable in his attributions of pamphlets to his father but Walpole himself tacitly acknowledged the authorship of this in the Commons in 1738, cf. Coxe, I, 43.

[2] *A Short History of the Parliament*, 1713, 25.

[3] *Ibid.*, 32.

Excellent propaganda, convincing and yet . . . it convinces less with each re-reading. Utrecht inaugurated a longer period of peace than this country had enjoyed for decades— its very moderation preventing a resurgence of French ambitions. Indeed, Walpole himself was to build on these foundations, and friendship with France, which he here denounced, was to become the keystone of his own foreign policy. And a further irony of history was that Bolingbroke was to jibe at Walpole's weakness in not insisting on the demolition of Dunkirk's fortifications, as Walpole now jibed at him.[1] But the accusations and justifications of politicians have almost as little to do with the realities of life as the quarrels of lovers. Peace was needed, but peace could not be achieved without making a mockery of Marlborough's victories. The terrifying implications of Bolingbroke's bid for power were so great that the virtues of the peace had to be scorned, so both sides battled with smears and slanders and lies.

Because of what followed it is easy to belittle Bolingbroke's achievement, for Utrecht was certainly his triumph. He understood public opinion instinctively—a gift not given to many in the world of politics and certainly not to Walpole. Bolingbroke knew how the public at large hated the endless war, and it did not care if the last possible concession were not wrung from France or if the peace had to be passed through the Lords by the creation of twelve peers. Englishmen wanted peace and they were prepared for the price.[2] And Bolingbroke, with only the lukewarm support of Harley and the Queen, succeeded against the violent opposition of many of the ablest and most powerful men in politics. His strength lay in the jealousies and hatreds of the great world, which were cherished by the independents and by the rural tories, who reflected truly enough the feelings of the nation

[1] Henry St John had been raised to the peerage as Viscount Bolingbroke after the signing of Utrecht.

[2] *Wentworth Papers*, 327–8; HMC, *Bagot MSS*, 342–3; Trevelyan, *The Peace*, 228.

at large. Yet there was another side to this question, which the influential whig merchants well appreciated. England's trade, and with it her prosperity, was flourishing as France grew weaker through defeat. A generous peace must inevitably restore her power and once more render her formidable. The Spanish trade, so dearly sought, would slip from England's grasp and enrich France. In 1712 Marlborough, had he been well supported, might have crushed France and imposed such terms that never again would she have been any threat to Britain. That this should be done was the firm belief of the City; England's treasure had been spent in the hope that the war would bring future wealth and prosperity. The squires could not or would not understand this. They paid heavy taxes, whereas the merchants lent their money at a profit. Nor were they impressed by the growth of England's trade during the war. They were more familiar with the sullen resentment of their tenants and their inability to pay their rents. In such men Oxford and Bolingbroke put their trust, only to find them difficult taskmasters.

In 1712, however, their support had given Bolingbroke the greatest victory of his career. His success tasted sweeter, perhaps, because of Walpole's disgrace. Expelled from the Commons, branded with the stigma of corruption, Walpole seemed to have little chance against this brilliant and daring statesman unless the Queen should die soon, before Bolingbroke could weld the tories and his administration into an unshakable unity. And the Queen's life was a gamble; a huge, moribund bulk of a woman, she was rotting away in Kensington Palace, obstinate, indecisive, in terror of death.

4

IF 1712 was a bad year for Walpole, 1713 was little better. The general election, due under the Triennial Act, took place in the autumn. Walpole, of course, busied himself in Norfolk, trying to find a whiggishly-minded candidate who would appeal sufficiently to the moderates so that the tories might be baulked of one seat.[1] He failed. The ministry had become very popular in all but the most prejudiced whig circles, and his uncle Horatio even thought that he might be able to prevent Walpole's election at Lynn. Walpole was, however, re-elected, and the prospect of once again denouncing the ministry in the Commons must have been some compensation for the decline of his power in Norfolk. To give them a taste of what they might expect he wrote a short trenchant pamphlet, addressed to the electors of King's Lynn, in which he denounced the Treaty of Utrecht as a threat to the nation's future prosperity and hinted broadly that the ministry was a danger to the protestant succession. Indeed he seemed almost to be inviting a fresh martyrdom.[2]

His weeks in Norfolk were not spent entirely in electioneering and the happiest event of the summer was Dorothy's marriage on 6 July 1713 to Townshend, made possible at last by the death of his first wife.[3] Since her 'scrape' with Lord Wharton, Dorothy had lived quietly in the country, seemingly as devoted to Townshend as he to her. Her settlement put a strain on Walpole's finances, which were as rickety as ever, but they were eased somewhat by the death of Lady Philipps. No burden, however great, would have prevented his accepting this match. He held Townshend in the highest regard, looked to him as his greatest supporter and patron. Nor could he have denied Dolly her choice. For her he had deep, abiding affection. He forgave easily her wayward, wilful ways and delighted in her wit and charm and beauty.

As ministries did not lose elections in the eighteenth century, Walpole on returning to Westminster in November to

---

[1] *Felbrigg MSS*, Walpole to Ashe Windham, 21 April 1713. He was also very much concerned about the fate of his colleague, James Stanhope, who had been turned out of his seat at Cockermouth by the Duke of Somerset. Walpole entered into negotiations to get him a seat in Scotland, but Stanhope was found a seat at Wendover by Wharton. *Chevening MSS*.

[2] *The Speech of R— W—p—le, Esq, at his election at Lynn Regis*, 31 *August* 1713. Cf also HMC, *Portland MSS*, V, 333.

[3] *Houghton Parish Register*.

take over the leadership of the whig party in the Commons, found the tories still crowding the back benches. Among them, however, there were many new faces and he must have hoped that these new men might prove more independently-minded than their predecessors. Although successful, the tories were gloomy, for an obvious deterioration had taken place in the Queen's health. Their gloom turned to alarm at Christmas when she fell so desperately ill that her life was despaired of. Slowly she recovered but it was obvious to all that her hold on life was growing ever more tenuous. Time, as Walpole knew, was the tories' dilemma. If the Queen died soon, Bolingbroke had no future, although Oxford might save himself by ratting to the moderates. As sly as ever, Oxford began to put out his feelers, hinting of the need to avoid a crisis, blandly assuming that he had always been a whig, and urging a broad-based ministry. Yet he clung to office and refused to throw down an open challenge to Bolingbroke. He drank harder than ever and frequently appeared at the cabinet so sodden with drink that he was useless at business. Bolingbroke pleaded for his dismissal. He hated Oxford for standing in his way; above all he feared his influence with the Queen. Sick as she was, she detested the passionate conflict which these two men engendered in the cabinet. She was worn down by the intrigues and the remorseless double-dealing. And yet she would not let Harley go. He belonged to the past as so few of her advisers did; she could not bring herself to trust Bolingbroke; few could.

The elimination of Oxford was but one part of Boling-broke's scheme. He knew that he must uproot as quickly as possible those whigs or moderates who still lurked in places of trust either in London or the provinces. He wanted above all to secure loyal adherents as justices of the peace and deputy-lieutenants, for their hostility might ruin any scheme and plunge the country into civil war. With regard to the succession, Bolingbroke made his preferences clear enough to his intimates. He wanted the Stuarts, not the Hanoverians; not, however, Roman Catholic Stuarts. Their religion had to be changed. They could only return as honest Anglicans. On this point Bolingbroke was adamant, for he knew that religious passion would decide the issue. He was sure that an Anglican Stuart would command far greater popularity than the whigs' German, and he was probably right. James would naturally be dependent for a time at least on the ultra-tories, long enough for Bolingbroke to consolidate his hold on the machinery of government. In December 1713, such a plan was not the wild fantasy that it has seemed to posterity. To a man of Bolingbroke's worldliness and agnosticism, a change of religion was a paltry matter. His attachment to this scheme grew stronger the more he contemplated the loathsome alternatives. He knew that although compromise with the whigs might preserve a few offices for the moderate tories, it would ruin him, for his power was based on the Octobrists —the High-Flyers—those rabid rural tories whose social and economic discontent he had so cunningly exploited. Their leader would not be forgiven.[1]

Bolingbroke's aims were not secret, and when Parliament, deliberately delayed, met at last on 16 February 1714, the question of succession was uppermost in men's minds. Naturally, the government wished to avoid an open debate as ardently as the opposition wished to force them to it. And in the hope of securing a trump card, Bolingbroke enthusiastically, and Oxford reluctantly, were beseeching James to change his religion. To gain time, in the hope of a favourable answer, they engineered an attack on the whig pamphleteer, Richard Steele, who had been bluntly outspoken in the *Crisis* and the *Importance of Dunkirk Considered*, boldly attaching his signature to both. Tom Foley, Oxford's cousin, raised the matter on 11 March, but Steele prevaricated: 'The answer was he had caused several books to be printed and that he knew not but the errors of the printers might be misconstrued as his and therefore desired time to compare what

[1] *Brabourne MSS*, Parliamentary Diary of Sir John Knatchbull, is invaluable for Bolingbroke's policy and his relations with the High-Flyers. Cf. also Trevelyan, *The Peace*, 266–307.

he charged him with in order to confess it, if they were his, and make his defence.'[1] The House gave him time. Immediately the whig leaders went into conclave and Walpole took over the management of Steele's case, which he realized could be used to arraign the entire policy of the ministry, foreign as well as domestic.[2] The next move was beautifully planned. The Commons had given Steele a week to prepare his case, but on the Monday before it was due to come up, Steele rose in his place and moved an address to the Queen that her directions touching the demolition of Dunkirk, and how far they had been complied with by France, should be laid before the House—a neat tactic which greatly irritated the tories, who stood to lose either way. The address was rejected, for at least this stopped Steele justifying himself out of their own mouths. The rejection, however, damaged them both in the House and outside it in the eyes of independently-minded men, which was precisely what Steele and his friends intended. The debate itself came on Thursday, 18 March. Addison had been commissioned to prepare Steele's own speech, since his friends, knowing his reckless and impulsive nature too well, feared that he might damage rather than further their cause if left to his own devices. The burden of his defence was undertaken by Walpole and Stanhope, assisted significantly enough by Lord Finch, the eldest son of the tory Earl of Nottingham, who was still standing out firmly against the ministry and giving his support to the opposition.

For Walpole this debate was an occasion. He had been out of the House for two years and this was his first opportunity

[1] *Brabourne MSS*, Knatchbull's diary, 11 March 1714.

[2] Walpole's notes and memoranda on Steele's case are to be found in *C(H) MSS*, 90. They are very scrappy but invaluable, and his ideas and arguments can be reconstructed from them. They were known to Coxe and used by him, Coxe, I, 43-5, but his use of the material is not entirely satisfactory for he preferred to use Chandler's account of the speech rather than the rough notes. Rae Blanchard, *Correspondence of Richard Steele*, 294-5; also Steele's dedication to Walpole in his pamphlet, *Mr Steele's Apology for Himself and His Writings*, ibid., 489-93, in which he speaks of Walpole's 'generous defence'.

to survey fully the whole range of the ministry's policy, and he made one of the most forceful and eloquent speeches of his career. Firstly, he dealt with Steele's accusations and showed in each case how thoroughly justified they were, and how they could only be resented by men bent on gratifying France at any price and plotting for a popish successor. Perhaps, he asked sarcastically, the ministry took exception to the doubts expressed about the Pretender's legitimacy. The truth was that Steele had attacked the enemies of the Constitution and that was resented. And, furthermore, why was Steele answerable in Parliament for what he wrote in his private capacity? Why could he not be left to the due processes of the law? Parliament was being used by the ministry as a scourge for the subject whereas it had hitherto been used as a scourge only for evil ministers. And then Walpole turned to the crux of the matter—that the punishment of Steele was an attack on the protestant succession, an attempt to prejudice it, and at the same time, a useful way of gauging the temper of Parliament. And he asked the pertinent question: 'How comes writing for the succession to be a reflection upon this ministry?' Skilfully he drew the debate away from Steele's justification of the war (the point upon which the ministry wished to concentrate) to the question of the Hanoverian succession, the support of which was after all the whigs' trump card. Naturally, the ministry could not let Walpole, and Stanhope who supported him, go unanswered and the debate was furiously maintained until nearly midnight when Steele was expelled by 245 votes to 152, a comfortable and encouraging majority for both Oxford and Bolingbroke.[1]

Their satisfaction was quickly clouded by anxiety. By the end of the month they knew that James would not change his religion for the sake of winning a kingdom. He would return

[1] C(H) MSS, 90. The salient points of Walpole's speech only are given: it would be too difficult to attempt to reconstruct the speech and too tedious to transcribe all of Walpole's jottings. Chandler V, 63–5; 67–71. Brabourne MSS, Knatchbull's diary, 18 March 1714.

as a Roman Catholic or not at all, and the arguments of the Abbé Gaultier, who stressed that Rome would gain in the end by his apostasy, failed to move him. He refused to be a renegade or a hypocrite and by his refusal he sealed the fate of Oxford and Bolingbroke as well as his own. Oxford accepted this; Bolingbroke would not. Oxford continued to profess sympathy with Bolingbroke's renewed determination to destroy the whig party before it was too late and at the same time he put out stronger feelers than ever for a compromise solution with the whigs; but, by now even a strong feeler from Oxford was so cryptic that no one knew what his intentions really were. He baffled Lord Cowper, the former whig Chancellor, by slipping a note into his hand in the House of Lords on 12 May 1714, in which he regretted 'the heat which prevented a real friendship between the Elector and the Queen' and finished by assuring Cowper of all people that 'I do speak the sense of many sober whigs'. Five weeks earlier Cowper had received a letter upbraiding him and his friends for their extravagance and warning them that they were ruining their future.[1] Such contradictory sentiments were at least evidence of the incoherence of the tory leadership.

The whigs, of course, sensed the dilemma of the tories; they had also heard of the secret negotiations with James, and, in consequence, introduced the motion in both Houses that the succession in the House of Hanover was in danger, which, if carried, might have destroyed the ministry. Aware of their predicament, some weeks before, the leading ministers, Oxford, Bolingbroke, Harcourt, and Hanmer, the Speaker, had met, on 4 April 1714, about thirty back benchers at Secretary Bromley's, amongst them Sir Edward Knatchbull, who made notes of the discussion in his diary. The ministers proposed 'that we should exert ourselves; not lett a majority in P[arliament] slip thro' our hands, and that

---

[1] Herts RO, *Panshanger MSS*, C.3, 5, Oxford to Cowper, 30 March 1714; C.3, 6, Oxford to Cowper, 12 May 1714. Oxford was also trying to explain himself away to the Elector, *Stowe MSS*, 227 ff. 67–8.

wee should meet twice a week for a mutual confidence and that any facts wee wanted to be apprized of they would furnish, and that the Queen was determined to proceed in the interest of the Church, etc. and my Lord Bolingbroke farther added afterward that he would not leave a whig in employ'.[1]

A few days earlier, on 5 April 1714, the ministry only just scraped home in the House of Lords by thirteen votes—a moral defeat. The whig lords immediately drove home their advantage. They proposed two addresses to the Queen, one that a price should be put on the Pretender—dead or alive, a phrase afterwards deleted by amendment in consideration for the Queen's feelings, and another that she should discuss means of securing the protestant succession with her allies. But the weakness of the ministry was amply demonstrated by their failure to divide the House; both addresses were carried *nemine contradicente*. The ministry was rapidly losing strength now that the independents were wavering. The back benchers needed every possible encouragement. Walpole had been greatly heartened by the success of his friends in the Lords. When he arrived at Westminster on 16 April for the debate in the Committee of the House on the state of the nation, he found four hundred and sixty-seven members present, the greatest number recorded since the Revolution, except on the occasion of Lord Somers's impeachment.[2] The debate was the most critical of this desperate session, and after Bromley, Secretary of State, had spoken first on the motion that the Hanoverian Succession was in danger, attempting to prove that it was not, Walpole rose in his place and answered him in a great speech full of vivacity and zest.[3] His arguments and his eloquence drew such applause that the ministry grew nervous of the outcome. They proposed, therefore, that Freeman should leave the Chair in order to prevent the motion being put to a vote in case they lost it. This was scotched by

[1] *Brabourne MSS*, Knatchbull's diary, 11 April 1714.
[2] *Ibid.*, 16 April 1714.
[3] Chandler, V, 124. Unfortunately nothing is known of the arguments which Walpole used.

H

the Speaker, Sir Thomas Hanmer, a moderate tory, who thus signalized publicly his break with Oxford and Boling- broke. Thirty tories followed him into the opposition lobby but even so the ministry got home by forty-eight votes.[1] Yet, considering the complexion of the House, the majority was small, and the Speaker's defection critical. Backed by a united and determined party, Bolingbroke might possibly have allowed himself the luxury of hope; a divided party meant his ruin, a fact realized by Walpole, who applauded the public spirit which the Speaker had shown. But Bolingbroke had the natural resilience and optimism so essential to a politician, and he drove ahead, determined, as Knatchbull related, 'to push the point of the succession notwithstanding our whimsical friends differ from us'. And he swore to his followers that he would have every whig out of employment by the end of the session.[2] His followers needed more than promises and exhortations and on 12 May his loyal friend, Sir William Wyndham, introduced a Bill into the Commons to prevent Schism. The object of the bill was to destroy the nonconformist schools and academies which had grown up since the Revolution. Many of them were exceptionally well run and provided an education more fitting to the require- ments of the age than either the grammar or public schools and, in consequence, many Anglicans were sending their children to them. In this the Church saw danger to its monopolies and preferred suppression to the provision of equal or better education in those academic preserves which it controlled. For the generality of members the educational aspect of the Bill was irrelevant; it provided an outlet for the rancorous hatred which they harboured for dissenters. And

[1] *Brabourne MSS*, Knatchbull's diary, 16 April 1714. At this time the Speaker took part in debates when the House was in committee and frequently voted. There was nothing exceptional in Hanmer's behaviour as Speaker, except that he went against the ministry.

[2] *Ibid.* Although there had been fairly thorough purges of the administration, many moderate whigs lingered on as deputy-lieutenants and justices of the peace and some still had senior office about the court. Somerset, for example, was still Master of the Horse and a member of the Privy Council.

Bolingbroke, himself a sceptic, knew the political value of religious prejudice. It was a popular move. In spite of Walpole's and Stanhope's eloquence, the Bill moved steadily forward, and the majorities which it commanded gave the public a wrong idea of Bolingbroke's position.

Victories in the House of Commons might be a tonic to the spirits of the tories, but they created a false illusion of strength. The final decisions about the succession would have to be taken at Court and there Bolingbroke was at a disadvantage. The influence of men such as Shrewsbury, Somerset and Argyll could only be obliterated by exile or death; otherwise they could not be stopped from exercising what they felt to be their natural rights in a crisis. And behind these three were the ranks of the whig aristocracy whose power was proved by the fact that the Schism Bill passed the House of Lords by only five votes, carried, in fact, into law on the shoulders of the tory bishops. In the crisis of the succession the leaders of the aristocracy would have to take action, otherwise their power and wealth might be in peril. Their continued existence about the Court threatened Bolingbroke's future. Their strength was further shown on 8 July 1714, when they struck at Bolingbroke's friend and confidant, Arthur Moore, on a charge of corruption. The weakness of the ministry was dangerously exposed and so fearful was Bolingbroke of the consequence that he persuaded the Queen to prorogue Parliament the next day.

The whigs watched the struggle between the tories for leadership with mounting anxiety. Bolingbroke worked with dynamic energy and found time, obsessed as he was with the problem of Oxford, to negotiate a new treaty with France against the whigs' ally, Austria—a bold, original stroke of diplomacy, carried through with magnificent confidence and dexterity. Ironically, this alliance was to become one of the main supports of Hanoverian foreign policy, and one which Walpole was to defend against the vehement criticism of Bolingbroke himself. Obsessed by his feud with Oxford, Bolingbroke became increasingly reckless and cabinet councils degenerated into private brawls. Oxford knew—no one better—the value of immobility. He ignored insults, committed himself to nothing and to no one, clung to his Treasurer's staff, and drank deeper. Resign he would not. The conflict between them was resolved in the end by the dying Queen. On 27 July 1714 she dismissed Oxford. Bolingbroke waited for her summons to receive the Treasurer's staff of office. No summons came. The whigs had the Queen's ear, not he. Foolishly the tories had allowed the Duchess of Somerset to remain Mistress of the Queen's Robes. Now Bolingbroke paid for their folly. The leading whigs of the middle party were kept immediately informed about the Queen's condition and they were able to take decisive action. The Dukes of Somerset and Argyll appeared (as they had every right to do) at the Privy Council which had been summoned to make arrangements in case the Queen became incapable. That meeting was fatal to Bolingbroke, for it passed the resolution to move the Queen to make Shrewsbury Treasurer. Dying, and scarcely able to speak, she handed the staff to him, thereby sealing Bolingbroke's fate and rendering certain a protestant and whig succession.

In the two days of power which Bolingbroke enjoyed between the dismissal of Oxford and Shrewsbury's appointment he had made one last desperate gamble. The Shrewsbury-Argyll-Somerset group was strongly disliked by the Junto whigs for their desertion in 1710 and for the support which they had given to Oxford. Bolingbroke, well aware of this, summoned Stanhope, Craggs, Pulteney to dinner on 28 July 1714—Walpole would have been asked had he not left for Norfolk on 14 July.[1] Bolingbroke offered an alliance. Stanhope, in Walpole's absence, presented their terms with brutal frankness: Marlborough to be immediately restored as Commander-in-Chief; the navy to be placed in Orford's hands; on King George's accession places to be equally divided. Bolingbroke could not bring himself to accept. He chose a wilder, more dangerous course. Perhaps he could not

[1] Trevelyan, *The Peace*, 297–305. Rae Blanchard, *Letters of Richard Steele*, 303.

so easily betray his most ardent supporters—those rancorous, crypto-Jacobite squires. Perhaps the crisis had come too suddenly upon him. The Queen's illness trapped him; her death betrayed him.

5

ONCE MORE the promised land stretched before Walpole's eyes, but he could only be temporarily relieved of the anxiety to which he was a prey. Nottingham and his tories had stood out loyally for George; Hanmer and his tories had ratted for Hanover's sake; Oxford had in the end turned his coat. Shrewsbury, Somerset, Argyll had little love for him or Townshend. There was no guarantee that the King's German advisers, nervous of whig strength, might not advise a mixed ministry and so resuscitate the struggle of Court factions.[1] Mixed ministry or not, Walpole was certain, however, to be offered a place, and for the first few weeks after the Queen's death on 1 August, he could dwell with delight on the future.

The years of exile were over; the frustrations of power denied were dissolved. He was thirty-eight years of age, and behind him lay fourteen years' experience of politics. He had the maturity, wisdom and public stature which compelled the admiration and devotion of those men, who, like himself, stood both for Hanover and for toleration. His power in debate, his experience in administration, and the force of his personality all marked him out for leadership.

Life must have seemed sweet to Walpole as he watched George I land at Greenwich in the September twilight, the magnificent buildings of Wren gleaming rose-pink in the torchlight. Marlborough, back from exile, was there to greet his new sovereign. The King acknowledged his presence graciously. 'My dear Duke,' he said, 'you have now seen an end of your troubles.' To Walpole's brother-in-law, Townshend, fell the task which, no doubt, they both relished of telling Ormonde and the rest how the King had no further

[1] Cf. BM *Add MSS*, 32, 686, fo. 20. Horatio Walpole was still very doubtful as to how the ministry would be constructed as late as 17 August 1714.

use for their services. Oxford lingered on the fringe of those making their court, hoping against hope that the King might notice him and his disgrace be avoided. Bolingbroke stayed away.[1] He recognized that all was lost. As he wrote sadly to Atterbury, his most ardent supporter amongst the bishops:

'I see plainly that the tory party is gone. . . . Numbers are still left and those numbers will be increased by such as have not their expectations answered, but where are the men of business that will live and draw together.'[2]

But the difficulty of finding 'men of business that will live and draw together' was not a problem peculiar to the tories. In the relief and gaiety which the accession engendered, the future glittered and sparkled for the place-hungry whigs and their letters to each other glow with benevolence. Their unity and friendship was a mirage, quickly dispelled; great events might hold them together for a few months, but all too soon they were to be divided by factional strife as furious as any they had experienced with the tories. In the autumn of 1714, Walpole cannot have suspected that the greatest struggle of his life lay in the immediate future or that his career would be in greater jeopardy than when he was imprisoned in the Tower. During the brilliant pageantry of that autumn night Walpole's mind can only have dwelt with delight on the profits of office and prospect of revenge.

[1] A. C. Edwards, *English History from Essex Sources*, 1550–1750, 129.

[2] PRO, *SP Dom.*, 35/1, No. 31b. Bolingbroke told Cowper on 11 September 1714 that he hoped to retire from politics for good. Herts RO, *Panshanger MSS*, C.3, 5.

BOOK THREE

THE STRUGGLE FOR POWER

CHAPTER SIX

THE PROMISED LAND, 1714-17

Q UEEN ANNE was dead, George I reigned in her place, and the change was momentous. The old sick Queen had lingered in a gloomy oppressive Court; doctors, chaplains, pious women had been her daily companions and those in search of wit and gaiety had to look elsewhere for their pleasures. Bolingbroke's flamboyant lechery and free-thinking had done him irreparable harm whereas Oxford had ingratiated himself by his grave manners and chaste living. George I, aged 54, arrived with two old and ugly mistresses, one excessively fat, the other excessively lean, to whom he had been loyal after his fashion. His wife, kept in captivity for suspected adultery, was never mentioned, and her son, the Prince of Wales, did not dare to display her portrait. George I hated society and shunned it; few courtiers saw him except when he returned rapidly to his private apartments after Chapel. He spoke rarely to any of the dense throng which lined the corridors, never resting by the great fireplace in the audience chamber as the old Queen had done. He took his meals in private, waited on by his two servants Mohamed and Mustapha—whom he had captured in his Turkish campaigns. He had grown so used to them that their influence even on political decisions was far from negligible and at times was as great as the two mistresses'—Schulenberg and Kielmannsegge. George I was not, however, a recluse. Neither was he pious nor an enemy of pleasure. Most nights he slipped out to the opera or the theatre with a small party of intimate friends, mainly women, with whom he talked and flirted. On other occasions he went to his friends' houses, for he enjoyed playing cards for modest stakes, and these evenings, too, were notorious for their informality. His personality was intricate, and in no way commonplace, but his lack of intelligence prevented him from playing an effective part in affairs, for like many stupid people he was highly suspicious. In consequence he placed his confidence in his German advisers—Bernstorff, Bothmer and Robethon—who had long served him. This German group, the King's most intimate friends, created a new factor in English politics. Even though the tories might be destroyed, the situation was no simpler for the whigs.

Indeed there was a further complication—the Prince and Princess of Wales. The King disliked his son almost as much as his son disliked him. George I found the Princess's plump charms very engaging but her sharp tongue and intellectual airs frightened him away—*cette diablesse Madame la Princesse*, he called her. The Prince and Princess held their separate Court. They were gay, worldly, eager to please. The Princess enjoyed gossip and fancied herself, not without justification, to be an adept politician. They both spoke English, loved company, and provided a centre of attraction which should have been occupied by the King. He knew it, and hated them. They underlined his stupidity, his malaise in society, his negligence and lack of regality. They had seized the opportunities of their new position. He could not or would not. Here was a dangerous, explosive situation, ready made for the discontented, place-hungry politicians.[1]

Many historians have found the reason for George I's difficulties in his inability to speak English rather than in his character. He had, however, little trouble in communicating with his ministers. He spoke and wrote adequately in French, which was the language of his Court, and one which most English statesmen knew sufficiently to converse or write in. Dispatches, cabinet minutes and other documents which the King needed to see were usually duplicated in French. Naturally, facility in this language was very useful in securing the King's attention and regard, but the effects of his lack of English were not very important. Walpole had adequate

---

[1] An admirable description of the Court in 1714 is to be found in Bonet's dispatch of 24 December 1714, printed in W. Michael, *England under George I*, I, 'The Beginnings of the Hanoverian Dynasty', 372–8.

working knowledge of French and Horace Walpole's story of his father and the King struggling to converse in dog Latin is most probably apocryphal. True, he lacked Townshend's or even his brother Horatio's dexterity, yet he could, if need be, maintain a conversation in French.[1] No, the chief stumbling-block between the new King and the politicians was his ignorance and his stupidity; one he did nothing to dispel, the other was incurable. In consequence, politicians quickly learnt to cultivate the King's mistresses and his German advisers, who greatly enjoyed their increased power. Their influence was powerful, and frequently decisive. Their frank and insatiable greed corroded what little remained of political morality.

Before the King's landing, the Regents, who had taken over the administration on the Queen's death, had discussed the disposition of places with Bothmer and Robethon. It may have been a disadvantage to Walpole that he was away in Norfolk when the Queen died, but the story that he deliberately chose to become Paymaster-General 'because he was very lean and needed to get some fat on his bones' may be in essence true.[2] By 1714 the dunning letters with their strange mixture of bellicosity and pleading had started again.[3] His debts were high: his coffers nearly empty. Four years of opposition and three elections had eaten into the profits which he had made during his first period of office. And there were other reasons, perhaps of greater weight. Walpole's leadership of the Opposition in the Commons had given him a mastery of parliamentary methods which few other poli-

[1] Evidence of Walpole's knowledge of French is scattered throughout his papers. As Secretary-at-War he ordered the *Gazette de France* for his own use. Diplomatic documents and letters in French abound and they are never translated for him. He also possessed about six French-English dictionaries and a number of French books. They are at Houghton. Against this there are the statements of his son Horace, who declared in his *Reminiscences* that his father knew no French and of Bonet who wrote in 1714 'il y a d'excellentes têtes comme celles du . . . Sr Walpole, etc., qui ne l'entendent point'. Michael, I, 374.
[2] Hardwicke, *Walpoliana*, 5.
[3] *C(H) MSS*, particularly Eleanor Richardson, 26 January 1714.

ticians possessed. Yet it would have been difficult for him at this time to accept a higher office without taking a peerage, an expensive honour which might have sadly cramped his abilities. And again, in some ways, he had been too successful. The ageing members of the Junto—Somers, Halifax, Orford and the rest—looked forward to ending their days in the promised land; their juniors could wait their turn. By the time Walpole reached London, the best offices had been decided; no doubt it was considered by them that his best interests were to be served by his remaining in the Commons in a comparatively minor post. And, in any case, it is unlikely that he would have considered anything but the First Lordship of the Treasury, which was pledged to Halifax.[1] His less able brother-in-law, Townshend, was appointed Secretary of State, an office of the greatest importance as it controlled foreign affairs, in which the Court had an abiding interest, sharpened now by George I's dual role as King of Great Britain and Elector of Hanover. Townshend's success had been obtained only by deeply disappointing Sunderland, who naturally expected to be appointed to his old office. He resented the slight offered him and neither forgave nor forgot.[2] And Townshend and Walpole were never closer than in these early years of Townshend's marriage with Dorothy, who loved and admired her brother. Their friendship was such that Walpole could be certain of making his views felt in the cabinet.

2

CERTAINLY, THE office of Paymaster had its compensations. It was the most lucrative of all government posts, and—equally valuable—controlled a great deal of patronage which Walpole immediately used for the benefit of his loyal friends and relatives. His brother, Horatio, had carved an inde-

[1] Marlborough may have tried, although not very hard, to get this office for him. Lord Cowper, *Diary*, 58.
[2] BM, *Stowe MSS*, 227, ff. 404–5.

pendent position for himself in politics and diplomacy, and his appointment as Minister and Plenipotentiary to the United Netherlands in January 1715 probably owed more to Townshend than to Walpole himself. Galfridus was appointed Treasurer of Greenwich Hospital, a sinecure which can only have been secured by his brother's influence. It was, however, at Chelsea Hospital, which Walpole as Paymaster virtually controlled, that he was able to exert his greatest influence. The dismissal of tories had not been confined to those in high office, for the tories themselves had been too meticulous in 1710 in rooting out the whigs to expect any mercy. Walpole, probably with a good deal of satisfaction, cleared them out of Chelsea, and it must have given him greater pleasure still to appoint Robert Mann Deputy-Treasurer of the Hospital. His old school friend Henry Bland, to whom he had given the living of Great Bircham on Parson Booty's death, was made Chaplain. His Norfolk doctor, Hepburn, was brought in as Surgeon's Mate, and his friend Henry Parsons, MP, who was soon selling him the Hospital's victualling bills at five per cent discount, became Purveyor.[1]

Chelsea was to give Walpole greater pleasure than that of providing for his friends. The Treasurer's official residence had been lost to the Hospital when it had been granted by the Crown to Lord Ranelagh, a former Paymaster. Lord Orford, Walpole's friend and patron, had made use of a little house and garden at the back of the Hospital, gradually enlarging it to meet his needs. He was unceremoniously turned out of his home during his disgrace and failed to get it back later. Walpole himself had no difficulty in 1714 in expelling the tory occupant, Jack Howe. Walpole was so delighted with his house and with its garden which ran down to the river that he managed to retain possession of it even after he had ceased to be Paymaster.

For the rest of his life Orford House—he never changed its

---

[1] C. G. T. Dean, *The Royal Chelsea Hospital*, 192–9; *C(H) MSS*, Account Books, 20A. Walpole bought £5,012 worth of victualling bills from Parsons for £4,761 12s.

name—became his chief London residence. He at once set about its embellishment for which he obtained the services of John Vanbrugh. He gradually expanded his empire at the expense of the Hospital, adding about nine and a half acres of land which he laid out as a garden, planting rare shrubs and flowers, costly items which figure frequently in his account books. He built an orangery, embanked the fore-shore, and laid out a noble terrace upon which he loved to walk in the evening air, talking and scheming with his friends, and no doubt casting a baleful eye across the river to Battersea where Bolingbroke lived on his return from France. A fine octagonal summer-house, from whose windows could be seen the wide stretches of the Thames, stood at one end of the terrace. In another corner of the garden Walpole placed his 'vollery', filled with singing birds—goldfinches, linnets and with brilliantly coloured parakeets. The need to adorn Chelsea first led him to indulge his taste for pictures. In 1718 he bought two at Graffier's auction. It was at Chelsea that he entertained the Queen and her children in 1729 to a lavish feast—food and wine in profusion, fireworks to gild the sky, music floating in from the moored barges on the Thames. It was at Chelsea that the most secret cabinets were held, the place where Walpole fought his hardest battles. It became dearer to him than even Houghton itself and when his time came to leave the Commons, it was from this house—Orford House—that he took his title.[1]

Walpole, seemingly secure for the future, was in an expansive mood. He gave up the house in Dover Street in

[1] Dean, *op. cit.*, 201–7; *LCC Survey of London*, II, 3–7. The Orangery, much restored, still exists. *C(H) MSS*, Account Books, 20A, various items. It is probable that the structural alterations were carried out by the Hospital, for Captain Dean points out that there is a sharp rise in the Hospital's building accounts for 1720–3 when much of the work was being done. Nevertheless, there are plenty of entries in Walpole's account book to show that he himself spent a great deal on his Chelsea house and he seems to have been entirely responsible for structural changes in the garden and out-buildings and for all 'making good' work, e.g. plastering, panelling, painting. As the Hospital was the owner of the property and would ultimately benefit by the improvements, Walpole's practice was not, perhaps, quite so sharp as Captain Dean implies.

Pieter Tillemans

V. A VIEW OF ORFORD HOUSE ACROSS THE THAMES

which he had lived for over ten years, although the lease had not expired, and moved down to a bigger house in Arlington Street which brought him a little closer to St James's.[1] This house was more in the nature of an office and it was constantly thronged with place-seekers, politicians, sycophants. Without Chelsea he would have found it difficult to secure the quiet he needed in order to discharge the formidable tasks he accepted with such alacrity. These were gay, carefree days, and Walpole, who loved to spend, flung out the guineas with a lavish hand. Richardson was commissioned to paint Sir Charles Turner, brother Horatio and himself, as a gift for the Corporation of Lynn. Horatio, to whom Walpole was always devoted, was also given a handsome gold repeating watch by Quare. On the Prince's birthday the Chelsea pensioners received a generous tip and Walpole adorned himself in an expensive new suit with silver lace trimmings. A legacy of £250 left to him by his old War Office clerk, James Taylor, was spent on a diamond ring. Presents of wine and the best green tea were sent off to Eton for his sons, Robert and Edward, and their masters. And even his difficult and disagreeable wife had her presents—dresses, trinkets and a 'parrakeet'. Not all of his money was dissipated in lavish living and expansive generosity. Some of the torrent of wealth was used for more serious purposes. Debts were paid off, the old mortgages discharged, and thousands wisely invested in annuities, victualling bills, lottery tickets, East India and Bank Stock. Suddenly, however, he had become vastly rich. From 3 August 1714 to 3 October 1717, £109,208 4s. 9d. passed through Walpole's hands, and of this £61,778 14s. 9d. was invested, the rest spent, and for the money spent was little to show, practically no pictures, jewellery or furniture; the sums spent on building were trivial. Walpole's great expenditure on these counts still lay in the future.

Walpole, of course, almost certainly did not own the sixty thousand invested; perhaps the major part was surpluses

[1] Walpole paid £300 per annum for Arlington Street; in the end his brother Horace took over his Dover Street house.

which the Paymasters were allowed to use for their own benefit, although the investments do not really begin until 1716 after he had ceased to be Paymaster, a fact which must cast a little doubt on this hypothesis. The question naturally arises—where did these vast sums come from? Unfortunately, the credit side of Walpole's account throws little light on the sources of his wealth. The interest of the investments alone brought in a fair sum of money, more was made by advantageous sales of stock and the adroit handling of short-term loans on the tallies, but the bulk seems to have arrived in the following way:

Jan. 10 1716	Reced of Your Honour in Bank	[notes]	300 0 0
„ 20	Reced of ditto ditto		300 0 0
Feb.ʳʸ 11	{ Reced of Your Honour		5,000 0 0
	{ Reced more		500 0 0
22	Reced more		500 0 0
March 5	Reced more		500 0 0
20	Reced more		2,000 0 0
22	Reced more		500 0 0
April 24	Reced more		500 0 0
May 11	Reced more		1,500 0 0
	Reced more		5,000 0 0[1]

And where Walpole obtained the bank notes will never be known; treasury surpluses, perhaps, which he could legitimately invest, but apart from £5,000 in Land Tax tallies on 7 March, no money was invested during this period. Over £11,000 was on call with Robert Mann. Owing to the delays in accountancy, old Pay Office surpluses could account for much of it; and some of it could be Chelsea Hospital money drawn from the Treasury, used in transit for speculation

[1] C(H) MSS, Accounts, 20A. 'Walpole's Account with Robert Mann'. One can be reasonably confident that his Norfolk rents were being more than absorbed by the cost of running Houghton for John Wrott, his Norfolk steward, was drawing large bills on Walpole in London. The only financial benefit he derived from Houghton was from the occasional sales of sheep and cattle at Smithfield. The money was promptly pocketed by his steward, Edward Jenkins, for housekeeping. Walpole's salary, of course, firstly as Paymaster and secondly as Chancellor and First Lord, would account for a fair portion of the money.

before it reached Mann's official account book as Deputy-Treasurer. These sharp practices by our standards were legitimate enough by the standards of Walpole's day, although these methods, when employed by former Paymasters—Ranelagh and Brydges—had caused a great outcry. But, even so, suspicion must linger: so much money was reaching Walpole's banker in bank notes—not in bills drawn on other men or in tallies which were so often used for transferring large sums, but in immediately negotiable bank bills. Yet it is hard to believe that Walpole can have set about corruption immediately he achieved office, and more particularly since its stigma had already marked him at the time of his forage contract scandal. Although the mystery remains, the facts of Walpole's sudden wealth are impressive and important.

Before 1714 he was a country gentleman living in modest circumstances in Dover Street, a man of obvious ability, a fine speaker, a shrewd parliamentary tactician; but he was not a dominating social figure. The great expansion of his wealth after 1714 enabled him to indulge in the lavish hospitality and opulent magnificence which were expected of a man of power. His domestic circumstances no longer hindered him from playing a leading role in political society. The flowering of Walpole's grandeur did not pass unremarked either by society or by the public, and accusations of brazenfaced peculation were soon circulating in private squibs or in the Press; malicious, exaggerated, but, perhaps, not without substance.

3

AS SOON as supplies had been voted, and the King crowned, Parliament was dissolved and Walpole went down to Norfolk to re-establish whig power at the elections, a task which he relished, for there was no restraint in his enjoyment of his enemies' defeat. The county was difficult to secure, because the tories were numerous and determined to maintain their hold on both seats, but Walpole campaigned vigorously,

spending over £100 on transporting his freeholders to Norwich. They left Lynn in a cavalcade, each freeholder having
7s. for himself and 8s. for his horse. They were preceded by
a drummer, and the aged lumbered behind in a wagon, but
the party stopped so frequently for refreshment that the
wagon had no difficulty in keeping pace.[1] Their return must
have been more riotous, for Walpole and Townshend had
been astute enough to put up Sir Jacob Astley, a comparatively moderate, independently minded tory but a firm
Hanoverian. He romped home with an orthodox whig,
Thomas de Grey of Merton.[2] Elsewhere the whigs' victory
was equally complete. Robert Britiffe, Walpole's family
lawyer, was returned for Norwich along with Waller Bacon,
another whig, by a handsome majority of three hundred
votes. There was even an improvement at Castle Rising,
where Walpole was at last able to get rid of his tory uncle,
who was consoled by being allowed to keep his office of Commissioner for the Irish revenues. In his place Walpole brought
in his great friend, Charles Churchill. At Yarmouth the
tories were forced out of one seat, which went to Townshend's uncle, Horatio. But the greatest joy of this election
battle came twelve months later when Richard Ferrier, the
rejected tory at Yarmouth, who had been a thorn in Walpole's side for five years past, wrote to him as follows:

'YARMOUTH, 19 MARCH 1716.
Sir,
    I am advised by some of my friends that there has lately
been application made to you and the other Lords of the
Treasury to supersede my son's patent, granted by the late
Queen, and renewed since his Majesties' happy accession,

[1] C(H)MSS, vouchers.
[2] Townshend MSS, James Calthorpe to Lord Townshend, 24 September
1714; Coxe, II, 49. Walpole wrote to Townshend as early as 8 November
1714, 'I dine tomorrow at Sir Jacob's who is very stout and resolute,' which
indicated clearly enough that these pillars of the whig party were backing a
tory for their own ends, but, of course, they knew that they had him in their
power. Astley had been promoted to the Board of Trade in September 1714,
and he became a whig and remained tied to their coat tails for the rest of his
life. He went out of office with them in 1717.

of one of the King's waiters in the Port of London, in favour either of a Captain Symonds a gentleman upwards of sixty years old or of my nephew Lodge who is at present deputy to my son and who, as such, makes as much or (if he be diligent) more of it than the principal doth.

I do humbly desire from your goodness and justice, that no *fiat* may pass till it appears that by some act of misconduct he has forfeited those hopes of your favour which an innocent man may lay claim to. With respect to the publick no body has a truer zeal for his Majesties service than he, and which he cheerfully demonstrates on all occasions. And if I have had the misfortune formerly to incur your displeasure I would hope that my late conduct and influence in this town and neighbourhood (by which not only the publick peace was eminently preserved, but by which also had it pleased God to have suffered the Rebellion to spread we should have appeared an example of loyalty to the best of his Majesties towns) will in some measure atone for me. Of this behaviour of mine my neighbour Mr. Fuller will if desired make I doubt not faithful and just representation.

You will by this act of goodness for ever ingage to your service a young fellow just entered into world (*sic*) who will I doubt not in time prove an usefull man, and I shall labour to acknowledge the favour in any way you please to command me. And which should no sooner offer, by having in a solemn agreement with all our people, my option of the next turn for this town to Parliament. I heartily pray you will give my son protection on this occasion with great truth, Sir,

Your most faithfull and obedient servant,
Richd. Ferrier.'[1]

But neither son nor nephew was spared, nor did Ferrier ever again sit for Yarmouth where the Walpole-Townshend caucus became predominant. Ferrier had sat in the Parliament which had sent Walpole to the Tower, and he was a

[1] *C(H) MSS*, R. Ferrier, 19 March 1716. For Ferrier, cf. E. Hughes, *North Country Life in the Eighteenth Century*, 184, 189. He was Mayor of Yarmouth in 1706 and 1720. His splendid seventeenth-century house, known as Drury House, still stands on the South Quay at Yarmouth.

Norfolk man. For that folly he was crushed into political oblivion.

4

BY THE time he received Ferrier's letter Walpole had tasted deeper satisfaction. He quickly realized that George I's accession gave him an opportunity to condemn the leadership of the tory party, if quickly done, before its value as a counter-poise was discovered by George's German advisers. Events alone did not condemn the tories; there were several groups which had weathered the crisis comfortably. A place had been found for Nottingham who, indeed, had been rewarded for his opposition to Oxford with the important office of President of the Council. His career had not been a model of political constancy, and if he ran true to form the whigs could expect him to be intriguing against them as soon as the King was firmly settled on his throne. If the tories were to be made impotent for the future, action had to be taken quickly, a fact which Walpole realized better than any man, and no one liked taking action more than he.

Walpole was determined to destroy the late ministry, and to destroy them in the most public fashion. He had insisted on writing into the King's proclamation for the new Parliament a reference to the danger which the Protestant succession had undergone during the last years of Anne's reign.[1] When the new Parliament met, Walpole moved the Address. This had probably been drawn up by himself and his friend, Stanhope; many of the phrases have a clear Walpolian ring, for it was very much more outspoken than anything which had gone before. It condemned the 'secret practises' of Bolingbroke and Oxford and asserted that it would be the government's business 'to trace out those measures whereon he (the Pretender) placed his hopes and to bring the authors of them to punishment'. This was a clear declaration of war; the leading tories of the old ministry could expect no quarter.

[1] Michael, I, 114; Wharncliffe, *Letters of Lady Mary Wortley Montagu* (2nd ed., 1837), I, 128.

The change in the political atmosphere was quick and remarkable. The tories overcame their inaction, which had
been based on anxiety and hope; hope that their indiscre-
tions might be ignored for the sake of unity; anxiety that they
might be called to account. No sooner was the Address
moved and carried than Sir William Wyndham, Bolingbroke's closest ally, rose in the Commons and denounced the
King's Proclamation for a new Parliament as an unwarrant-
able interference with the freedom of elections. A sharp bitter
debate followed, so sharp, indeed, that Walpole himself was
constrained to advise moderation, sarcastically suggesting
that to send Wyndham to the Tower, which several members
had proposed, might make him too considerable a figure.
When Wyndham was finally ordered from the House, 128
tories followed him in a body; an action impressive in its unanimity and strength. The game could not be saved by brave
gestures. All was lost, and Bolingbroke, for one, knew it. On
6 April 1715 he was at the theatre, but he slipped out before
the end of the play. Next day he landed at Calais. Historians
have condemned him for lack of courage. He knew, however, that he would be the central target for whig animosity;
he knew his half-treasonable intentions, and his more than
treasonable utterances to his cronies; he knew Walpole's implacable hostility; that his head might roll on Tower Hill could
not be dismissed as an idle fear. But there were far more than
immediate personal reasons for his decision. He was not only
saving his life, he was also making another bid for the future.

Discontent was rife. What Bolingbroke and his tories had
intended was now being put into speedy practice; but, instead of whigs, tories of every hue were being weeded out of
office. With the utmost care Townshend, Stanhope and Cowper were going through each county, vetting each deputy-
lieutenant and justice of the peace.[1] Departments of State
were being equally thoroughly purged, and many men lost
their livelihoods and future prospects.[2] Many of these were

[1] Herts RO, *Panshanger MSS*, C.1.
[2] W. R. Ward, *The English Land Tax in the Eighteenth Century*, 64.

completely loyal tories and their bitterness grew intense. In the counties and in London knots of discontent were thereby formed which could provide the leadership for a national movement against the Hanoverians. And such a movement remained a possibility. During the election there had been riots in London with a strongly Jacobite twist. There were mobs in Lancashire crying 'down with the Rump' and grave disturbances in Shropshire, Colchester and elsewhere.[1] There was a great deal of unfocused animosity which the tories and Jacobites began to exploit for their own ends. By 30 May 1715 the cabinet was so worried that it passed the following resolution:

'That the Jacobite spirit being encouraged and formulated with so much industry and impudence it is necessary for the King's service and security that a strict enquiry should be made into the dispositions of officers of the Army and that those who with reason may be suspected to be disaffected to the Government be immediately removed.'[2]

Bolingbroke, who possessed a stronger sense of public opinion than Walpole, was well aware of the extent and depth of anti-government feeling. Locked up in the Tower, he could not exploit this to his purpose. To stand his trial would be a fruitless gesture. In person he might persuade James to cast aside his religion and appeal to the common people against the greed and the graft of the Hanoverian Court. The same reasons prompted Ormonde; the unrest in England was creating a crisis in which a decisive blow might be struck for the Jacobites. It was neither cowardice nor folly which drove these men to France. Bolingbroke was a shrewd politician. And there was no other course left for him. Because he failed, and failed so abysmally, it is a temptation to dismiss his action as folly and ignore the potentialities of the situation for one who was ignorant of the future.

Bolingbroke's flight was very welcome to Walpole. It

---

[1] *Stowe MSS*, 288, pp. 61–2, quot. Michael, I, 130: *Townshend MSS*, Townshend's cabinet minutes, March and April 1715.

[2] *Townshend MSS, ibid.*, 30 May 1715.

justified completely his reiterated charges of Jacobitism which he had levelled so constantly at the old ministry, so convincingly indeed that it excused all but the most sceptical of reading the evidence. The mere statement that tory and Jacobite were one became sufficient to carry conviction. Walpole also avoided the difficulty of a public trial, for difficulty there would have been, as Bolingbroke had very skilfully covered his tracks. Although there was plenty of hearsay evidence against him, there was little more. Nevertheless, Walpole was determined to make out a strong case and secure his condemnation in absence. He wanted to break Bolingbroke; so did his colleagues. For this purpose a committee of the Commons was formed to investigate the grounds for proceeding to an impeachment and Walpole was made chairman of this committee. In spite of illness, he attended innumerable meetings and sifted a vast mass of evidence; and finally, on 9 June, he read the report which he had drafted to a crowded House. This was everywhere admitted to be a masterly performance, and Walpole relieved the tedium of the long indictment by making great play of the politics of Lord Strafford, which made the House laugh 'as often as any passages were read in his letters which Mr Walpole humoured very well in the repeating of them'. For a sick man the effort of reading for five hours must have been very great, but Walpole immediately rebuffed the tories' demand to delay consideration of the report. There and then he proceeded to move for Bolingbroke's impeachment, a motion which was quickly carried.[1]

This was the first great triumph of Walpole's career. He had provided the forceful energy necessary to secure the in-

[1] Parliamentary Reports, I; W. Graham, *The Letters of Joseph Addison* (Oxford, 1941), 336–43; Michael, I, 123–9. Also for parliamentary affairs in 1715 and 1716, there is a most valuable series of newsletters from Anthony Corbière, a Treasury clerk, to Horatio Walpole at The Hague. Corbière, although not a Member of Parliament, was able to attend debates. He is always careful to state whether he himself was present or not. These letters are in the *Walpole MSS* at Wolterton and the references in the rest of this chapter to the *Walpole MSS* refer to them. They are more valuable than Bonet's reports which were used by Michael, because Bonet's were second-hand.

dictment of the past. For fifteen years he and Bolingbroke had fought for power, and for most of them the tide had run against Walpole, but he had been sustained by his faith in his own judgment. He had written in the Tower: 'I shall one day revenge what I heartily despise.' And the day had come. The thoroughness of preparation, the incisive, unrelenting speeches of condemnation, bespeak the inner satisfaction with which Walpole took his revenge. The insubstantial mercurial wit and charm of Bolingbroke were alien to Walpole's temper. It is not remarkable that they hated each other. Bolingbroke wrote with elegant ease, indeed with such grace that he bewitched men into thinking him a philosopher; Walpole wrote dull, solemn, heavily argued common sense. Bolingbroke was sensitively alive to the changing mood of the people; Walpole never understood it, for he blundered time and time again, and was bewildered, frustrated and made angry by his unpopularity. But Walpole had weight and power, two qualities which the chameleon Bolingbroke lacked. For all his brilliance, for all his insight, Bolingbroke could never evoke in other men a sense of security, of competence, of dependability. In Walpole's life there is as much hypocrisy, as much double-dealing, as much treachery as in Bolingbroke's, yet he remained a solid, four-square man in whom other men put their trust. Indeed, one could with justice maintain that there is a greater consistency about Bolingbroke's career and ideas; but temperamentally he was shiftless. Bolingbroke was a man of small character but brilliant gifts; Walpole a man of commonplace ideas with the stature of a giant. The combat between these men could only end with death, but Walpole was too shrewd not to realize his present advantage. There could be no compromise, no suggestion of mercy. Bolingbroke, the traitor, had to be condemned fully and finally. This day he took his revenge on what he 'so heartily despised'.

Although he regarded Bolingbroke as his arch-enemy, he was equally impacable towards Ormonde and Oxford; indeed when the debate on Ormonde seemed to be going in

VI. HENRY ST JOHN, 1ST VISCOUNT BOLINGBROKE

his favour, he intervened decisively, sharply reminding the House that no minister or general could plead the orders of his sovereign as a defence to a charge of treason. The case against Oxford was admittedly thin, and the brave old man, not himself unsatisfied by Bolingbroke's flight, was determined to stand his trial. His courage aroused pity, and pity bred a desire for mercy. This, too, was quickly checked and Oxford was bundled off to the Tower.

5

THE REMORSELESS destruction of the old ministry helped to bring the restless discontent to a head. Rebellion broke out in Scotland. But the revolt was formless, badly timed, and ill-supported. It had been provoked partly in an attempt to commit France before her policy to the Stuarts could be changed by Louis XIV's death, partly by the anxious need to exploit the growing unpopularity of the Hanoverians, but mostly by the thoughtlessness of men like Mar, who lacked patience and judgment.

The ministry acted promptly. Argyll, the ablest commander after Marlborough, was dispatched to Scotland. The Dutch were called upon for the troops which their treaty obligations compelled them to provide. Notorious Jacobites and tories were quickly rounded up and at the same time the Habeas Corpus Act was suspended. A strong force of troops was maintained around London. Rebels wandering about Scotland could be dealt with at leisure, but London had to be kept completely loyal. Never was the wisdom of this ministry more clearly demonstrated than in the way in which it handled the Jacobite rebellion. The country was seething with discontent, yet, with a few regiments of troops to back their quick decisions, they were able to choke the rebellion in the south. They were aided by the ineptitude of James. Bolingbroke, now his Secretary-of-State, implored James to change his religion and make an appeal to the common people, who were to be promised a ministry free from corruption. Both he and Ormonde wanted a landing in the south to avoid arousing the violent national prejudice which an invasion from Scotland must bring. All to no purpose. James was a convinced Catholic, whose religion could not be changed for the sake of any kingdom. Like so many Stuarts, he distrusted England, and, in any case, Mar had forced the issue. As to an appeal to the common people, that was a subtlety beyond his simple grasp. He went to Scotland to concentrate what forces he could, taking with him the little help he could muster in France. Preston, Sherrifmuir and the army's flight to the Highlands have stamped the 'Fifteen with the air of a fiasco which it was far from being. Sherrifmuir won half Scotland for James for that winter and, had energetic measures been taken, the campaign of 1716 might have been arduous for the Hanoverians. Britain was in grave danger and it was saved as much by the ineptitude of the Jacobites as by the skill and courage of the ministry.

No sooner was the rebellion over than the ministry were faced with the problem of what to do with the Jacobite lords who had been captured. Once the danger of the rebellion was past, the desire to vex the King and his ministry sprouted afresh, and pleas for mercy were heard on all sides. And for mercy there were other more solid arguments. The national pride of Scotland was chafed by the yoke of the Union; its advantages were not immediately discernible but its humiliations were obvious, and many saw that the success of the 'Fifteen in Scotland had been due to the sense of frustration which it had created. The public execution of six Scottish noblemen could only exacerbate the animosity which was already there and strengthen the Jacobite cause, whereas mercy would clearly demonstrate not only to Scotland but also to France the security of the Hanoverians.

This was not Walpole's view. He stood for the utmost rigour of the law, and he was now in a far stronger position to get his own way, for, a few months after the death of Halifax, he had become First Lord of the Treasury, which gave him a seat in the cabinet. But it was not easy to make his views prevail, for the Scottish lords had many friends at

Court and a strong advocate in Lord Nottingham, who also sat in the cabinet. The Act of Settlement was invoked by the whigs in favour of execution in order to protect the King from being attacked as brutal and at the same time to make certain that the death penalty was carried out. One clause of the Act of Settlement ran 'That no pardon under the Great Seal of England be pleadable to an Impeachment by the Commons of England'. This Act had come into operation with George I's accession and the whig lawyers held that the clause was effective in cases of treason by impeachment. Hence, clemency was outside the royal prerogative.[1] But the whigs soon realized that this was a dangerous argument, for both Houses were assailed with petitions for mercy. Walpole, appreciating that sentiment was rapidly strengthening in favour of the condemned men, proposed the adjournment of the Commons until 1 March, by which time the executions would have taken place. This speech was marked by its implacable hostility to clemency. He had strong grounds for demanding the destruction of the traitors in the Tower and he did not spare them, but he only just managed to carry the House with him, scraping home by a bare majority of seven votes.

In Walpole's reported remarks there is a hint of a savagery which may seem at variance with his character. But this is not so. Walpole was a curious compound of directness and subtlety. He could withhold his hand, dissimulate, restrain his hatreds and jealousies when policy demanded, but once the need was past, then he preferred to be ruthless. He was not squeamish, and politics were a rough game. Derwentwater, Nithisdale and the rest must have known where failure would lead them, and the block, according to Walpole, was their rightful destiny. A dead man could no longer plot and mercy was too easily mistaken for weakness. And furthermore, he had his own rectitude to sustain him: others might be inclined to charity by the uneasiness of their own

[1] Philip Yorke, later Earl of Hardwicke, wrote a short argument in support of the whig case which received a fairly wide circulation, cf. BM. *Add MSS*, 36088. A copy which belonged to Chief Justice Lee is in the possession of Mr D. E. C. Yale of Christ's College.

consciences for there was scarcely a politician who had not dabbled in Jacobite intrigue. Walpole had never done so, and in his demand for death there is a hint of aggressive moral pride.[1]

To others it was a less simple question. These men had been their friends, and in those frantic months before the Queen's death so many had toyed with Jacobitism either in thought or word or deed. Had James enjoyed but a little more success, then many of them might have been in a like case to those traitors in the Tower. And to their inner doubts were added the cogent arguments of State—blood demands blood, and what was begun with such ferocity might end in renewed war. No one had any doubts of the unpopularity of the dynasty and mercy argued strength and benevolence. It was arguments such as these which carried the Lords in a contrary direction to the Commons. They refused to vote for an adjournment and an Address to the King was carried, largely due to Nottingham's intervention; but the situation was partly retrieved by Lord Islay and the Address asked the King only for a respite and for mercy 'to such as he judged might deserve it'.[2] The King, realizing the delicacy of the situation, pursued a middle course. Three were respited, three ordered to the block, of whom one, Nithisdale, escaped. Nevertheless, the executions were received uneasily, an uneasiness which was strengthened by popular superstition when London witnessed a violent display of the *Aurora Borealis*.[3] Anthony Corbière described the scene in his letter to Horatio Walpole of 9 March.

[1] *Walpole MSS*, Letters of Corbière; Chandler, VI, 67; Oldmixon, *History of England* (1735), 631; Coxe, I, 72; Herts RO, *Panshanger MSS*, contain the careful drafts of Lord Cowper's great speech on the verdict. These papers of his increase one's admiration for his wisdom and temper. He deserves to be studied in more detail.

[2] *Ibid*. Corbière, 28 February 1716.

[3] Spencer Cowper (ed.), *Diary of Mary Countess Cowper* (2nd ed., 1865), 90–1. The King was pleased at Nithisdale's escape. The original of Lady Cowper's Diary is at Herts RO amongst *Panshanger MSS*. The editor took liberties with the text and omitted much. All quotations have been corrected by the original: references are to the printed version.

'When I went out at ten o'clock, I found the whole town in a consternation; some were at their prayers, and expected the Day of Judgment; others could see armies engaged in the air, and not a few could distinguish trunks of bodies and their heads near them. I got amongst the rabble out of curiosity and having asked one what people that of this strange think (*sic*), he answered it was looked upon as a judgment upon the King for intending to execute the Lords the next day[1] (which had been appointed for their death) but it happened they had been reprieved that very morning, and I told him it was a judgment because they were not to dye though they had so much deserved it. . . . The next day we were told that this was a common sight in Muscovy and the North of Scotland, and was called Lux (or Aurora) Borealis. However the uncommonness of it here affected the inferior people who would needs say that this with the last eclipse portended dire events, and I am sorry it gave occasion to observe too much disaffection amongst them.'[2]

Dissatisfaction was not only to be found amongst the inferior classes. Nottingham's open opposition had displeased the King, yet his dismissal, welcomed by Walpole, did not resolve the situation, for, as he wrote to his brother Horatio on 6 March:

'You will be surprised at the dismission of the family of the Dismalls;[3] but all the trouble we have had in favor of the condemned lords arose from that corner, and they had taken their plea to have no more to doe with us, and so the shortest end was thought the best. I don't well know what account to give you of our situation here, there are storms in the air, but I doubt not they will all be blown over.'[4]

[1] These were the three who had been respited; their execution was expected.
[2] *Walpole MSS.*
[3] The Finchs, they were known also as 'the black funereal Finchs'.
[4] *Walpole MSS*, quoted. Coxe, II, 51. Also Coxe, II, 52. In trying to dissuade the King from visiting Hanover, Townshend wrote to Bernstorff of Nottingham's 'strong disposition in favour of the rebels, which has already shewn itself in different shapes ever since the defeat at Preston, and which appears not only by that open and barefaced obstruction of justice which is at present offered in the tryals in the inferiour courts, but likewise by that excess of tenderness which has been expressed for the criminals on every occasion, even in places where his majesty had the least reason to expect it (i.e. in the cabinet); which shews at once the strength and riches of the faction'.

The storm clouds were not so easily dispersed; indeed every day they grew thicker and more ominous.

6

THE UNITY of the whigs was more apparent than real; jealousies everywhere abounded, particularly in the army, where Argyll hated Cadogan, Marlborough's protégé. Matters had not been improved by the reappearance of Charles, Earl of Sunderland, in the ministry, whom, at the King's accession, Townshend had managed to get appointed Lord Lieutenant of Ireland, thereby keeping him clear of the intrigues of the Court.

This marked, perhaps, the beginning of what was to develop as a struggle for supreme power in the whig party. Sunderland had expected much from the arrival of George I. A man of sanguine temperament and soaring ambition, he was baffled by the offer of the Lord Lieutenancy of Ireland, a post which, except for an Ormonde, carried with it a hint of derogation. He could not understand how his father-in-law, Marlborough, had allowed him to be passed over. The Marlboroughs, however, had never warmed to him. His strong, decided views often clashed with theirs and towards their daughter he was too possessive, too passionately uxorious for their taste. He lacked humility and the desire to please, his own views were too imperative. Yet it was unlikely that he could be kept long from influence. His ability was too clear, his wit and his charm too obvious to be ignored; and his capacity for intrigue was even greater than that of his distinguished father, who had served James II as a Catholic and William III as a Protestant. Sunderland, reluctant to leave St James's, did not hurry his preparations, and before he set foot in Dublin, his path to advancement had been cleared by sudden death—Wharton, the Privy Seal, collapsed and died. Had he been in Ireland it is more than likely that Townshend and Walpole would have prevented his recall—the fear of a Jacobite invasion would have been a politic reason for not changing the Lord Lieutenant so soon after appointment. Sunderland's presence at Court left them no alternative but to accept his appointment to Wharton's office. In the few months which had elapsed since the King's accession he had won the friendship of Madame Schulenberg, George I's *maîtresse en titre*. No one ever knew better than he how to exploit the wit and charm which nature had bestowed on him so copiously. Assiduously he began to court Bothmer, Bernstorff and Robethon. He cherished his growing hatred for Walpole and Townshend, two Norfolk upstarts, thrusting themselves into places to which he had been destined by birth and breeding, and waited for his opportunity for revenge.

Whatever the internal strains and stresses may have been, the ministry pursued its policy of thoroughly destroying all vestiges of Jacobite influence with seeming unanimity. Lechmere in the Commons directed an attack on the non-jurors and Catholics with such ferocity that many Catholics thought it was prudent to retire abroad.[1] At the same time, considerable lobbying was undertaken to test opinion in the Commons about the desirability of repealing the Triennial Act, for the government wished to avoid a new election which would be due in 1717. Whose idea this was is not known, but Walpole was certainly an ardent advocate of longer Parliaments; however, before the measure could be brought before Parliament, Walpole had fallen desperately ill of fever. The tories quickly spread the rumour that this illness was due to excessive drink but, according to Corbière, 'he got it by walking one night along the river side with a certain tory whom he was bringing over to the Parliamentary Bill now in agitation. It was a double concern that so good a cause should have such a fatal effect.'[2] His illness was greatly magnified by Jacobite agents who kept him at the point of death long after he was not only on the way to recovery but at Houghton convalescing.[3] This is at least a tribute to his

[1] Margaret Blundell, *Blundell's Diary and Letter Book*, 1702–28, 158–9.
[2] *Walpole MSS*, Corbière, 10 April 1716.
[3] HMC, *Stuart MSS*, II, 83–4. These letters are used uncritically by Stirling

importance. Actually, the illness was short, though severe enough to put him out of business for most of the early summer. He missed the great struggle about the Septennial Act which the ministry obtained after a hard-fought debate, their victory made easier by the support of some twenty-six tories.[1] The passing of this Act did not ease political tension at Court, for the removal of the need to hold a general election with its danger of an increase of tories, allowed the factional strife amongst the whigs to flourish with greater intensity.

As Walpole fought his way back to health and strength he discovered a situation of great complexity and even greater obscurity. The whig oligarchy was a small inbred world, full of jealousy, distrust, malice, sense of grievance. That was the perpetual background to politics, and one with which Walpole had been familiar since he first entered Parliament. He was wary and distrustful by nature, unless he had long-standing and convincing proofs of friendship, when the warmth of his nature could obscure his intuition. He had known James Stanhope intimately for more than ten years. They had fought together the same battles, and their attitude to politics was uniform and consistent. Walpole trusted Stanhope implicitly—only to be betrayed. But Stanhope's treachery was well conceived and throughout the summer of 1716, Walpole wrote trustingly to Stanhope in Hanover of his difficulties.

The situation which Walpole found was a new one, although it was to become the pattern of court politics during the eighteenth century. Queen Anne's heirs had not lived in England, and therefore disgruntled politicians had no natural focus, no subsidiary court where they could plan and plot and brood about the future. But George I's heir was very much in evidence, and not at all averse to making trouble.

Taylor, *Walpole*, 146–7. By 13 April, Walpole was mending, and by 16 April he was well enough to leave London. He was back at Chelsea by 1 May, although he was not yet fit for business for several weeks. *Walpole MSS*, Corbière, 13–17 April and 1 May. Also Coxe, II, 62.

[1] *Walpole MSS*, Corbière, 20 April 1716.

The Prince of Wales had been encouraged to expect a leading part in affairs.

He had attended all meetings of the formal cabinet with his father, where his sound knowledge of English put him at a great advantage.[1] And when his father decided to visit Hanover in the summer of 1716, he hoped naturally enough to rule with full powers. The King, fully appreciating this and heartily disliking the idea, attempted not only to impose rigid restrictions on the Prince as Regent, but also to associate others with him in the office. This put the inner cabinet, who were consulted, into a quandary, and they pleaded for the King to stay in England. Indeed, they had good reasons of State for doing so. The rebellion was scarcely over, the situation of foreign affairs so delicate that the time lost sending back and forth to Hanover for instructions might endanger the country—or so they argued. However, if the King insisted on going, they were quite clear that the Prince must be left as sole Regent and that his powers should be according to 'ancient practice'.[2] When the King departed, the Prince was left as Regent, but he had neither the right to make appointments nor to call Parliament; indeed, in essentials, he was merely a caretaker. Nevertheless, the Prince determined to make what he could out of his position and in this he was strongly encouraged by those malevolent whigs— Argyll principally—who viewed the ministry with dislike because they too had been rejected.[3] If the Prince became a nuisance, the ministers in England were bound to be blamed either for a lack of loyalty or wisdom.

This situation was difficult enough, but it had been made worse by the carelessness of Townshend. During Walpole's illness the King's senior mistress, Fraulein von Schulenberg,

---

[1] *Townshend MSS*, Cabinet Minutes, e.g. 3 March 1715; 4 May 1715.

[2] Coxe, II, 51–4. It is a little difficult to see what they meant by this as Regency in England was practically non-existent. It was probably a face-saving phrase used in the hopes of pacifying the Prince without unduly irritating the King.

[3] *Townshend MSS*, Cabinet Minutes. The Prince continued to preside at formal cabinet meetings.

I

wished for an English title, and Townshend had fobbed her off with an Irish one—Duchess of Munster—which infuriated her intensely and filled her with rancour against Townshend. At once she began to work for his downfall, a prospect which was not entirely unpleasing to the King's German advisers, whose early enthusiasm for Walpole and Townshend was beginning to cool.[1] And, finally, Sarah, Duchess of Marlborough, put her tongue and money at the service of her son-in-law, Sunderland—neither was a despicable ally. Sunderland himself was quick to realize the delicacy of the situation and the fatal danger of staying in England. His health was quickly pressed into his service and he obtained the King's permission to take the waters of Aix. But once his office was placed in commission, and his *congé* arranged, he found it more prudent to forgo his cure for the more strenuous charms of Hanover. This was the welter of intrigue, malice, animosity and treachery which faced Walpole as he slowly climbed back to health in June 1716. By the time he was fully recovered in July, rumours were already circulating that he was to be 'laid aside'.[2]

Fortunately, we can watch the development of this crisis through Walpole's own eyes, for his letters to Stanhope survive at Chevening. He placed absolute trust in Stanhope—his 'dear Don', so called in memory of Stanhope's childhood spent at Madrid. He held back none of his suspicions, fears and anxieties. These heartfelt letters must have stirred Stanhope's conscience as he plotted Townshend's downfall with Sunderland and Bernstorff in Hanover, for he knew well enough that Townshend's fall must necessarily implicate Walpole. Yet so trusting were both Walpole and Townshend that they opened a secret channel to the King through Stanhope via Stephen Pointz, an Under-Secretary of State, in order to exclude the German ministers, hoping thereby to

[1] Lady Cowper, *Diary*, 107–11; also *Walpole MSS*, Corbière, June, reported that rumours of a ministerial crisis had reached the public and depressed the stocks.

[2] *Walpole MSS*, Corbière; Coxe, II, 54 *et seq*.

secure a hearing for their personal views with the King direct, an unwitting act of great folly.

On 30 July, some two or three weeks after his return to full political activity, Walpole sketched his situation as follows:

'Although you were very sensible how affairs stood among us here at your departure, and were acquainted with the heats and divisions betwixt the King's servants, yett we have picked up some particular accounts which may a little contribute to your better informations, I thought it not improper to write to you a little at large, that you may know in what situation we apprehend our matters stand at present.

We conceive then there is reason to believe that the designs of Lord Sunderland, Cadogan,[1] &c. were carried further, and better supported than we did imagine whilst you were here, and that all the foreigners were engaged on their side of the question; and in cheif that the Dutchesse of Munster entered into the dispute with a more than ordinary zeal and resentment against us, insomuch that by an account we have of a conversation with the King at the Dutchesse of Munster's, they flatter themselves that nothing but the want of time and the hurry the King was in upon his going away, prevented a thorough change of the ministry, which they still proposed to carry on upon the whig foot, exclusive of us, and by the account we have, there was no difficulty at all in removing me; you, it was thought might be taken care of in the army, but they were at a losse about my Lord Townshend. That this was discoursed of there seems to be no room for doubt, how far the King gave into it is not sufficiently explained, or whether he was more than passive in hearing the conversation; but it seems to me so contradictory to the accounts I allways had of the King's behaviour to Lord Townshend and you upon this subject, that I am at a losse how to question what is positively affirmed, or to believe what is so very extraordinary and irreconcilable with all other parts of the King's conduct, but now you are informed of this, I think you will be able to learn or guesse

[1] William, Earl Cadogan, Lieutenant-General of the Ordnance, a great soldier and close friend of Marlborough and bitter antagonist of Argyll.

what foot we stand upon. That the Dutchesse of Munster was very angry at her not being an English dutchesse is most certain, and that she imputes the whole to my Lord Townshend, and has expressed a particular resentment against him; I fear old Bernsdorff has given into these matters more than we are willing to believe, but yett I cannot be persuaded that he had any thoughts of entering into their thorough scheme, which to me must appear impossible, when I recollect the discourse I had myself with him upon these topicks: Robethon's impertinence is so notorious, that we must depend upon it he does all the mischief he possible can; but if the Heads can be sett right, such little creatures must come in in course, or may be despised.

Lord Sunderland talks of leaving England in a fortnight, and to be sure will not be long from you; he seems very pressing to have instructions from us how to behave at Hanover. His professions for an entire reconciliation and a perfect union are as strong as words can expresse; and you may be sure are reciprocall; and when I consider that common interest should procure sincerity among us, I am astonished to think there is reason to fear the contrary. What to my conception is first and cheifly necessary is the King's return, if practicable, which must determine these doubts one way or other, for nobody can answer for the successe of any thing, as long as nobody durst undertake, or knows, he shall be supported in what is found necessary for carrying on the King's businesse. I find Lord Sunderland and they persuade themselves the King will come back before the Parliament sitts; the Prince talks of nothing but holding the Parliament. It were very materiall to us to know which will be the case, because I think a different management will be necessary according to this event, and such measures must be kept with the Prince, if he is to hold the parliament, as may perhaps be misrepresented with you, and may be declined if the King comes over himself.

And now I have mentioned the Prince, 'tis fitt you should know how it stands with him, which is in appearance much better than it was, and instead of pretty extraordinary treatment, we meet civill receptions. He seems very intent upon holding the Parliament, very inquisitive about the revenue, calls daily for papers, which may tend to very particular informations; and I am not sure, they are not more for other people's perusall than his own. By some things that daily drop from him, he seems to be preparing to keep up an interest of his own in Parliament independent of the King's; but if that part is to be acted, I hope 'tis not impossible to bring him into other and better measures, but for this I do not pretend to answer. As for our behaviour to his highnesse we take care not to be wanting in duty and respect, not to give any offence or handle to such as are ready to take any opportunity to render businesse impracticable, and we hope we demean ourselves so, that neither they who would misrepresent us to the King for making our court too much to the Prince, nor they who would hurt us with the Prince for doing it too little, can have any fair advantage over us, but this is a game not to be managed without difficulty. Lord Townshend goes to-morrow to live at Hampton Court, I shall go twice a week, and on those publick days we both shall keep tables. This is a burthen not to be avoided, and what is expected from us, since 'twas determined that neither King nor Prince would keep a green cloth table, and the white staffs are generally gone to their respective homes except Lord Steward.[1] The Duke of Argyll comes constantly to Court, appears in publick and has his private audiences, and not without influence.

Count Quirini has lately had some conferences with Lord Townshend and self, he has made great tenders of his good offices at Hanover, and given the strongest assurance of his friendship; we have engaged him and obliged him enough to meritt his service if he can render any: he will apply to you as a freind and confident, and you must receive him as such, but take care not to trust him, nor make any other use of him, than to learn what you can from him.

This correspondence is a secrett to all the world except Lord Townshend and Mr. Methwyn.[2] He is acquainted

[1] The Duke of Kent.
[2] Paul Methuen (1672–1757), Lord of the Admiralty, 1714–17, Acting Secretary of State *vice* Stanhope.

with every step we take, and has indeed entered into businesse with us with so much friendship and honour, that we are in the same confidence and intimacy with him, as we were with you: what comes from Mr. Poyntz[1] you are in all respects to treat as from ourselves, and 'tis desired your private letter may for the future be directed to him; this saves the trouble of denying and chicaning about the correspondence both to and from you; and I promise you 'tis necessary to say every post something that shall look like truth upon the subject of the private correspondence. I am ever dear Don, &c.'[2]

A week later, he wrote again to Stanhope, but just as despondently; Argyll, he thought, was gaining strength steadily, and planning to run a faction of his own in the next parliamentary session, whereas their own situation was in no way improved. The Prince was civil to them, but that was all, and, concluded Walpole gloomily, 'no man can serve in this nation, whose creditt with the prince is supposed to be lost or declining'; and two days later he wrote: 'We are here chained to the oare, and working like slaves, and are looked upon as no other; for not only the behaviour and conduct of the prince are a weight upon us; but the industrious representations that are made of our being lost with the King reduces our creditt to nothing.' He pleaded for the King's early return, for a demonstration of his favour which was essential to restore their credit. 'If he is otherwise disposed, and has thoughts of fixing another scheme of ministry, not to advise him to determine one way or other, is to betray him, for in the present state of affairs his businesse will moulder to nothing, and whilst all the world is in a gaze to see which way the wind will blow and settle, nobody cares to putt to sea in such a storm and hurricane as we are in at present.'[3]

But the King did not return; indeed, Stanhope did not

---

[1] Stephen Pointz, client of Townshend, Under-Secretary of State.

[2] Coxe, II, 58–61, checked by the original at Chevening.

[3] *Ibid.*, II, 61, 64–5, also Lady Cowper, *Diary*, 114. The Princess of Wales called Townshend 'the sneeringest, fawingest knave that ever was' and said she preferred Sunderland.

mention the possibility until the end of August, and even then it gave rise to much 'uneasiness'.[1] By this time Walpole's hopes had begun to rise a little—the Prince was more civil; indeed, he had been invited to join him and the Princess in a hunt,[2] and he was beginning to believe that they might weather the storm. And with his usual boldness he fought back at his enemies. He presented the Prince with a patent revoking Argyll's pension of £2,000 per annum, and when the Prince refused to sign Walpole refused to pay, but the Prince did not take this amiss.[3] Walpole was also encouraged by the news which he received from Stanhope, who reported that he had had very great difficulty in obtaining permission for Sunderland to come to Hanover from Aix. With rising hopes Walpole, Townshend and Methuen began to plan for the winter session of Parliament, and they settled on a broad outline of policy.

Walpole, blind to the true situation in Hanover, was principally concerned with the growing alliance of such disgruntled whigs as Argyll and Shrewsbury with the tories. His political experience had given him a healthy fear of such manoeuvres and he knew their danger to any ministry in the Commons. In order to split this alliance, the ministers proposed to take further steps against the tory strongholds—the Church and the Universities. Walpole also decided to take the national debt in hand. His short experience as Chancellor had been sufficient to convince him that there was an unnecessary wastage of public money. He had also learnt that the Hanoverians delighted in a full purse.[4] When he set out for Houghton at the end of September in order to build up his health, look to his estates, and to work out a detailed financial policy at his leisure, his spirits were higher than they had been since his illness. When he returned five weeks later, he faced the prospect of a ruined career.

[1] Coxe, II, 79.
[2] *Walpole MSS*, Corbière, 21 August 1716.
[3] Coxe, II, 78–9.
[4] *Ibid.*, II, 80–2.

THE TROUBLE was twofold. Townshend, bluff and boisterous as ever, had got into difficulties over foreign affairs, and Stanhope, possibly owing to tittle-tattle retailed by Sunderland, had developed the suspicion that Walpole and Townshend were seeking an accommodation with Argyll and the Prince's whig friends which, if true, could only mean that it was a matter of some urgency who betrayed whom first.[1] The suspicion was most convenient for Stanhope, for it eased his own conscience, and he seized on it avidly. But, of course, this was in no way sufficient to set the King against Townshend. For this purpose the delay in signing a treaty with France was effectively used. When the King first went to Hanover, many prognosticated difficulties in carrying on diplomatic negotiations at both Hanover and London. As the King was very much more personally concerned in foreign affairs—it was still regarded constitutionally as his official province—the *Schwerpunkt* became the Hanoverian Court. Stanhope, who was supposed to represent English interests, was inevitably more concerned to stand well with the King, whereas the ministers in London approved or disapproved of what was done in the light of whether it would make their work of getting supplies through the Commons lighter or heavier. Added to this, there was the further complication that formal negotiations for a treaty between France, England and the United Provinces were being held at The Hague, where the British representative was Walpole's brother, Horatio. At the same time, secret negotiations were on foot at Hanover for the same purpose. The King, as Elector of Hanover, was also deeply involved in the Northern War, but there he was very much at a disadvantage, and needed both British subsidies and British naval support to strengthen his

[1] Coxe, II, 145; B. Williams, *Stanhope*, 245, quotes Philip Yorke, afterwards Lord Chancellor Hardwicke, as reporting this rumour, but there is no other shred of evidence to give it substance. Yorke at the time was a young lawyer far from the centre of politics. A ministerial crisis was known to exist and therefore rumours of every sort were bound to fly about.

Sir Godfrey Kneller

VII. JAMES, 1ST EARL STANHOPE

hand. The ministry at home were terrified that he would involve them in a costly war with Sweden, and perhaps with Russia, which would have been immensely unpopular in the Commons, in the City and in the country at large.[1] This was a situation complicated enough to tax the most patient diplomats and offering infinite scope for misunderstanding, particularly when it is remembered that communications were difficult and slow and that there were plenty of willing hands and tongues eager to make mischief and foster misunderstanding.[2] Added to this were the difficult temperaments of the two major politicians—Stanhope and Townshend. Stanhope was a soldier, not a diplomat; he liked action, prompt decisive action and a clear-cut policy. He was indifferent to risk, quick-tempered and ready to take offence.[3] Hervey, who detested Townshend, described him as 'rash in his undertakings, violent in his proceedings, haughty in his carriage, brutal in his expressions, and cruel in his disposition; impatient of the least contradiction, and as slow to pardon as he was quick to resent'.[4] After making allowances for Hervey's waspish malice and the need to balance his sentences, there is a considerable stratum of truth in his description. His best friends found him hot-tempered, rash and obstinate.[5] But he was a capable man of business—the efficiency of the ministry at the time of the Jacobite rebellion was largely due to him—and he had a considerable experience of diplomacy, a far greater one than Stanhope, which, of course, exacerbated the conflict of their wills.

Naturally, the Northern War seemed far more urgent to George than any other problem of foreign affairs, for it

[1] For the complexities of the diplomatic situation in the North, cf. J. F. Chance, *George I and the Northern War*.

[2] Bothmer sent a secret report, compiled by Schrader, to the King in Hanover, in which the actions of the Prince and the ministers were minutely described. Some of these are amongst Robethon papers, *Stowe MSS*, 229–30, cf. B. Williams, *Stanhope*, 237.

[3] Stanhope referred to his own character as 'ever inclined to bold strokes', B. Williams, *Stanhope*, 235.

[4] Hervey, I, 80.

[5] Chesterfield, III, 1408.

deeply concerned Hanover, to which he was naturally attached. Therefore it was a matter of great urgency to him that a treaty between Great Britain and France should be signed as quickly as possible. His advisers in London thought otherwise. Precipitate action might strengthen France at the expense of Britain, and they wished to see outstanding difficulties between the two countries resolved before any signature was appended to a treaty. The Pretender was still in France and it did not appear that he was unwelcome. Furthermore, the French had failed to carry out the destruction of Mardyke in accordance with the Treaty of Utrecht. Here were two problems, large in London, insignificant in Hanover, which caused misunderstanding and delay. On these matters the diplomats at Paris, Vienna, London, Hanover and The Hague expressed themselves in elaborate and beautifully constructed dispatches, embellished, after lengthy cogitation, with apposite quotations from Cicero or Demosthenes. The couriers crossed and recrossed the Channel, often carrying answers to questions which had ceased to be asked by the time they arrived at their destinations. At length exasperation was scarcely concealed by the courteous language of diplomacy. Time was vital to Hanoverian interests: George I knew it and found these interminable delays intolerable. Freed from the possibility of war with France, George intended Great Britain to direct her full attention to the Baltic and so restore the balance in the North which was endangered by the Tsar's successes. When the Abbé Dubois appeared in Hanover to conduct secret negotiations, George was eager to settle differences with France as promptly as possible. Owing to the Regent of France's own insecurity, he too wanted Dubois to secure a decision without delay and he showed willingness to accommodate. But there was further delay. Horatio Walpole tried to avoid signing the treaty with the French at The Hague before the concurrence of the Dutch had been secured. He pleaded to be allowed to return home, acquired violent colic as a further excuse; all to no avail. Letters passed slowly: Hanover–London; Lon-

234

don–The Hague[1]; and tempers grew short, so short that on 17 November 1716 (N.S.) Horatio himself was at last sent off to Hanover to explain away all the delays to the King and Stanhope, and to make them easy. That round, ebullient little man returned full of self-satisfied optimism and joy. All was well. The King was satisfied; Stanhope remained a true friend. A courier from Hanover followed hard on his heels and delivered a letter to Walpole, dated 15 December 1716 (N.S.), which brought news of the King's intention to make Townshend Lord Lieutenant of Ireland, which was the politest possible way of sacking him. At last the crisis, which both sides had half wanted, was open and avowed. The trouble was that what seemed like necessity to one side, appeared suspiciously like treachery to the other. Walpole and Townshend knew that they needed the Prince's support, and royal powers at their command, if they were to succeed in carrying the King's business through the Commons during his absence in Hanover; furthermore, their experience had taught them that an aggressive and expensive foreign policy in the North was likely to alarm the Commons and undermine their authority. Seen from Hanover, Townshend's reluctance to please the King, the dilatoriness of his diplomacy, his harping on the necessity of a Parliamentary session, his demand for increased powers for the Prince, all could be, and were, used as arguments for the thesis that he and Walpole were creating an independent party. The impatience of Stanhope, the insistence of Sunderland, the malice of Bothmer and Bernstorff, the hatred of the Duchess of Munster, and the interference of Robethon gave heightened significance to their occasional courtesies to the Prince. Difficult as conditions were, the ministry might have survived had no decisive action taken place before the return of the King. The blow had now fallen.

Townshend's appointment as Lord Lieutenant was not quite equivalent to disgrace, for Stanhope still hoped to avoid splitting the whig party. This office was an extremely lucra-

[1] Coxe, II, 105–6.

tive one, and carried with it a seat in the informal cabinet when the holder was present in London. Townshend's removal from the Secretaryship indicated certainly a loss of face and a weakening of the power of the Walpole-Townshend faction in the cabinet, but, if Townshend could be persuaded to accept the office and Walpole be retained as Chancellor, then whig unity might still be maintained. This was Stanhope's aim and with this in mind he wrote to Walpole on 4 December 1716, sending his letter by a special messenger, Brereton, 'who is a very sensible young man, and I have ordered him to manage it so that this letter be delivered to you four and twenty hours, before the messenger who goes along with him, deliver my dispatch to Mr Secretary Methuen [which contained Townshend's dismissal] that you may have so much time to reason with my Lord Townshend'.[1]

Although Townshend and Walpole half expected this blow, this letter caused great consternation. Sunderland and Stanhope had made their move with consummate art and Stanhope's letter was a masterpiece of veiled threats and cajolery. He was careful to make it quite clear to Walpole that the King intended to have an entirely whig ministry, that if he and Townshend should insist on resigning then there was a scheme prepared. He was to take the Treasury and Sunderland the vacant Secretaryship, so that if Walpole and Townshend went into opposition it would be they who would have to ally with tories, not the ministry. Furthermore, the letter contained a strong warning that Walpole had enemies at Court. The King had been displeased over Walpole's refusal to pay promptly some German mercenaries, and his displeasure had been most carefully exploited by Robethon and others. Only his own loyalty, Stanhope broadly hinted, had saved Walpole from being ejected with Townshend, but Stanhope knew his worth. There was no one comparable to him as Chancellor and Stanhope would only succeed him with the utmost reluctance—a situation from

[1] Coxe, II, 139–141.

which he hoped Walpole would rescue him by persuading Townshend to accept Ireland.[1]

Adroit as this letter was, Stanhope was writing to a master politician who had this advantage, that he trusted the instincts of his heart as well as the dictates of his head. His answer—dignified and moving—parried the blow and carried the attack into the Hanover camp, which naturally wished to avoid, if it could, a split ministry.

'Your private letter to me, I have not let one mortal see,' he wrote on 12 December 1716. 'I never read it, but some parts of it astonish me so much, that I know not what to say or think. What could prevail on you to enter into such a scheme as this, and appear to be chief actor in it, and undertake to carry it through in all events, without which it could not have been undertaken, is unaccountable. I do swear to you, that Lord Townshend has no way deserved it of you; and even after the letter that came with the King's, I do protest to you, he never treated your conduct in that matter, but as a mistake; which, when you were sensible of, your friendship for him would easily prevail upon you to retract. Believe me, Stanhope, he never thought you could enter into a combination with his enemies against him.

I find you are all persuaded, the scheme is so adjusted, that it can meet with no objection from the whigs. Believe me, you will find the direct contrary true, with every unprejudiced whig of any consequence or consideration. I, perhaps, am too nearly concerned in the consequences to gain any creditt with you. However, I can't help telling you, you don't know what you are a doing. 'Tis very hard to treat my Lord Townshend in the manner you have done, but 'tis more unjust to load him with imputations to justifie such ill treatment. Such sudden changes to old sworn friends, are seldom looked upon in the world with a favourable eye. What is given out here and published, from letters from among you, in regard to the Prince, I cannot but take notice of, and will stake my all upon this single issue, if one instance can be given of our behaviour to the

[1] Coxe, II, 139-141.

Prince, but what was necessary to carry on the King's service; and we never had a thought, but with a just and due regard to the King as our King and master; and as for any secret intimacies or management undertaken with the two brothers, if there be the least handle, or one instance can be given of it, call me for ever *villain*; if not, think as you please of those that say or write this.[1]

I will say no more, but give you one piece of advice. Stop your hand till you come over, and can see and hear, how what you have already done, is resented here. I am very sensible in what a manner Lord Townshend's refusall may be represented to the King. Think a little coolly, and consider how possible it is for men in a passion to do things, which they may heartily wish undone. I write this as an old acquaintance, that still desires to live in as much friendship, as you will make it possible or practicable for me. And lett me once more beg of you to recollect yourself, and lay aside that passion, which seems to be so predominant in all your actions. I have heard old friends were to be valued like old gold. I never wished any thing more sincerely than to bear that title, and to preserve it with you.'

And he sent along with this a more formal letter, intended for the perusal of Sunderland and the Germans, in which the phrases ring like hammer-blows.

'When you desired me to prevail with my Lord Townshend to acquiesce in what is carved out for him, I cannot but say you desired an impossibility; and 'tis fitt you should know, that there is not one of the cabinet councill, with whom you and Lord Sunderland have agreed in all things for so many years, but think, that considering all the circumstances and manner of doing this, no body could advise him to accept of the Lieutenancy of Ireland; and that it cannot be supposed, that the authors of this scheme either thought he would, or desired he should. And believe me, when I tell you, this matter is universally received here by all men of sense, and well wishers to the King, in another manner than you could imagine, when you gave

[1] This refers to the rumours that Walpole and Townshend were plotting with the two Campbell brothers, Argyll and Islay.

into the measure. And be assured, that whoever sent over the accounts of any intrigues or private correspondence betwixt us and the two brothers,[1] or any management in the least tending to any view or purpose, but the service, honour, and interest of the King, I must repeat it, be assured, they will be found, pardon the expression, confounded liars, from the beginning to the end.'[2]

The news was quickly all over London. The disgruntled whigs were delighted, for they hated Townshend and looked eagerly for some privileges in a reconstituted ministry. Poor Horatio was distracted. He had returned full of himself, the wise diplomat, the born negotiator, strutting with self-importance and self-esteem—only to have his rosy optimism blown to pieces! He wrote a letter to Stanhope complaining of his duplicity and lack of candour. Horatio's anger was as much due to his own simplicity as to Stanhope's guile. This was not to be the last of Horatio's diplomatic follies, for he responded at once like a warm and friendly spaniel to the proffered hand and never learnt to fear the whip behind the back. To many wiser heads than his this crisis in the ministry was not so unexpected, or entirely unwelcome. It was realized that the King's German advisers had played too large a part in it, and there were many who were willing to see a trial of strength between the Germans and the English, and from the moment the crisis broke, Walpole knew that he had strong support amongst his friends, who would be willing to follow his lead.

When Stanhope received Walpole's letters he was probably disturbed by the aggressive confidence which Walpole displayed about the support of the rest of the cabinet. It might be bluff, but at that distance there was no telling, for Schrader's reports were gossip, not fact. It was a threat, however, which could not be ignored, and contained what Stanhope considered dangerous constitutional implications which he thought highly improper and said so. He told Walpole on 1 January 1717 (N.S.) that the King was so determined to

[1] The Duke of Argyll and the Earl of Islay.
[2] Coxe, II, 143–6.

239

get rid of Townshend that no arguments would move him. 'Ought I,' he went on, 'either in my own name or in the name of the whiggish party, to have told the King, that my Lord Townshend must continue to be Secretary of State, or that I, nor any of our friends, would have anything to do? I really have not yet learnt to speak such language to my master.'[1] And he made it quite clear that under no circumstances would the King be bullied into taking Townshend back. Having allowed time for this to get home, he followed it by another letter agreeing to a further suggestion of Walpole's that Townshend should not be pressed to make a final decision about Ireland until the King had returned. But in the hope of maintaining a united ministry he had put out the further bait that 'when my Lord Townshend shall have accepted of Ireland, if in six months or a twelvemonth, he should like better some other post at home in the cabinet council, that his majesty will very readily approve of any scheme that his servants shall concert for placing my Lord Townshend where he shall like'. And for this he had the King's word. Townshend must lose face. There was to be a public demonstration of Stanhope's and Sunderland's power. These terms accepted, then kindness would be shown in return for good behaviour—hard terms, yet not ungenerous in the battle of politics.

Townshend and Walpole decided to appear to comply and wait for the King's return; it was difficult to make a final decision until they had had an occasion to sum up the situation for themselves. When the Court arrived from Hanover all was friendly, explanatory, bonhommous. The King behaved with great courtesy to Townshend, who was persuaded to take Ireland. All the ministers—even Sunderland—dined and drank together. The new Parliamentary session was, of course, about to begin, and there was much practical busi-

[1] Coxe, II, 154. This attitude is of interest to students of constitutional theory. There are no signs here of cabinet solidarity or that the King should be forced to employ servants he disliked for the sake of policy. These ideas hinted at in Walpole's letter were obviously as repugnant to Stanhope as they were to become to Walpole—when he had the whip hand.

ness to discuss in addition to their own misunderstandings, and it was essential that the ministry should give the appearance of unity when Parliament met.[1] These junketings may have deceived the plain country gentlemen as they rode through the mud and filth into London, but they certainly failed to heal what was beyond cure—the broken confidence of Townshend and Walpole in Stanhope. The session opened and at first they gave support. They agreed to the arrest of the Swedish ambassador, Gyllenborg, whose intercepted correspondence showed that he had been plotting with the Jacobites. Walpole even spoke in support of Stanhope's demand for energetic measures against Sweden, but his speech was short and lukewarm; in any case his henchmen must have been told to ignore his words, for they voted against the government which had a bare four votes' majority.[2] Behind the scenes the moderates were doing all they could to patch up the breach, and the Duke of Newcastle gave a dinner to Sunderland, Stanhope, Walpole and Townshend at the Kit-Cat on 30 March. To no purpose. Townshend had been behaving with flamboyant independence by voting against the Mutiny Bill, and by joining a protest against it. He cannot, therefore, have been surprised to receive notice of dismissal from the Lord Lieutenancy of Ireland. The next day Walpole waited on the King and returned his seals of office. Long afterwards old Horatio recalled how reluctant the King was to receive them; his warm and loyal imagination pictured the King pressing the seals again and again into the hands of the kneeling Walpole—an unlikely story and more probably the figment of an old man's memory, for the King's German advisers upon whom he relied had grown to hate Walpole. His mistress loathed Townshend, and it is all too probable that their departure was not regarded with much sorrow.[3] But fear cannot have been absent from their

[1] B. Williams, *Stanhope*, 246. HMC, *Polwarth MSS*, I, 160.
[2] The Prince's servants behaved also with ostentatious opposition, walking out of the Chamber in a body before the vote. HMC, *Polwarth MSS*, I, 212.
[3] Horatio's story is in Coxe, II, 169-70. There is no corroborative evidence.

hearts. Walpole's power in the Commons had been demonstrated too often for the new ministry to relish his opposition.

It was a grave decision for Walpole. He had tasted real power for the first time. He had set about putting his country's finances in order with energetic insight. This work he had to quit at the very moment of its introduction into the Commons. In his short time as Chancellor he had mastered fully the detail of the Exchequer's administration, and he knew what he wished to do. For the first time he had secured a position commensurate with his ability. Yet no sooner had he settled to this task, than he was forced to abandon it. And the loss, too, was a personal disaster. He had felt so safe, so secure that his expansive nature had indulged itself in all the appurtenances of greatness. He had formed opulent establishments, spent vastly and saved little. To retrench was not only against his nature but an admission of failure which he could not afford. He had to continue to live like a great man who was destined shortly to return to great office. Hence in his opposition to Stanhope there is a note of urgency as well as fury. That he should resent this abrupt break in his success was natural, but the unremitting hostility with which he pursued the ministry was due to his urgent need to get back into office on his own terms as soon as possible. For this end he was prepared to be both opportunist and ruthless, thereby creating a pattern of opposition which was to last a century.

CHAPTER SEVEN

THE STRIFE OF FACTION, 1717-19

THERE were many members both of the King's and of the Prince's Courts who regarded Walpole's fall with undisguised pleasure, for the German ministers, who had quickly lost their early regard for him, had now transferred their allegiance to Sunderland and Stanhope. Lady Cowper did what she could to prejudice the Princess of Wales against him, and certainly at this time the Princess, an ardent theologian, felt that her inclinations lay towards the tories, possibly because, like herself, they had a sincere interest in religion. Although the Prince did not dislike Townshend, he had little use for Walpole. In the casual correspondence and gossip of these years there is very little that is favourable to Walpole.[1] He was at a turning point in his career. His enemies had secured his disgrace. Nor is it difficult to discover why they had done so. Walpole did not belong to the small group of families who had come to regard themselves as the predestined rulers of their country. Neither did Townshend. In the first flush of success after the King's accession both of them had flaunted their power, pushed forward their relations, struck up an ostentatious friendship with the Germans, talked loudly and boastfully, and busied themselves with promotions and appointments that were no concern of theirs.[2] Their desire for power was frank in expression and unbridled in action. When their difficulties arose they discovered fewer friends than they expected and enough enemies to make them tremble for the future. They did not lack assets. East Anglia —and they and their friends controlled most of it—was a powerful factor in politics, and although most of the Court strongly disliked Walpole's thrustful personality his capacity

---

[1] Coxe, II, 119.
[2] Collins Baker and Muriel I. Baker, *Chandos*, 109.

for business was universally recognized; after all it was this, and this alone, which had carried him so far in his political career. But his skill in debate, his excellent judgment in parliamentary tactics, his knowledge of finance and administration seemed no longer to be so important. And for this reason the government had sailed through its troubled waters. The Jacobites were defeated, the tories broken, and the ministry had a large, and probably dependable, majority in both the Commons and the Lords. Walpole, indispensable to them in opposition or during the difficult months of the succession, could be dropped, they felt, without serious danger. They were wise enough to know that their own political fortunes depended on their mastery of Walpole, for it was inconceivable that he should be kept for long in a subordinate position.

But for Walpole the situation was bleak. He was nearly forty-one years of age, and he had been forced from office by men who had been his friends throughout his political career. To be out-manoeuvred by a St John or a Harley, as he had been in 1711, was a political experience for which he must have been prepared, but to be rejected by the weightiest section of his own party created a novel situation.

In 1717 the bulk of the men with whom Walpole had long been associated in politics were still in office and Walpole was faced, therefore, with a difficult decision. It is true that, during the reign of Anne, party distinctions were not clear cut, but a close alliance in opposition between groups holding strongly different attitudes to politics had been quite rare. It is true that in 1711 the whigs had discarded their views on Occasional Conformity in order to secure the adherence of Nottingham and his faction to their general scheme of opposition, but this was regarded as most exceptional, and gave rise to much adverse criticism. In 1717 the bulk of the opposition in the Commons was tory, and the group which crossed over with Walpole was small by comparison. It was neither large enough nor important enough to be able to impose itself on the opposition already in being; furthermore, these tories

were not eager to become a cat's-paw in the fratricidal warfare of the whigs.[1] Walpole, therefore, was faced with the
problem of either carrying on an intermittent, sniping opposition of his own, concentrating on these points of debate where
he differed from the ministry, or jettisoning the views which
he had hitherto voiced in order to enter wholeheartedly into
the general opposition of the tories in the hope of becoming
the opposition's leader.

At first Walpole may himself have hesitated about the
course to take, and, naturally, he had his friends to consider.
William Pulteney and Paul Methuen had quitted the ministry with him; and so, too, had the Duke of Devonshire,
already a close and devoted friend not only of Walpole but
also of the Princess of Wales, and his old patron, Edward
Russell, Earl of Orford, kept him company. Along with these
high-ranking politicians, a number of lesser figures had entered the wilderness either voluntarily or involuntarily. Walpole and Townshend's Norfolk friends and relatives were
naturally turned out of office and Sir Jacob Astley, who had
only recently turned to ardent whiggery, lost his seat in the
Board of Trade, whilst Sir Charles Turner, Walpole's
brother-in-law, was dismissed from the Admiralty Board.
These were natural victims, doomed to suffer for their close
personal allegiance, but the purge was more thorough than
that and reached down to men like Sir William St Quentin,
MP for Hull, who lost his place in the Treasury. Although
Walpole's threat to Stanhope, that 'every unprejudiced whig
of any consequence or consideration' would be on their side,
was not borne out, yet the split amongst the whigs went deep
enough to create anxiety for the future. The weakness of the
ministry was illustrated by some of its appointments. Joseph
Addison might be a writer of outstanding merit and of
reasonable administrative ability, but he lacked followers,
and he was thoroughly inept in the House of Commons. His
promotion to Secretary of State indicated the lack of choice
open to Sunderland and Stanhope. Addison's appointment

[1] Swift, *Correspondence* (ed. Elrington Ball), II, 360–1.

was not the only demonstration of weakness, for the young, gauche, anxiety-ridden Duke of Newcastle was made Lord Chamberlain, and many minor offices were filled with men of little weight, lacking not only experience but also a following in the Commons. Indeed the frailty of Stanhope's ministry was an encouragement to Walpole to attack at once and in earnest; but there were other factors which rendered such a decision less easy to take.

During the summer and autumn of Stanhope's sojourn at Hanover there had been many private meetings of the chief ministers left in England to plan the Government's policy for the next session of Parliament. They had decided to press for a closer alliance with the Czar in order to intimidate Sweden from giving help to the Jacobites. The forces necessary to support their foreign policy they realized would be costly, and they had no doubt that the expense would be unwelcome to the Commons, for 'the nation is so sett upon reducing her forces, and upon easing themselves of the burden of taxes'. The ministers had also been greatly troubled by the unrest in the country, which they felt was in some ways due to the clergy, whom they wished to place more effectively under the control of the Crown by statute. The Universities, too, were scheduled for regulation. But the ministers were quick to realize that the country's unease sprang from deeper causes. The demobilization of Marlborough's forces, the economic dislocation brought about by the peace, the anxiety caused by a new threat of war, these were more fundamental and more difficult to alleviate. One palliative they were determined to try—the reorganization of public debts by a scheme which might give hope of discharging them at a future date. This task had been entrusted to Walpole. He had spent the summer at Houghton, building up his health, and perfecting a plan for the national finances.[1] This had been drawn up in detail by the time of his resignation, and was awaiting an early presentation to Parliament; in-

[1] Coxe, II, 120–32.

deed, some of the details of the scheme had already been before the Committee of the House.

It was obvious that Walpole could not abandon a scheme to which he had devoted so much care; indeed, he had no intention of doing so, and he seconded the Redemption Bill which Stanhope introduced, saying that 'it would not fare worse for having two fathers'. The scheme was straightforward: a new loan was to be raised at five per cent; old stock was to be converted, or redeemed by the loan, or by the Sinking Fund which was to be established. This fund was never to be alienated from its prime purpose of extinguishing the National Debt. What Walpole hoped to achieve was a consolidated debt bearing a uniform rate of interest, for many of the old stocks had carried rates as high as seven or nine per cent, and at the same time by the foundation of the Sinking Fund to create confidence amongst the nation's creditors that their debts would be repaid. By this device Walpole showed great originality. It was the first general sinking fund to be established in this country, although a similar scheme had been employed by the Dutch in 1655 and by Pope Innocent XI in 1685. It bears the mark of so much of Walpole's administrative work, for it was simple, practical and sound. Stanhope delayed considerably the final passage of the three acts by which this plan was established, maybe hoping to give the impression that he had thoroughly reworked the scheme, for he made one or two minor alterations which angered Walpole.[1] During the debates he went out of his way to cast aspersions on Walpole's period of office at the Exchequer, accusing Walpole of giving his own relations and friends not only places, but the reversions of places, as well as securing for himself gratifications from the great financial companies in return for bargains made with them. Phrased in strong sarcastic language, the accusation infuriated Walpole, who leapt to his feet and, purple with rage, treated the House to a tirade of self-justification. 'He frankly owned that

[1] N. Brisco, *The Economic Policy of Sir Robert Walpole*, 30-40; B. Williams, *Stanhope*, 261-3.

while he was in employment, he had endeavoured to serve his friends and relations: than which, in his opinion, nothing was more reasonable, or more just. That as to granting reversions, he was willing to acquaint the House with the meaning of it. That he had no objections against the German ministers whom His Majesty brought with him from Hanover, and who, as far as he had observed, had all along behaved themselves like men of honour; but that there was a mean fellow, of what nation he could not tell,[1] who took it upon him to dispose of employments; that this man having obtained the grant of a reversion, designed for his son, Mr Walpole thought it too good for him, and therefore kept it for his own son. That thereupon that foreigner was as saucy as to demand of him the sum of £2500 under pretence that he had been offered so much for the said reversion; but that he was wiser than to comply with his demand. And that one of the chief reasons that made him resign his places, was, because he would not connive at some things that were carrying on.'[2] This last thrust infuriated Stanhope, never the coolest of men, to cast more aspersions, which in turn goaded Walpole further, stung doubtless as much by the sense of Stanhope's treachery as by what he said. The quarrel was so violent that their friends feared that it would end in a duel to prevent which the House commanded Walpole and Stanhope to take no notice of what had passed.

This made the breach between the whigs open, avowed and irreconcilable, although between April and May Walpole had made up his mind to oppose the ministry at all points, in spite of the fact that he and his friends had largely been responsible for the programme which the ministry proposed to undertake—the one exception from his outright opposition being the financial proposals. It was a grave decision. After all, it meant that the ministry could condemn his opposition as factious, as based on the pursuit of power rather than principle, and assert that he was betraying whig

[1] This was Robethon.
[2] Chandler, VI, 133–4.

principles as well as endangering the succession not only by an open alliance with the tories but also by the adoption of their views. Nor was his attitude of outright opposition on all points to the taste of some of his supporters, in particular, William Pulteney, who went out of his way to condemn Walpole's action in associating so wholeheartedly with the tories.[1] Indeed, it was from this difference of opinion that a coolness developed between them and it is one of the ironies of history that by his disapproval Pulteney jeopardized his own future and, being excluded from office by Walpole, was driven in 1726 to take the very same action that Walpole was now taking—full alliance with the tories, and was condemned in turn by Walpole for his desertion of whig principles. But the innovator of this type of opposition was Walpole himself. It was to become the pattern of all oppositions in eighteenth-century parliaments, a pattern which it is difficult for men versed in the parliamentary politics of recent times to judge sympathetically.

In the months of opposition that were to follow Walpole and his friends were to denounce the Septennial Act which they had done their utmost to promote. They were to support the continuation of the Schism Act, which in Queen Anne's reign they had vigorously opposed because of its discrimination against dissenters. They were to attack Stanhope's liberal tendencies towards religious toleration and to confound his attempts to render the Universities less tory. They voted against making Bills which kept in being that small standing army which had become a symbol of whiggery and a guarantee of the Protestant Succession. They refused to proceed with the prosecution of Oxford, on which Walpole had insisted with all the vehemence of which he was capable. No country gentleman could have appeared more rabid than Walpole in his attacks on placemen and pensioners or more ardent in his support of the Church. It is not surprising that Stanhope and Sunderland were bewildered and strengthened in their

[1] Stair to Stanhope, 23 January 1718, quot. Mahon, *History of England, 1713-83* (1858), II, app. lxi.

hostility to him, or that the apologists of Walpole should pass over this period of his political life as quickly as decency allows. But to do so falsifies the picture of Walpole and of the politics of his day.

2

THE MAJOR business of eighteenth-century governments was administration, the conduct of foreign affairs, and the method and incidence of taxation. Great legislative principles were rarely at stake, except perhaps with regard to religious toleration, where Walpole was reasonably consistent. He was not in favour of extending greater liberty to dissenters or of reforming the Universities. When in office, he left both questions alone. The principal business of any ministry was to get its money bills through Parliament, avoid trouble over foreign affairs, and keep parliaments as short as possible. But more important than the absence of great legislative issues was the fact that Walpole could not appeal to the electorate. He could not be *voted* back into power, for he had been in politics long enough to know that governments did not lose general elections. He could only be *taken* back into power by the King. And the situation here was very different from what it had been in Queen Anne's reign. Her sickly health had kept the whigs to the narrow path of political virtue, for they had adopted George I in the same way that opposition politicians later in the century were to adopt the heir to the throne, whereas the tories in Anne's reign had pinned their hopes on the Queen's life lasting long enough for them to root out the whigs and to make their own terms with the Hanoverians, or bring in a Stuart. In fact the Queen's health helped to keep party divisions sharper than usual. In 1717 George I was reasonably young and healthy; and even if he had dropped dead, his successor would have been obliged to choose his ministers from the whigs. There could have been no question of a complete reversal of parties. There were, therefore, three courses open to Walpole. He could accept his lot, give support to the government and hope to be forgiven. Or he could try to become the Prince of Wales's prime minister and wait such time in the wilderness until the King died. And, lastly, he could make the maximum nuisance of himself, and embarrass the King's business in the Commons to such an extent that the King would be forced to take him back into the ministry for the sake of peace and security. The first course was beyond Walpole's means and alien to his ambitious nature; so, too, was the second, for the King was healthy, and there was also the added difficulty that the Prince of Wales did not like him overmuch. Therefore Walpole was driven to the last course. And it was obvious that his line of action could only hope to succeed if it was carried out with complete consistency. It was pointless to approve of the government one day and oppose it the next. The only exception was the Sinking Fund, for Walpole needed a share in the glory of this to maintain his reputation as a man of business. And finally there was this consideration. Walpole wanted to secure power not in order to put forward a great political programme of reform but quite simply in order to administer the King's business, which he thought, not without justification, that he and his friends could do far better than the rest of the politicians. For the sake of this supreme prize any tactic of embarrassment was worth adopting, even if it meant joining forces with the Jacobites and Hanoverian tories, or giving voice to sentiments to which Squire Western would have given a grunt of approval.

Nor was Walpole the only cynic. Stanhope was as quick to realize the need of the ministry for support, and he had no hesitation in opening secret negotiations with Bolingbroke, who had been quickly converted to the Hanoverian succession in 1716, after the failure of the Fifteen. Stanhope's father-in-law, Governor Pitt, saw Bolingbroke for him in Paris, and Lord Stair, the Ambassador, was also told to keep in touch with him. Bolingbroke welcomed these approaches, hoping to get his pardon: Stanhope, on the other hand, aimed to neutralize the Hanoverian tories, who might be reluctant to give full support to Walpole whilst the question of Bolingbroke's pardon remained a live issue.[1] But the prospect of the King's chief servant negotiating with an attainted exile, convicted of treason is, perhaps, in its way, as remarkable as tory sentiments in the mouth of Robert Walpole, and no less cynical. Stanhope realized that his own position in the Commons would be very insecure and he had been in politics long enough to know that failure to check Walpole could only end in disaster for himself. As with Walpole, the end justified the means.

It took a little time for Walpole's full-scale opposition to get under way, for he himself was eager to see Stanhope's financial measures for the Sinking Fund pass through the House. Also, aware as he was of the Jacobite intrigues in Sweden, he was prepared to accept the Government's motion to vote the King a quarter of a million pounds to concert measures with foreign princes to check the designs of Sweden, although this measure aroused the isolationist fury of the country gentlemen, who saw in it a needless and expensive sop to allay Hanoverian fears. They regarded rumours of Jacobite intrigue as a mere excuse to extort money to pay for alliances which were useless to Great Britain although a protection to Hanover. It would have been easy for Walpole to have exploited these prejudices and he did nothing to prevent one of his chief supporters—John Smith—from doing so, but at the end of the debate he rose in his place and made a short statement, saying that he would vote for the Court. That having been said, the opposition did not press a division and the motion was carried.[2]

If these closing days of April led Stanhope to hope that Walpole's opposition might be confined to a few explosions of rage on personal issues, he was soon disabused by a carefully laid attack on the government. On 8 May 1717, Pulteney acquainted the Commons that he had reason to suspect that there had been serious mismanagement and

[1] B. Williams, *Stanhope*, 258–60; Mahon, *History of England*, app. lviii–lix.
[2] Chandler, VI, 121–5.

possible embezzlement of the public money which had been spent on the transport of Dutch troops at the time of the Jacobite rebellion. This was an old-fashioned but popular move. The independent country gentlemen had no doubt that the King's servants richly buttered their own bread out of the public funds. They enjoyed nothing better than the exposure of corruption; indeed, they enjoyed it so much that they were willing to delay their return to their estates, which naturally called them as the summer advanced. Their presence at Westminster was essential if a large opposition was to be maintained against the government. Walpole and Pulteney could not have devised a more popular move. The accusation having been made the government had no alternative but to allow an investigation to proceed; the weeks ahead began to hold out little prospect of quiet for the ministry.

But a more trivial incident disturbed them more profoundly, for it illustrated the strength of the opposition when it was thoroughly united. Sir William Wyndham proposed that Dr Snape, the Headmaster of Eton, should preach before the House at St Margaret's, Westminster. It was customary to accept preachers proposed by any member without debate, but the proposal of Dr Snape was deliberately provocative, for he had been the champion of the High Church in a recent pamphlet battle with Benjamin Hoadly: indeed the quarrel between these two divines had been so ferocious that the King had been impelled to end Convocation. Although it was proposed by the tories, Snape received strong support from Walpole and his brother Horatio. Walpole declared his complete faith in Snape—'he had not only entrusted him with the education of his own sons but also recommended the sons of the Duke of Devonshire and Lord Townshend to his care'. This, no doubt, was said with firm conviction, firmer, perhaps, because it was but a half-truth. Although Walpole's sons—Robert and Edward—were at Eton under the immediate care of Dr Henry Bland, Walpole anticipated his advice to Devonshire and Townshend, for their sons were not admitted to Eton until 1718.[1] Doubtless prepared, the dissident whigs were present in force and defeated the Court who may have been caught unawares—141 voted for Snape, 131 for the Court, an ominous ministerial defeat. It implied that the government needed to be at full strength in order to combat successfully the combination of tories and Walpolian whigs.[2] Trivial though the motion was, for Stanhope it was an unpleasing omen of the difficulties which lay ahead.

The trial of the Earl of Oxford had long been deferred. Walpole had been the active chairman of the committee which investigated his crimes; indeed he had been very ardent in his demands for punishment of those guilty of treasonable intentions at the death of Anne. He had set his face resolutely against clemency when the tories had demanded it for the Scots peers, convicted of treason for their part in the Fifteen. He had opposed suggestions for the pardon of Ormonde. But the case of Oxford had proved difficult; evidence of his guilt was not easy to find. Walpole's serious illness, followed immediately by his quarrel with Stanhope and Sunderland, had helped to delay matters further. But Oxford, comfortable as he was, grew tired of the Tower, and on 24 May 1717 he petitioned the House of Lords for a speedy trial; also, the division of the whigs created troubled waters in which he could happily fish. Walpole did not welcome the petition; indeed it was an embarrassment to him. To prosecute Oxford with his old vigour would mean alienating his new friends and making Stanhope's life too easy for him: to spring to Oxford's defence was more than he could stomach. He allowed Stanhope to place him in his old post as chairman of the committee which was to manage the Commons impeachment. Then he stayed away from most of its meetings. Not an ideal solution, but a skilful one, and skilful enough to prevent Stanhope making capital out of the issue. He could not claim that Walpole had deserted the Hanoverian

[1] C(H) MSS, Account Book, 20A; R. A. Austen-Leigh, Eton College Register, 63, 340, 341, 342.
[2] Chandler, VI, 130.

succession and given his support to his old enemies, yet the tories could hardly be offended by his negative attitude. But if Walpole played a negative attitude to Oxford's trial, Townshend did not. He threw his hand in with the tories, demanding the shortest possible time for the Commons to prepare their case. When the trial came on with all its macabre splendour in Westminster Hall, the tories in the Lords hit upon an ingenious method of scotching the trial. Oxford was on trial for high crimes and misdemeanours as well as treason. The high crimes and misdemeanours covered most of his foreign policy during the last years of Anne's reign, and the charges against him were to be used for an exposure of the folly of that policy; and by implication the government would justify not only its own warlike past but also its present intentions. Only two of the charges referred to high treason. Lord Harcourt, the friend of Bolingbroke, secured an interruption of the trial soon after John Hampden (for the Commons) had laboriously justified the need for an impeachment. Back in their own House, Harcourt proposed that the Commons should be instructed to proceed directly to the two charges of treason upon which Oxford's life depended. Harcourt argued, and Townshend with him, that the trial would be indefinitely prolonged if the Commons were allowed to pursue Oxford charge by charge. In spite of the government's opposition, Harcourt and Townshend carried the day. As no doubt they expected, the Commons were furious at this noble interference with what they regarded as their ancient rights of procedure. They expressed forcibly their intention of proceeding with the high crimes and misdemeanours and demanded a free conference of both Houses when the Lords refused. There the trial stuck until the Lords resolved it by finding Oxford not guilty.[1] The fiasco of this trial was due entirely to the action of the Walpolian whigs in the Lords; without the energetic support of Townshend and Devonshire, Harcourt could never have succeeded. It was a hard blow for Stanhope: his weakness

[1] W. Michael, *Quadruple Alliance*, 21–4.

had been underlined, and weakness in eighteenth-century politics bred its own dangers. Members back in their neighbourhoods for the summer recess would argue his chance of survival, and decide how much they would trim their sails when Parliament met again.

Nor was the Oxford fiasco the only cross which Stanhope had to bear before the session closed. During the period of the trial Pulteney's accusations of corruption against Cadogan had been fully debated. The ministry had given in to the demand for papers about Cadogan's transport costs for the Dutch troops used in the Fifteen. These were presented and taken into consideration by a Committee of the whole House on 4 June. Much to its consternation the ministry realized that it was in a minority. To gain time to whip in members, the Court proposed that a money Bill should be read for a third time—an astonishing suggestion as it flouted the long accepted procedure of the House. Naturally it gave rise to indignation; indignation which required such time for its expression that the Court was able to root out its supporters, but not in such sufficient numbers to press their choice of Chairman on the House; and so their tactical victory was partly offset by Walpole's moral victory in obtaining Edgecumbe as Chairman. The House became very full and the debate very warm. Pulteney, who opened the attack, proved peculation to his own satisfaction, even though he hesitated to accuse Cadogan by name; but eighteenth-century accounts could be made to prove almost anything and Craggs, the government's apologist, had as little difficulty in spiriting away to lawful uses figures which Pulteney found so peculiarly damning. Walpole supported Pulteney with such vehemence that he broke a blood vessel in his nose and had to be led from the House. This gave Lechmere an admirable opportunity to be sarcastic at Walpole's expense—pointing out that Walpole of all men should know that accusations of peculation were too readily made out of party pique. Walpole, pale and rather shame-faced, scrambled back in time to vote when the Court decided to force the issue by proposing that the Chairman leave the chair. They just managed to secure this closure of the debate by ten votes, 204–194. The ministry tried puffing this up as a great victory, a pretence which can have deceived no one. To get home by only ten votes in a crowded House after whipping up every available supporter was a bleak prospect for future security; a sign which discreet and wavering men needed little help in interpreting. When the time came for Parliament's prorogation Stanhope and Sunderland must have viewed the future uneasily. Walpole had shown a formidable strength in opposition; he had dexterously exploited their weaknesses and with equal skill evaded their attempts to set him at loggerheads with his new friends.[1]

3

BEFORE THE session reached its formal end on 15 July Walpole had gone to Norfolk with his sister and Charles Townshend; indeed they had left London two days after the end of Oxford's trial. Dolly was seven months gone with child, and they made their way slowly to Norfolk.[2] Walpole was alone; for many years now he and his wife had lived their separate lives. Even when he had been desperately ill in April 1716, his wife had kept to her arrangements and gone to Bath for her yearly jaunt. She lived mainly at Chelsea, and her interests were those of the wealthy women of her time—music and the opera, clothes, jewels, an amusing collection of exotic birds—and, if her contemporaries are to be believed, gallantry—for Egmont wrote in his diary at her death: 'Sir Robert it is likely is not very sorry: she was as gallant, if report be true, with the men as he with the women, nevertheless they continued to live together and take their pleasures their own way without giving offence.'[3] It was this reputation which gave rise to the rumour that the child

[1] Chandler, VI, 135–9.
[2] C(H) MSS, Account Book, 20A. Dolly's son was born on 20 September according to the Historical Register, 1717, 'The Chronological Register', 39.
[3] HMC, Egmont Diary, II, 431.

which she was now carrying was not Robert's but Carr, Lord Hervey's[1]; a rumour which gained credence because the child—the celebrated Horace Walpole—was so unlike his father either physically or mentally. Modern historians have discredited the rumour and dismissed it as malicious.[2] But the rumour may not have been without substance, for there is no evidence of any reconciliation of Walpole and his wife; there is little doubt that they had continued to live as they had done for the last ten years—sharing the same houses but living their lives apart.

In 1716 they had spent hardly any time together. Robert went to Norfolk alone; Catherine by herself to Bath. In December, about the time of Horace's conception, she went off to visit Lord Conway, at Sudbourne Hall in Suffolk, not far from the Herveys. And this summer, when she was far gone with child, Walpole was off on his own again to Norfolk. Nor did he return directly to London. On 17 August he made his only recorded visit to Bath and stayed there for at least a month and returned only just in time for his wife's confinement.[3] Dolly's son was born about the same time, and so was a daughter to Sir William Wyndham; both births were announced in the Press whereas Horace's birth was passed over in silence. This, of course, is far from conclusive evidence that this son was not his. Horace may have been premature; the Walpoles may have had a brief reconciliation in the winter. But at least it argues for caution, strengthening as it does the gossip of Lady Louisa Stuart; more important,

[1] *Montagu Letters* (1837), I, xcii–iii.

[2] R. W. Ketton-Cremer, *Horace Walpole*, 26–8.

[3] Huntington Library, *Chandos Letter Books*, XV, 52–4. Duke of Chandos to J. Arbuthnot, 25 September 1717, quot. A. Ross, *The Correspondence of John Arbuthnot*, unpubd. Ph.D. thesis, Cam. Univ. Lib. Walpole had returned in a somewhat sententious and hypocritical mood. 'Mr. Walpole,' Chandos writes, 'is returned and I wish he could as easily tell you how you might be restored, as he did, how you came to be turned out. (Arbuthnot had lost his place as royal physician in 1714.) I am indeed persuaded what he says is true, that in many cases he was not the cause but the unhappy instrument of bringing about those misfortunes; the constant effects of a divided nation when violence in party matters supplies the defect of merit, and is allowed to be sufficient cause for doing unjustifiable hardships.'

however, it illuminates the broken happiness of Walpole and his wife. If reconciled they were, the reconciliation was brief and meaningless. She had behaved heartlessly when he lay at death's door, going off for her gay season at Bath; he was almost as indifferent. The child which she bore failed to bring them together. He acknowledged Horace but ignored him, leaving him entirely to his mother's care. They went on sharing the same houses but they remained indifferent to each other's happiness. For ten years the marriage had been a failure and a failure it remained until death parted them.[1]

No doubt in Norfolk and at Bath, Walpole found his consolations, for he was a sensual man; but they can have meant little to him, for not a name remains behind, either in the gossip of the day or in his account books. Most of his time was spent with his fellow politicians or with Townshend and Dolly, to whom he was deeply attached. In spite of his air of gallantry it is unlikely that the erotic life meant much to him; a man, already so famous, could not have avoided the inevitable gossip which any intimate or prolonged liaison must have given rise to. Fortunately the future was to bring him greater happiness.

4

AFTER WALPOLE returned from Bath towards the end of September events at Court became of dramatic importance for the course of English politics; the smouldering quarrel between the King and the Prince of Wales flared up. The King thought that the Prince had threatened the life of the Duke of Newcastle at the christening of the Prince's son. The incident had all the quality of high farce. The King, to show his authority, had insisted that the traditional right of the Lord Chamberlain to be a godparent of the Prince's child should be honoured. This infuriated his son, who detested all his father's servants. Fury once felt needed expression

---

[1] The movements of Robert and Catherine Walpole can be worked out from *C(H) MSS*, Account Books 20A and 22. The *Historical Register*, 1717, contains the announcements of births.

and at the christening he grabbed Newcastle's arm and said: 'Rascal, I find you out.' The Prince's accent was never very clear and Newcastle's intelligence rarely exact. Bewildered and confused, Newcastle understood the Prince to have said: 'I fight you.' He rushed back to the King in an irrepressible state of excitement and said that his life had been threatened. The King called a cabinet meeting; ministers of State were sent to interrogate the Prince, who called Newcastle a liar, and this promptly led the King to place his son under what was virtually close arrest. The ministers began to talk of *Habeas Corpus*; the Prince, with perhaps memories of his mother's long imprisonment, began to express contrition. The King would not listen to his son, but the fears of his ministers worked on him sufficiently to call off the Yeomen of the Guard. However, he relieved his feelings by expelling his son from St James's Palace but insisted on his grand-children remaining; in future he himself would be responsible for their education.[1] The Princess naturally followed her husband into exile; they were devoted to their little daughters whom they had left behind and after a time paid a clan-destine visit to them.[2] Immediately they had a sharp rebuke from the King.

'Monsieur Coke[3]

Vous dites de ma part à mon fils que je trouve fort mauvais qu'il soit venu à S. Jaimes sans ma permission, moy y etant, et que luy et la Princesse ayent a me la faire demander à l'avenir quand il voudront y venir voir les enfans, ce quy leur sera accordè un fois par semaine.

GEORGE R.'[4]

[1] The right of the King to educate his grandchildren and take them from their parents was put to the Judges who decided in his favour, Judge Eyre being the chief dissident.

[2] W. Michael, *Quadruple Alliance*, 25–7.

[3] The King's Vice-Chamberlain, and Walpole's neighbour at Holkham.

[4] Herts RO, *Panshanger MSS*, C.1, 6, not before printed. Spelling and gram-mar as in the original. The letter is in George I's handwriting. Stanhope's copies of the correspondence between the King and Prince, printed in 1717, are at Chevening. Michael, *op. cit.*, 309–10, prints the copies in the Vienna archives.

This was too much for the Prince and for the future he left the visiting to his wife.

The Prince hired a house in Leicester Square where he set up his Court; naturally the King forbade his friends attending and just as naturally the opposition, who had little to hope for at St James's, flocked to Leicester Square; Walpole and Townshend were in the van, along with their old friend Spencer Compton, the Speaker, whose sympathies were with them rather than with Stanhope, Sunderland and the Court. This quarrel aroused immense interest, for it occurred when the members of Parliament were coming up to London for the new session which opened on 21 November. Walpole and Townshend were quick to realize that this quarrel strengthened rather than weakened their hand. The future belonged to the Prince of Wales and no young ambitious politician would lightly alienate his regard. Furthermore the Prince had his own friends and dependants at his Court—Argyll for one—who possessed parliamentary influence which would now be brought into full opposition to the ministry. It was understandable, therefore, that in these circumstances the Court should wish to avoid all controversy and to keep parliamentary business to the minimum, for they were doubtful of their ability to carry the Commons with them on all points.

The session 1717–18 is notable both for the ready spirit of compromise shown by the ministry and for the strength of the opposition when led by Walpole. The main weight of Walpole's attack was aimed at the supply for the army which was about the only measure which allowed of controversy. The standing army since the Revolution had been legitimized each year by the passing of a Mutiny Bill. It was a singularly English compromise. Standing armies were regarded as alien to the constitution, a potential threat to the liberties of the country gentlemen, who had learnt during the seventeenth century to fear a well-armed central government. Yet the army could not be abolished; civil war raged in the early years of William's reign, only to be followed by long years of struggle against France, during which time Jacobite invasions were either a potential or actual danger. The memory of the 'Fifteen was too recent for Walpole to demand the abolition of the standing army—although for the sake of the country gentlemen he began his speech on 4 December 1717 with a few platitudes on the danger of a standing army to a free people. Shrewdly, he concentrated on the weaknesses of the army's organization. He complained that the army was larger than any previous army in peace time—a popular point with the back benchers, who always suspected any ministry of being too complaisant to the King. George's predilection for his army was well known; and, of course, such criticism implied that when Townshend and Walpole were in the government matters had been better arranged. But, Walpole maintained, the composition of the army was worse than its size; no due proportion had been observed between cavalry and infantry or between officers and men, and this led him to his peroration in which he denounced the excessive numbers of general officers as an altogether needless expense.[1] Walpole's criticism was both penetrating and dexterous, for he had the detailed knowledge to substantiate his criticism. It was difficult for Craggs, the Secretary-at-War, to answer him, but the effect of Walpole's speech was partly lost through faulty timing. Walpole found it difficult to wait; more often than not he was one of the foremost speakers in any debate whether he was in office or out of it; and he spoke as frequently as the rules of the House permitted—indeed on occasion more frequently. It was partly a lack of patience, partly a conviction of the relevance of his ideas, partly a need for dominance and leadership. At times this eagerness brought him rewards, for it brought the debate round to his own grounds of argument, but for once it betrayed him. He was followed by William Shippen in one of his most daring and provocative moods. He insulted the King; he insulted the ministers not by implication but openly and unequivocally, so openly and unequivocally that the

[1] Chandler, VI, 154 *et seq.*; Coxe, I, 112–3.

House was bound to take notice of the offensive nature of his remarks. It was proposed to send him to the Tower. Walpole attempted to excuse him but Shippen did not wish to be excused. He was quite happy to go to the Tower—no one enjoyed a fracas more, so to the Tower he went. By the time the House recovered its temper Walpole's speech was forgotten.

But Walpole had stamina, and in the days which followed he maintained his attack on the army so effectively that the government were forced to compromise with him. On 9 December 1717 a Committee of the Whole House accepted his figure for the supply allocated to garrisons although it was a reduction on the amount demanded by the government, and the next day, when the Committee reported to the House, the ministry did not attempt to reverse the decision. The real struggle came on 22 January 1718 over the retention of half-pay officers and the amount of the supply which was to be allocated to them. The ministry wanted £130,361; after a day's debate they would gladly have accepted £115,000, but Walpole pressed remorselessly his criticisms of detail. Why should not Ireland pay the half-pay officers of the thirteen Irish regiments recently disbanded? Why should chaplains without regiments be paid? What was the use of maintaining officers under sixteen? (At this moment did the embarrassing memory of his own son, Robert, who, as an ensign in the Footguards, had drawn a steady £75 per annum from the age of eight, cross his mind?)[1] These were questions which Craggs found difficult to answer, and in the end on 25 January 1718 the Court willingly accepted Walpole's figure of £94,000 for these half-pay officers in order to bring to a close these debates on the army supply, which had been prolonged for nearly seven weeks. But throughout these debates it was Walpole who had led the Commons—time and time again it was his proposal or his figure which was accepted as a

[1] C(H) MSS, Account Book, 20A. Robert Walpole junior's commission in the Footguards was superseded on 16 April 1718; a rebuke presumably for his father's opposition, if not the effect of conscience on his father.

compromise. With Stanhope in the Lords the ministry lacked leaders of ability in the Commons; lacked men who had Walpole's mastery of detail or his immense stamina in debate. Although he had opposed the ministry in the session forcibly, and even at times heatedly, yet the opposition could not be dismissed as factious. He had avoided general principles and kept to arguable questions of detail. He followed the same course when the Mutiny Bill itself came to be debated. He spoke strongly against permitting courts martial to inflict the death penalty but took himself and his supporters into the government lobby for the Bill as a whole. Although he was willing to criticize the standing army, he was still a little reluctant to accept the full tory demand for its abolition. There was in fact a hint of moderation about his opposition to the Court; the same was true of Townshend and Devonshire. They spoke in debate against the ministry but never first or for long; they, too, had the air of waiting.[1]

After the close of the session the Court took stock of its position, as did the opposition. Stanhope, Sunderland, the King's mistresses, particularly the Duchess of Munster, were quite capable of interpreting the opposition attitudes and hopes. Townshend and Walpole had displayed their strength but never once used it to jeopardize the ministry; they hoped to be taken back into the ministry on good terms. Stanhope and Sunderland could not afford to allow the opposition either an actual or moral victory. They were deeply conscious of their own weakness, so they developed a line of approach which offered them the greatest accession of strength in exchange for the minimum of concession. They recognized that Walpole was their greatest danger, so they attempted to buy him off. By midsummer this was common knowledge, for Walpole made no secret of it to his friends or his enemies, and Lady Cowper wrote as follows to her husband, who had recently quitted his office of Lord Chancellor owing to the quarrel in the Royal Family:

'. . . The Speaker [Spencer Compton] and Walpole were

[1] Chandler, VI, 171 *et seq.*; Timberland, II, 74–94.

here yesterday.[1] You'll be surprised when I tell you that the latter has had personal offers from the K[ing], but I'm ordered to desire you to say nothing of it to anybody. The first offer, he says, was made him from the D[uches]s of Munst[er] by a Romish priest that was their spye when they were in place. He told him, he could not believe she could send such a message by him, and would give him no answer, but since the King has sent a general to him (whose name he would not tell) to make him what offers he would have. He excused himself and said the same reason was in being for which he quitted; that the Munster had used him and all his freinds so ill that he could not believe that they durst do it without his Majesty's leave; and that truly whilst this quarrel[2] was in that posture it is, nobody would care to engage in business, for it made the whole family contemptible in the eyes of the people, and let himself into arguments to persuade a reconciliation. These offers (to explain myself) were only for himself and not for any of his friends.'[3]

By August the rumours of these negotiations had reached the Jacobite Court at Paris.[4] However, by the time the new parliamentary session opened all prospect of reconciliation had faded. The quarrel between the King and Prince showed no signs of healing. Although Walpole was far from happy in opposition he could not possibly join the ministry upon the terms which it offered. It meant deserting not only tories but friends with whom he had been closely associated in politics for over ten years to join Sunderland whom he had always distrusted and Stanhope who had betrayed him. Political necessity did at times drive Walpole to sacrifice his friends; at times even ambition got the better of his loyalty, but in the present situation there was no necessity and little temptation, although the ministry had achieved a certain popularity by its success in forming the Quadruple Alliance and by the vic-

[1] Probably Leicester Square because Lady Cowper was in waiting to the Princess of Wales.

[2] i.e. of the King and the Prince.

[3] Herts RO, *Panshanger MSS*, Lady Cowper to Lord Cowper, June 1718.

[4] HMC, *Stuart MSS*, VII, 102.

tory of English naval forces at Passaro. These successes, however, pleased the City rather than the country gentlemen,
who feared that increases in the land tax would be the inevitable result of a renewed war. In any case, Walpole had
been in politics long enough to know that the security of a
ministry did not rest on its success in diplomacy. Ability to
control the King and his personal advisers was the secret of
power and Walpole was far from certain that Sunderland
and Stanhope had that ability.

When Parliament met on 11 November 1718, however, it
was the ministry and not the opposition which took the
initiative. Stanhope had decided on a dangerous course. The
last years of Queen Anne's reign had witnessed a renewed
attempt to prevent the dissenters playing their full part in
social and political life. By occasionally partaking of Communion many dissenters qualified themselves for office.
There were a dozen or so avowed dissenters in Parliament.
But the High Anglicans resented keenly what they considered
to be a mere hypocrisy for the sake of office. During their
triumph in Anne's reign the practice had been condemned
in the Act against Occasional Conformity. From the time of
the Revolution, dissenters' schools had come to play a dominant part in the educational life of the nation, and their
success had aroused great envy, so much so that severe
limitations had been placed on dissenting academies by the
Schism Act, which came into force with the accession of
George I. Naturally these repressive measures had caused
bitter feeling amongst the dissenters; and they had begun to
organize their political influence to try and bring pressure
on the government in order not only to get these Acts re-
pealed but also to have removed all the civil disabilities imposed on them by the Test and Corporation Acts. Calcula-
tions, and very generous ones, had been made of the influence
of dissenters in parliamentary elections; individual members
of Parliament had been lobbied, and in March 1717 a
general meeting of members interested in the repeal had been
called. Although two hundred members were present the

managers for the ministry succeeded in persuading the conference to take no action, but to collect further information
of the dissenters' hardships.

Although there was considerable sympathy for the dissenters amongst the whig bishops, the bulk of the Anglican
clergy were strongly opposed to further concessions to them.
They argued cogently that the dissenting interest had steadily
declined since the Restoration, and that this was due to the
fact that they had been excluded from public life. If these
restrictions were removed, the dissenting interest would revive. There was force in this argument. There were no longer
any dissenting peers; dissenting gentry had dwindled to an insignificant number. There were still influential dissenters
amongst the City merchants—Shute Barrington, Samuel
Holden, and others—but there were far fewer than there had
been. Undoubtedly the High Anglican argument that the
social influence of dissenters had declined was a true one.

Although the influence of dissent had declined it was still
important, certainly important enough for Stanhope to wish
to secure its unqualified support. If his foreign policy had
done much to reconcile the City to his ministry, his position
even so was weak; there were many whigs who held back
their interest and regarded Walpole as the more effective
politician. But Stanhope's policy of securing further concessions for dissenters may not have been due so much to his
need for support. The mainspring of his action may, perhaps,
have been his hope that such a policy would place Walpole
himself in a dilemma. If he supported Stanhope he would
alienate his new tory friends. If he opposed the policy of
clemency surely he would expose himself as a factious self-
seeking politician to whom personal power meant more than
principles. And would not this exposure lower him in the
esteem of other men? It must have been considerations such
as these which led Stanhope to embark on what proved to be
a singularly disastrous parliamentary session.

The dissenters who were well organized and expert at
lobbying had been sending deputations to all parliamentary

groups to solicit their interest before the sessions opened; and reports of their reception circulated about London. Dudley Ryder, afterwards an ardent supporter of Walpole and his Attorney-General, was at that time a young lawyer with a strong nonconformist background. Naturally he was intensely interested in the success or failure of Stanhope's project and he kept a diary of all that he heard during the debates in the House of Lords when Stanhope introduced his scheme on 13 December 1718 'very much contrary to the expectation of the people at that time'.[1] As soon as the debate came on, the dissenters' lobbying became more active. 'The Bill was adjourned for a second reading to the Thursday following,' Ryder wrote in his diary. 'In the meantime the dissenting ministers and others among them thought it proper to solicit several of the noblemen, and among the rest the Prince. He received them civilly, but told them he believed their application to him would do them more harm elsewhere than he could do them service. . . . Some of the dissenting ministers waited upon the D. of Argyll. He received them mighty civilly and told them he was for the bill both by inclination and principle and should do them all the service he could. But he believed the Prince would be against them, not so much out of his own inclination as by the [importunity][2] of Walpole and Townshend, who would mix Heaven and earth together rather than not be at the head of the party.'[3]

The petulance of Argyll gives us an insight into the difficulties which faced Walpole in opposition and also shows how skilfully Stanhope had calculated his risks. As leaders of Scottish opinion it was difficult for Argyll and his brother Islay to be anti-dissent yet their support of the dissenters' cause was bound to weaken their influence with the Prince and make their uneasy alliance with Walpole more than ever

---

[1] *Harrowby MSS*, Document 29. 'The proceedings in the House of Lords in relation to Act of Parliament against occasional conformity and schism,' transcribed for me by Mr K. A. Perrin. This is the fullest account of the debate which exists.

[2] Reading doubtful.

[3] *Harrowby MSS*, Document 29.

precarious. It was this split in the ranks of the opposition which enabled Stanhope to carry his Bill through the Lords. 'The Prince voted himself against it and did it with a peculiar forwardness as if he had a mind to make everybody take notice of it. Argyll and Lord Islay were for the bill.'[1] The ministry's position had never been very strong in the Lords, and a majority of eighteen for committing the Bill indicated that Stanhope had been more successful with this measure than many had expected—even so dispassionate an observer as Bonet, the Prussian minister, had expected the measure to cause divisions.[2]

The defection of Argyll seems to have strengthened Walpole's influence with the Prince rather than weakened it; indeed the Prince's passionate interest in this controversy is rather remarkable. No doubt he wished to embarrass the King's servants as much as he could; but even so, he took a most exceptional step in listening from the Peers gallery to the debate in the House of Commons on 7 January 1719, when he was treated to the spectacle of Walpole explaining himself away.[3] He argued that the Bill would create dissatisfaction—a point with which both sides could agree—but from that point onwards his argument became stranger and stranger. He maintained that behind this Bill was a secret design—that it would give rise to an attempt to bring toleration to Catholics and so reverse the Revolution. Odd though the argument was, it was subtle and played most effectively on rumour, for through the Abbé Strickland the government was exploring the possibilities of opening negotiations with the Papacy about the position of English Catholics. The ministry was trying to neutralize Catholic opinion in England and elsewhere and render it less Jacobite; Strickland was attempting to win concessions from the ministry by playing on its fears of Jacobite invasion from

---

[1] *Harrowby MSS*, Document 29.

[2] W. Michael, *Quadruple Alliance*, 51.

[3] W. Michael, *op. cit.*, 55; Chandler, VI, 192; HMC, *Portland MSS*, V, 575-6, which contains a report of Walpole's speech.

Spain. Intensely secret though these tentative approaches were, Walpole was well aware of them; the fears which they naturally engendered amongst the old-fashioned country gentlemen were valuable to his purpose, and they were curiously used to give force to the denial of toleration to dissenters. Walpole's speech was subtle tactically, but perhaps oversubtle in its main argument at least. Furthermore it was interspersed with biting sarcasm about Sunderland's father and about the King, for Walpole remarked that it was a consolation to have an heir to the throne who had shown that aversion from the Church of England was not hereditary in the Royal family.[1] It was not a good performance and from this debate Walpole lost rather than gained. The Bill quickly passed through the House.

Stanhope's bid had proved successful. The debates had damaged the opposition rather than strengthened it. Even more important, perhaps, was the fact that Stanhope had played successfully on the jealousy of Argyll, who, unknown to the Prince, was negotiating secretly with the ministry for return to office. This was not accomplished until 6 February 1719, when he was gazetted Steward of the Household. The terms offered to Argyll were not generous, for he was to be excluded from Scottish affairs. The fact that the ministry could impose such conditions implied great confidence; that Argyll accepted them is a further tribute to their strength. The defection of Argyll was a blow to the opposition, for he materially strengthened the ministry both in the Lords and Commons.

Another bold move by the government was less successful. Stanhope and Sunderland realized that their ministry was not as strong as it might be in the House of Lords; furthermore the German faction at Court had strengthened its interest by exploiting its influence with the King to secure peerages for its friends. They both wished to see this stopped. By some means they had persuaded the King, without the Germans knowing, to accept a limitation of his prerogative

[1] W. Michael, *Quadruple Alliance*, 56.

of creating peers. In future, creations were to be limited to replacements of peerages which had become extinct. It may have been easy to obtain the King's consent because throughout Europe nobility was defined far more rigidly than in England, where the aristocracy had never become a closed caste; indeed the majority of peerages had been created since the Restoration. George I with his European outlook can only have deplored the fact, which may have encouraged him to support the measure. The Duke of Somerset introduced the Peerage Bill in the Lords on 28 February 1719; immediately it aroused strong passions. The opposition naturally disliked a Bill which was to abolish the sixteen representative Scottish peers and replace them by twenty-five hereditary ones, chosen by the ministry, for this could only mean twenty-five certain ministerial votes instead of sixteen. But supporters of the government did not like it either, nor did the public at large, which immediately imagined that it was to be governed by a tyrannous aristocracy. Wisely Stanhope allowed the project to drop, and the Bill never reached the Commons.

Stanhope handled his foreign policy more successfully. In the previous summer the English fleet, under Byng, defeated the Spanish fleet at Passaro; this battle had taken place even though the countries were not formally at war. It was a preventive action, fought to stop Spain from seizing Sicily, contrary to the Treaty of Utrecht. Since Passaro Stanhope had tried his utmost to avert war and bring Spain to an accommodation; but by the time Parliament met the Spanish Ambassador had packed his bags and quitted St James's. War seemed merely a matter of weeks. The King alone might declare war but Parliament provided the money, and Stanhope therefore devoted most of the King's Speech to the development of relations with Spain and a demand for adequate supplies for the forthcoming war. The dissident whigs attacked his policy with the utmost vigour. Orford, Walpole's old patron, accused Byng of violating the law of nations; Townshend pleaded time and time again for moderation and negotiation. In the Commons, Walpole was equally vehement; he used the same arguments as Orford had in denouncing Byng's action at Passaro; ministerial incompetence had led to this war—and here he jibed at Stanhope's fruitless mission to Madrid—and now Parliament was asked to pay for the folly of the King's servants. But in these denunciations of Stanhope's policy there was the ring of sincerity, or at least of potential sincerity. For the rest of his life Walpole was to try to prevent war with Spain. Nevertheless Walpole's diatribes availed little, the ministry obtained the Address which it wanted and the supplies which it needed. When Walpole packed up for his summer jaunt to Norfolk he could not look back on the past year with much satisfaction.

5

TWO YEARS' opposition had made little impression on the ministry. The King remained estranged from the Prince; there were no signs that the government were unduly worried by the united opposition of tories and dissatisfied whigs. Parliament had done the King's business; Stanhope had been forced to modify his programme of full religious toleration. Yet it is doubtful whether he ever expected it to be successful. So long as the ministry continued to enjoy the King's confidence there was no reason at all why Stanhope should not remain in power and Walpole be excluded from it.

Walpole left London early in May. His stately cavalcade made its way through Epping Forest, and then along the chalk ridges covered with young corn to the lonely brecks of Norfolk. The journey took him three days, with two nights on the road, and he had time enough to think over his position. It was not easy. He had grown out of the way of life of a simple Norfolk gentleman. He was a great man and lived like one. Each summer the party which he took with him to Norfolk had grown larger; now he had a chef, Solomon Sollis; a butler, Grantham; his personal footman, Harry Yardley; his steward of the household, Edward Jenkins. Wherever he went they travelled with him—Norfolk cooks and Norfolk servants were no longer good enough for his fashionable existence.[1] The loss of office seems to have made little difference to his personal expenditure. The masons and carpenters were busy that year in the old house at Houghton; considerable sums were being spent on the garden at Chelsea; jewellery, snuff-boxes, silver dishes, fine clothes; wine in ever-increasing quantities; the best Bohea tea for the boys at Eton; pictures painted by Richardson; loans and subscriptions to Heidegger and the opera; the account books read as if there had been no change in Walpole's fortune. He was investing astutely—he had managed to secure a share of £1,000 in the first Assiento voyage in 1717; he was buying and selling East India stock and making a good profit; dabbling with success in tallies and annuities. But he was selling far more than he was buying, and his capital, made as Paymaster, was slowly wasting away.[2] Another two or three years of opposition would reduce him to desperate straits. He could not continue to live as he did without office; to sell his houses and return to the simple life of an independent country gentleman was to acknowledge defeat. To give up the splendour with which he surrounded himself would be tantamount to giving up his ambition. In his world wealth was power; yet his wealth, expressed so vividly, rested as yet on slender foundations.

Back in Norfolk he farmed his estates, discharged his servants' accounts, settled the bills in Lynn; entered his rents and his tenants' debts in the great ledger, which was marked in his own hand '*Noli me tangere*'. He acted his part as justice of the peace, rode to his neighbours and brought them in to Houghton to taste his fine hogan. He talked with them of hounds and horses, hunted with them across the heaths, chasing either the hare or fox. The gentlemen of Lynn were

---

[1] *C(H) MSS*, Account Books and Vouchers, various dates: Sollis was taken into Walpole's employment in 1714. French chefs were just becoming highly fashionable. Sollis's first visit to Houghton was in 1718, after which he always went with Walpole. Sollis was allowed £15 per week for purchases of food other than that bought in bulk.

[2] *Ibid.*, particularly Account Book 20A.

royally entertained; haunches of venison were dispatched with judicious care. Everywhere he went there was talk of harvests, rents, taxes and war. The great man was eagerly listened to; the great man eager to please. And so the summer days passed amidst the scenes of his childhood in the great house where so many of his ancestors had lived and died. But there must have been closer, less expansive conclaves, when he sat with Townshend in the small high-ceilinged library at Raynham and argued their future policy. They badly needed a victory, a public and resounding victory; only with that could they hope to get back into office on reasonable terms. Both of them were shrewd enough to know that the longer Stanhope and Sunderland survived, the more powerful they would become. Their weakness was in the House of Lords; yet even there time was bound to help them, for bishops were neutral and the bench, twenty-six strong, could be a decisive factor.[1] And there were deeper causes for gloom. Foreign policy was being well handled—the alliance against Spain was popular in the City which hoped for increased trading concessions in the event of a successful war. But even more depressing for Walpole and Townshend was the financial buoyancy of the government; stocks were high, the South Sea Company a success. These were uncomfortable factors in their situation, but there were others, more cheerful to contemplate as they tasted their claret in the warm afternoon. London society was small and power at Court its favourite topic, so that rumours ran fast; and, of course, Walpole and Townshend were not without their own channels to St James's[2] where the situation was uneasy enough to give them grounds for hope; and hope is never far from the politician's heart, eager to spring up on the flimsiest pretext.

The trouble was the Germans. They had always been the trouble. Unfortunately the evidence of their activities comes either from prejudiced sources or from ambassadorial re-

[1] In 1718 Stanhope and Sunderland had strengthened themselves in the Lords by the appointment of two new bishops, at Carlisle and Peterborough.

[2] The French Foreign Office thought that Bothmer had secret contacts with Walpole. *Arch. Aff. Etr. Corr. Angl.*, 323.

ports which are little better as they are based largely on gossip. Lady Cowper would have it believed that Bernstorff, Bothmer, Robethon and the rest were little better than brokers selling honours and offices to the highest bidder. Pendtenriedter, the Austrian Ambassador, however, had the highest opinion of Bernstorff's integrity and regarded him as being in effect the King's first servant both for German and English affairs, and much the ablest. But neither rumour did the Germans much good; and there was probably substance in both, certainly the latter, for it was natural that the King should rely upon men whom he had trusted for most of his life. It was just as natural, but no less maddening to his English ministers, that the Germans should try to put Hanoverian interests first and that in order to do so they should keep the initiative in the complicated diplomatic negotiations, which the affairs of Europe entailed, in their own hands. A *gaffe* of the Danes had made it quite clear to Stanhope that he had not been fully in the King's confidence in regard to Northern affairs. Nor was this an isolated case, and the warmth of the alliance between himself and Sunderland on the one hand and the Germans on the other which had been fostered by the need to dish Walpole and Townshend in 1716 had steadily cooled. By the end of 1718, London was full of rumours of the conflict at St James's between the two groups. In the ministry itself there were men who were willing to exploit the growing hostility of the two factions for their own ends; in such troubled waters Walpole and Townshend were expert fishermen.[1]

Had they known the secret designs which Sunderland and Stanhope were concocting in Hanover, their spirits would have risen far higher. Both the ministers were determined on three measures for the new session of Parliament, which they considered to be absolutely necessary if they were to secure themselves against future contingencies. They had, of course, two major fears: that George I would turn against them, or that he would die, in which case they could expect little

---

[1] W. Michael, *Quadruple Alliance*, Chapter XII.

mercy. Their need, therefore, was to obtain so secure a hold on both Houses of Parliament that even a combination of the Germans plus dissatisfied whigs, plus tories, would be helpless against them and that their hold on the nobility would be so great that the Prince on becoming King would be unable to secure sufficient men to serve him without using their faction. It was most unlikely that they could ever achieve their purpose, yet this did not deter them. Both men were rash, wildly ambitious, and apprehensive of the future. They thought that they could achieve their end by four measures. The Peerage Bill had appealed to the nobility: no body of men with special privileges is averse from locking others out. The advantages of this measure to Stanhope and Sunderland were very great; twenty-five new Scots peers, six new English ones would give them an overwhelming majority in the Lords, whilst the inability of any new ministry to alter its composition by new creations gave them security for the future.[1] Such security was bound to breed a more independent attitude amongst the peerage, and make it far less easy for the Prince and his friends to get their own way in the event of his succeeding his father. Indeed it was the argument that this measure would hamstring the Prince, which made the King view this diminution of his own prerogative so favourably. The outcry against the Bill had been very loud, fanned by Walpole, who had written two very trenchant pamphlets, the best probably of his career; but outcries did not matter much in eighteenth-century politics. Stanhope thought the time would never be more opportune for such a measure since the King was so determined on it. 'When Your Grace shall see our good master you will learn from himself,' he wrote to Newcastle on 27 October 1719, 'how much he has at heart not to be baffled a second time in this matter.'[2]

---

[1] E. R. Turner, 'The Peerage Bill of 1719', *EHR* (1913), XXVIII, 243–59. The sixteen representative Scots peers were to remain in the House of Lords. The additional nine Scots peers were to be Hamilton, Queesnberry, Buccleuch, Douglas, Atholl, Tweeddale, Morton, Murray, Marchmont. *Blenheim MSS*, D. II, 10.

[2] BM *Add MSS* 32686, fo. 156.

Their position in the Commons was less secure than in the Lords, although ultimately the Commons were less dangerous, for they exerted little influence at Court and usually they could be managed. But it was natural that they should wish to strengthen themselves and they could conceive of no measure more calculated to do so than to abolish the Septennial Act and so revert to parliaments without any time limit. Stanhope thought that the security of tenure so created would make the Commons more complaisant towards the changes to be made in the peerage and more eager to belong to the majority which was likely to be the recipient of favours in perpetuity.

To weaken the tories in order both to prevent their revival and to render them ineffectual allies of the whigs, the Universities, which Stanhope regarded as forcing grounds of tory opinion, were to be drastically reformed. Grateful Lords, compliant Commons, a devoted City and a subservient Church, all to be accomplished in one glorious session; intoxicating thought! Sunderland's and Stanhope's letters to Newcastle bubble with optimism. It all seemed so easy at Hanover; in London the difficulties were more apparent. Newcastle's anxiety-ridden temperament, trapped in thickets of detail, could never rise to conceptions so bold and grandiose as these, yet he was more in touch with reality and had a far more accurate sense of what was both possible and desirable. Throughout his long life Newcastle found decisions desperately difficult to take but he had no doubt of the folly of attempting to repeal the Septennial Act. 'We shall lose much more by it than we can possibly get,' he wrote to Stanhope, for he realized that security of tenure would be more likely to breed ill-humour and dissatisfaction than quieten them. Discipline was better achieved by well-managed elections. His arguments convinced the ministers and the project was dropped. But even Newcastle was convinced that the rest of the programme would lead to the final discomfiture of Walpole and his friends whom he considered 'the most virulent kind of men, the most abandon'd to all pretence of principle . . .'.[1]

---

[1] Newcastle to Stanhope, 10 August 1719. BM *Add MSS* 32686, fo. 137.

Stanhope and Sunderland realized, of course, that the Peerage Bill would not be easy to get through the Commons, since the public outcry, led by Walpole in the spring, had been loud and long. And there was bound to be trouble from Scotland, where the majority of the peerage was unlikely to view with complacency its complete exclusion from affairs. Great secrecy was, therefore, maintained about the project and rumours only began to run about London as the members rode up for the opening of the session on 23 November 1719. The King recommended the Bill in his Speech and within a week it had passed through all of its stages in the Lords and been sent down to the Commons. The ministry hoped to catch the Commons below strength; independent members with no prospects were never in a hurry to leave their country houses for the discomforts of London lodgings. So opportune was the moment which the ministry had chosen that many of the leaders of the dissident whigs, who met at Devonshire House to discuss the measure, felt that it was hopeless to oppose it.[1] There were also some others who did not view the measure with real disapproval although, of course, willing to take any course that was likely to embarrass the Court. But Walpole was adamant. He had never been more convinced of the folly of any measure and he thought it the best opportunity they had ever had of winning over all the independent country gentlemen, even those who usually supported the ministry.

'He was sure,' he told them, 'he could put it in such a light as to fire with indignation at it every independent commoner in England; and that he saw a spirit rising against it among some of the warmest of the whigs that were country gentlemen, and not in other things averse to the Administration. That the first discovery of this to him was from what he overheard one Mr. —— member for —— say upon it, a plain country gentleman of about eight hundred pounds a year of a rank equal only to that and with no expectations or views to himself beyond what

---

[1] The account of the Devonshire House meeting is in HMC, *Onslow MSS*, 458-9.

his condition at that time gave him. But this person talking with another member about this Bill, he said with heat and some oaths (which was what Mr. Walpole overheard and catched at)—"What, shall I consent to the shutting the door upon my family ever coming into the House of Lords!" This Mr. Walpole told the company struck him with conviction, that the same sentiment might easily be made to run through the whole body of country gentlemen, be their estates than what they would.'[1]

He declared with great heat and force that do what they would he was absolutely determined to oppose the measure. In the end he carried them with him. The ministry were unable to rush the measure through the Commons and it was not until 8 December that the debate for its committal took place, by which time the vast majority of members had reached London.

It was a great debate. The House was packed and the excitement of the occasion quickened the atmosphere. The measure itself raised fundamental constitutional principles, sufficient in themselves to create an air of tension; but more than the fate of the Bill depended on this debate. Success for Walpole would not necessarily mean his return to office; so long as Stanhope and Sunderland enjoyed the full confidence of the King there was little hope of that. But it would improve his chances, for the King's intimate advisers might begin to doubt the ministry's capacity to do his business. Victory for the ministry, however, could blast Walpole's hopes of ever getting back into office, so that there was an undercurrent of personal drama to the debate, and this heightened its quality. Young Craggs opened for the government; it was his first great occasion. He knew it, and made the most of it, although he personally was opposed to the measure. He dwelt upon the abuse to which the King's prerogative of making peers had been subject, stressing particularly the creation of twelve by the tories to carry the Treaty of Utrecht, and he praised the magnanimity of the King in permitting the measure: 'That it was only in the reigns of

[1] HMC, *Onslow MSS*, 458-9.

good princes, that legislators had opportunities to remedy and amend the defects to which all human institutions are subject: and that, if the present occasion of rectifying that apparent flaw in our constitution were lost, it might, perhaps, never be retrieved.'[1] The appeal to old rancours, the urgency of 'now or never' were admirably used to allay fears and stampede a decision. Steele, who had played a leading part in dissident whig propaganda of the previous spring, put forward the obvious arguments against the Bill—that it was a violation of the Union with Scotland and that it would lead England into an aristocratic oligarchy which would hold both the King and Commons prisoners. The run of the debate went with Steele rather than Craggs and by the time Walpole rose to speak few could have any doubt as to the outcome of the debate. Perhaps the knowledge of a certain victory gave him that extra elation which made his speech one of the best of his life. Men who were in Parliament at that time told Onslow that his performance 'was very great, and had as much of natural eloquence and of genius in it as had been heard by any of the audience within these walls'.[2] Directed principally to bringing over any of the country gentlemen who were still wavering, his speech contained both more imagery and more sentiment than his usual practice, but they were singularly apt. 'That among the Romans, the wisest people upon earth,' he said, 'the Temple of Fame was placed behind the Temple of Virtue, to denote that there was no coming to the former, without going through the other. But that if this Bill passed into a law one of the most powerful incentives to virtue would be taken away, since there would be no coming to honour but through the winding sheet of an old decrepit lord, and the grave of an extinct noble family.'[3]

Indeed Walpole played admirably on the secret ambitions of men and their jealousy of power. The ineptitude of the

[1] *Chandler*, VI, 211; Onslow, *op. cit.*, 459. Chandler's sequence of speakers cannot be regarded as chronological; Onslow implies that Craggs opened the debate.

[2] *Ibid.*

[3] *Ibid.*; HMC., *Onslow MSS*, 459.

ministerial policy was dramatically demonstrated in the lobbies—the government mustered one hundred and seventy-seven votes, the opposition two hundred and sixty-nine. It was a splendid victory for Walpole and Townshend and throughout the Christmas season neither London nor the provinces could talk of anything else. Yet it did not ruin the ministry; they neither resigned nor were asked to resign. If the King continued to give them firm support such a defeat would in no way endanger them. The loss of the Bill was not in itself important; the real danger for Stanhope and Sunderland lay in what their enemies could make of their defeat at Court.

It was too good an opportunity to miss; the opponents of the ministry made what capital they could out of its blunders, but there were many politicians far less intransigent than Walpole or Townshend who made up their minds that this ministry ought not to continue, and naturally they exerted what influence they could muster. The King's German ministers were assailed with advice to tender to the King privately, of which this letter from Cowper, the former Lord Chancellor, is an admirable example. Cowper, although a close associate of Walpole, had a great reputation for independence, hence his views were bound to carry great weight with Bernstorff. He wrote as follows on 9 December 1719:

'As I would not do myself the honour of waiting on you while the Bill was depending, that you might not be hurt by the false suggestions of malice, so now it is over, I will not venture to ask that liberty, till you are pleased to think it prudent. But I beg upon this occasion I may be allowed in this manner to observe to you this further instance that happened yesterday to prove what I have always suggested to you. They are by no means men of good judgement, nor capable if they had but their dues of above a third, or at most a second, rate station in business. The last session showed them mistaken in everything, but making a mere course [?], as the necessary supplyes are in so good a Parliament, and to engage their Master so far this session in a project that fell of itself the latter end of the last is an inexcusable folly[1] Ther is no doubt, they must have suggested that the King, yeilding part with his prerogative in that point, would be a most popular act. What then must His Majesty think either of their sincerity or their judgment when he finds that this popular act would not be accepted by the representations of the people though enforced by the power of the Crown to make it pass. No doubt all arts will be used to divert His Majesty's eyes from the true causes of this disappointment: but when all is said, it has been affected principally by his Majesty's true and most disinterested friends, who thought him abused in the schemes and choose rather to have no power but that of saving him from dangerous attempts rather than acquire or support it by keeping up divisions in the Royal Family. I have more than ordinary reasons to be concerned at the weakness occasioned by that breach, having served the Crown in capital cases by which I shall be exposed to revenge in case of a Re-revolution. Pray God strengthen your hands for the good of the King and Kingdom, that your prudence may yet temper the rashness of some people; for indeed, Sir, if we are wholly left to their advice, I easily foresee what will be my lot in the common calamity.

Give me leave, Sir, just to mention that as much as I am for reforming the schools and universities: I think this miscarriage has made it at this time unseasonable to venture a second defeat: though for aught I know, rage with too great a degree of natural heat may forthwith undertake it. Methinks our good Master may excuse himself at least during this one session from going into any more projects on the credit of their judgments.'[2]

There were many who thought as Cowper did and there was one factor in this entangled situation which strongly increased the importance of their criticism. Sunderland, Stanhope and Craggs had aimed to destroy the German influence. They had made no secret of this. The attack on Cadogan, the closest ally of the Germans, had been solely for the purpose

[1] i.e., The Peerage Bill.
[2] Herts RO, *Panshanger MSS*, C.1, 12(5). No addressee is given but it is obvious that it is written to someone who can give the King advice behind the ministry's back; therefore Bernstorff or Bothmer were the most likely recipients.

of weakening them. Their policy for this Parliament had the avowed intention of making the ministry as safe as possible not only from the dissident whigs and the Prince but from the Germans. Bernstorff, Bothmer and the rest were well aware of these schemes and did not like them. The Duchess of Munster had been careful to keep in touch with Walpole. A rapprochement between the King's personal friends and the dissident whigs seemed to many a strong possibility so that when a scheme for such a union came to light no one questioned its truth.

The circumstances, however, were mysterious and odd. In April 1720 Sunderland was given what purported to be 'an extract of a project sent by Count Bernsdorff to Count Sinzendorf'. But the original does not exist amongst the papers of the Austrian Chancellery at Vienna.[1] No sooner had Sunderland received the information than the scheme became readily available in London. The French Ambassador obtained a copy of it; so did Townshend; so did the Earl of Oxford.[2] No doubt there were plenty of other copies circulating which have failed to survive. It is curious that a private communication of Bernstorff's to the Imperial Vice-Chancellor should have been so easy to secure, for his letters would not pass through the usual channels. Had they done so their contents would have been privately available to the ministers because their underlings in the Post Office would have intercepted them and taken copies. And the communication itself is rather curious:

'The disgusted whiggs,' it begins, 'have endevoured to convince his Majesty that the Cabal designe to alter the Constitution, to destroy the present establishment and the Quadruple Alliance, which was formed for the security of both, but it seems now they intend that allians[e] only to secure themselves in their places, the better to enable them to run the nation into an aristocracy as appears by the frame of the South Sea Bill.

---

[1] W. Michael, *Quadruple Alliance*, 303. Michael assumes that the original is lost.
[2] *Arch. Aff. Etr. Corr. Angl.*, 31 (29 April 1720). HMC, *Townshend MSS*, 104-6; HMC, *Portland MSS*, V, 594; *SP Dom*, 21 (43). Sunderland's copy is at Blenheim, D.II, 10.

That the Cabal designe to amuse his Majesty with a peace in the South in the same manner as they have done that of the North, but in the end will order it so as to establish themselves, and be able for the future to give laws to the King and his son, and even to remove him when they shall think proper.'

And then it goes on to outline what Walpole and Townshend had offered in foreign affairs, including money for Augustus of Saxony in order to make the Polish Crown hereditary and the even stranger proposal of buying territory in Germany for George I to strengthen his position in Northern affairs 'which would enable him to hold the ballance between the Northern powers better than by sending a fleet yearly to Baltick which gives umbrage to the people'. The King cannot delay long in giving attention to this scheme: Bernstorff and his friends realize that there is a necessity for a change of ministers. And finally he hopes that the ministerial designs 'will be brought to light and the eyes of the People will be opened, which will give the King an opportunity to part with them with honour and reputation to himself'. A list of the new ministry follows in which Walpole is designated Chancellor of the Exchequer and Townshend Paymaster-General of the Forces. Sunderland was to be packed off to Ireland as Lord-Lieutenant and Stanhope given the choice of becoming Lord Privy Seal or General of the Horse. The whole list is a nicely balanced combination of bribe and threat. 'There will be room left for 5 or 6 of the leading country tories to come in for the rest of the places and in case they refuse the other country gentlemen of god esteame and estates, that will accept of the Kings favours.' Now this reads much more like a manifesto than a private communication, and it makes much more sense if considered as a forcing bid. It indicated to Sunderland and Stanhope that the whigs in opposition were willing to outbid them in foreign affairs in order to secure the King and his Germans. Their willingness to join with tories and independents was intended to counterbalance the ministry's own secret negotiations with the tories. And finally there was the skilful move to divide Sunderland and Stanhope; lucrative exile for one whilst the other was offered the choice of co-operating with Townshend and Walpole or quitting political life. It seems highly likely that this document was intended for Sunderland and Stanhope, a deliberate leakage engineered by Walpole or Townshend in the hope of bringing them to terms. Subsequent events strongly confirm this view which if true turns this incident into one of the most dexterous of political manoeuvres, and timed to perfection.

Sunderland was convinced of the document's authenticity and was deeply perturbed. He went into conference at once with Stanhope and Craggs. They hated the Germans and they loved office. There was only one way of gratifying their emotions, although it took them three days to bring themselves to it, and that was reconciliation with Townshend and Walpole.

6

AT THIS point the sources of information about Walpole are suddenly enriched by the diary kept by Mary Countess Cowper, a lady-in-waiting to the Princess of Wales and wife of the Lord Chancellor who had quitted office after the Prince's quarrel.[1] Lady Cowper wrote to ease her heart, to ease it of the fury and rage which she felt towards Walpole, Townshend, Sunderland and even the Princess. She was a clever, ambitious woman, and a vain one. Her expectations rose very high. She saw herself as Mistress of the Robes to the Princess or as Governess of the Royal children. She lacked humour and all sense of reality. When the Princess, perhaps to gratify her vanity and soothe her unquiet spirit, mentioned the way the King had looked at her, she virtuously declined the prospect of becoming his mistress. She was as passionately attached to her husband's career as her own, and when he was scarcely consulted about the reconciliation and offered

---

[1] Spencer Cowper, *Diary of Mary Countess Cowper, 1714–20,* 2nd ed. (1865). Cf. p. 220. For a short but wise account of this crisis see also C. B. Realey, *The Early Opposition to Sir Robert Walpole* (Kansas, 1931), 4–6.

no place, her resentment was doubled. In the end she angrily packed her bags and followed her husband into voluntary exile at Cole Green, their country place in Hertfordshire. Her diary is not easy to use but the infuriated and prejudiced eye often sees clearly if not charitably; unfortunately she swallowed rumours wholesale and believed everything that she heard to the detriment of her enemies. Nevertheless she gives a glimpse of Walpole at work in the heart of a political crisis—the only really intimate view that we possess[1] until Lord Hervey takes up his pen in the 1730s.

'Walpole was every day this winter once, if not twice, at Leicester House,' wrote Lady Cowper. His influence with the Princess had steadily grown; it was the beginning of a long and enduring friendship. He was quick to realize that Caroline was a woman of real intellectual force who longed for power, that her husband loved her from the heart, that she cherished him with a cynical amused affection, that her coolness and her cleverness gave her the ascendancy in this strange marriage. 'Walpole let the Prince lye with his wife which both he and the Princess knew.'[2] A spiteful, jealous hit of Lady Cowper's? Perhaps, but it could be true, for both Walpole and Caroline were made of very human fibre; and in their own relationship there was a freedom, an intimacy and an exhilaration which were almost amorous in their intensity. Whenever Walpole arrived, Caroline saw him at once; together they concocted plans to lead the Prince; she was ready for sacrifices so that Walpole should succeed, even agreeing to let the King retain her children. And when Hervey's *Memoirs* illuminate their relationship twelve years later it is still the same. Their temperaments matched like two leaves from the same twig, and in this crisis they found each other. They both had their worlds to conquer; neither was squeamish and their tolerance in sexual matters at least matched that of their times.

---

[1] Lady Cowper, *Diary*, 134.
[2] *Ibid.*, 134. In the printed version 'lye' was changed by the editor to 'intrigue'.

The firm friendship of the Princess was Walpole's strongest weapon. He had been equally adroit with the Duchess of Munster, now Duchess of Kendal, an English title given to her by Sunderland and Stanhope to wean her from the German faction, a title for which she had yearned for many years past. Throughout his opposition Walpole kept a channel open to the Duchess. He considered her 'as much Queen of England as ever any was'; and he 'did everything by her'.[1] Her role was to bring the King to reason and at the same time prevent his consulting his German friends; a difficult task as the latter was against her natural inclinations, but one in which Walpole was successful—very largely because of what was offered, and because also of the Duchess's own position. She was not the King's sole mistress; *en titre* she might be, but there was also Kielmannsegge[2] with whom she had to share the King, a highly ambitious woman and much younger than the Duchess. Their rivalry naturally drove them to seek support in rival Court factions, and Kielmannsegge was strongly attached to the Germans. Their defeat would be a real humiliation for her, a prospect which the Duchess never failed to enjoy. Also it had to be worth the King's while. He hated his son and had not the least desire to see him back in St James's Palace. But the offer of £600,000 nourished a spark of paternal love and prepared him to listen to reason. That six hundred thousand was more or less in Walpole's gift. It represented the accumulated debt of the Civil List which the government were anxious to see written off by Parliament, but were quite unlikely to do unless Walpole was willing to support the measure. He knew it was a dangerous topic and he knew that his ability to

[1] Lady Cowper, *Diary*, 132.

[2] '... whom I remember by being terrified at her enormous figure, was as corpulent and ample as the Duchess was long and emaciated. Two fierce black eyes, large and rolling beneath two lofty arched eyebrows, two acres of cheeks spread with crimson, an ocean of neck that overflowed and was not distinguished from the lower part of her body. ...' Horace Walpole, *Reminiscences*, ed. Paget Toynbee, 29-30. Her wit and gaiety were much appreciated and she was a force to be reckoned with at Court.

secure it a majority in the Commons was his strongest card with the King and his Duchess. Cowper was very angry when he learnt from Walpole of his part in the negotiations. 'The very thing they engaged in,' he told Walpole, 'was betraying the liberties of the people for what use was limiting the civil list if they could run in debt and have it paid as oft as they would.' Walpole stammered and said: 'Truly it is not quite right.' 'No,' says Lord Cowper, 'for 'tis quite wrong but you of the House of Commons are to look to that, not the House of Lords who have no blame to share with you on that score.'[1] Cowper was shrewd enough to see just exactly where Walpole's power lay yet impotent to do anything but hope for disaster.

Greed secured the King; fear the Prince, who had little to gain from any reconciliation. He loved his Guards though he was not even certain that he could get them back. Both he and his wife adored the princesses even if it seemed unlikely that they would be returned to them. He hated St James's so much with his father there that he flatly refused to return, a concession which Walpole was able to secure easily enough as George I viewed the Prince's presence with equal distaste. It was a concession which Walpole quickly turned into an obligation. Why then did the Prince yield? The Princess wanted the reconciliation, and she did all she could to coax him into it. But fear of the future most probably carried the day. The Prince was told that his servants were ready to desert him for the Government, that the tories were eager to join the ministry, and if they did, they would be willing to act against the Prince.[2] Rumours, not without their roots in reality, were current of the King's desire to separate his Kingdom from his Electorate. A succession which had once been settled by Parliament could be unsettled to the Prince's disadvantage. Under such attacks the Prince's will began to crumble.

With the prospect of a royal reconciliation, Walpole was

[1] Lady Cowper, *Diary*, 132–3.
[2] *Ibid.*

able to negotiate in earnest with Sunderland and Stanhope, who had sent Craggs to him in the early days of April after Bernstorff's project had come so opportunely into their hands. In these negotiations Walpole acted more closely with his old friends; meetings were held regularly at Devonshire House, for the Duke was regarded at least as the titular head of their faction. Their formal business was to draft a letter of submission which they could bring the Prince to sign and the King to accept. The disposition of places was a longer task. At first Walpole insisted that he would not serve with Sunderland, but it quickly became clear that this was bidding too high; so they began the other way round and decided on who was to be removed. This, Lady Cowper thought, was a victory for Sunderland. 'One needs must own,' she wrote, 'Sunderland has the ascendant of these people, and has out-jockeyed Walpole though a Newmarket man.' At the time this was not unperceptive.

The victims for disgrace were chosen from the fringes; Argyll, who had in a sense betrayed the Prince by going over to the Court, and the Duke of Kingston, who had been more outspokenly hostile to the Prince's friends, were to be re-moved, but the principal changes were left until the recon-ciliation was accomplished and the Civil List debts safely paid.

On St George's Day, 23 April 1720, the King, who had been thoroughly bad tempered for days, saw the Prince privately to receive his submission. Lady Cowper's account, derived most probably from the Princess, is admirable.

'. . . The Prince took his chair and went to St James's, where he saw the King in his closet. The Prince made him a short compliment, saying it had been a great grief to him to have been in his displeasure so long; that he was infinitely obliged to H.M. for his permission of waiting upon him, and that he hoped the rest of his life would be such as the King would never have cause to complain of. The King was much dismayed, pale, and could not speak to be heard but by broken sentences, and said several times, "*Votre conduite, votre conduite*''; but the Prince said he could not hear distinctly anything but those words. The Prince went after he had stayed about five minutes in the closet . . . the Prince came back . . . with the Beefeaters round his chair, and hollowing and all marks of joy which could be shown by the multitude. He looked grave, and his eyes are red and swelled, as one has seen him upon other occasions when he is mightily ruffled. He immediately dismissed all the Company, and I was ordered to be there at five in the afternoon.

At five I went, and found the Guards before the door, the Square full of coaches; the rooms full of company; everything gay and laughing; nothing but kissing and wishing of joy; and in short, so different a face of things, nobody could conceive that so much joy should be after so many resolutions never to come to this. . . .'[1]

The next day the dissident whigs returned to Court. Their reception was chilling.

'The whigs of the late cabinet all met at Devonshire House to wait upon the King, as had been agreed the night before at a meeting to settle the ceremonial. The Duke of Devonshire made the King a short speech in the name of the rest (which had been made for him the night before; God having made him a very honest man, but no speechmaker). The King's reply was so low, few of them heard it; those who did, said the main of it was to say he was glad to see them all united. After which they came out of the closet, and then waited on the King to Chapel. The King went to Church a quarter of an hour sooner than usual; the Prince by that was but coming upstairs when the King went in. He followed, but they spoke not to one another nor look at one another all the time, which caused many speculations.

When the King came out, the Prince stood by him. The King spoke to most people except the Prince; they two only looked grave and out of humour.'

Such a reception must have damped even Walpole's ebullient spirits. The situation was very precarious, but he

---

[1] Lady Cowper, *Diary*, 142–3.

had chosen his way and there was no going back. He put the best face possible on his situation, drank hard and deep with Sunderland, Stanhope and Newcastle, showed himself with them, arm in arm, laughing, at both the King's and the Prince's Courts. He flung himself into making this a great triumph for himself, whatever doubts he had in his heart.

And he performed promptly and boldly, not perhaps without a certain effrontery, his duties in the Commons. He settled the problem of the Civil List, profitably for the King, profitably for himself, and with no trouble to the ministry. The King presented the Commons with an address on 4 May 1720, informing them that he had received many petitions from merchants asking him to create by Letters Patent two insurance companies for insuring ships and merchandise, but the King needed 'advice and assistance of the House in matters of this nature and importance. He hopes therefore for their ready concurrence to secure and confirm the privileges his Majesty shall grant to such corporations, and to enable him to discharge the debts of his civil government without burdening his people with any new aid or supply'.[1]

When Sir William Wyndham attempted to raise the question of how the Civil List debts had arisen he was swept aside and an humble address of thanks, seconded by Walpole, was promptly passed. The two following entries in Walpole's account book with Messrs Gibson and Jacombe are not without interest:

'26 April Paid Mr Jacombe the amount of his account of £20,000 Ram's insurance and £4,000 old insurance bought . . . .   £2,550'

'12 May Received of Mr Jacombe the amount of his account of £20,000 Ram's Insurance, & £4,000 old insurance sold £5,162–10–'[2]
This gave Walpole a clear profit of £2,612 10s. in sixteen days. Lady Cowper was, therefore, not speaking entirely

[1] Chandler, VI, 214–5.
[2] C(H) MSS, Account Book, 24, fo. 3.

from malice when she wrote in her diary of this project: 'These bubbles Walpole and Craggs had engaged in. They would hear no other proposals, though others offered double, which these did; and W[alpole] at a meeting of Commons the night before, had openly said to Poult. [Pulteney]: "By God! Sir, I tell you we will hear no proposals, for these shall do."' [1] A glimpse of the Duchess of Kendal's bank-book might be equally revealing!

Indeed, Walpole had played his part admirably; he had secured the reconciliation; he had helped to pilot the awkward Civil List debt through the Commons. His reward came on 11 June 1720, when he was once more gazetted Paymaster-General of the Forces. At the same time Townshend was appointed President of the Council and Paul Methuen Comptroller of the Household; none of their other friends received a major appointment. William Pulteney was bitterly resentful, feeling that Walpole had sacrificed him to save himself, a feeling which was not entirely without justification. Walpole tried to extricate himself by telling Pulteney that the Court had wished to make him a peer, which honour Walpole realized Pulteney could not accept. This was a lame excuse which Pulteney did not believe. Walpole probably spared little thought for Pulteney, yet this slight was to grow and fester in Pulteney's heart until his life was consumed with hatred for Walpole. [2] The trouble was that Walpole had been forced to a hard bargain and it had taken a major effort to get himself and Townshend, let alone anyone else, back into the ministry. Sunderland and Stanhope were still dominant at Court. Walpole had been kept out of the cabinet and the closet; Townshend's office gave him little power. Indeed it looked as if they had been outjockeyed. Why then, after the triumph of the Peerage Bill, were they prepared to accept such niggardly terms? One factor, usually overlooked, was undoubtedly the flourishing state of the South Sea Company.

[1] Lady Cowper, *Diary*, 159.
[2] *An Answer to One Part of a Late Infamous Libel*, 19.

CHAPTER EIGHT

THE BUBBLE, 1720

THE reconciliation of the King and Prince and the re-entry of Walpole and Townshend into the ministry had taken place against a background of mounting public excitement bordering on hysteria. The London money market was caught in a spiral of wild inflation. Few could resist the lure of quick profits. On 23 May 1720, Auditor Harley wrote to his brother the Earl of Oxford: 'The madness of stock-jobbing is inconceivable. This wildness was beyond my thought.'[1] The mania was short-lived, for the rocketing prices could not be maintained; the crash came in August, to be followed by a panic fear of national bankruptcy. These months have been regarded as the turning point in Walpole's career. Historians have praised his wisdom and sagacity for standing aloof from the wild and reckless schemes, secure in his knowledge that he alone could rescue his country from its desperate plight. This view of Walpole's role in the South Sea Bubble was first portrayed by Archdeacon Coxe. 'When the public distress,' he wrote, 'was arrived to a most alarming height, and despair pervaded all ranks of people, to Walpole every eye was directed, as the only person capable of affording assistance, under the pressure of immediate necessity.'[2] Nineteenth-century historians echoed Coxe; Lecky thought that 'his well known financial ability made men turn to him in the hour of distress, as of all statesmen the most fitted to palliate it'.[3] Morley concurred and so did Robertson.[4] And twentieth-century historians have followed so clear and confident a lead without hesitation; all but C. B. Realey, whose

[1] HMC, *Portland MSS*, V, 597.
[2] Coxe, I, 135–6.
[3] W. E. H. Lecky, *History of England in the Eighteenth Century* (4th ed., 1888), I, 324.
[4] J. Morley, *Walpole*, 64; J. M. Robertson, *Bolingbroke and Walpole*, 14.

reassessment of the evidence no one has listened to.[1] Realey thinks that Walpole had great luck and no foresight, but an outstandingly quick capacity to exploit the situation to his own advantage once it had arisen. Although Walpole's actions can be questioned, the result cannot be. By the spring of 1722 Walpole had become the most powerful member of the ministry; for the first time his future began to look really secure. These months, therefore, witnessed one of the great climaxes of his career, and it is essential that the story of the part which he played in the South Sea Bubble should be as accurate as possible, and all the more so as the account in most history books bears so little relation to the truth.

Towards the end of the seventeenth century wars became more widespread and of longer duration; the armies involved became larger and more complex; so their cost grew and grew. The need to keep great armies and navies in being multiplied taxes which led to an increased administration that burdened the national budget. Treasurers and financiers had to think in terms of millions rather than thousands, and had to devise new methods for securing short and long term credit for the governments which they served. Experience of handling great public debts and the newly devised instruments of credit was extremely limited and consequently this provided a happy field of speculation for economists, politicians and cranks. Governments found the greatest difficulty in securing credit or in preventing their credit instruments from being heavily discounted; in time of war—and in these years England was more frequently at war than not—there were also the difficulties of remittance to pay for the large armies and navies maintained abroad. The foundation of the Bank of England had done something to mitigate these difficulties; without it William's wars might easily have collapsed through a lack of credit.[2] But the establishment of the Bank

---

[1] C. B. Realey, *The Early Opposition to Sir Robert Walpole*, 1–67. See Basil Williams, *The Whig Supremacy*, 170; C. Grant Robertson, *England under the Hanoverians* (13th ed.), 40; W. Michael, *Das Zeitalter Walpoles*, 12, 107.

[2] For the foundation of the Bank of England, cf. Sir John Clapham, *The Bank*

of England had bred its own jealousies and difficulties at Court and in the City, for it had alleviated rather than solved the problems of public credit and national debt.

Naturally, through the creation of the Banks its Directors had acquired increased political power; government contracts came their way and they lived to see their friends in charge of the Government. The majority of these Directors were whiggish, not out and out intransigent whigs, but whiggish rather as William III was. They were for the wars, which they thought would increase England's trade; they were strongly protestant, for, after all, their European rivals were prejudiced and persecuting catholics; they had no use for the Stuarts at all, for they were unsound both in foreign affairs and religion. Moreover they wanted stability. Political and social disturbances were bound to lead to a run on the Bank and plunge them into difficulties. They were natural allies of the Court; indeed they saw very much eye to eye with Marlborough and Godolphin and with Walpole when he was in power. Of course they had their enemies. Oxford realized that they were a powerful factor in affairs and he wished to counterbalance them; there were merchants in the City who did not belong to the Bank group and they were pleased to support any scheme which offered them an opportunity of diminishing the Bank Directors' power. It was these political considerations which had led to the foundation of the South Sea Company in 1711.

Unfortunately 'South Sea' Company is a highly misleading name, for trade with the southern seas had little to do with the project at all. It was in essentials a finance company devised to take over a part of the national debt in order to strengthen public credit. Walpole opposed its foundation not because he had any doubts about its efficiency but because it had been Oxford's project and a likely menace to the Bank whose Directors were his friends. Not all the Bank Directors were opposed to the South Sea Company; from its foundation

of England, I, 1694–1797, and for the effect of the shortage of credit on the armed forces, J. Ehrman, *The Navy in the War of William III*, 1689–97.

Sir James Bateman and Sir Theodore Janssen, both Directors of the Bank, played an important part in the Company. Although Bateman left the Bank and became Sub-Governor of the Company, Janssen maintained both his interests.

By 1717 the South Sea Company had achieved an established place in the credit structure of the nation as a rival, and a potentially powerful rival, to the Bank. Political and financial factions naturally fought for the control of these companies. In 1711 the tories attacked the directorship of the Bank in the hope of changing its personnel—a retaliation for its attempt to unseat the tory ministry. In 1718, the Prince's party—alias Walpole's and Townshend's—pushed their candidates in the elections to the South Sea Company directorate with some success.[1] The reason for this thrust must have been the rumours which were already circulating of new schemes to take over the public credit. No financial groups wished to be left out of such a project—nor did the politicians.

They had before them the fantastic success of John Law in France, which seemed to justify the belief, held by many, that the credit resources of the nation had never been fully exploited. Backed by the authority of the State, credit, they thought, was capable of almost infinite expansion. In a few months Law had created a vast financial monopoly. He had created a bank, taken over the entire public debt, secured the monopoly of all foreign trade, and on the strength of this security circulated paper money. The effect had been magical; from the economic doldrums France had passed straight into wild inflationary prosperity. So delusive was Law's sleight of hand that hard-headed Dutch and English financiers were tumbling over themselves to get shares in the Mississippi Company which controlled his venture. Law's success had a twofold effect, but with the same result, on the

[1] HMC, *Portland MSS*, V, 544–5. Edward Harley junior to Abigail Harley 6 February 1718: 'The King's people and Sir George Caswell have lost it for sub- and deputy governors of the South Sea, and those that are reckoned of the Prince's party have carried it, Bateman, etc.' Bateman, however, died on 10 November 1718.

City and the ministry. Sunderland and Stanhope wished to stop the outward flow of capital to France; the City wished to emulate the French success. Law's triumph made it more than ever imperative that something should be done with the public debts.

The first secret negotiations between the ministry and the South Sea Company Directors took place in November 1718.[1] Then the Directors startled the government by offering to take over the entire public debt including that held by the Bank and the East India Company. They aimed at nothing less than the absolute control of the nation's finances. Sunderland and Stanhope realized at once that this could not be undertaken without a vast struggle with the Bank for which they were not prepared. For the next two months negotiations progressed on a less grandiose scheme. This the ministry accepted and it came before the House of Commons on 22 January 1720. At once Walpole opposed it on behalf of the Bank, maintaining that the Bank, which had helped the nation in difficult times, should be allowed to present its own scheme for taking over the debts. This received considerable support and the government acquiesced. The Bank was fully prepared and presented its terms seven days later. They were far more advantageous than those offered by the South Sea Company: they offered two millions more for the privilege of taking over the debts and bound themselves to secure their discharge at an earlier date. This was a strong forcing bid but the ministry secured a delay in order to enable the Company to make yet another offer. They at once took up the challenge and over-bid the Bank by another two millions. Walpole pressed the case of the Bank when both schemes were debated on 1 February 1720, but he could not prevail against Aislabie, the Chancellor of the Exchequer, and the solid ranks of the ministerial supporters.

---

[1] By far the best account of the South Sea Bubble is to be found in W. R. Scott, *The Constitution and Finance of English, Scottish and Irish Joint-Stock Companies to 1720*, III, 288–360. W. Michael, *Das Zeitalter Walpoles*, 13–119, provides a useful summary.

To understand fully what happened in the next few months it is essential to explain what the South Sea scheme implied.

During Marlborough's wars money had to be raised and the government had been forced to accept harsh terms. With peace prosperity had returned, and with prosperity cheap money. Hence the paradox arose of the government paying six per cent on its debts, tied up in long or short term annuities, when the current rate was from four to five per cent. Although some of the more outstanding anomalies had been set right by 1717 by Walpole's scheme of the Sinking Fund, this had only touched a part of the redeemable debt. The South Sea Company now proposed to take over the whole of the remaining debts of the nation, redeemable or irredeemable, upon which it would receive five per cent interest to 1727 and thereafter four per cent. In addition it was willing to pay the State heavily for the privilege of taking over the debts—its final offer, which was accepted, came to £7,134,906 0s. 4¾d.[1] Aislabie maintained that the savings on the reduced interest to be paid on the debt by the government would completely extinguish the national debt in twenty-five years. At first sight this proposal looks like an act of fatuous magnanimity on the part of the Directors. How could they ever hope to recoup, and how could they expect to lure hard-headed business men into converting their high interest-bearing annuities into South Sea Stock at five per cent?

There were several baits. The first and most important was the simple fact that a company with a working capital of forty millions, closely associated with the State, might successfully undertake almost any economic enterprise. No such concentration of capital had been achieved previously in England and this very fact was sufficient to whet the speculative appetite of prudent men. And for those who required a more concrete attraction there was the trade to the South Seas, guaranteed by Utrecht, and confirmed as a monopoly of the Company by the government. True enough, the trade

[1] Scott, III, 306.

had not developed, but it was a prime article of faith in English commercial circles that the Spanish trade would be fabulously profitable. Such were the reasonable grounds for speculation that might have led the most cautious and close-fisted holder of annuities to convert into South Sea Stock.

Unfortunately this is not the whole story. The Bank in its offer had named the ratio of stock it was to give in exchange for the annuities; the South Sea Company, by what must have been a deliberate and criminal neglect, did not. Therefore as the South Sea Stock rose in price, the Company could offer less script to the government bondholders; this created a surplus stock, over and above that required to convert the public debt, and this surplus represented the profit to the Company. So long as the South Sea shares continued to rise, men would be willing to sacrifice a higher yield on their annuities for the sake of immediate capital gains in South Sea Stock. The Directors stimulated the annuity-holders further by offering them advantageous terms in relation to the market price of their stock; for example, at the first conversion the annuitants were offered stock at 375 when the market price was over 400. The future prospects of the Company were entrancing; immediate gains were irresistible; South Sea Stock became the rage and the price soared. The Directors encouraged the rise by every means in their power, honest or dishonest, including an attempt to corner their own markets as well as lending on the security of their own stock. They enjoyed wonderful success; thus the price of their stock advanced astronomically, reaching 1,050 on 24 June; for five weeks it remained very high, hovering between 940 and 990, but during the first few days of August it began to sag ominously. The Directors having unleashed forces which they could not control, their reckless disregard of the simplest forms of financial honesty was about to have its inevitable consequences. Keen draughts, heralding the whirlwind, were blowing through 'Change Alley.

The quick profit made by the South Sea Company had given rise to an orgy of speculation; mushroom companies sprang up overnight for projects sane or insane. On 6 June 1720 the following companies were floated:

	Capital, if known
'Company to carry on a trade from Scotland for importing all manners of naval stores as masts, timber, deal, boards, turpentine, pitch, tar, etc.	£2,000,000
Company for the cotton manufacture in Lancashire.	£2,000,000
Company to trade in hair.	—
Company for settling the Tortugas.	—
Company for the better promoting and increase of American trade, the building of ships and importing of timber.	—
Company for the purchase of estates.	£4,000,000
Company for the supply of all kinds of grass seeds and the changing of seed-corn.'[1]	—

On the next day nineteen further companies, some vague, some sensible, some silly, but all demanding millions of capital, opened their books for subscription. So it went on day after day until 24 June, when the government, thoroughly alarmed, quickly passed the 'Bubble' Act which threatened with *praemunire* any company which acted without a charter. This checked the mushroom growth of companies but not speculation, which was merely diverted to those that could act under a charter; the fertile imagination of avaricious men soon made the charters stretch to cover a variety of economic enterprises, far remote from their original purpose.

Wise men and wise women read the signs of the times. Thomas Guy, reputed the meanest man in England after 'Vulture' Hopkins, sold out in June making the splendid profit of £180,428 with which he founded his hospital.[2] On 12 August 1720 Sarah, Duchess of Marlborough, was sure

---

[1] Scott, III, 452.
[2] H. C. Cameron, *Mr Guy's Hospital*, 29, n. 20.

'that this project must burst in a little while and fall to nothing'. She refused to exchange her annuities and kept her money in the Bank.[1] Auditor Harley called the scheme a 'machine of paper credit supported by imagination',[2] and throughout the summer thought that the nation was bordering on lunacy. He deplored that the child of his brother's invention should develop into such a monster. Other men nursed different fears. The Duke of Wharton was more alarmed by the Company's possible success than frightened by the prospect of its failure. 'The addition of above thirty millions new capital,' he told the House of Lords, 'would give such a vast pride to the South Sea Company as might endanger the liberties of the nation; since by their extensive interest they might influence most, if not all the elections, and consequently overrule the resolutions of the House of Commons.'[3] Lord Cowper thought the scheme was 'contrived for treachery and destruction'.[4]

2

SO MUCH has been said of Walpole's sagacity in these dangerous months that his actions must be subjected to a minute scrutiny. Until he left London towards the end of July 1720, only the following evidence for his opinions and actions is available. References to him in letters and memoirs; one significant letter addressed to him by Nathaniel Gould, a Director of the Bank of England; and, *mirabile dictu*, his account book with Messrs Gibson, Jacob and Jacombe of Lothbury Street, Scriveners and Bankers.[5] After he reached Houghton in August, letters to him, particularly from Jacombe, are plentiful, and his cheques take the place of his bank account, which was balanced on 28 July 1720. Unfor-

---

[1] Mahon, II, app., XCIII–IV, also *Blenheim MSS*, E.15, where she expresses strong distrust of the Company to Sunderland on 11 August 1720.

[2] HMC, *Portland MSS*, V, 599.

[3] Timberland, III, 125. Nevertheless Wharton speculated in South Sea Stock very heavily and lost.

[4] *Ibid.*

[5] *C(H) MSS*, Account Book, 24.

tunately no one has yet traced any of Walpole's own letters for this critical period, which detracts from the certainty, although it adds to the excitement, of the interpretation of his actions and motives.

Walpole's reputation was partly based on his knowledge of finance; every office which he had held had been associated with the Treasury. He was known to be a close associate of the Directors of the Bank of England.[1] It might be expected, therefore, that he would come out strongly, one way or the other, when the scheme was introduced into the Commons on 22 January 1720. He was, at that time, in bitter opposition to the ministry and fresh from his triumphs on the Peerage Bill. This did not happen. A detailed account of the debate, by Thomas Brodrick, a Member of Parliament, exists.[2] After Aislabie had introduced the scheme and Secretary Craggs had congratulated him on his lucidity:

'. . . a profound silence ensued for a full quarter of an hour; every body expecting who would first rise; when the Secretary getting up to make his motion in form, I rose, and was pointed to. I readily agreed with the two gentlemen who had spoake, that till the nationall debt was discharged, or att least in a fair way of being soe, we were not to expect making that figure wee formerly had. I sayd, I could goe farther, making use of the expression of a gentleman (Mr. Hutchyson) whoe told us in a former session, that till this was done, wee could not (properly speaking) call ourselves a nation; that therefore every scheme or proposal tending thereto, ought to be received and considered. But that the occasion of my now speaking was, that the first gentleman who spoake, seemed to mee to recommend the scheme nott onely in opposition, but even exclusively of all others; and that the next had chimed in with him; that I hoped, in order to make the best bargaine wee could, every other company, nay any other society of men might bee att as full liberty to make proposals as the South Sea company, since every gentleman

[1] Coxe, II, 194.

[2] *Ibid.*, II, 182–3. Thomas Brodrick, MP for Stockbridge, was the brother of Lord Midleton, Lord Chancellor of Ireland, to whom he sent this account.

must agree, this to be the likelyest way to make a good bargain for the publique.

Our great men lookt as if thunderstruck, and one of them in particular, turned as pale as my cravate. Uppon this ensued a debate of above two hours. Our ministers (as they might in a committee) spoake again and again; for their auxiliarys proved faint hearted. Mr. Aislaby, in heat, used this unguarded expression; Things of this nature must bee carried on with a *spiritt*; to which Sir Joseph Jekill, with a good deal of warmth, tooke very just exception; this *spiritt*, sayes hee, is what has undone the nation; our businesse is to consider thoroughly, deliberate calmly, and judge of the whole uppon reason, nott with the *spiritt* mentioned. Mr. Aislaby desired to explaine; sayd hee only meant that creditt was to bee soe supported; which caused some smiling. Mr. Walpole applauded the designe, and agreed in general to the reasonablnesse of the scheme, wherein however something wanted amendment, and others (although but few) were unreasonable; but concluded strongly for hearing all, as indeed every body did, three or four onely excepted. Mr. Lechmere answer'd him but little, God wott, to the matter in hand; for quitting that, he fell into invectives against Walpole's former scheme, giving great preferences to this. The town says, the bargaine with the South Sea company was agreed att his chambers, between Mr. Aislaby, Sir George Caswell, and three or four other South Sea-men; since which, they say Mr. Aislaby has bought 27,000 l. stock.

We often observe how far passion carrys men beyond reason, and certainly interest has generally the same effect; for Walpole being irritated, rose again, and began with shewing, by papers in his hand, how very unfairly Letchmere had represented facts, then proceeded to shew his fallacious way of reasoning, and concluded with going more particularly into the scheme, which in severall materiall parts he exposed sufficiently. Letchmere rose up, butt he took time to consider, whilst another had spoke, in order to reply; but this was prevented by the whole committee rising att once, and going into the floor; the chairman tore his throat with "to order, hear your mem-

ber", butt all to no purpose, other than to mortifie Letchmere, by the members crying out, "wee have heard him
long enough".'

The significance of this report lies in this. Walpole entered
the debate late; he only spoke strongly when provoked by his
enemy Lechmere's aspersions on his Sinking Fund arrangements of 1717, but then, as before, he criticized the South
Sea scheme in detail but not in essentials, which he considered reasonable and sound. The proposal which the Bank
made a few days later differed in two important points from
the South Sea scheme but fundamentally the idea was the
same, and similar to Law's, namely, the creation of a huge
financial monopoly in close association with the State, and
trading on its credit. Walpole spoke strongly in favour of the
Bank's scheme, partly because he preferred it in detail and
partly because he was a close friend of the Directors.[1] At no
point in these debates, for which reports exist, did Walpole
attack the whole structure and policy of the South Sea Company as he had done in the Commons at its inception in 1711,
an attack which he and his friends were to inflate into 'fore-
knowledge absolute' later in his career. There can be little
doubt that by 1720 he had come to accept the South Sea
Company as a part of the financial structure of the nation.
He had not opposed the extension in 1713 of the Company's
interest in the public credit and in 1717 he had obtained for
himself a share of £1,000 in the first of the Assiento ships to
sail. His behaviour in these debates was in tune with this
attitude, which is confirmed by what followed. After the
Commons had voted in favour of the South Sea Company,
Walpole did nothing to hinder the passage of the Bill which
was necessary to give the scheme legal form. There was no
rousing of the Commons, no skilful tactical manoeuvres in
committee, no attempt to delay the measure and embarrass
the ministry. This is hardly the behaviour of a man who fore-
saw his country's ruin.

That Walpole was as blind to the full implications of the

[1] Chandler, VI, 213.

South Sea Scheme as most politicians is confirmed by the
letter which Nathaniel Gould sent to him in April.[1] He puts
forward the obvious objections to the failure of the South
Sea Company to fix the ratio of stock for the conversion; the
extravagant sum offered to the government. And he deplored
the behaviour of 'these Projectors who act in concert with the
commands of great stocks, who by resolutions of their own
making, expresses of their own contriving, reports of their
own invention, can raise or sink the price of stock at their
own pleasure, at least whilst the vulgar believe 'em masters
of all arenas'. He could only foresee ruin for hundreds of
families even if the projectors themselves avoided it, and if
they did there was this further danger: 'What I formerly
hinted to you of the S[outh] Sea's getting even all like corporations into their hands is worth your considering. So
much wealth amassed in one body in conjunction with, or in
opposition to, any future ministry may produce events
hitherto unknown or unthought of.' And he concluded: 'I
will trouble you, Sir, but with one thing more. You have
heard me charged with calling this scheme a chimara. 'Tis
true I did so and sorry I am to own myself mistaken. For I
could not beleeve that such a project (at least as it was in
its original design) could ever have made entry into, much
lesse have passed through the place I have seen it do.' This
long self-justifying letter, thoroughly condemnatory of the
project and of Parliament's acceptance of it, cannot have been
written merely to ease Gould's conscience. It is a letter written
to convince, to allay doubts and arguments that have been
expressed about Gould's attitude which can only have been
made by Walpole himself or with his approval. It could never
have been written to a man who hated the scheme lock, stock
and barrel. Easy money, already gained or in prospect, had
bemused Walpole and stilled the voice of criticism; there
were no scruples to overcome. It is time to turn to Walpole's

---

[1] *C(H) MSS*, 18 April 1720. On this letter Coxe has scribbled: 'May it not be
Nathaniel Gould one of the Bank Directors.' This attribution is almost a
certainty.

bank account with Messrs Gibson, Jacob and Jacombe of Lothbury Street.[1]

3

THEY WERE not ordinary bankers, for Robert Jacombe was Under Secretary-at-War, closely associated with the Pay-master-General and Gibson, a scrivener, had affiliations with the Treasury. Robert Jacombe became Walpole's principal deputy for handling the army accounts when he took over the Paymastership on his return to the ministry, but Walpole had banked with him during the period that he was out of office.

In June 1719, Walpole possessed £18,760 7s. in South Sea stock which may have been his own personal fortune, but was more probably old surpluses not yet called in for settlement belonging to his account when Paymaster. On 23 June he sold £6,000; in September another £1,000, but the money from this sale was transferred immediately to Horatio Walpole; a further £2,000 was sold on 27 October. By 1 January 1720, Walpole had reduced the holding which he controlled to £9,760 7s., and knowing that either the Bank or the Company would be bidding for the public debts, he was buying annuities. On 25 January 1720, a further £18,000 was sold for £24,383 15s.: a mysterious transaction as he only possessed stock to the value of £9,760 7s. Twenty-one days later, on 15 February, Walpole received from a Mr Sloper £9,000 in South Sea stock, bearing interest up to Christmas 1719, for which he paid £8,770. This, undoubtedly, provided the stock which Walpole had already sold. The last sale of South Sea stock was that of £760 7s., his remaining holding, at 194½ on 18 March 1720. At that date Walpole had no South Sea stock at all, and he did not again invest in the Company until June 1720.

These investments are interesting in a number of ways. Firstly there is the lack of foresight shown by Walpole. His sales of stock were inopportune. Had he held them for three or four weeks longer, he would have made a vast fortune.

[1] C(H) MSS, Account Book, 24.

Both Thomas Guy and Sarah, Duchess of Marlborough, displayed far greater appreciation of the stock market. There was no compulsion for Walpole to sell since, during this period, Messrs Gibson, Jacob and Jacombe received £16,500 from him. It is true that he wisely invested the proceeds from his South Sea sales in Bank stock, the Royal African Company or Insurance shares, all of which did well. His eagerness to get back into the South Sea's shares in June when they reached their highest price, argues that Walpole felt that he had misjudged the situation. This was the time when hard-headed investors like Guy were getting out. But before turning to Walpole's behaviour in relation to South Sea stock during the summer months, the transactions of January and February need a closer investigation. On 25 January Walpole sold stock which he did not possess; on 15 February, when the price of shares touched 187,[1] he obtained £9,000 worth at slightly below par. During those weeks the directors had been busy issuing stock to members of Parliament and to the ministers who favoured them.[2] Sometimes this stock was sold at par, sometimes it was a fictitious book-entry by which the profit of the sale went to the nominal owner, sometimes the stock was given as a direct bribe.[3] Walpole's transaction might be thought to belong to the first category, but there are difficulties even here. The stock which Walpole received and sold was old stock, whereas all of the bribes which have been traced were in the new stock which the Company were about to offer for sale. There may be a simple explanation of this strange transaction. Sloper had a place at the Treasury: Walpole had been Chancellor of the Exchequer: often the settlement of accounts dragged on for years.[4] The key which could unlock this mystery might well lie hidden in a semi-

[1] Scott, I, 411.

[2] On 6 February 1720, James Craggs senior received from Knight, the South Sea Company's cashier, £30,000 of stock for £25,930. *C(H) MSS*, 88/19.

[3] Scott, III, 314–7. 'The Secret History of the South Sea Scheme' and Report of the Committee of Secrecy, *CJ*, XIX, 425–51, and below.

[4] Sloper had also been in the Paymaster's office during the time Walpole was Paymaster-General.

official arrangement the evidence for which has disappeared, leaving behind treacherous clues all too easily misinterpreted. Nevertheless he received stock at well below market value; his outlay to Sloper of £8,770 netted a profit of £3,691 17s. 6d., including the Christmas dividend of 3 per cent which he drew on it. Furthermore this profit was made without the slightest risk having been incurred by Walpole who had already sold the stock.

These private transactions must now be matched against his public behaviour. He did not spring to his feet when the South Sea Scheme was first introduced in the Commons; usually Walpole was not backward in debate, but on this occasion he allowed a quarter of an hour's silence to elapse; others intervened long before he spoke. When he did address the Commons it was already clear from the drift of the debate that the Bank would be invited to make a bid against the South Sea Company's offer. Walpole stressed in his speech that he saw nothing against the South Sea Scheme in essentials and criticized only its detail. Later he supported the Bank more strongly, but once the decision was taken to accept the Company's offer, his opposition quickly came to an end. His public behaviour and his private transactions might not have been uncorrelated. He had done well out of South Sea stock and his attitude, in consequence, was not intransigent; he was prepared in the circumstances to show a certain benevolence to the Company, although he did not cease to support the Bank. The speed with which he realized his profits implies that he had little faith in the Company's scheme. As the weeks passed, however, he began to lose confidence in his own judgment; by the time that the third subscription of stock was launched in June, Walpole was attempting to obtain a large share in it, although the inflation of South Sea stock had carried it to 1,000. His belief in the capacity of the shares to yield higher profits had become so strong that he was investing for his friends and relations—James Hoste, Sir Charles Turner, William Allen and others.[1] About this time,

[1] C(H) MSS, Account Book, 24; HMC, Ketton MSS, 200.

he was encouraging the Princess of Wales to dabble in the South Sea shares.[1]

By June 1720, Walpole had seen no farther than the majority of his fellow men; there is no evidence whatsoever that he expected a crash to take place, indeed he was eager to re-invest at a time when the shares of the Company were outrageously high. Yet even then Walpole's cautious temperament did not entirely desert him. He limited his own speculation to about £9,000.[2] Nor during these weeks of April and May had he sat by, idly watching the boom; he had invested with great profit to himself in insurance and in the Royal African Company, whose shares experienced an even more rapid rise than those of the South Sea Company. Indeed, the late spring of 1720 witnessed as dramatic a turn in his private fortune as in his public career. He had netted a small fortune—not, however, as historians have thought, by a realistic exploitation of the weaknesses of the South Sea Company's scheme. He made his money by skilful speculation in other stocks and by one transaction which on the present evidence can only be regarded as dubious, even by the standards of his time. It must be stressed, however, that Walpole, contrary to the assertions of most historians, did not see through the South Sea Scheme. He saw no farther and no more clearly than most of his contemporaries.

4

WHEN WALPOLE left London on 28 July 1720, the situation in the stock market was strained and uncertain; the price of South Sea shares had begun to sag but they were still very high; the public at large had every confidence that the ingenuity of the directors would lead to a further spectacular increase in its price. A new subscription was in the offing and there were rumours of a large dividend about to be de-

[1] Lady Cowper, *Diary*, 158.

[2] It is difficult to be exact; applications for stock in the name of Walpole's wife, children and servants can be taken as his own, but, of course, it is possible that some of the investments in the names of his relations or friends also belonged to him.

clared, perhaps as great as 50 per cent, rumours much encouraged by the directors, who were at their wits' end to keep the inflationary curve spiralling upwards. Walpole, however, cannot have expected any dramatic change, otherwise he would not have left London, anxious as he was to get to Norfolk to view the large new estate at Crostwight which he had just bought from Major Le Gros for £21,000. Robert Britiffe, the Norwich attorney, had concluded this purchase after a great deal of difficulty, for as usual, the estate was heavily mortgaged and loaded with life interests so that Major Le Gros and his wife displayed a natural reluctance to sell when prices showed signs of soaring rapidly upwards. Britiffe had been alarmed by learning from another attorney that estates in West Norfolk were being sold at thirty-seven years' purchase, and, as he wrote to Walpole, hoping perhaps to check his keenness to buy: 'At present people make such demands for estates that purchasers must be very sanguine to buy.'[1]

The news that Walpole had entered the land market quickly spread about Norfolk and his post bag filled up with offers great and small. Edward Spelman, a relative of Walpole's through his aunt, wrote that he was willing to negotiate the sale of his estate at Massingham, worth £300 per annum.[2] William Turner reported two small but choice bits of property, entirely enclosed, at Happisburgh, going for a mere twenty and twenty-five years' purchase respectively.[3] Britiffe advised Walpole to buy out Alderman Jonas Rolfe from the lordship of the manor at East Ruston to which the estate at Crostwight paid its dues; he suggested a price at twenty-two years' purchase.[4] Walpole was far more interested in the offer of a large estate at Hickling and Palling belonging to the Calthorpes, with a rent toll of £488 per annum,[5] but he was prepared to buy almost anything which

[1] *C(H) MSS*, R. Britiffe, 18 and 31 July 1720.
[2] *Ibid.*, E. Spelman, 30 July 1720.
[3] *Ibid.*, William Turner, 18 July 1720.
[4] *Ibid.*, R. Britiffe, 10 June 1720.
[5] *Ibid.*, R. Capper, 6 May 1720.

he could lay hands on and he was not very troubled by the price. He boggled at forty years' purchase, but was quite prepared for terms between twenty-five to thirty years which represented a very considerable increase in land values. He expected his attornies to beat down the seller as far as they possibly could, but once resistance was reached then there was to be no hesitation. Although Walpole was still speculating heavily on the Stock Exchange he was furiously eager to get his gains into the solid indestructible fields of Norfolk. Throughout the summer he bought an immense amount of property, more than doubling and possibly trebling his rent roll. Here is a list of the places where he bought land.

Crostwight	North Runcton
Hickling	Stalham
Palling	Massingham
East Ruston	Sloley
Worstead	Brumstead
Stanhoe	Burnham Thorpe[1]

Most of this property lies to the south-east of North Walsham, almost equidistant from Norwich and Great Yarmouth. Walpole's choice of East Norfolk was quite deliberate. The influence of his party in this area was comparatively weak, and needed strengthening. The proximity to two boroughs which returned members to Parliament was another factor of importance. His brother, Horatio, who had recently married the daughter and heiress of Peter Lombard, was also looking for an estate in Norfolk. He considered taking over Lord Londonderry's mortgages on the Paston property in this area, but could not get his money in quickly enough.[2] A year or two later, however, he purchased the Wolterton estate, only a few miles from Crostwight, where Walpole established his son as soon as he was married. The purchase of estates in this part of Norfolk was a political move. By such means they were able to strengthen their hold on the county

---

[1] *C(H) MSS.* Letters for 1720, particularly of Thomas Gibson, Robert Britiffe and John Fowle.

[2] *Ibid.*, Thos. Gibson, 29 October 1720.

vote; from 1720 onwards their influence was also much greater at both Norwich and Yarmouth.

It is difficult to understand why Walpole was in such a hurry to buy land at a time when prices were so high. The myth that he doubled his property in Norfolk when land values crashed with the bursting of the South Sea Bubble is quite untrue. Between April and September 1720, he had either purchased, or had committed himself to purchase, almost all the land he was ever to own in Norfolk. At no time in his life would these farms and estates have cost him so much. There were rumours circulating in London in May that Walpole was about to be ennobled.[1] As the highest honours of the State were rarely granted to commoners, Walpole may easily have wished at this time for a peerage. The ministerial arrangements which had been made were known to be temporary. That Walpole was rapidly equipping himself with the property necessary to support the dignity of a peer would explain the speed with which he acquired land in a seller's market. The bursting of the South Sea Bubble, perhaps, not only gave Walpole a chance of obtaining supreme power but it may also have saved him from the House of Lords.

5

ALTHOUGH WALPOLE was spending money like water, his reserves were sufficiently great to permit him to speculate. Robert Jacombe handled his investments, but he was so apprehensive of the future that he wrote to Walpole every other day to keep him in touch with conditions. The posts were slow, and it took nearly a week for Jacombe to get a reply to a letter, which in the fateful days towards the end of August meant that he had to take decisions for Walpole on his own initiative. Fortunately for Walpole, Jacombe was an exceptionally shrewd man of business. His letters sent to Houghton in the first few days of August betray a lack of faith in the South Sea Company's prospects. 'Our affairs here

[1] HMC, *Portland MSS*, V, 597.

are very dull,' he wrote on 4 August, 'South Sea is under 900 and all the subscriptions are proportionally fallen, and all people begin to be concerned at the falling of the exchange for Holland and the great exportation of gold. We are told that when the present subscription for annuities etc. is over we shall see a great turn in stocks, but I see so many watching to gett out on another rise that I cannot consider they can carry it much longer by any art.'[1]

Each day the situation worsened and the country moved inexorably to the disastrous consequences of its folly. The Bubble Act had effectively quenched the more inane promotions but it had failed to check the rage for speculation. New promotions took cover under the protection of a company which possessed a charter, even though the promotion had little to do with the business pursued by the chartered corporation. The insurance companies—'Onslow and Chetwynd's bubbles' which Walpole had so effectively helped in the Commons—decided to ignore the limits set to their capital by the Act of Parliament which established them and to float a vast new issue. The South Sea Directors were bitterly opposed to these companies, as they drew away good capital which they felt would be better used chasing South Sea stock and keeping its price high. Walpole had a warm sentiment for the insurance companies, and as soon as he had heard of the new issue he had written off to the Chairman of the insurance companies, Sir William Chapman, to make sure that he would receive preferential treatment and be allotted a solid block of shares, which he expected to be oversubscribed.

Sir William Chapman's reply when it came on 19 August made gloomy reading.[2]

16 August 1720

'Dear Sir,

By many continued obligations as well as by inclination I find myself inviolably attached to your service and

---

[1] *C(H) MSS.* Robert Jacombe, 4 Aug 1720.

[2] *C(H)MSS.* Sir William Chapman, 16 Aug 1720. The post took three days from London.

having the honour of your letters have accordingly placed your friends in my list and am desired by Mr Hawes to acquaint you that he shall take care of whatever relates to your self. I cannot omit acquainting you that fresh Bubbles like Hydra heads have multiplied, their shapes have been changed, and have raised their value to hundreds of pounds per centem whereby millions are diverted from the South Sea Company, and thereby the stock meets with a check, but it is our misfortune (of the Insurances) always to incurr from some gentlemen of the South Sea Company a censure in the same nature as the Bubbles, though upon the same Parliamentary foundation, and by inclination as well as by interest their fast friends and ready to concur in any measure (not destructive to our selves) to their advantage. I cannot say the Court of Directors has as yet done any thing as to us, but I hope all things will be prudently managed and that we may be permitted in our little corporation to enjoy our morcell.'

Walpole did not scent danger; he wrote off at once to Jacombe telling him to go straight to the Directors and invest £5,000. By what must have seemed a lucky chance to Walpole, William Allen of Lynn was going up to London that day, and agreed to carry the letter with him to save time. It was not long before Walpole regretted his haste. On 23 August his post-bag contained a letter from Townshend who was up in London, acting as a regent during the King's visit to Hanover. Walpole was expecting the letter, for his sister was about to have a child. He was delighted to read that she had been safely delivered of a girl, but the rest of Townshend's brief note brought ominous news. 'The South Sea,' he wrote, 'has sett us upon the Bubbles which we have near demolished. This, I think from my heart, is a right measure for the publick but very ill taken at Richmond.' Walpole took it no better than the Princess, and for the next few days he was a prey to anxiety until he heard from the wise and cautious Jacombe, who had saved him from the dangers of his importunity by taking matters into his own hands. Jacombe held the money back 'desiring first that you

would consider that this method the two Insurances take of
raising subscriptions *à la mode* South Sea has been complained of to the Regency by the South Sea Company that
thereupon the Regency have interposed to discourage it . . .
it has had so much influence that both the Insurances are
fallen much upon it which induced me to stop till I had your
directions'. He asked Walpole bluntly enough, whether he
wished to be obliged to the Insurance directors for preferential treatment if the matter were to become a parliamentary affair—a singularly pertinent question. But Jacombe
was a far-sighted man and the Insurance companies were not
his only worry. He had grave doubts about the prospects of
the new South Sea subscription, and wanted Walpole to
consider the matter very carefully again before investing.
'However,' Jacombe wrote, 'I have writt to Mr Hawes [a
South Sea Company Director] that he would take care for a
proper reserve for you and your friends. They pretend they
will make no regard to lists yet I am satisfied they will make
a distinction and that you will not be putt to take your fate
with the multitude.' Though Jacombe indicated that he was
willing to risk a little money himself if Walpole decided to
invest, yet he begged to be allowed discretion 'to add or
reduce the list for your own particular. I will doe it according to the best of my judgment as the price of stocks or other
accidents shall make prudent or reasonable'. But the real
object of his thoughts can be judged by his final comment:
'Ready money is a valuable thing.'[1]

But Jacombe was forced to act once more without the
benefit of Walpole's advice. Back in Norfolk he had come to
two important decisions on the basis of the information which
he had; one was to sell out his holding of the third subscription. He had £6,500 invested, and Walpole fixed his price
at £250 advance; the other was to invest, and to encourage
his friends to invest in the new, fourth, subscription of South
Sea stock. He sent his orders to sell on 22 August and Sir
Henry Bedingfield himself took Walpole's subscription list

[1] *C(H) MSS*, Robert Jacombe, 23 August 1720.

to Jacombe on 27 August, so it was probably completed at Houghton on 24 August. All the names on the list but one are lost, but very probably the same people whom Walpole had encouraged to invest in the third subscription were on it—his brothers, his uncles and his friends in London and in Norfolk.[1]

Neither of these decisions was shrewd. In the conditions of the market £250 was an optimistic value to set on the third subscription and Jacombe never had a chance of selling anywhere near it. But to be prepared to invest heavily, and to encourage others to invest in the South Sea Company as late as 24 August 1720, showed either a thirst for a gamble or a lack of common sense or both—at least when conducted from Norfolk. The chronic difficulties of the money market, the unreliability of the antics of the South Sea Directors, had been stressed by Jacombe and Gibson time and time again in the letters which went by every post to Houghton. These decisions must dispel for ever the old legend that Walpole saw through the South Sea Bubble from start to finish and skilfully exploited it to create a large personal fortune. His losses, as we shall see, were not inconsiderable. That they were not larger was due entirely to the actions of Jacombe.

He had been very suspicious of the South Sea Company's attitude towards this new subscription. Previously they had been only too willing to reserve stock for their friends in the ministry and accept their lists without question. On 24 August 1720, Jacombe, with his senior partner, Thomas Gibson, went round to South Sea House to question the Directors about Walpole's list—to inquire whether they would receive it if one arrived from Norfolk. The Directors refused. They had refused to accept any from ministers. Jacombe knew them well enough to realize that this was not a sudden conversion to virtuous stock-jobbing but a desperate attempt 'to make a crowd' at the books.[2] They were terrified that the new sub-

[1] *C(H) MSS*, Robert Jacombe, 25 and 27 August 1720.
[2] *Ibid.*

scription would not be fully subscribed. As well as refusing
lists they were bolstering up the credit of their company by
the wildest measures. On 30 August 1720, they declared their
intention of offering a dividend of 30 per cent for Christmas
1720, and thereafter a guaranteed dividend of 50 per cent
for twelve years, maniac actions which lifted the stock from
750 to 780, albeit only for a few hours. Gibson and Jacombe
held them in great contempt. 'We did not subscribe anything
for ourselves,' Gibson wrote complacently to Compton on
25 August, 'not thinking it worth the bustle.' When Sir
Henry Bedingfield arrived in Lothbury Street with the
packet of Walpole's orders Jacombe was delighted that they
'did not come till 'twas too late to make use of it, for if your
list could have been received, as things are at present you
and your friends would have been sufferers by it'. With the
books closed and the Directors unwilling to take private
lists Walpole was safe. Yet it is very doubtful whether
Jacombe would have invested for him had the books been
open or the Directors willing, though it was obviously a
comfort for Jacombe in dealing with a character so powerful
as Walpole's to be able to shuffle his decision on to ineluctable
circumstance. Walpole's friends were relieved at being saved
from calamity by a hair's breadth and his old drinking and
hunting companion, Charles Churchill, wrote to him full of
gratitude. 'I give you a thousand thanks for your kinde
indeavours and am now glad that we did nothing for since
I have bin offered one att par but would not tutch.'[1]

But Walpole was far from being out of the wood. The first
days of September witnessed a rapid deterioration in the
value of stocks. Although Jacombe had received Walpole's
consent to sell everything, even he did not realize the magnitude of the disaster which was about to overtake the
Company, for he held on to the shares from day to day,
expecting that the unscrupulous ingenuity of the Directors
would give the market a fillip which would enable him to sell
reasonably well. But the Directors' last bid—the declaration

[1] *C(H) MSS*, Charles Churchill, 3 September 1720.

of a 50 per cent dividend guaranteed for twelve years—failed, and by 6 September, Jacombe was quite despondent.

'These two days,' he wrote to Walpole, 'all sorts of stocks have been falling so very fast and there appears such a deadness in all that used to deal in it that I am afraid all opportunities are over.'[1]

Feeling that it was time to summarize the position he set down Walpole's total investment in the South Sea Company for which he and his partner were responsible. £777 per annum in annuities had been converted into stock; on paper it was worth £24,864—but its real value was anyone's guess. Unfortunately Walpole's holding was probably larger than this, for Jacombe speaks of the stock belonging to Walpole with Hawes, a Director of the Company. No record exists of how much Hawes held or whether it was entirely in South Sea stock. For a man who was spending money like water on estates and farms the probable loss of nearly £25,000 must have been a grievous blow, but this was not the whole of the sorry story.[2]

Jacombe and Gibson, wise and cautious as they were, had blundered. £50,000 belonging to Walpole as Paymaster-General had been released to Jacombe at the end of August. He did not like idle money. So on 29 August he made a short-term loan of £18,000 to Sir Cesar Child on the security of £2,500 South Sea stock and £1,000 East India stock.[3] In the early days of September, however, they were not very worried about Child, who was a very rich man, and they were ignorant of the nature of his vast losses, which only became apparent at the end of the month. At this time Jacombe was more concerned for sales which Walpole himself had made, particularly to Lord Hillsborough, who flatly refused to pay the £9,000 which he owed. Hillsborough, already bankrupt, had fled to Newmarket in the hope of

[1] C(H) MSS, Robert Jacombe, 6 and 8 September 1720.

[2] Ibid., 6 September 1720, enclosure headed: 'An Account of Mr Walpole's Annuities.'

[3] Ibid., Robert Jacombe, 30 August 1720: for the rest of the Child story cf. Jacombe's letters for October.

recuperating on horses what he had lost on the shares. He failed. To offset the gloom created by Child and Hillsborough, Selwyn had paid up cheerfully what he owed Walpole.

Nevertheless Walpole's position was grievous and he was faced with the possible loss of over £50,000. This situation demanded his presence in London and on 5 September he informed Jacombe of his intention to leave Norfolk at the end of the following week.[1] By the time he reached London the price of stock had fallen alarmingly. When Gibson and Jacombe waited on him on Monday, 19 September, South Sea Company stock had reached 380, dropping two hundred points in four days.[2] Panic was widespread in London and countless families were faced with bankruptcy and ruin. The holders of the third and fourth subscriptions were in a very desperate condition, for they had pledged themselves to pay £900 or £1,000 for stock now worth under £400, and many of them had no means whatsoever of meeting the calls which would be made upon them. They demanded, naturally enough, in one insistent voice a revision of the terms of their subscription. On the other hand, investors who had bought their shares in the Company's early days—and many, like King's College, Cambridge, had done so and never sold— were bitterly opposed to a reduction of terms, which would waste their Companies' assets. The loss of their paper profits seemed of little importance compared with the loss of capital. But matters had gone too far. The Company's bankers, the curiously named Sword Blade Company, were tottering into bankruptcy, and the Directors of the South Sea knew that their bank would not be able to continue payment much

---

[1] There is no evidence whatsoever that Walpole was recalled from Norfolk as suggested by Coxe, I, 136, who writes: 'he was called from the country, and importuned to use his influence with the governors (i.e. of the Bank).' Walpole decided to leave Houghton either on 4 or 5 September, as soon as he heard of his own serious position from Jacombe. There was no suggestion that the Bank should aid the Company until the middle of September by which time Walpole was in Arlington Street. Walpole's decision was taken before the panic set in.

[2] Scott, III, 326.

longer. So grave a crisis for the country's financial structure could not be ignored.

6

THE AUTUMN of 1720 proved a grievous time for Walpole for, in addition to the anxieties about the South Sea Company, he was amply troubled by the health of his eldest daughter, Catherine. She had been sent to Bath by Sir Hans Sloane to be under the care of Dr Cheyne. He had tried the Bristol waters, but her symptoms had become so alarming that Mrs Bedford, her governess, had hurried her back to Bath. Her condition tended to worsen—she was prone to violent fits, fainting and prolonged sickness—and yet there were times in August and September when she seemed to rally long enough for Walpole to cherish the hope that she might recover. Such hopes were all too quickly extinguished, and Dr Cheyne's letters, which arrived regularly at Chelsea in October and November, described an increasingly deplorable state in which the girl was so tormented by pain that her life became utterly wretched. Even Cheyne, who had lived for many years with chronic invalids, was moved to pity.[1] In the midst of such grief Walpole found it difficult to give his financial affairs the undivided attention which they required. Nevertheless the South Sea Company was in such a desperate plight that even its obstinate and arrogant Directors realized that some action had to be taken to avert disaster, and Walpole had to play his part.

The South Sea Directors asked for help from the Bank on 16 September, before Walpole had arrived in London; they had been reluctant to discuss what they could do, for at the height of their arrogance the South Sea Directors had spurned the Bank and used the Sword Blade Company as their financial agent. The government exerted pressure—the leading conciliator may have been the elder Craggs, at whose house a meeting was held on Monday, 19 September, be-

---

[1] BM, *Sloane MSS*, 4034, ff. 319–36; 4046, f. 6. Catherine's condition steadily grew worse and she died in 1722.

tween the Bank, the Company and the ministry, at which
Walpole was present. At this meeting Walpole played a leading part, for he was one of the few present who still exercised
considerable influence over the Bank Directors. The meeting
proved difficult but Walpole in the end was able to find a
formula which the Bank would accept; the draft in his own
handwriting still exists.[1] South Sea bonds were to be circulated by the Bank, which also agreed to subscribe a part
of its public debt into South Sea stock at 400. Although both
Companies ratified the agreement on 23 September, it was
never implemented. The optimism created by the negotiations, which had lifted the stock to 400, was soon dispelled.
The stock started sagging again on 23 September and
plunged downwards the next day, when the Sword Blade
Company stopped payment; by 29 September its price had
fallen to 190. The Bank's contract to buy at 400 had become
absurd; in any case a number of the Directors were expressing very loudly their doubts as to the legality of the Bank's
aiding the Company without parliamentary sanction—
doubts which were naturally enough immensely influential
at such a time. The intervention of the ministry, and of Walpole, and their attempt to stave off the crisis failed absolutely.
It did not take long for Walpole to realize that any action
was useless and that there was nothing which he could do
either to repair his own fortune or to save the country's
finances. He filled his bags with gold and set out once more
for Houghton to await the return of the King and the recall
of Parliament. Shortly afterwards Townshend followed him
and brought yet more specie for Walpole, who had grasped
the wisdom of one piece of Jacombe's advice, namely 'ready
money is a valuable thing'.[2]

[1] C. B. Realey, *Early Opposition*, takes considerable pains to belittle Walpole's
part in these negotiations. There is no doubt that historians such as Coxe, I, 135,
have greatly exaggerated Walpole's influence and his reputation at this time,
but Realey has gone to the opposite extreme. Walpole's draft of this famous
'contract' is to be found in the records of the Bank of England. Cf. *C(H) MSS*,
88/20, for Coxe's copy.

[2] On 27 September, Walpole drew 1,000 guineas in gold from Gibson &

Walpole had stayed in London little more than ten days. By chance he had arrived at a critical juncture, but his efforts to stem the disaster which had overtaken his country had been quite unavailing. His contribution was small and ineffective. He was disinclined to bother himself further and none of his colleagues seems to have exerted any pressure on him to stay in London. Few eyes at this point seemed turned towards Walpole, and the ministry at least did not expect him to save the country, otherwise they would have kept him with them. Why then did Walpole return so abruptly to Norfolk? The short answer is that there was nothing that he could do in London, and prudence argued withdrawal. The South Sea disaster was the responsibility of the government, which he had only recently joined. The magnitude of this disaster had been impressed on him during his brief stay in London and he must have felt that the less he was seen to be connected with it the better for his reputation. Furthermore, his retirement to Norfolk was a lofty way of dissociating himself from the crisis. Indeed, this withdrawal can be interpreted as a most dexterous move. During his few days in London he demonstrated his influence with the Bank Directors; by so doing he created the illusion of power and purposeful action, even though it had come to nought. His subsequent absence and silence inflated his credit. He could not lose face by being wrong and many came to feel the need for his advice when they could not get it. His return to Norfolk—for which there was no personal necessity[1]—was the most skilful way of drawing attention to himself. This may not have been a conscious motive in Walpole's decision, for politicians are often led unconsciously to take steps which afterwards reek of Machiavellian foresight. Yet it is curious

Jacombe, C(H) MSS, Vouchers, 1720. On 5 October, Walpole wrote for another £1,700 which Jacombe had difficulty in raising, C(H) MSS, Jacombe, October 1720. Walpole treated this sum in gold as a reserve, for he continued to draw on Gibson & Jacombe for his current expenditure.

[1] The business created by his land purchases could be as easily conducted from London as from Norfolk. Thomas Gibson had been engaged on it from his office for most of the summer.

that no sooner had Walpole got back home than his name was on everyone's lips. His post-bag began to fill up with projects for saving the country's credit; Dutchmen, Frenchmen and Englishmen were only too eager to secure his support for their schemes.[1] And when, towards the middle of October, the sober, cautious Jacombe wrote: 'Everybody longs for you in Town, having no hopes from any but yourself,'[2] he was not aiming at flattery but speaking the truth. No better demonstration is needed of the effectiveness of Walpole's withdrawal. But Walpole stayed on in Norfolk, and the clamour for his return grew even stronger. 'They all cry out for you to help them,' Jacombe wrote on 1 November, 'so that when you come, you will have more difficultys on you than ever you had. For though you are perfectly clear of this sad scheme yet you will be prodigiously importuned by all the sufferers to doe more than any man can doe; and more than you in your judgment would think ought to be done, if it could be done.'[3] Of course, he was not the only man in the public mind; many politicians out of office, Thomas Winnington, William Bromley, Matthew Prior and others, confidently expected that the aged Oxford would be called for 'to extricate us out of these difficulties and prevent a relapse'.[4] But Walpole's retreat had been effective both in dissociating himself from the ministry and in calling attention to himself.

7

WALPOLE WAS probably glad to flee from the clamours and distractions of Town to consider by himself or with Townshend what policy they should pursue. The King had been asked to return from Hanover. Parliament was to be recalled and the session could only be stormy; many members

[1] C(H) MSS, Henry van der Esche, 20 October 1720; P. Godfrey, 27 October 1720; unknown Frenchman, 27 October 1720; Thomas Houghton sent a scheme via Mann, ibid., 24 October 1720.

[2] Coxe, II, 193.

[3] C(H) MSS, Robert Jacombe, 1 November 1720.

[4] HMC, Portland MSS, V, 606; Realey, Early Opposition, 10–11; W. Michael, Das Zeitalter Walpoles, 105.

of Parliament had lost heavily; their friends and relations were ruined, or would be ruined if they were forced to find the price which they had pledged themselves to pay for South Sea stock. Walpole knew enough about the dealings of the Company with the ministry and the Court to know that they could not bear close scrutiny. He must have asked himself how he could turn this situation to his own advantage. How could he enhance his own reputation and secure for himself and his friends an increase in place and power? His enemies had blundered: he would have been less than human had he not considered the crisis in relation to his own opportunities. But the decisions would not be easy ones. He could resign and give political leadership to the outcry for retribution which was already arising on all sides. Although some of his own transactions were of a doubtful character he had at least paid for what he had received, and he could have championed the martyrs without undue hypocrisy. But the dubiety of some of his dealings was such that they must have caused him uneasiness at the thought of ruthless exposure of all the Company's dealings. Nor was he built on that heroic scale which thrives on public drama. By instinct Walpole was drawn to the arts of management and the politics of the *couloir*. But management for whom? For Sunderland, for Stanhope, for Aislabie, for Craggs, for men who had done their utmost to wreck his career and keep him from office? The need for revenge lies very deep in the human heart, and no matter how greatly Walpole loathed demagogy there must have been times when his imagination roamed untrammelled, picturing the public disgrace of his enemies, wrought by his own words. The relish and savour of their ignominy must have been hard to resist. But Walpole was born to success, not glorious failure, and at forty-four he had learnt to check a lust for immoderate advantage. And his knowledge of the world of politics for which he lived and breathed was deep enough to make him realize that the citadel of power would still be the King's so long as he continued to sit on the throne. To clamour for the public disgrace of his mistresses and servants was not likely to put the key to it in Walpole's hands. If the turmoil of the times turned to revolution—and for men who had grown up in the seventeenth century such a prospect was far from chimerical —then Walpole's career would stop dead in its tracks. The Jacobites had as little use for him as he for them. Rebellion, renewed civil war, could lead only to his country's ruin. Public need and personal ambition both directed him to a policy of restraint.

Apart from the necessity of deciding the broad lines of action which he and Townshend would take in the coming months there were also practical steps which had to be decided upon. The financial crisis was real and urgent, and required solution. If the South Sea Company's affairs could be retrieved, even on a modest scale by Walpole, his position would be formidably strengthened both with the public and the House of Commons. Before he had time to give this matter much thought he received a proposal from Jacombe to which he was immediately attracted. Jacombe had first tried his ideas out on Townshend, who realized at once their importance.

'When I waited on Lord Townshend,' Jacombe wrote on 11 October 1720,[1] 'he was very pleased to talk with me on what could or ought to be done for the Company. I mentioned a thought of mine that twould be best for the interest of the nation if instead of adding more to the Company, their capital were divided amongst the three great bodys, the Bank, the South Sea and India Companyes thereby making them more equall but upon seperate interests as checks on one another and consequently lesse powerfull and less dangerous to the State. He was pleased with the thought and comanded me to consider how it might be practicable. I promised him to doe so against your return to London. I have since thought more closely of it and doe believe though there are difficultyes yet that it is practicable and advisable. When you come to

[1] C(H) MSS, Robert Jacombe, 11 October 1720. Jacombe had taken Walpole's gold to Townshend on 8 October. Ibid., Robert Jacombe, 8 October 1720.

town I believe I shall be able to lay a short plan of it before you and submitt it to your judgement.'

Walpole, who had great faith in Jacombe's financial ability, and was secure in the knowledge that he was working on the right lines, was able to dismiss technical considerations from his mind in order to concentrate on the more involved and delicate task of assessing the full political implications of the crisis.

Walpole set out from Norfolk about 5 November, by which time he had probably decided on the policy which he was to adopt in the session which had been called. But before turning to the way in which he handled the political crisis which was consequent on the failure of the South Sea scheme, there is another valuable piece of evidence to be derived from Jacombe's letters, which unfortunately come to an end with Walpole's arrival in London.

Walpole's contemporaries, who were immensely cynical about the motives of all politicians, accused him of being the creature of the Bank of England. His policy, they thought, was dictated by the mercenary consideration that he held a vast amount of Bank stock. He could offer harsh and brutal remedies to the sufferers in the South Sea crash because he himself was not involved in its disorders. Such accusations were made repeatedly for the next two years, and intermittently throughout Walpole's life. As late as 1735 the *Craftsman* printed a leader asserting the truth of this accusation in such violent terms that Walpole himself was constrained to reply.[1]

Walpole was certainly friendly with a number of Bank Directors. Nathaniel Gould, who had a great regard for Walpole's ability, told Jacombe on 20 October 1720 that he very much wanted to have a long talk with Walpole about the crisis. Sir John Williams and Sir Peter Delmé, both

---

[1] *An Answer to One Part of a late Infamous Libel* [W. Pulteney], 1731, 43; *Craftsman*, 19, 26 July and 9 August 1735; Mahon, II, app. CXVII. Walpole's reply to this accusation is to be found in *Some Considerations Concerning the Publick Funds*, 1735.

Directors of the Bank, had known Walpole for many years. Nevertheless his association was no closer than friendship. Although Walpole had particularly asked the Bank to discount tallies for him so that the army could be paid, the Directors refused him £20,000 on 14 October, much to Jacombe's chagrin. He wrote at once to Walpole, asking him to send pressing letters to Gould and Delmé, but afterwards thought better of it and did not use the letters when they arrived. Jacombe managed to raise the money elsewhere. This delighted him because, as he stressed to Walpole, it avoided putting them under any obligation to the Bank, and this was particularly desirable at such a juncture.[1] Furthermore, Jacombe's letters and Walpole's account book with his firm give a precise picture of Walpole's holding in Bank stock. During August 1720 Walpole had sold the majority of his shares—£6,000 at an average of £227 5s. 6d. per cent.[2] On 6 September 1720 Walpole still had £1,622 10s. in Bank shares, but their value had dropped much below 200.[3] At the same time he held South Sea shares to the paper value of £24,864. Also he had many friends among the South Sea Directors—Hawes was a very close friend of many years' standing; Sir William Chapman and Sir Theodore Janssen were as much his friends as Gould and Delmé. If personal considerations were to dominate Walpole's actions exclusively then his favour would have been shown to the Company rather than to the Bank.

Walpole was on the threshold of the most momentous weeks in his career; and it is necessary to summarize his position. He had shown no more foresight than anyone else about the South Sea affair. He had sold and bought at the wrong time, but his operations had not been vast. They had been discreetly managed by Jacombe, whose skill and devotion had saved him from major blunders. His absence from

---

[1] C(H) MSS, Robert Jacombe, 13, 14, 20 October 1720.
[2] Ibid., Robert Jacombe, 27 August 1720.
[3] Ibid., Robert Jacombe, 6 September 1720. J. H. Clapham, The Bank of England, 1, 87.

London had helped to foster the illusion that he himself had been unmoved by the prevailing hysteria of speculation; that he had exploited the folly of mankind to his own advantage but evaded the disasters which had overwhelmed others. His reputation was therefore high, if unjustified, and there were many men of affairs who wished to see him taking an active part in setting the country's credit on a firmer basis. Yet it would be nonsense to say with Coxe that every eye was directed to Walpole as the only person capable of affording assistance to the public. In the political confusion which the crisis was bound to create, each faction looked for a saviour who would not only rescue the public but also place it in power. By his withdrawal to Norfolk, Walpole had created the impression of being somewhat independent from the ministry, yet he had not resigned, nor did he intend to resign. And he had this advantage over other potential saviours; he was in office, a member of a government in which every other minister of ability was so deeply involved in bribery and corruption that it was unthinkable that they should be called upon to do anything but defend themselves. And he had this further advantage; his invaluable assistant Jacombe had cooked up a scheme which seemed to offer an adequate solution to the nation's desperate affairs. As soon as he arrived in London, Walpole began at once to work for the re-establishment of public credit and supreme power for himself.

CHAPTER NINE

THE SKREEN-MASTER GENERAL, 1720-1

W ALPOLE reached London about 8 November, just before
the King, who was hurrying back from Hanover, for
the Council of Regency had decided that Parliament must be
summoned at once to deal with the financial chaos. Public
opinion was inflamed and no matter how much the ministry
loathed the prospect of a public inquiry they could not delay the calling of Parliament. The King was therefore forced
to return. Walpole set to work at once to discuss with Jacombe
his ideas of breaking up the capital of the South Sea Company and engrafting parts of it into the Bank and India
Companies. Jacombe had prepared a scheme for Walpole's
consideration; this Walpole adopted almost unchanged and
set about convincing others of its wisdom.[1] He began with
the Bank Directors, whose concurrence was essential for the
scheme's success, for if they agreed the India Company would
follow. The views of the South Sea Company's Directors
were hardly relevant, since it was likely that they would
gladly accept any solution which saved something from the
wreckage. If they proved obstinate, they could easily be
coerced. The Bank set up a committee of directors to discuss
the proposal with Walpole. By 28 November he had achieved
the first necessary step for his success and he was able to
draft the following minute, to be sent, presumably, to the
South Sea and India Companies for their approval.

'Nov: 28th 1720.

At a meeting at the Bank with a Committee of Directors,
the Governour acquainted me, that the court of Directors
of the Bank had authorised the said Committee to proceed
and treat upon the following proposall, the same, if

[1] *C(H) MSS*, 88, 25/10. Jacombe's draft.

accepted by the South-Sea-Directors, to be laid before a generall court of the Bank for their approbation.

That nine millions of the capitall stock of the South-Sea-Company, together with an annuity of £5. per cent per annum issuing from the Exchequer and payable weekly, be ingrafted into the Bank of England, and added to the present capitall stock of the Bank amounting to £5,560,000. or thereabouts. That every proprietor of the said nine millions so to be ingrafted, be entitled to a share in the capitall of the Bank at the rate of £120. per cent viz. for every £120. in the nine millions to be ingrafted, each proprietor to have £100. stock in the Bank. The remaining £20. per cent, part of the nine millions, making in the whole one million and a half, to be referred for the common benefitt and advantage of the Bank.'[1]

This is almost identical with Jacombe's draft and to him, therefore, must go the credit for having invented the scheme.

To secure the concurrence of the three Companies was the first and most necessary step in Walpole's plan of campaign, but he also needed the backing of the Court and a favourable reception by the public. Naturally he set about both as soon as he arrived in London. Walpole's rivals, however, were as quick as he was to see the necessity of getting control of the situation. Sunderland, who had been with the King in Hanover, summoned the Bank Directors to his house as soon as he arrived back. But Walpole had the advantage over Sunderland, partly because he was not associated in men's minds with the South Sea Company, and partly because much groundwork for his scheme had been done already by Jacombe. Naturally enough rumours of these negotiations were on everyone's lips. Walpole, some said, was in the pay of the Bank; Sunderland, others reported, had threatened to break the Bank and Walpole unless they came into his scheme; and a few were confident that Walpole and Sunderland had united to press forward a common scheme. By the end of November, Walpole had created great public interest in his scheme: rumours of the Bank's acceptance were suffi-

[1] *C(H) MSS*, 88, 26/1. Walpole's minute.

cient to drive up the price of South Sea stock from 140 to 215.[1]

The speed with which Walpole secured the acceptance of his scheme by the Bank argues that they were favourably disposed to it; the rise in the price of stock indicates that the City and its investors had some faith in Walpole's ability. What the Court or the ministry thought is harder to discern. It is significant that as late as 28 November he was negotiating alone with the Directors of the Bank and that no other member of the ministry was associated with him. Furthermore, Walpole found it necessary to draw up a long memorandum about his scheme for the personal attention of the King.[2] Walpole took a great deal of trouble about this memorandum, which was written for the King's private advisers as much as for the King himself, but the fact that this appeal was necessary implies that Walpole was having some difficulty in securing full ministerial support for his ideas. The difference of opinion on the merits of the scheme, or the reluctance of Sunderland and Stanhope to allow Walpole to take such a leading part, may have led to the postponement of the recall of Parliament from 25 November to 8 December. Many years later Hervey suggested that Sunderland permitted Walpole to take over the leadership of affairs in the hope that it would effectively ruin him,[3] and his suggestion has been accepted by a recent historian.[4] Such an action, however, seems scarcely credible. Sunderland hated Walpole, and no doubt he would have contemplated his ruin with cheerful equanimity, but he had lived long enough at Court to know that it was unutterably dangerous to push anyone forward; temporary assumption of leadership could

[1] For rumours: Coxe, II, 194–7; HMC, *Portland MSS*, V, 606; *ibid.*, VII, 284; HMC, *Carlisle MSS*, 26; for stock prices, *C(H) MSS*, 88, 27. Realey, *Early Opposition*, 12–15, is not reliable and he places far too much weight on gossip, often from sources highly prejudicial to Walpole.

[2] Coxe, II, 197–201. Notes for this in Walpole's hand are in *C(H)MSS*, 88: a fair copy, not in Walpole's hand but in Jacombe's, is in the *Walpole MSS*, volume marked 'Letters of Sir Robert Walpole'.

[3] Hervey, I, 33.

[4] Realey, *Early Opposition*, 15. Cf. also W. Michael, *Das Zeitalter Walpoles* 106, n. 8.

so quickly develop into absolute possession. Although there can be no certainty, the rumours of rival schemes, and the elaborate memorandum of Walpole to the King do imply that the struggle between Walpole and Sunderland for control of the ministry had begun in earnest and that Walpole had won a partial victory. Although he was to be allowed to try to get his scheme adopted ministerial sanction for it had been withheld. Walpole negotiated alone with the Companies and when he announced his scheme to Parliament when it finally met on 8 December 1720, it was in these terms: 'That for his own part he had never approved the South Sea scheme and was sensible it had done a great deal of mischief; but since it could not be undone, he thought it the duty of all good men to give their helping hand towards retrieving it: and that with this view, he had already bestowed some thoughts on a proposal to restore publick credit, which at a proper time, he would submit to the wisdom of the House.'[1] In the course of a month Walpole had achieved considerable success and displayed his great skill in negotiation; the Companies had agreed to his terms, the scheme had been given a semi-official blessing, and the public had been encouraged to direct their eyes to Walpole as a possible saviour of his country.

But the scheme was only one part of Walpole's policy and by far the easiest part of it. The rest was more difficult and fraught with risk. Ruin had overtaken many men and women. Lord Londonderry had lost over £50,000[2]; the Dukes of Bolton and Wharton were in a similar plight; many squires and younger sons had lost their patrimony.[3] For months men and women had wallowed in the wild fantasies begotten by the prospect of wealth raining on them like manna. They had talked and written of the great estates soon to be theirs, built palaces in their dreams, married their daughters to the noblest blood. Now they were landed in debt and frightened

---

[1] Chandler, VI, 221.
[2] C(H) MSS, Thos. Gibson, 29 October 1720.
[3] Coxe, II, 196; R. W. Ketton-Cremer, Norfolk Portraits, 69–84.

of the future. They craved not only for salvation but for revenge. The lobbies of the House of Commons swarmed with
rioters clamouring for justice, and the South Sea Directors
went in fear of their lives. In so dangerous a situation the
Court itself could easily be imperilled; its safety depended
upon the skill with which its servants could placate those
angry men who insisted on retribution, and at the same time
preserve the ministry. It was to this task that Walpole addressed himself, for unlike many losers he wished 'to skin the
wound over rather than probe it'. At such a time he had no
use for revenge and little for justice.

The motives for Walpole's policy are clear enough, and
they are both personal and public. The personal motives are
easily disposed of. Walpole wanted supreme authority for
himself and his friends, as any politician must who feels within himself that he has the power to rule. To obtain it he
needed the wholehearted, undivided allegiance of the King,
and that could not be obtained by an exposure of corruption
which would stain the reputation of the King, his mistresses,
and ministers to whom he was obviously attached. It was unlikely that all would escape unscathed, so Walpole and his
friends would be in a position to demand their just rewards.
To battle therefore for the King and his ministry must lead
inevitably to advancement unless the Commons got completely out of hand. In that case anarchy and revolution
would engulf all. Walpole loathed chaos as much as he hated
the Jacobites who would be the only gainers from it. Temperamentally Walpole was antagonistic to any policy which
was rooted in emotional attitudes, but there were sound
reasons of State for his policy of protection, and the insecurity
of the Throne was the most powerful of all. Walpole had
grown up in an atmosphere of plots, revolutions, attempted
assassinations. During his life there had already been three
rebellions, two frustrated invasions, and prolonged civil war.
The prospect of yet another rebellion was not a childish fear
for men of Walpole's generation but an ever present danger.
To weaken the authority of the Crown for the sake of re-

venge was far too perilous for one who had never wavered in his adherence to the Protestant succession. There were equally powerful reasons for Walpole's attempting to maintain the whigs in power. The mixed ministries of Anne's reign had bred instability and hamstrung decisions. Sunderland and Stanhope's destruction could only lead to a mixed tory and whig government which would bring Bolingbroke back to play a leading part; and Walpole had as little use for Bolingbroke as he for him. That a policy of Walpole's should lead to Bolingbroke's recovery of power was not an irony which Walpole wished to savour. He had struggled in and out of the wilderness for long enough. He was quick enough to realize that the future of men who thought like himself depended on their thwarting the tories in their inevitable attempt to exploit the South Sea crisis to their own advantage.

2

ALTHOUGH THE reasons for Walpole's policy were cogent enough at both levels, it was a far from easy policy to pursue, and could only lead to bitter criticism and personal abuse. This was made clear enough to him when the members favourable to the government met at the Cockpit to hear the King's Speech on Wednesday, 7 December 1720. No mention was made either in the Speech or the Address of any inquiry into the causes of the crisis, an omission which was seized upon at once. The Secretary tried to dodge the issue by reading on, but this subterfuge was quickly exposed; although Walpole displayed his hand and spoke strongly against this insistence on an inquiry, his argument that the Directors would at once run away was a feeble one and carried no weight. For once he seems to have been caught unawares, having underestimated the strength of feeling even in the Court party! It was as well that he was overborne and the words inserted, for the attack by the tories on the Address was exceptionally vigorous. They were supported by such rugged individualists as Governor Pitt and Sir Joseph Jekyll;

334

by radicals like Lord Molesworth, who wanted the South Sea Directors sewn up in sacks and thrown into the Thames; and by knights of the shire, compelled at last to break their six years' silence. Even the amended Address proved too lukewarm for this passionate House and the Court accepted a further clause, which demanded the punishment of the 'creators of our present Misfortunes', without attempting to force a division.[1]

Emboldened by his success, Governor Pitt pressed on with the attack on the Court, and the next day in a wild speech proposed that the South Sea Directors, their Secretary and Treasurer and 'their great Scanderbeg' should attend the House at once for cross-examination. He misjudged his moment, for the House was about to attend the King with their Address, so the ministry had little difficulty in getting the motion delayed a couple of days. But members were quick to sense that this motion would be a serious test for the Court. The lobbies and drawing-rooms sparkled with rumour; and some confidently asserted that Walpole was in favour of an immediate prorogation to give time for men's tempers to cool. Such a dangerous expedient was not attempted and the debate came on. Walpole said what he was to say over and over again to the Commons during the next few weeks: that the prime necessity was to repair the public credit, and that investigations and inquiries would inflame passions further and wreck his scheme. But the Court had lost control of the Commons and rather than risk a vote the ministry bowed to the storm, and the South Sea Company Directors were sent for with their books and papers, which were to be presented on 15 December. Hoping that these successes might be sufficient to ease the tension, the ministry plucked up enough courage to check Sir Joseph Jekyll's de-

[1] Coxe, II, 201–19. The letters of Thomas and St John Brodrick are one of the best sources for this critical session, but they need to be used carefully as they both hated Walpole. The 'great man' in this letter was Walpole. It was his common nickname, arising partly from his great bulk—he weighed twenty stone—and partly from his manner. The other source used in the reconstruction of these debates is Chandler, VI, 218 *et seq.*

mand for a select committee of inquiry into the Company's affairs. Encouraged by their success in this Walpole took his first hurdle, which was to insist that all contracts with the South Sea Company should be declared valid and not set aside except by the general court of the Company or the due course of law. Such a statement was necessary, for many men were hoping to forget the consequences of their folly by obliterating their obligations. But it was not until 21 December that Walpole introduced his scheme to the Commons. His approach had been practical, in fact rather dilatory, as if he feared to place his scheme squarely before the House. With the Court so insecurely in control Walpole's delay is understandable. As Christmas drew near there was a slight but perceptible drift of independent members away from Westminster which steadily strengthened the ministry. When the debate came on, Walpole was far below his usual form. He was prolix and obscure. His manner was infectious; speaker after speaker expressed his doubts about the scheme in vast but tedious speeches, which Walpole started to annotate for his reply and then gave up in despair.[1] His main antagonists were Milner and Hutcheson, the latter an amateur economist of some ability who had pondered long but inconclusively on the South Sea Company's mistakes; but, though they were quick to criticize, they offered nothing constructive in exchange for Walpole's scheme. This was accepted without enthusiasm as the basis for further negotiations.

The scheme was no more popular with the City or with the public. Many, like Arthur Onslow, thought that it should be accepted because there was nothing better.[2] But any scheme was bound to have a bad Press, for only magic could conjure back lost fortunes, and any settlement would merely underline what many were reluctant to acknowledge—that their losses were final and irrevocable. Walpole's aim was to create a sense of security, no matter how modest or tentative, in which confidence could begin to flourish. That, too, is why

[1] C(H) MSS, 88/34(a).
[2] HMC, Clements MSS, 297.

the King's Speech had deliberately drawn attention to the flourishing nature of British trade and of the ministry's intention to encourage it. In many ways these gestures were more important than the technical adjustments involved in Walpole's plans; and they were successful, for by the end of the year the South Sea stock had risen from its lowest point, 124 on 14 December to 200.[1] Ten days before Christmas the demand for retribution had been at its height; a week after Christmas it looked as if the ministry might evade an inquiry. Walpole's scheme and policy had induced a tentative buoyancy in the City.

It did not last. The delays had begun to exacerbate those irascible men, Sir Joseph Jekyll and Governor Pitt. They enjoyed their moral fervour and would not be denied their victims. Their suspicion of the government's intentions was intense, and they thought that the ministry would use the need to settle the year's supplies as a means of evading the question of punishment.[2] When the Commons returned after the brief Christmas recess on 4 January 1721, they were horrified to find that the Court had thought up a better stratagem. The yearly Mutiny Bill was introduced. Never, stormed Jekyll, had the Bill been introduced so early in a session. 'Such a hurry,' he went on, 'seemed to be intended to stop the prosecution of the authors of the present misfortunes.' He hinted darkly that the session's days were numbered, that it would not be long before members were dispatched home. He judged accurately the temper of the House, and although the government were allowed to introduce their Bill, it proved no advantage. The initiative was with Jekyll and he took it, demanding that the Directors and officials of the South Sea Company should be forbidden to leave the Kingdom and that an inventory should be made at once of their fortunes. Horatio Walpole supported Jekyll; so did Philip Yorke, a young client of Newcastle's who was already a devoted and reliable supporter of Walpole. Their

[1] Scott, III, 320-1.
[2] Coxe, II, 204.

late support represented a desperate attempt by the Court to regain control of the Commons by falling in with its temper, a tactic quickly recognized by the Jacobite Shippen, who ironically complimented the House on its unanimity and then nettled Craggs by proclaiming that men in the ministry were as culpable as the Directors. Foolishly Craggs flew into a rage and offered to give satisfaction to any man who should question his integrity. Never was temper more out of place or the calm irony of Shippen more successful. The affront to the dignity of the House was seized upon by Molesworth, and a discredited front bench lost all hope of checking the hounds now in full cry. They continued to fight hard, but in the end they were overwhelmed and forced to agree to what they feared most—a select committee, to be elected by ballot, to investigate the Company's affairs. Only at the very end of this day did the government secure a small victory. They evaded Lord Hinchinbrooke's proposal to commit the South Sea Directors and officials to the Tower. To the dispirited and exhausted ministers this cannot have been much consolation, though in time it was to prove the salvation of some of them.[1]

Evasion had failed. The Commons were committed to a full investigation of the Company's affairs and Walpole could no longer hope to save the ministry. Nevertheless it was as essential as ever for him to salvage whomsoever he could, no matter how vilified he might be in doing so. His financial 'scheme' became of secondary importance. It was useful for showing Parliament's good intentions—an aid to maintaining confidence—but politically it had become a side-issue. The measure passed slowly through both Houses. Its main opponent was Archibald Hutcheson, whose own scheme proved so fantastic that the House turned back with relief to Walpole's. No one was enthusiastic, probably not Walpole himself, and when finally his permissive measure passed into law it was shelved and not put into operation. And in the next session of Parliament (1721–2) Walpole had to begin all over again,

[1] Chandler, VI, 226–8.

but by that time the country's finances had recovered from the worst consequences of the South Sea disaster. Walpole has been inordinately praised for his financial skill at this juncture. Time was the healer, not Walpole. The scheme which goes by his name was invented by Jacombe and never put into practice. What Walpole can be praised for is wisdom or downright common sense. The prime necessity, as he saw it, was to avoid panic and restore confidence. While many had lost money, others had gained; and if bullion had flowed out of the country, it had also poured in. Wealth had not been destroyed but bizarrely redistributed as in a monstrous lottery. The trade of the nation was in a flourishing condition. The danger, if any, was psychological. Like Walpole himself, men had obtained what gold they could and hoarded it.[1] The London market was very hard pressed for ready cash.[2] His scheme coaxed men to part with their gold once more. In this lay its value. As a financial operation it had absolutely no importance. And its psychological effect should not be overestimated. No one, certainly not the City men, was enamoured of it.[3]

Few reputations have such strange or inaccurate origins as Walpole's. Generations of historians have praised him for repairing his country's ruined finances, yet for this there is no foundation in fact. The finances repaired themselves. This is not intended to belittle Walpole's part in the crisis. By tenacity of purpose and undeviating courage, exercised at the expense of his public reputation, he rescued the Court and the ministry from utter ruin, and in so doing he secured that stability of government which had eluded England for generations past. The battle was bitter, and his role as a champion of cheats and swindlers was neither heroic nor godly, but greatly to his country's good.

[1] Throughout the crisis Child's Bank kept a cash balance of £80,000 *ex inf*. Mr D. C. Joslin.

[2] HMC, *Clements MSS*, 297. '. . . no money is stirring, and as difficult to borrow fifty pounds now as it was five thousand six months ago'. 4 February 1721.

[3] *Ibid., Carlisle MSS*, 27.

The days that were devoted to Walpole's scheme were the few days of respite which the ministry enjoyed during this unhappy session, for not only did they fail to stave off the parliamentary inquiry but they also lost the election of their nominees to the committee. Lechmere, Molesworth, Brodrick, Jekyll, Hutcheson, the fiercest critics of the government, were successful in the ballot. They set to work with a will, toiling from nine in the morning to eleven at night, Sundays and the feast of Charles, King and Martyr, alone excepted.[1] At first all went smoothly. The Bill against the South Sea Directors, forbidding them to leave the country or to alienate their estates, passed through all its stages by 19 January when it was sent to the Lords who were no less prompt than the Commons. Two days before the measure received the royal assent, the inquiry was dealt a staggering blow. Naturally the Committee began their examination by interrogating Robert Knight, the cashier of the South Sea Company. After two exhausting sessions of cross-examination he realized his danger. His colleagues encouraged him to flee after destroying or taking with him as much of the incriminating evidence as he could lay his hands on. Sir Thomas Pengelly announced his flight to the Commons, who exploded with anger at the news. They offered a reward of £2,000 for his capture and ordered the ports to be closed. At this time Knight was in Dover but he was able to embark without hindrance in the yacht which he had hired. He landed in the Netherlands and went straight to Brabant, a most cunningly chosen refuge, for the *Joyeuse Entrée* gave him complete protection from extradition.[2] Frustrated, the Commons directed their rage against those Directors who sat in the House— Sir Robert Chaplin, Sir Theodore Janssen, Eyles and Sawbridge. They were summoned to attend in their places. Only Janssen and Sawbridge could be found. The doors were

[1] Coxe, II, 207.
[2] HMC, *Carlisle MSS*, 30. The privileges of the Netherlands towns were enshrined in the *Joyeuse Entrée* which was jealously guarded against infractions by the Emperor.

locked and the keys solemnly laid on the table. Then General Ross, a member of the Committee, told the House that they had 'already discovered a train of deepest villainy and fraud that Hell ever contrived to ruin a nation'. Janssen and Sawbridge were expelled and committed to the Tower; Eyles and Chaplin followed them the next day.[1] Men recalled the stirring days of Parliament's not too distant past—the days of war and plot when passionate men fought for liberty and justice for themselves. The Court no longer possessed control of the House and Walpole played no part in these angry scenes. He pushed steadily ahead with his scheme, which aroused less feeling, against strong but ineffectual opposition, and waited on events.

Although the flight of the cashier and the disappearance of important ledgers hampered the Committee in their investigations, they were aided by the breakdown in the resolution of Sir John Blunt, one of the Directors. His evidence was sufficient for them to uncover a number of dubious transactions with members of the ministry. On 18 February the Commons passed ten resolutions in which they condemned the South Sea Directors as having been guilty of a gross breach of trust, to the detriment of the nation, and ordered that their estates should be sequestered for the use of the unfortunate speculators in their Company. This was expected and caused no debate; a single voice raised in their defence would have been sufficient to cause a tumult both within and without doors. The Directors having been condemned, the Committee moved on a week later to attack the ministry. Aislabie, Chancellor of the Exchequer, and Charles Stanhope, Secretary of the Treasury, were named as guilty of corrupt practices. They at once declared their innocence and demanded that a day should immediately be set aside to prove their innocence by refuting the evidence set out against them in the report. This the Committee of Secrecy tried to prevent. They still had hopes that Knight might be extradited, and they knew that his evidence, if extracted from him,

[1] Chandler, VI, 230-1.

341

would be conclusive. As it was, the accusation rested almost entirely on the evidence of one man, Sir John Blunt.[1]

At this point the ministry decided to make a stand. For six weeks they had permitted the Commons to follow their own course of revenge, reserving their strength to press Walpole's scheme. This could not go on, if the government were to survive. And although the evidence against Charles Stanhope was powerful it was far from being conclusive. Also circumstances were favourable to his defence, his cousin, Earl Stanhope, having dropped dead a few days previously of an apoplexy, induced by the anxiety of the crisis. Charles Stanhope's defence was that he had paid for what stock he had received from Knight or alternatively that his money held by his bankers had been used without his knowledge. His bankers, Turner and Sawbridge, with an eye to the future, acknowledged that they had used his money without his consent. It was a thin defence and did not meet in detail the bulky accusations of the prosecution, which can be found in the Committee's Report. But it raised a doubt which was strong enough to satisfy the conscience of many courtiers and so permit them to vote for his acquittal. Others were prevailed upon to abstain out of sympathy for his dolorous plight. All arts of persuasion, including, some hinted, bribery, had been used by the ministry which just scraped home by three votes.[2] The people of London were enraged; riots and disorders expressed their impotent frustration at what they rightly considered a travesty of justice.[3] Venomous abuse was hurled at Walpole, who from this time became known as the Skreen-Master General.

Politically a demonstration of the ministry's strength had been very necessary. The loss of Stanhope, although it had removed a rival of Walpole's, weakened the ministry in the Lords. But this was not the only blow of fate which fell on

[1] Chandler, VI, 234–6. C(H) MSS, 88. 'Report of the Committee of Secrecy', JHC, XIX, 425–51, for what follows.

[2] Three members of the Committee, Jekyll, Molesworth and Sloper, decided that discretion was the better part of valour and abstained from voting.

[3] Coxe, II, 209; Swift, Correspondence, III, 74.

them. James Craggs, Senior, broke down under the examination of the Committee and probably killed himself, thereby proving his guilt in the eyes of the opposition. His son, the Secretary of State, equally suspect with his father, contracted smallpox and died. These deaths, coming as they did so closely together, weakened the ministry to such a degree that its collapse might have followed if the Court had not demonstrated that it still retained a hold on the Commons. Yet it lacked the strength to repeat its effort on behalf of Aislabie. Probably Aislabie had been marked for sacrifice as soon as the evidence against him had been placed before the Committee; for Walpole had begun to inspect all Treasury business at the beginning of February when the Court learnt that he was to succeed Aislabie, who had prudently resigned, at the end of the session.[1]

Aislabie, reconciled to his doom, had treated his examination both by the Committee and the Lords very light-heartedly, making jokes about screens which were not in the best of taste; but he cannot have felt much gratitude to Walpole, who long before had decided not to defend him. When his case came before the Commons, Thomas Brodrick noticed that 'Walpole's corner satt mute as fishes'.[2] Realizing that they had been tossed a victim, the opposition wished to make the most of it, and a member suggested that a Bill of attainder would be appropriate in Aislabie's case. Walpole then rose, but not to defend. He remarked dryly that the proper procedure would be by impeachment; this infuriated Jekyll, who misinterpreted what was probably intended as a sarcasm. He suspiciously regarded it as a sly design to get the Lords to sit in judgment on the delinquents of the Commons. Jekyll's anger had the same result as Walpole had hoped to obtain by his bleak sarcasm: the House contented itself with packing off Aislabie to the Tower.

As his coach rolled through the City he saw bonfires springing into flame and heard the noise of the jubilant mob

[1] HMC, *Carlisle MSS*, 28-9.
[2] Coxe, II, 210.

who were delighted by his downfall. The same uncontrolled joy greeted Sir George Caswell, who followed Aislabie to prison two days later. Once more Walpole and the Court stayed their hand. Caswell was disliked more than any other Director, and the mob had already shown its hatred by nearly tearing him to pieces as he went to his examination. These outbursts of public violence were very useful to Walpole. They created uneasiness, a sense of insecurity, a feeling that the structure of social order was tottering. The wild and wanton talk in the Commons of attainder and impeachment did him a similar service. Many men had dreaded what might be the outcome of this crisis. Like Sir John Vanbrugh, although they were losers, they did not wish to see the safety of the Kingdom jeopardized for the sake of revenge.[1] The orgiastic delight of the mob and the reckless venom of the opposition confirmed the doubts of those who believed that authority should be upheld even at the expense of righteousness.[2] Necessity of State grew larger in men's thoughts, and made them hesitant, a mood which Walpole and his henchmen were quick to exploit, for they were faced with their toughest task—the salvation of Sunderland himself.

Walpole must have reflected on life's irony during these difficult days of March. He had it in his power to crush Sunderland, his most dangerous and ruthless enemy in the whig party, a man of tortuous ambition and uncertain judgment, whose responsibility for the country's catastrophic plight was heavy indeed. Yet Walpole was impotent. Sunderland was beloved of the King, he was liked by both the King's mistresses. About the Court and in the ministry were many men who owed what little patronage they enjoyed to Sunderland. They knew of the past rivalry between the two men, which knowledge bred of itself a distrust of Walpole. They had supported his scheme in the lobbies, helped him and Stanhope, waited with him in patience whilst Aislabie and Caswell were condemned; but they would not have

[1] HMC, *Carlisle MSS*, 29.
[2] *Ibid.*, *Clements MSS*, 297.

countenanced a sacrifice of Sunderland. This Walpole knew, so he used every art to avert it.

In preparation for the debate in the Commons on Sunderland's guilt a whispering campaign was started. Sunderland had lost heavily in the Bubble and this was used to arouse pity. It was explained that he was the dupe of others and that the worst excesses had taken place during his absence with the King in Hanover. And the argument of expediency was used to reinforce sympathy. If Sunderland fell, the ministry would crash. If that happened the King would have no alternative but to ask the tories to govern. A tory administration would entail a purge of office-holders high and low. At such a crucial moment the ministry could not allow a placeman to ease his conscience by abstaining from voting. But courtiers, willing or unwilling, were not numerous enough to secure Sunderland's acquittal and Walpole needed to exploit the fears of those cautious men, like Arthur Onslow, who trembled at the thought of anarchy.[1] Even so, he felt that he could leave nothing to chance and used a tactic which he was often to employ in his parliamentary battles. On 14 March, the day arranged for the debate, he moved its adjournment for one day and secured it, on the grounds that he needed the presence at the Bar of witnesses who had testified against Sunderland. The advantage of this move was threefold; firstly, the temperature of the Commons was lowered, men keyed up to the excitement of battle found their spirits and energy deflated by delay; secondly, it enabled Walpole and his friends to lobby energetically those men who had come to the Commons but who had previously evaded them; thirdly, it was likely to diminish the members of the opposition at the next day's debate. Lukewarm men could argue imperative engagements to explain their absence, whereas the discipline of place would

[1] HMC, *Carlisle MSS*, 33; HMC, *Clements MSS*, 294-5, 308; HMC, *Onslow MSS*, 508; HMC, *Portland MSS*, V, 618; Coxe, II, 192, 195-7. Lechmere took to his bed on 14 March; his father-in-law, Carlisle, thought that he had done this to save himself from voting. HMC, *Carlisle MSS*, 32-3.

ensure the presence of courtiers. Even so, on 15 March St Stephen's was far fuller than it had been for many weeks, and the Prince of Wales listened to the debate from the gallery. Thomas Brodrick, the Chairman of the inquiry, was confident of success. Walpole, aided by Henry Pelham, conducted the defence and astonished the opposition by completely denying the validity of the evidence set out in the Committee of Inquiry's report. This Brodrick had not expected, for he believed the evidence so cogent as not to be denied. The evidence was derived from Sir John Blunt, who swore on oath that Knight told two witnesses in his presence that 50,000 stock had been given to Sunderland. Walpole concentrated his attention on the witnesses who were called to the Bar of the House, and he exploited adroitly the discrepancies in their recollections; one said that Sir John Blunt was not in the room when Knight spoke to him; the other was brought to admit that though Blunt was in the room he was not within hearing distance of the conversation. Brodrick thought that this was silly, trifling stuff and a waste of the Commons' time as there were three witnesses irrespective of Blunt who admitted hearing such a conversation with Knight, yet he was mistaken.[1] With the flight of Knight, Blunt had become the chief witness of the prosecution and any doubt which could be created about his evidence was a most valuable gain for the defence. And the discredit of Blunt was sufficient to permit some members to ignore the evidence of the three humbler witnesses. The wisdom of Walpole's conduct of the defence was demonstrated at the division, which did not take place until eight in the evening. Sunderland was acquitted by 233 votes to 172. The majority was substantial, but so was the number who had voted against the Court, too great, Edward Harley thought, for Sunderland to remain a Prime Minister.[2]

This debate proved to be the crisis which could only have been prolonged to the further discredit of the ministry if Old

[1] Coxe, II, 213–4.
[2] HMC, *Portland MSS*, V, 618.

Craggs had lived to face his trial; but the day before the debate he died, either through apoplexy at the prospect of it or by taking an overdose of opium for fear of it. The public decided unhesitatingly in favour of suicide and promptly condemned Craggs as guilty.[1] As far as the ministry were concerned the inquiry came to an end with the death of Craggs.

3

THE ORDEAL was over for the Court. Violent skirmishes and strong rearguard actions would be needed before the battle finally ceased and the ministry secured its control of the Commons. The government had never suffered complete defeat. Discretion and sacrifice had been forced on it but it had survived, and survival in eighteenth-century politics carried with it immense advantages. On the other hand individuals had suffered. Death or disgrace had overtaken Stanhope, the two Craggs and Aislabie. These removals had greatly strengthened Walpole's position. Indeed so much so that he could regard cheerfully the public abuse which was hurled at him, or sit comfortably in his corner as Shippen and his Jacobite cronies denounced his turncoat nature and screening activities. When the crisis began Walpole and Townshend had been junior members in Sunderland and Stanhope's ministry. By the end of March their faction had achieved parity. They had been, of course, quite unable to dislodge Sunderland and his friends, and nothing displays the immense hold of that adroit statesman better than the way he survived the shames and humiliations of the South Sea crisis. The reconstruction of the ministry had proceeded piecemeal, but it was more or less complete when Walpole took over the Chancellorship of the Exchequer, which had been promised to him much earlier, on 3 April 1721. By then Townshend had already succeeded Stanhope in his old post as Secretary of State, but the Sunderland group retained

---

[1] HMC, *Portland MSS*, V, 618. Walpole was interested in the evidence against Craggs, cf. *C(H) MSS*, 88/19, but there is no indication in his papers whether he would have defended him or offered him as a sacrifice for Sunderland.

its hold on the other Secretaryship when young Craggs died. Carteret, a brilliant friend of Sunderland, obtained the office, much to Walpole's and Townshend's chagrin. The real struggle came over the control of the Secret Service money. Although the amount of money disbursed to needy aristocrats or members of the Commons was not great, the person who distributed it mattered a great deal, for he was rightly regarded as the head of the government's patronage system, and therefore the chief figure in the ministry. At the time of the previous reconciliation with the King, Walpole had made a bid to wrest it from Sunderland's hands: he had failed. Now Walpole felt his position was strong enough to claim it. He could point to the insecurity of the government's position in the Commons and the necessity for the leader of the ministry there to be able to enforce discipline by promise or threat of royal favour or displeasure. It was the key to power: Walpole knew it and insisted. Yet, once again, he failed. Sunderland resigned the office of First Lord of the Treasury, which went to Walpole on 3 April 1721 with the Chancellorship. Sunderland nevertheless kept control of the Secret Service funds.[1] Moreover Sunderland retained the office of Groom of the Stole, a most honourable Court office, to which he had been appointed in 1719; this gave him a seat in the Cabinet and access to the King. Such an arrangement underlined to all who knew how to interpret appointments that Sunderland was far from being a spent force. Carteret's promotion made that clear: so did the appointment of Lord Carleton to be President of the Council in place of Townshend. Indeed, Sunderland's faction maintained a strict equality with Walpole's in all the major offices. To keep the balance the Postmaster-Generalship was divided between Edward Carteret, brother of Lord Carteret, and Galfridus Walpole, Robert's sailor brother, who had never held a government office before. The Post Office was a vital Department, for letters were opened there, read and sometimes conveniently misdirected—particularly at election times. It was

[1] *Blenheim MSS*, D. II, 4.

essential to each faction that neither should steal an advantage. Although Walpole failed to secure control of the Secret Service money, he was able nevertheless to consolidate his power at the Treasury. He secured places for two important friends—Richard Edgecumbe and Sir Charles Turner. Better still, one of Sunderland's nominees there, Henry Pelham, was beginning to see very much eye to eye with Walpole himself —and Pelham was the brother of the Duke of Newcastle, whose electoral interest was very great. If the struggle between Walpole and Sunderland had to be fought out in the parliamentary boroughs—and under the Septennial Act a general election was due in 1722—then the Pelhams would be a key factor. Edgecumbe, who also possessed great electoral influence in Cornwall, was Walpole's answer to the Pelhams. These appointments demonstrate Walpole's systematic approach to the question of power, for although Sunderland maintained parity for his faction, Walpole had disposed his forces more strategically. His control of the Treasury gave him an immense advantage in the struggle for supremacy, and this was only partly offset by his failure to secure the Secret Service money.

Although Walpole had greatly strengthened his position at Court, the Commons were still far from docile. Naturally his enemies wished to continue the crisis as long as possible, whilst public-spirited men felt that the evasion of justice had gone too far. So long as Robert Knight remained abroad further evidence against ministers and the Court was unlikely to be forthcoming. Towards the end of March, therefore, the opposition pressed the ministry to do more than it was doing. Gossip sneered at Colonel Churchill's mission to the Emperor which was said to have been undertaken merely to get the Court's money out of Knight and not to insist on his extradition. On 29 March 1721 the ministry very willingly placed before the Commons the exchange of letters between Churchill and the Imperial Chancellor, in which the Emperor had insisted that he must show a proper respect for the rights and privileges of Brabant. This Lord

349

Molesworth denounced as a frivolous pretence. The next day three hundred members with the Speaker trooped off to St James's Palace to present the King with their resolution, praying the King to use 'his most pressing endeavours' to get Knight out of the Netherlands. These were harmless enough junketings, which eased the consciences of the country gentlemen and caused little embarrassment to the ministry. They also absorbed enough of the Commons' time to carry it to the Easter recess.

4

A SUMMER session was needed by the Court to establish its control of the Commons, or at least to reassert its influence: furthermore the King required subsidies for Sweden and his Civil List debts demanded settlement. Neither of these pieces of business could be attempted so long as the Commons showed a truculent and independent spirit. As the summer wore on the heat and stink of London could be counted on to drive the weary backbenchers to their country seats. Time ran strongly against the ill-disciplined opposition.[1]

When Parliament reassembled on 19 April 1721, the tories immediately attacked Walpole. According to Shippen nothing had been done to alleviate the distress of the nation which still cried aloud, though in vain, for vengeance. He demanded a full inquiry into the nation's indebtedness, an extravagance quickly supported by Sir William Wyndham. Walpole did his best to evade their motion, but the weakness of the government was laid bare by his failure. Gratified by their success, the opposition set about Craggs's estate and demanded its sequestration. It had devolved by inheritance on two members of the House, Samuel Trefusis and Newsham, who immediately begged to be allowed counsel to defend them, owing to their lack of skill in debate. Trefusis, who had sat for twenty years in Parliament, had scarcely ever spoken and Newsham had not yet opened his mouth. This plea, suggested (the opposition hinted) by Walpole's

[1] HMC, *Carlisle MSS*, 34; Chandler, VI, 258.

cunning, was disallowed after Lechmere's sneer that Walpole would sit by them in any case to advise them, and he would do as well as any counsel. Once more the Court failed, but it is worth noting that each time Walpole refrained from forcing a division. If he was willing to accept what was forced on him, he was not prepared to allow the opposition a victory in the lobbies, which did a little to deflate their sense of success. The next day Craggs's estate was forfeited. Very few leading ministers of the Crown can have experienced so bleak a beginning to their administration. In his first week Walpole had been defeated on every issue and his suggestions had been completely ignored by the Commons.[1]

Furthermore he had a thankless and difficult duty to perform. Aislabie had gone cheerfully to his doom and the ministry were bound in honour to try and rescue some of his estate. Walpole first displayed his hand when the opposition tried to out-jockey him. Although the Directors' estates had been confiscated, as yet only a declaration of the full value of Aislabie's had been demanded, so that the Commons could decide how much it wished to take. On 21 April the opposition tried to consolidate Aislabie's Bill with that of the Directors, and treat him in the same way. Walpole regarded this as a low trick and said so. He spoke with great passion, pleaded for Aislabie's wife and children, but to no effect. The Commons received his oratory 'like soe many statues'. Realizing his failure, he did not press the House to a division.[2] Walpole's next move was to attempt to exclude Aislabie's paternal inheritance from the forfeiture of his estate. Again he was defeated. But worse was to come. Thomas Vernon, a brother-in-law of Aislabie, and member for Whitchurch, attempted to bribe the choleric General Ross, a member of the Secret Committee, to do what he could for Aislabie on the grounds that the Commons were becoming more charitably inclined towards him. Vernon was immediately expelled.

[1] Chandler, VI, 241-5.
[2] Coxe, II, 214-5.

It was not until the end of May that Walpole began to gain ground in the Commons. The business before the House was the allowance to be made to the South Sea Directors out of their estates, for it was recognized that some were more guilty than others. Walpole in every case but one tried to secure as much as possible for the Directors and used his great knowledge of parliamentary procedure to spin out the business and wear down the opposition. On occasion he cheerfully kept the House going for five hours without achieving a single decision.

These tactics wearied and baffled the opposition, and their frustrated rage can be imagined when one day the Commons were side-tracked into a discussion of the libellous character of *Mist's Weekly Journal*. Some thought that Walpole would ask the King to prorogue Parliament rather than allow the Directors' Bill to pass. But this proved unnecessary, for Walpole was in many cases enabled by his skill and ingenuity to secure a reasonable allowance for the Directors; even Aislabie in the end obtained all of the estates which he had possessed on becoming Chancellor of the Exchequer and for this he expressed his deep gratitude to Walpole. There was one Director, however, who was denied Walpole's benevolent protection—Sir John Blunt. Blunt had been responsible for providing the evidence which had so damaged the credit of the ministry, particularly Sunderland's. When his case came to be debated Horatio Walpole accused him of a lifetime's fraud, and laid the ruin of innumerable families at his door. Out of an estate of £183,349 10s. 8¾d. he was allowed to keep but £1,000, and he suffered the largest confiscation of all the Directors.[1]

[1] Chandler, VI, 247–52; Coxe, II, 216–9; *C(H) MSS*, Sir Theodore Janssen, 24 May 1721, asking Walpole for help in preserving his estates and speaking of his [Walpole's] 'kind and powerful assistance under this terrible state of Providence'. And a very begging letter of 21 May 1721 from Sir George Caswell: 'There never was a law so severe made against the greatest villans yet extant and the foundation as false as the cruelty extravagant. I beg your Honour's pardon for the length of this but a wife, children and many dependents are to be stript of all the comforts of life and reduced to utmost necessitys.—Plead for me!' Walpole did.

This policy of leniency brought Walpole great odium, and for the rest of his political life the nickname, already mentioned, which he acquired at this time, of Skreen-Master General, or simply the Skreen, stuck to him.[1] There can never have been a Prime Minister who rose to power in such a welter of denigration. At first sight Walpole's continued resistance to the will of the parliamentary majority and his unceasing support of a policy of moderation may seem to have involved both an unnecessary waste of effort and a useless loss of public reputation. Certainly the gains were small and the loss of goodwill immense. Nor did Walpole use the full power of the Court to secure his policy. As we shall see, when he wanted to force through a measure, no matter how strongly disliked in the Commons or in the City, he got his way. In these debates on the Directors the whips seem to have been off, for placemen such as Sloper and Clayton sometimes spoke and voted with Walpole, sometimes against him. Walpole's attitude in May and June needs explanation.

Walpole's motives can, of course, only be surmised, but knowing his character they are not hard to guess: usually they were a compound, arising from the necessities of his own ambition and what he felt was required for the country's good, disciplined by his strong sense of reality. Many Directors of the South Sea Company were men of wide commercial interests. Sir Theodore Janssen had business relations with firms in Amsterdam, Antwerp, Geneva, Paris, Dublin, Genoa and Leghorn; he dealt in tin, china, paper, mortgages, loans, foreign exchange.[2] Some Directors had larger, some smaller interests, but there were thirty-three of them and amongst them over two millions of capital at the most conservative estimate were involved. They were intimately concerned with the entire economic life of the nation, and the confiscation of their wealth could only lead to a sharp contraction of trade

[1] HMC, *Portland MSS*, V, 619; *Mist's Weekly Journal*, 8 April 1721; *The Naked and Undistinguished Truth* (1721), 28. These are typical examples of the virulence of the attack on Walpole.

[2] *C(H) MSS*, Sir Theodore Janssen, 24 May 1721. 'Particulars of Real and Personal Estate.'

and enterprise. Common sense dictated that they should not be so crippled that they would be forced to abandon business, for this could only be detrimental to national prosperity which Walpole had very much at heart. In the King's Speech at the beginning of this critical session he had stressed the need to encourage trade, for a revival of commerce and the renewal of confidence were likely to repair the disasters of the Bubble more quickly than inquiries and revenge. The destruction of some of the wealthiest merchants of the City was unlikely to encourage a quick renaissance. Furthermore, Walpole was not without humanity. It must be admitted that he could be ruthless when the nation was in peril or his own career in jeopardy. He had handled Bolingbroke and Oxford with the same relentless persistence with which Brodrick now hunted the South Sea Directors. He had set his face against clemency to the Jacobite peers. But in Walpole's view there was a vast difference between treason and peculation; towards the one he was remorseless, towards the other always tender. And again, the guilt of the Directors varied; even the most prejudiced members of the Commons realized that this was so. But the assessment of guilt from one Director to the next depended very much on personal prejudice, and prejudice rarely worked in favour of the convicted. Also there may have been what may seem to some a far less respectable motive. Walpole wanted supreme power. He had never denied this and had always sought it, so flagrantly indeed that many had come to hate him. He was involved in a great struggle with Sunderland which could end either in victory or defeat. Aislabie possessed important electoral interests in Yorkshire; Craggs's heirs owned boroughs in Cornwall; the South Sea Directors were connected with many merchant families who had their representatives in the Commons. Parliament had but a year to run. The gratitude of Aislabie was far more important to Walpole than the impotent hatred of a back-bench squire. And finally there was the Court. The King himself had speculated in South Sea stocks; his mistresses had been bribed as well as his ministers.[1] The inquiry was utterly distasteful to the Court; the instability of the English throne had been a byword for generations. The violence of the London mob, the uncontrolled vituperation of the Press, the vehement anger of the Commons, bred fear. In this shifting world Walpole's persistent policy of moderation made him a favourite at St James's. But he refrained from making his policy an issue of confidence. He cheerfully accepted defeat after defeat in the Commons. Afterwards he gained as much from pursuing this policy as he would have done from success. It was important, furthermore, to allow the placemen a free vote, for all of them did not come from closed boroughs which would elect them no matter how they voted. Some were accountable, many more feared that they might be. To have driven his screening policy through Parliament willy-nilly would have been disastrous. He allowed freedom on a number of issues, involving people of secondary importance, but kept a tight rein on matters of substance.

There were three occasions during these summer months when Walpole felt impelled to use full ministerial pressure to secure the government's majority in the Commons. In the middle of June, Methuen put forward the government's demand for supply to pay a subsidy to Sweden. The tories and old whigs attacked the ministry on what was rapidly becoming traditional grounds—the sacrifice of English interests for the sake of Hanover. It was a good rallying-cry which never failed to stir the hearts of the back-bench squires. Nevertheless the administration secured its supply with a steady majority of about forty. On this occasion office-holders such as Jekyll and Lechmere, who were usually found in the opposition lobby on questions relating to the South Sea, spoke strongly in support of Walpole. But his strength was more amply demonstrated when he called for a reduction of sixpence in the pound on all salaries, wages and pensions paid

[1] C(H) MSS, 88, 36a/1 and 2. For the King's account with Aislabie in Walpole's own handwriting, 16 September 1721. The King had purchased £20,000 first subscription which had been sold for £106,400.

by the Crown, in order to discharge the debt on the Civil List. Throughout his life Walpole remained very proud of having piloted this measure through the Commons at such a time, for naturally it created no enthusiasm amongst the placemen. It gratified many of the independents, with the result that his majority rose and in one division reached a hundred.[1]

Wisely, however, Walpole reserved the completion of the most difficult of all measures to the very end of the session. Parliament had been sitting nearly six months, and this bore very heavily on those ministers who needed to attend to the business of their estates yet had to stay on at Westminster. Nor did many relish the sultry and evil-smelling streets of London, particularly as bubonic plague was raging across the Eastern Mediterranean towards the West. The Privy Council had in June ordered the burning of two ships and their cargoes which had arrived from Smyrna.[2] Quite early in the session Walpole had attempted to secure a remission of the money owed to the government by the South Sea Company but he had been narrowly defeated in committee. He let the matter be for a month—an astonishingly long time to delay a committee's report. When at last it was introduced, he managed to get the motion negatived—a very rare and, some thought, irregular practice in money bills—by the narrow majority of eleven. Once more Walpole delayed the measure, and the Bill did not pass its final stages until August. The other half of the final settlement of the Company's affairs— the thorny question of what terms should be allowed to the holders of annuities—was also left to the very last days of the session. The terms were severe and aroused bitter opposition from the City, and though the holders tried to petition, Walpole would not permit them to do so. He secured the rejection of the petition by 78 votes to 29, a clear enough indication of the effect that his Fabian tactics had on the composition of the House. The infuriated mob swarmed into the lobbies, and was only with difficulty ejected by the justices

[1] Coxe, I, 157.
[2] Chandler, VI, 253–60.

and constables of Westminster.[1] Walpole insisted and got his
way. Harsh the terms might be but they were a final settlement and they put an end to uncertainty which in itself
destroyed confidence. From the moment the Bills which were
concerned with the South Sea crisis received royal assent
public credit began to revive.[2]

5

WALPOLE MUST have listened with relief to the speech pro-
roguing Parliament. Not until 1733 was he to face so difficult
a session. He had lost what little reputation he enjoyed with
the public. Curiously enough he was very sensitive to the
abuse which showered on him, and the King's speech at the
end of the session, probably drawn up by him, went out of
its way to animadvert on the malicious and seditious libels
spread abroad to create dissatisfaction. Although Walpole
resented the lampoons and their mockery they were irrelevant
to his political strength, as irrelevant as the vituperation and
sneers of the opposition in Parliament. His triumph in the
session was intimate, not public, for his role in the South Sea
crisis had been largely misunderstood. None of his financial
measures was constructive. The engraftment scheme, Jacombe's and not his, was not put into operation. The sequestration of the Directors' estates was forced on him, and he
never liked the measure or gave it much support. The settlement of terms for the annuitants was purely an administrative act and called for strength of character, not dexterity.
The only ingenuity in finance which he displayed in this
session was in his method of discharging the King's debts—
and this had nothing to do with the South Sea. The pane-
gyrics which historians have lavished on him for rescuing the
nation's credit have been wide of the mark. Tribute should
not be paid to his skill as a financier but to his indomitable
will as politician. Remorselessly he set about making bygones
bygones, setting his face resolutely against revenge which so

[1] Coxe, II, 218; *Parl. Hist.*, VII, 908-10; HMC, *Portland MSS*, V, 556.
[2] Scott, III, 346-53.

often masqueraded as justice, and even prepared to reject justice for the sake of a speedy and final settlement. At the same time he steadily ingratiated himself with the Court, seized every office which he could for his friends and relatives, and finished the session in as strong and as effective a position as Sunderland. Although Walpole had used the South Sea crisis to climb to the highest point he had yet reached in his political career, he was far from being supreme. The King was attached to Sunderland and enjoyed Carteret's company; Carleton was an old friend; Carteret and Carleton were popular with his German advisers. And Sunderland had the Secret Service money. Walpole's marked desire for power and Townshend's hasty temper did not endear them to their friends and infuriated their enemies.[1] The battle between Sunderland and Walpole was far from being over. Contemporaries did not misunderstand Walpole's position in 1721. They did not regard him as supreme nor as the King's first servant nor as prime minister. They knew that he shared power with Sunderland, who, they thought, would hold his ground.[2] Some prophesied that Walpole would be out again within twelve months and relished the prospect.[3] The whig control of the Court had been preserved at great cost, but peril had not bred harmony; the struggle for leadership remained intense and could only end in the death or defeat of Walpole or of Sunderland.

[1] C. B. Realey, *Early Opposition*, 54–5.
[2] HMC, *Carlisle MSS*, 31.
[3] Chandler, VI, 259.

Stephen Slaughter after Sir Godfrey Kneller

VIII. CHARLES, 3RD EARL OF SUNDERLAND IN 1722

CHAPTER TEN

THE END OF SUNDERLAND, 1721-2

WALPOLE slipped away to Norfolk a day or two before the formal closing by the King of the parliamentary session. He was exceptionally eager to return to Houghton because he had been continuously in London for rather more than nine months. The South Sea Bubble could not have blown up at a more awkward time for Walpole's private affairs, for not only was he busily extending his estates but he was also planning to change the face of Houghton itself. Sometime in 1720, probably during the long summer, which in spite of the financial crisis he was so eager to spend in Norfolk, he had come to the decision to pull down the old house and build a new Palladian mansion, far greater and finer than Norfolk had yet seen. He had chosen his architect, Colin Campbell, and appointed Thomas Ripley, whom he had befriended earlier, as supervisor of the building.[1] The house was designed to stand in a vast park with semi-formally disposed plantations, which were to create large vistas of exceptional grandeur, a project the fulfilment of which would require the village to be removed. Bridgeman, one of the earliest exponents of landscape gardening, was responsible for the park. By the summer of 1721 much had already been done; most of the plantations had been set and were giving employment to twenty-nine men and fifty women. The heaviest task, nearing completion, was the fencing of the park; hitherto it had been partly enclosed, and partly open and protected by ditches; now its extent was to be greatly increased.[2] In order to make a start on the new Houghton

[1] H. M. Colvin, *Dictionary of British Architects*, 504.

[2] Ripley was viewing timber for the house at Lincoln and Gainsborough towards the end of June 1721. Robert Hardy was appointed Clerk of the Works by 19 August 1721. *C(H) MSS*, Jonas Rolfe, 19 June 1721; Jonas Rolfe, 19 August 1721. For the plantations and increase of the park, *ibid.*, Edmund

the old stables had been torn down and new ones erected.[1] The influx of labourers and artisans had created considerable difficulties at Houghton. The village inn was too close to the work in progress, so that tippling in working hours became so excessive that Jonas Rolfe, acting as Walpole's steward (old John Wrott having died the previous year), was forced to threaten Dunsmore, the publican, with eviction and made him promise to close his house at ten o'clock every evening. Rolfe did not carry his anxieties easily nor did Edmund Cobb, who was acting as bailiff; in consequence Walpole was assailed with a stream of questions for decision, many of them trivial, throughout the difficult months of the debates on the South Sea crisis.

To add to his burdens a fierce quarrel had sprung up with his uncle, James Hoste of Sandringham, whose behaviour for a long time had not been friendly to Walpole. He was a bustling, cantankerous man and as justice of the peace he had forced himself into Walpole's Hundred at Bircham which, naturally enough, irritated Walpole's steward, as he saw his fees disappear. Hoste's servant picked a quarrel. Hoste joined in and reflections were made about Walpole himself. Letters of inordinate length swelled Walpole's postbag and frayed his temper. He tried evasion, but Hoste kept the quarrel going until at last Walpole was constrained to write sharply to Rolfe: 'As to Mr Hoste I have no answer to give but that I am fully satisfied what he has said is utterly false, and has cast such reflections upon me all over the country without the least pretence or provocation as are not to be endured, and if a servant of mine had said anything unbecoming, which in this case I am sure is not true, it gives him no title to take such liberties with me.'[2] That silenced Hoste but made him an inveterate enemy and he set to work with a will to undermine Walpole's parliamentary influence at Castle Rising, where he possessed some property.

Cobb, 5 June 1721; Robert Walpole to Jonas Rolfe, 13 July 1721; Fulke Harold, 17 July 1721.

[1] These are not the stables now at Houghton, which were built in the 1730s.
[2] C(H) MSS, Robert Walpole to Jonas Rolfe, 9 June 1721. For the quarrel see also ibid., Jonas Rolfe, 3 and 12 June 1721; also cf. p. 46.

And finally there were the negotiations, in which Walpole was deeply involved, for the purchase of land. He might take the decision to buy an estate, as he did with Lady Seaman's at Rudham, but as soon as his attorney got to work on the deeds he usually discovered a highly complex problem. Lady Seaman declared herself to be her father's heir-at-law. Her father was old Alderman Framlingham, the land-tax collector. (The first job that Walpole tackled as a Member of Parliament was to make certain of Framlingham's being in the land-tax commission.) But Britiffe, Walpole's attorney, was very wily and always insisted that Walpole should buy an estate only if the title could be proved clear at law, and Britiffe knew old Framlingham too well to believe that he had died intestate. So he rooted round the offices of the London attornies and unearthed a will, which proved Lady Seaman was not heir-at-law but only tenant-for-life, the estate being entailed in a highly complex way on her children. True, one had died and this cleared the way a little, but Britiffe was strongly against Walpole banking on either the mortality of the others or being able to extract their consent at twenty-one to a sale that had taken place many years previously. Yet the estate was valuable, Walpole wanted it, and Lady Seaman did not look a good life to Britiffe. The solution he suggested was for Walpole to get an Act of Parliament as quickly as possible to break the entail. But Walpole, and not Britiffe, would have to conduct that business. Then there was Pigg's estate at Anmer—should a guinea be given for two new ladders? And a lengthy report on Lord Fitzwilliam's farms at West Winch which Walpole was after.[1] There were problems enough to keep him busy in Norfolk for months, but no sooner had he arrived at Houghton than he received disturbing news from Jacombe.

2

THE DIRECTORS of the South Sea Company were intending

[1] *C(H) MSS*, Robert Britiffe, 10 July 1721; Jonas Rolfe, 12 June 1721; Philip Hart, 10 June 1721.

to exploit Walpole's absence and wreck his engraftment scheme. As soon as he heard of the Directors' intentions, Jacombe had rushed round to South Sea House and bearded Sir John Eyles, who admitted that many Directors hated the engraftment scheme; but Eyles promised not to hold a general court until Walpole returned. Jacombe, however, had his suspicions about Eyles and urged Walpole to write at once to those Directors whom he could trust. Jacombe's doubts were strengthened the next day, for Eyles had gone at once to see Townshend who had been very alarmed by Eyles's cold manner in speaking of Walpole's scheme and feared that he would doublecross them. Jacombe, in a panic, wrote again to Walpole in urgent terms, for he had found many other Directors '. . . in suspense, whom you could fix if you were here, no doubt of it—your enemys take advantage of your absence to counterworke you and I should be glad if your affairs would permitt you to return sooner than you intended that you might prevent any sudden step . . .'.[1] He also reported that Townshend seemed very uneasy at Walpole's absence. He was; but it was not entirely due to the sly deceit of the South Sea Directors. Sunderland was at work.

The rescue of Sunderland by Walpole had not bred a sense of gratitude but rather the reverse. Sunderland was a man of long memory and restless, fretful ambition. Like his father before him he revelled in the tactics of politics and paid too little attention to the principles which governed his strategy. It is true that eighteenth-century politics did not require much consistency in debate, or even of attitude to specific problems of government, but they did require a consistency of temperament, and the ability to create a sense of dependability in political friendships was of inestimable value to a statesman. Whereas Sunderland lacked this, with Walpole it was a part of his nature. Both were markedly ambitious men, but Walpole bred trust and by the warmth of his character drew a responsive loyalty from other men.[2] Sun-

[1] *C(H) MSS*, Robert Jacombe, 10 and 12 August 1721.
[2] BM, *Add MSS* 47117, fo. 334.

derland's hatred of Walpole had been intensified by recent events. It must have fretted his vanity to have been in need of Walpole's protection and to have been saved by his efforts. And though at times they seemed to be drawing together, Sunderland's mind was full of schemes to rid himself of Walpole. Townshend was to be forgiven—at the price of sacrificing his brother-in-law.[1]

Although the intrigue against Walpole had been brewing for some months, it became very active the moment he left London. Details of the plot have never come to light, but from the hints in Carteret's talks to Newcastle and from the actions of both Sunderland and Walpole, much may be surmised. Newcastle was a key figure in any ministerial reshuffle, for he controlled more borough patronage than any other nobleman.[2] Both Walpole and Sunderland were acutely conscious that the next general election could not be far distant. Walpole, worried by the shortness of time, had given serious consideration to the idea of prolonging the present Parliament, a move which Sunderland had been quick to counter, since he knew that every month that Walpole spent at the Treasury would make his victory in a general election more certain. Newcastle's allegiance, therefore, was of vital importance. Neither Sunderland or Carteret had any reason to doubt his loyalty in August 1721. After the end of the session Newcastle, like Walpole, had gone to his country house, but Carteret and Sunderland were shrewd enough not to ignore him and though they did not give him any details of their scheme, they did their best to give him the feeling that he was essential to their purpose and most highly valued. On 17 August, Carteret bemoaned his absence, and no doubt with a keen relish of the hypocrisy of his re-

---

[1] Torrens, *History of Cabinets*, I, 304.

[2] S. B. Nulle, *Thomas Pelham Holles, Duke of Newcastle* (Philadelphia, 1931), 23–53, 137–47. B. Williams, *Carteret and Newcastle*, 38, grossly exaggerates his influence in elections. He could influence strongly twelve seats according to L. B. Namier, *Structure of Politics*, I, 13, but Newcastle himself wrote on 19 October 1719: 'I will take the liberty to say that I myself will make the difference of 16 votes.' BM, *Add MSS*, 32,686, fo. 152.

marks went on to say that he was 'uneasy to have no one near to whom I can open my thoughts'. He opened his heart, he told Newcastle, to no one so freely because there was no one he loved so much.[1] In the same letter Carteret confidently reported that Sunderland's position with the King was as strong as it ever had been, and when they told the King how they intended to arrange matters, he had replied: '*Je veus qu'ils sachent que j'aurai toujours une particulière distinction pour Milord Sunderland et vous.*'[2] As Newcastle always responded with the lavish affection of a spaniel to any sign of human warmth, he wrote at once to Sunderland professing eternal loyalty in words that tumbled in a torrent from his pen. 'I have no one thought in the world but for the interest of the King, the whigg cause, and, if you will allow me to say so, your Lordship to which I shall ever be bound by the strongest tyes imaginable. . . . For God's sake, my dear Lord, give me leave for to hope for the sake of the King and all your faithful servants that you will continue at the head of the King's affairs, that the source and direction shall come from you, and that all others should act in the manner the King intends they should, and since they are convinced of that point, I verily believe they will. You know I neither love their persons nor court their interest. . . .'[3]

Whilst this welter of sentiment was flowing from London to Sussex and back again, Walpole had ridden post haste to London, arriving about 20 August. He cannot have spent more than three or four days in Norfolk upon the urgent problems which waited his attention there. Jacombe's letters, Townshend's obvious concern, and his own anxieties impelled him to return far sooner than he had intended. He was aware, of course, of Sunderland's dislike. He hated the man and expected no quarter, and some of his moves were obvious and easy enough to forecast. Walpole knew that Sunderland was intriguing with the Hanoverian tories, per-

[1] BM, *Add MSS* 32,686, ff. 185–7.
[2] *Ibid.*
[3] *Ibid.*, ff. 189–90.

haps even with the Jacobite tories, for his carriage had been seen frequently outside Francis Atterbury's house, and Carteret was said to be a daily visitor.[1] Towards the end of June, Walpole had called on Atterbury himself, either to ask his terms or to warn him of Sunderland's inability to help him. Whatever the motive, the visit did not stop Sunderland's approach to the tories. But by the end of August some of the shrewder leaders had grown sceptical of his power to accommodate them. William Bromley, a staunch country tory who had spent a lifetime of vicissitude without wavering from his old-fashioned Church-and-King principles, wrote to his former leader, Oxford, on 22 August 1721:

'I had a great deal at second hand of the project then pretended to be carrying on, but wanting faith, I absolutely declined the opportunities offered and pressed upon me of receiving all possible assurances. . . . Promises were made to me so extravagantly large, that it was affronting me to imagine that I could think them sincere, and be imposed upon by them.'[2]

Of course, the tories were only a part of Sunderland's scheme and probably not the most important; his need to come to terms with them arose from the fear that they might once more combine successfully with Walpole if the latter were driven from office.

The test of strength between Walpole and Sunderland arose over the question of the promotion of Charles Stanhope. The proposal, backed by Carteret as well as Sunderland, was to make him Treasurer of the Chamber, an office which had been half promised to him when he had resigned the Secretaryship of the Treasury during the South Sea crisis. It will be remembered that he had been deeply implicated in the Company's affairs. The evidence against him was very strong and his acquittal had been secured by the narrowest of margins—three votes. He was the first cousin of Earl Stanhope, whose death had so weakened Sunderland. His pro-

[1] H. C. Beeching, *Francis Atterbury*, 274. HMC, *Portland MSS*, VII, 295. Dr Stratford thought that Atterbury was duped by Sunderland.
[2] HMC, *Portland MSS*, V, 625.

motion, therefore, at this time would show that the King's trust was firmly placed in the Sunderland group. There could be no other interpretation of his being granted office after his near disgrace. Furthermore, the fact that he was to be given office in the Treasury of which Walpole was the head would undermine Walpole's importance. The move to promote him was nicely calculated to display where the real power lay at Court. Finally it was timed to take place during Walpole's absence in Norfolk. But Walpole had become aware of his danger. He returned precipitately from Norfolk, for he fully understood the nature of the crisis and from the moment he arrived in London he bitterly opposed the suggestion of giving Stanhope office. Naturally he did not oppose Stanhope outright. That might have led to a showdown which he did not want. He asked for the matter to be delayed until the following March, arguing that the promotion of Stanhope would 'revive matters in Parliament concerning the South Sea'. This convinced the King of the need to refuse Stanhope, which, as Carteret admitted to Newcastle, 'mortified Lord Sunderland and me not a little, but when Mr Walpole has taken upon him that all South Sea matters shall be kept out of Parliament next sessions, we could not persiste in a point which would bring us to answer for any ill event in Parliament that should happen on such an occasion'.[1] Walpole's temper was frayed by this subtle attack on him in his absence, but a break between the leaders was prevented by Townshend, whom the King liked and trusted. 'If,' wrote Carteret on 22 August 1721, to Newcastle, 'he could govern Mr Walpole, all would answer his engagements. The King was resolved that the First Lord should not govern, but it was hard to prevent it.'[2]

3

THAT, INDEED, was the dilemma. No one, apart from Townshend, and perhaps the Princess of Wales, wanted to see

[1] Torrens, *History of Cabinets*, I, 305; BM, *ADD MSS* 32,686, ff. 183, 185–7, 191.
[2] BM, *Add MSS* 32,686, fo. 193.

Walpole continuing long in power. The fashionable stories that were circulating about him were to his discredit and strengthened the belief that George I did not like him. Chesterfield, many years later, related that the King at this period was only waiting on events to get rid of him, and that the Duchess of Kendal was equally antipathetic to him. Undoubtedly these reports were exaggerated, but they must contain a substratum of truth, and it is easy to see why they should.[1] Walpole irradiated power and no one who had spent any time with him could doubt his intention to use to the full any opportunities which he might make for himself. But, and this is important, his desire for power was not entirely personal. He had a profound conviction that he knew how to lead the country back to prosperity and make it wealthier than it had ever been. The accent was on wealth rather than glory, and the King's Speech drafted by him and Townshend for the new session, opened on 19 October 1721, made this very clear.

'In this situation of affairs,' it ran, 'we should be extremely wanting to ourselves, if we neglected to improve the favourable opportunity which this general tranquillity gives us,[2] of extending our Commerce upon which the riches and grandeur of this nation chiefly depend. It is very obvious that nothing would more conduce to the obtaining so publick a good, than to make the exportation of our own manufactures, and the importation of the commodities used in the manufacturing of them as practicable and easy as may be; by this means, the balance of trade may be preserved in our favour, our navigation increased, and greater numbers of our poor employed.'[3]

This was a positive policy, a clarion call to London and the principal merchants, and a bait to the independent country gentlemen, who would scent low taxes in commercial prosperity. It was a positive and creative policy, and Walpole's restless energy longed to be fully employed on its ful-

[1] Sir G. H. Rose, *A Selection from the Papers of the Earls of Marchmont*, I, 3.
[2] The Northern war had just been concluded.
[3] Chandler, VI, 263.

filment. Until the struggle between Sunderland and himself was finally resolved there was little he could do except bait the appetite and stir the imagination of those solid men who sat mutely on the back benches. Silent they might be yet they were alive to the struggle raging above and about them. They had little liking for any King's servants; they had detested Walpole's actions in the previous session. They relished the lampoons and calumnies against him in the Press. And yet their minds and hearts were not quite closed to him. He was, after all, in origin, in manners, in looks, one of them. His florid countenance and direct coarse speech, even the way he munched little red Norfolk apples to keep him going during the debates, helped to create that deceptive air of rusticity, of Norfolk squiredom, which he knew how to exploit so artfully. And in these critical months, when he could never be certain how the Court vote might go, when his colleagues themselves were involved in so many intrigues against him, this link between himself and the back benchers strengthened his hand. Perhaps its most valuable quality was the fear which this relationship aroused in Sunderland, Carteret and others. They had spent their lives in the House of Lords; there and at Court the friendship between them had grown and strengthened. The Commons were a different, turbulent world in which they had no colleague of any ability. In consequence their letters are full of their fear of Walpole's power. And that fear is the key to Walpole's success. He had incurred odium with the public. The King did not like him, neither did Kendal nor Kielmannsegge. Sunderland and Carteret loathed him. And yet they lacked the courage to go through with their scheme. They gave way on Charles Stanhope, whose promotion was the critical test of power. And by the end of September, Carteret was writing defensively to Newcastle: 'no ground has been lost since your absence' [i.e. during the summer]. But they had gained none and in that lay Walpole's hope. Time was on his side. Yet it is important not to exaggerate the strength of his position in the government even as late as the autumn of 1721. He was

THE END OF SUNDERLAND, 1721-2

not Prime Minister either in fact or in name. Sunderland still held that position, for he still controlled the Secret Service money, disposed of a great deal of patronage, and still possessed the King's ear.[1] A general election in accordance with the Septennial Act had to take place in 1722, and that election would be controlled by Sunderland and Newcastle as much as by Walpole. They could not destroy all his friends nor clear the Commons of its independents, but they could, and they intended to, reduce his strength. Of that Walpole was aware; in reply he began to press for a repeal of the Septennial Act, in order to perpetuate the existing Parliament. Sunderland, who had contemplated the same measure with equanimity as a *quid pro quo* for his Peerage Bill, now argued for an immediate dissolution and pressed his views on the King.[2]

The struggle between Sunderland and Walpole was not openly avowed; appearances of harmony were kept up at the most critical times. Even when the struggle about Charles Stanhope was at its height, Walpole and Townshend with Sunderland and Carteret, went off together on a day's outing to Richmond to visit the Prince.[3] They were seen together at both Courts; they dined and drank together and on all issues spoke as one voice either in the Lords or Commons. No one was deceived. Court, town and countryside knew that Sunderland and Walpole hated each other and neither could rest until the other was disgraced or dead. And Sunderland possessed the advantage in October 1721. Although he was only Groom of the Stole, he was, in effect, the principal minister. If he had lost reputation with the public by his South Sea ventures, so too had Walpole.

4

WALPOLE'S POSITION was difficult and allowed him little

[1] For Secret Service payments cf. *Blenheim MSS*, D. II, 10. Cf. also W. Michael, *Das Zeitalter Walpoles*, 212-5.

[2] Coxe, II, 217.

[3] BM, *Add MSS* 32,686, fo. 187; *Blenheim MSS*, D.II, 1. Sunderland's letters to his wife in 1721 contain several references to dinners with Walpole at Chelsea.

room to manoeuvre. Mostly he waited on events and played for time, crossing Sunderland only when, as in the case of Charles Stanhope, his own position was threatened. Otherwise he tried to demonstrate as clearly as possible to the King his capacity to carry through the King's business in the Commons. Fortunately there he had no rival, and the problems which he was called upon to handle required both his boldness and skill. Naturally, he made the most of his work in the Commons for it was essential if he was to survive that he should still be in control of the Treasury at the general election which was to take place in the spring of 1722.

Before turning to the way he handled the government business during this session, it is necessary to note one factor which worked considerably in Walpole's favour and with which he himself had nothing to do. In the redistribution of offices during the South Sea crisis, the old Lord Chancellor, Cowper, had been ignored and his self-avowed retirement accepted without question. Lady Cowper, who had lost and not gained from the reconciliation of the King and Prince, was an embittered woman, and her resentment, together with her husband's disappointment, was sufficient to stimulate Cowper into an out-and-out opposition to the ministry in the Lords during this session. In this he was helped by the brilliant and impulsive Duke of Wharton, whose losses in the South Sea Bubble had destroyed what little sense of restraint he had hitherto possessed. They opposed every possible issue and invented a new technique of turning their protests into effective propaganda. Any peer had an ancient right to have his written protest against any measure entered into the Journals of the House of Lords; the custom, although ancient, was more or less moribund. Cowper and Wharton revived it and what is more had their protests printed. The novelty of being able to read about the conflicts of opinion in the House of Lords caught the fancy of the public and these protests secured a wide circulation and helped to maintain the bitterness against the government which the South Sea crisis had created. Cowper and Wharton were whigs, Cowper a highly respected one, and they commanded some support. The defection of Wharton to the government, early in December, made little difference to Cowper's 'cabal' which remained about twenty strong. Although it was merely an irritant so long as the ministry remained united, it would have become of vital importance were the ministry to split, a fact which Cowper must have well understood and which fortified him in his intransigence. The effect on Sunderland, however, was to increase his hesitation in bringing his struggle with Walpole to a decision. There can be little doubt that Cowper's violent opposition, curiously enough, helped to preserve Walpole in office.[1]

Walpole, however, was his own best advocate, and his handling of the Commons must have strengthened his position with the King, whose interest in English affairs had been sharpened by the recent crisis. Although this session of Parliament was kept short, two problems of great difficulty arose in which the Court was sorely pressed—one was the final settlement of the South Sea Company's affairs in a new engraftment scheme; the other a sordid tale of bribery which involved one of His Majesty's judges. Fortunately, for the latter there exists a detailed account of the parliamentary debates which gives a closer view of Walpole in action than any other source at this time and displays admirably his tactical dexterity in debate.[2]

On 1 February 1722, Sir John Cope, an Oxfordshire gentleman who was Member for Tavistock, rose in his place and accused Sir Francis Page, a Baron of the Exchequer, of attempting the wholesale bribery of the Corporation of Banbury where a by-election was taking place. The accusation was judiciously timed, for only a few days previously the

---

[1] For Cowper's opposition cf. C. B. Realey, *Early Opposition*, 81–4; also *Arch. Etr. Corr. Ang.*, 338, ff. 204–5, 233–5.

[2] *Harrowby MSS*, Doc. 29 (Part I), by Dudley Ryder, entitled *Memoirs of my own and facts happening in my time*. Ryder obtained his account of the debates 'from Mr Philip Ward who was in the House all the time'. Ward was not a Member of Parliament but access to the House was easy enough. Also Chandler, VI, 275 *et seq*.

House had committed a private Bill, sponsored by that sturdy independent Archibald Hutcheson, for the better securing of freedom of elections. As the ministry were embarrassed by this Bill (for it was difficult to oppose it openly) they were allowing it to proceed, but in so dilatory a fashion that it was most unlikely to pass both Houses before the session came to an end. Cope's accusation, which 'set the House in a flame', might easily create a sense of urgency in the House and so make the passing of the Bill a matter of immediate necessity which the ministry might find difficult to prevent. The implications of Cope's attack were quickly appreciated and the Banbury case became a *cause célèbre*.

Tempers were short in the Commons, and many members were eager to censure Page there and then on Cope's testimony. Walpole, however, sprang to his defence and pleaded for time. He asked the House to defer all inquiry until the election was over, and then to hear what Page had to say for himself. At length the House agreed, but some damage was done, for the members settled down to work with a will on the Committee stage of Hutcheson's Bill. In order to expedite it, the country gentlemen accepted a number of ministerial amendments with disheartening promptitude. However, the Court was not unduly worried as they had no doubt of the ultimate fate of the Bill if they were unable to delay it until the dissolution. They failed to do this, so the Lords with strong episcopal support secured its rejection. Cope, however, proved more difficult to deal with. On 13 February he informed the House that his witnesses had been tampered with, and asked the House to take evidence on this point first. Walpole vehemently opposed the suggestion, maintaining that it must prejudice Page, who should be heard first. This move failed, and the House insisted on hearing the witnesses, whose story was clear enough. After Cope's first accusation a relative of Page had slipped down to Banbury, called the Corporation together, and pointed out that witnesses examined by the Commons were not put on oath; the Corporation took his point at once—they would not be liable for perjury whether they told the truth or not. The back-benchers grew angry at such an affront to the dignity of the House and heartily endorsed Archibald Hutcheson's demand to put the witnesses on oath. Walpole would not have it. His arguments were far-fetched—that to put witnesses on oath would provoke a quarrel with the Lords, who regarded the power to put witnesses on oath as belonging to them alone. Shippen quickly made hay of his flimsy argument and the Speaker was forced to admit there were precedents of putting witnesses on oath, but (he maintained) only by a committee of the House and not by the whole House—a most adroit move, for it split the back-benchers, who knew what the answer would be once the case went to a committee; so the motion to discharge the House of this examination and put it to a committee was lost. After that had been decided Hutcheson moved for the House to proceed to put the witnesses on oath, though not in committee. Walpole, who thought he had outmanoeuvred the opposition by the previous vote, lost his temper. What they proposed was unprecedented and they were voting on the same motion twice for the 'meaning of the present question is but the same with the last'. His force and certainty may have baffled some of the slower-witted squires, for the motion was lost by two votes. The witnesses were heard without oath; whether they spoke the truth or lied they told a sorry tale. The corporation had offered to elect Page's candidate in return for his paving the streets, augmenting the vicarage and erecting a school. The discharge of a debt of £500 which they owed the judge for help in obtaining their new charter was also expected. The money, of course, was to be paid to the Corporation of fourteen who were Banbury's sole parliamentary electors. Page's defence was not denial but the contention that as these payments were for the good of the public, they could not be described as either bribery or corruption. After two days' wrangling on the evidence, Walpole managed to save Page by four votes.

It had been an unseemly scandal—more unseemly to

us than to the eighteenth century, for it was the type of exposure which might have happened to anyone who dabbled in the affairs of small corporations. Archibald Hutcheson, who at this time was speaking with such moral fervour about the horrors of corruption and bribery and posing as the leader of the independent country gentlemen, was himself Member for Hastings, whose handful of electors were of no stronger moral fibre than those of Banbury. Corruption might have been rife amongst the supporters of the ministry, but certainly the opposition stank of hypocrisy. Probably the leaders on both sides cared little about the issues involved; these were left to the knights of the shire on the back bench. What was critical, however, was the closeness of the government's defeat. In the avoidance of that defeat Walpole had shown a skill and resilience in debate which no one else could equal. It was neither the first time nor the last time, but it demonstrated to the Court at a critical moment his capacity for extricating the ministry, caught unawares and placed in jeopardy.

During this session Walpole gave evidence not only of his tactical skill in handling the Commons but also of his immense stamina, than which there are few more valuable attributes in political life. A settlement of the South Sea Company's affairs had still to be reached. The scandal had been dealt with, new Directors installed, the old ones punished. Though no one felt that justice had been done, time had quietened the rage and the fury. Gold had come out of hiding and the market had recovered some of its old buoyancy. The scheme which Walpole had pushed through Parliament had served its purpose as a sedative. He was not content, however, to let the matter rest there. He wanted the engraftment scheme to go into operation. Before it could do so, it required the consent of the Company. Suspicions that the Directors would not advise this course of action had reached Jacombe early in August and he had warned both Townshend and Walpole, and it was intrigue against his scheme as well as intrigue for Charles Stanhope which had

brought him rushing back from Norfolk.[1] In his interviews
with Townshend, Sir John Eyles, the new head of the Company, had prevaricated about engraftment, but on 1 September at a meeting of the General Court he came out
strongly against it, maintaining that the assets of the Company with the forfeited estates of the old Directors were
sufficient to discharge its debts without recourse to other
corporations. Since Jacombe had first outlined his scheme to
Walpole he had been convinced that the nation's financial
stability depended upon its acceptance. He at once began,
therefore, to create a Court party in the Company in the hope
of securing the acceptance of the scheme when it came to its
final vote on 1 December 1722. Naturally, Walpole's attitude
was widely misinterpreted. The crusted tories at Oxford
thought that the aim was to aggrandize the Bank and 'by
that to govern the other companies and consequently the
whole Kingdom'. A sight of Walpole's bank book would have
been quite unlikely to convince old Dr Stratford of Walpole's
honesty, but it would have shown that Walpole's investment
was far, far higher in the South Sea Company than in the
Bank.[2] In his struggle to secure the acceptance of the engraftment scheme Walpole was moved by conviction, not interest. The vote on 1 December was known to be critical;
some rumours suggest that Sunderland supported Walpole;
others that he would use an adverse vote to get rid of him.[3]
It is hard to believe that Sunderland could have given Walpole help on any issue at this time and behind the Court's
defeat by 178 votes may lie a story of duplicity and chicanery.
But Walpole was not so easily overborne. He held his hand
and waited his opportunity. It came appropriately enough towards the end of February, when Parliament was drawing

[1] *C(H) MSS*, Robert Jacombe, 12 August 1721.
[2] Walpole had £16,717 17s. in South Sea Stock invested in the names of
Jacob, Gibson and Jacombe on 30 August 1721; in addition he was still owed
£18,000 by Sir Cesar Child, secured on South Sea stock. He had £2,000 in
the Bank, though his wife probably had more. *C(H) MSS*, Financial Jottings.
[3] HMC, *Portland MSS*, VIII, 309-10. The rumour that Walpole was to go
raised South Sea stock by ten points. Cf. also Realey, *Early Opposition*, 73-4

near to its close. As Walpole expected, the sanguine expectations of Sir John Eyles proved false; the South Sea Company was unable to meet its debts and the Directors were forced to apply to the government for an Act of Parliament to enable them to sell some of their assets. When the Bill was in committee Walpole secured the addition of a clause which would enable the Bank or any other corporation to purchase a part of the Company's capital fund. There were cries of 'engraftment', and Pulteney denounced the clause and accused Walpole to his face of being in the pay of the Bank. Walpole did not bother to deny the charge that what he was proposing was engraftment which, he maintained, had always been to the interest and advantage of the Company; but he hotly resented Pulteney's accusation of secret and dishonest motives. His speech was as dignified as it was forceful and carried the House; his clause was incorporated in the Bill and engraftment crept in through the back door. The whole of this story is mysterious; the underlying theme is as hard to piece together as notes of music scattered by a gale. Contemporaries found it easier to interpret these strange battles, which flared with such intensity so suddenly and often about issues with seemingly only an oblique reference to the main theme. They recognized that these conflicts were the bones of contention seized on almost arbitrarily by the two great factions warring for power. Who provoked Cope's exposure of a Baron of the Exchequer, of which Walpole was the Chancellor? Who strengthened Eyles's dislike of engraftment, which in August he had been ready to accept? There is no evidence; yet suspicion must rest on Sunderland. If that is true, then Walpole's skill is heightened and his dexterity in avoiding these pitfalls commands respect. He survived and maintained himself as Chancellor of the Exchequer. That gave him a chance at the election of 1722, for although Sunderland retained his hold on the Secret Service money Walpole could use to his own great advantage the influence which the Treasury exercised through the Customs and Excise.

EVERYTHING DEPENDED on the result of the election which started in March 1722. Preparations had been long and very devious. The tories hoped to gain both from the divisions of the whigs and from the obloquy of the South Sea scandal. Sunderland and Walpole tried to preserve the whig supremacy, but neither of them preferred a client of the other to a tory. Sunderland secretly supported J. Brinsden at Wootton Basset against Chetwynd, although Brinsden was the agent of Bolingbroke.[1] Walpole had been up to exactly the same trick at Beeralston where he had 'quit his countryman, Sir John Hobart', and engaged his friends for St John Brodrick, a tory.[2] Both went out of their way to placate Archibald Hutcheson. Walpole secured a quick, fair trial for Hutcheson's Jewish friends in the Court of the Exchequer; Sunderland received with gratitude long-winded statements of his political creed. Hutcheson thanked both profusely but their time was wasted, for nothing would deflect him from his self-satisfied course of intractable independence.[3] Anxiety pressed so heavily on Walpole that he felt that he could not risk a trip to Norfolk to attend his own election at Lynn. His uncle, Hoste, too, had been intriguing against his influence at Castle Rising and his presence was highly desirable. He could not bring himself to go; greater injury might be done him at Court, so he left his affairs in the none too capable hands of Jonas Rolfe, and pleaded 'Extraordinary Businesse' as his excuse.[4]

The Duke of Newcastle spent hugely on Sunderland's behalf both in Sussex and in Nottingham. He made long

[1] Blenheim MSS, D.I, 38, J. Brinsden to Sunderland, 22 March 1722. Wm. Chetwynd, Brinsden's opponent, was a Courtier and at the time inclined to Walpole.

[2] Coxe, II, 217. Shaftesbury seems to be another borough where they clashed. C(H) MSS, Charles Withers, 13 May 1722.

[3] C(H) MSS, A. Hutcheson, 8 August 1722; Blenheim MSS, D.I, 33, A. Hutcheson to Sunderland, 3 and 11 April 1722.

[4] Ibid., Jonas Rolfe, 19 August 1721; Robert Walpole to Jonas Rolfe, 17 March 1722.

slow electoral tours in which he was rarely sober for days on end, but the outcome was outstanding success ior his candidates, and he urged Sunderland to convey at once the results of this triumph to the King.[1] Sunderland himself was busy everywhere, and his correspondence (if one can judge by the replies) must have been full of directions, exhortations and advice. As the results came in he began to draw up his lists; yet before either he or Walpole could know precisely how they stood to each other he was struck down with pleurisy and died on 19 April 1722.[2] His death, more than any other single event—certainly far more than the crisis of the South Sea Bubble—brought supreme power within Robert Walpole's grasp. The King was deeply disturbed by Sunderland's death, because he feared Walpole, feared the power which he irradiated and resented the sense of inferiority which his presence created. But there was no one else. Carteret lacked followers and Newcastle, who had the followers, lacked the courage and the necessary mastery of men. On the day after Sunderland's death Robert Walpole became the first servant of King George I, and his Premiership began.

6

THE RISE of Robert Walpole to power now appears to be part of an inevitable historical process. The failure of the Stuarts, the folly and incoherence of the tory party, the ascendancy of the whig attitude both amongst the merchants and the nobility, the lack, in fact, of any alternative, gave the Hanoverian Court into whig keeping. And yet the men who lived through these times never enjoyed the sweet relish of certainty. For they lived through tumultuous days, days when England knew civil war, insurrection, rebellion, plots, assassinations and traitors' deaths. To them the Stuarts were not the object of romantic nostalgia but of a desperate

[1] *Blenheim MSS*, D.I, 33, Newcastle to Sunderland, 31 March 1722; also S. B. Nulle, *op. cit.*, 137–46.

[2] *Ibid.*, D.I, 38, contains Sunderland's election correspondence. D.II, 10, contains a list of members marked 'doubtfuls'.

loyalty or a gnawing fear. Politics were still cruel and still dangerous: the journey from Westminster to the Tower short and well-trodden. Such times breed harshness. And the ferocity of political life arose partly from the deeper fears and anxieties which corrupted the motives of men who struggled for power. Since the Revolution of 1688 England had failed to achieve political stability; disintegration had been rendered worse by the weakness of the Queen and the growth of factions which flourished at the expense of party. So long as the whigs were sharply divided, both the tories and the Stuarts had a chance of returning to power. Long ago Sunderland's father had stressed the necessity of the government of the country being in the hands of a small closely allied group, but no set of men had achieved such dominion until Walpole replaced Sunderland in 1722. Walpole was able to consolidate the immense advantage which the deaths of Stanhope and Sunderland so fortunately gave him, and the country enjoyed a stability of government such as it had not known for a hundred years; a pattern of politics came into being which lasted long beyond the century which brought it into being.

Walpole's emergence was a triumph of character, strongly aided by luck; his role in the South Sea crisis has been widely misinterpreted, the strength and power of Sunderland belittled. Until April 1722, there was no certainty that Walpole would ever become the King's first servant. His qualities were known—his mastery of complex details, his ability with figures, his capacity for work, the range of his memory, the quickness of his judgment, the strength of his resolution. Yet the King, and his courtiers, and most men in office, feared, disliked and envied him. He liked power too openly. He knew too decidedly what he wanted to do. He was impatient of restraint and frankly contemptuous of lesser men, and these qualities might have prevented his rise to power, but for the happy accident of the deaths of his enemies. No picture is falser than that which portrays Walpole riding to power on the crest of a wave of public opinion. In 1721 he

379

was the most execrated and despised man in public life, hated, indeed, far more intensely than Sunderland or the South Sea Directors. The Bubble certainly made Walpole, though only by providing him with unlooked-for political opportunities which he seized and exploited. In his handling of the crisis he showed qualities of statesmanship of the highest order. He preserved the structure of government at a time when it could easily have dissolved in chaos. The skill displayed in his financial arrangements at this time is, however, a myth of the historian. They were technically useless. What he should be praised for is this: he checked a return to the chaotic politics of Anne's reign. Vengeance and justice, so morally satisfying, could only have destroyed the growing strength of the monarchy, jeopardized the Succession, and split the whigs for a generation. True, his policy was in line with his own interests. Walpole never denied it. As he himself said, he was not 'a saint or a reformer'. His ambitions were narrow—pre-eminence for himself; peace and prosperity for his country. After a long, and frequently discreditable, struggle, he had achieved the power he sought. It remains to be seen how he used it.

A NOTE ON SOURCES

The most important source for this volume is Sir Robert Walpole's own archives belonging to the Marquess of Cholmondeley, formerly at Houghton, Norfolk, and now deposited until 1960 at the University Library, Cambridge. These papers were arranged by A. G. Chinnery and a full description of them is to be found in a *Handlist to the Cholmondeley (Houghton) MSS* published by the Cambridge University Library. A few detailed letters from this collection are in the University of Chicago Library and in the possession of Dr W. S. Lewis. Regrettably many papers have disappeared. Letters from members of Walpole's family are abundant from 1700 to 1706, after that they become exceedingly rare. Except for the years 1720–2 there is very little other personal correspondence of importance and Walpole's official papers are not numerous for this early period. Fortunately Walpole's brother, Horatio, carefully preserved his own correspondence and his archives, in the possession of Lord Walpole at Wolterton, have proved invaluable for this volume. Many of Townshend's papers have been dispersed but much remains at Raynham, including the valuable run of cabinet minutes from 1714–16.

Walpole's rivals, however, preserved more papers than his friends. Although many of Charles, 3rd Earl of Sunderland's papers were destroyed, a vast quantity still exists at Blenheim. Many of these, particularly his letters, have been printed either by Coxe or Churchill, but there is still a considerable quantity unpublished. The papers of Stanhope are to be found at Chevening. These were used extensively by Basil Williams in his life of Stanhope. He missed little of importance, but there are one or two letters at Chevening which

throw considerable light on Walpole's marriage. The *Cowper*
(*Panshanger*) *MSS*, now deposited at the Hertfordshire Record Office, have proved richer in unpublished material. The
manuscript of Mary Lady Cowper's Diary differs considerably from the printed version; her letters, too, are of great
value for the period 1716–20, which is rather deficient in
material. Other collections of importance are at the British
Museum: the *Portland MSS*, in which there are a great
number of letters and papers which were ignored by the
editors of the Historical Manuscripts Commission's report on
these manuscripts when they were at Welbeck; the Hanoverian State Papers in the *Stowe MSS* and the Newcastle
papers in the *Additional MSS* have yielded little that has not
been used by other historians of the period; the same is true
of the State Papers Domestic at the Public Record Office.
Other collections which have yielded a few letters of value
are the *Howard MSS* at Castle Rising; the *Harrowby MSS*; the
Felbrigg MSS; and the *Chatsworth MSS*.

As excellent bibliographical guides exist for this period of
English history there is little point in listing all the printed
books which have been consulted in the writing of this
volume. Readers are referred to Stanley Pargellis and D. J.
Medley, *Bibliography of British History, The Eighteenth Century,
1714–89* (Oxford, 1951), and W. T. Morgan, *A Bibliography
of British History, 1700–15* (Bloomington, Indiana, 1934–42).
There are, however, one or two books which call for comment. Archdeacon William Coxe's *Life and Administration of
Sir Robert Walpole* (1798), has not been bettered by any subsequent historian. Other lives of Walpole have been marred
either by a lack of scholarship or by the attempt to see him
as the first modern prime minister. The shrewdest comment
on any part of Walpole's career is by C. B. Realey in his
Early Opposition to Sir Robert Walpole, 1720–7 (Kansas, 1931),
a book of real value, which, however, places too great reliance on Jacobite sources. Most of Walpole's colleagues and

rivals still await their biographers. W. Sichel, *Bolingbroke and His Times* (1901–2) is ludicrously adulatory. No serious attempt has yet been made to write a life of Harley, Sunderland or Townshend although materials exist in abundance for all of them. B. Williams, *Stanhope* (Oxford, 1932), is scholarly if pedestrian.

The period is better served by its general histories. The most outstanding is W. Michael, *Englische Geschichte im Achtzehnten Jahrhundert* (Leipzig, 1896–1945). The first two volumes were translated under the editorship of Sir Lewis Namier; their English titles are *The Beginnings of the Hanoverian Dynasty* (1936) and *The Quadruple Alliance* (1939). It is to be hoped that the work of translation will be completed. Michael also published a number of illuminating papers of great importance to students of early eighteenth-century history, and, after Coxe, I am more indebted to his work than to any other. For the period before 1714 I placed a similar reliance on G. M. Trevelyan's *England under Queen Anne* (1930–4). Coxe's *Memoirs of the Duke of Marlborough* (1818–9) and Sir Winston Churchill, *Marlborough, His Life and Times* (1933–4), contain a vast amount of valuable material.

Special studies, where used, are mentioned in the footnotes and I have relied on other scholars, particularly for Chapters I and II; without the work of Sidney and Beatrice Webb on Local Government, Sir Lewis Namier on Parliament, Professor Norman Sykes on the Church and Professor Mark Thomson and Professor Edward Hughes on Administration, these chapters could not have been written. The articles of Professor H. J. Habakkuk have illuminated the social and economic history of this period and deepened our understanding of it. My debt to him in Chapter I will be obvious to all. The most serious lacuna for a political historian is the absence of an up-to-date study of the South Sea Bubble by an economic historian. W. R. Scott, *The Constitution and Finance of English, Scottish and Irish Joint Stock Companies to 1720* (Cambridge, 1910–12), remains the most reliable guide, supplemented by A. B. DuBois, *The English Business Company after the Bubble Act, 1720–1800* (New York, 1938). N. Brisco, *The Economic Policy of Sir Robert Walpole* (Columbia, 1907), is of little value.

What merit this book may have springs largely from the work of these scholars and from others whose works are mentioned in the text. This note is not intended for a comprehensive bibliography; it is merely an expression of a debt of gratitude.

ABBREVIATIONS

Add. MSS.	Additional Manuscripts.
Arch. Aff. Etr. Corr. Ang.	Archives des Affaires Etrangères, Correspondance d'Angleterre. (Quai d'Orsay.)
BM.	British Museum.
Cal. Treas. Bks.	*Calendar of Treasury Books.*
Cal. S.P. Dom.	*Calendar of State Papers, Domestic.*
Chandler.	Richard Chandler. *The History and Proceedings of the House of Commons from the Restoration to the Present Time*, London 1742-4 (14 vols.).
C(H)MSS.	*Cholmondeley (Houghton) Manuscripts.* *Note:* as letters are chronologically arranged, all references are by writer and date. The addressee, unless otherwise stated, is Robert Walpole.
Churchill.	Sir Winston Churchill, *Marlborough, His Life and Times* (ed. 1947) 2 vols.
CJ.	*Journals of the House of Commons.*
Coxe.	William Coxe. *Memoirs of the Life and Administration of Sir Robert Walpole, Earl of Orford*, London 1798 (3 vols.).
DNB.	*Dictionary of National Biography.*
Ec. Hist. Rev.	*Economic History Review.*
EHR.	*English Historical Review.*
GEC.	George Edward Cockayne. *The Complete Peerage*, new ed. Revised and enlarged by

	Hon. Vicary Gibbs and others. London 1910 —.
GEC. Barts.	George Edward Cockayne. *The Complete Baronetage* (1611-1800), Exeter 1900-6 (5 vols.).
Hervey.	John, Lord Hervey. *Some Materials towards Memoirs of the Reign of King George II.* ed. Romney Sedgwick, London 1931 (3 vols.).
HMC.	Historical Manuscripts Commission.
LCC.	London County Council.
PCC.	Prerogative Court of Canterbury.
PRO.	Public Record Office.
RO.	Record Office.
SP.	State Papers.
Timberland.	Ebenezer Timberland. *The History and Proceedings of the House of Lords from the Restoration to the Present Time*, London 1742-3 (8 vols.).
Trans. R. Hist. Soc.	*Transactions of the Royal Historical Society.*
VCH.	*Victoria County History.*
WO.	War Office.

INDEX

Abingdon, 142

*Account of the Examination of R. W.
Esq. for Bribery and Corruption
(Anon)*, 183

Addison, Joseph, MP, 115, 190, 245

Africa Company, cf. Royal African Company

Aislabie, John, Chancellor of the Exchequer, 297, 347, 354, 355 n. 1; and South Sea Company, 302–3; accused of corruption, 341–3; imprisoned, 344; estates partially restored, 351–2

Aldred, Capt., 119

Allen, William, 308, 314

Amelia, Princess, 123

Anmer (Norfolk), 361

Anne, Queen, 20, 43, 66–7, 94, 118, 138–9, 186, 193, 201, 380; and Hanoverian Succession, 172; and Marlboroughs, 117, 128, 139, 141–2, 146, 151, 153, 166, 175; and whigs and tories, 110–11, 128, 143, 148, 157–60, 175, 196, 250, 379; and Harley, 128, 163, 188, 196, 201; and Bolingbroke, 185, 188, 195–7; health, 161, 188, 250; death, 197

Arbuthnot, Dr John, 258 n.3

Archdale, Thomas, 121

Argyll, John Campbell, 2nd Duke of, 157, 195–7, 229–30; and Sacheverell's trial, 152–3; and the Fifteen, 217; and Cadogan, 222; and Prince of Wales, 225, 261, 270, 289; and tories, 231; and Walpole and Townshend, 232, 238 n. 1, 239 n. 1; and

repeal of Test and Corporation Bill, 268–70; rejoins ministry in 1719, 270; removed, 289

Aristocracy, 6–9, 12–15, 18–20, 25, 29; and patriarchal theory of monarchy, 39; influence on local government, 52; and Commons, 64; and Walpole, 137; and succession, 195; and dissenters, 267, 268; and Peerage Bill, 270–1, 278; European, 271; and whigs, 276, 378; and Secret Service money, 348

Army, 21, 72, 78, 155, 166, 167, 214, 222, 246; and Walpole, 131, 132, 133, 136, 140, 143, 144, 261–4, 306; in Scotland, 136, 178–80; estimates for, 140, 143; and recruiting, 132, 140, 143–4, 157–9; mutinies in, 157, 157 n. 1; promotions in, 159; and the Fifteen, 217–18, 256–7

As Bob as a Robin (Anon), 183

Ashby v. White, 112

Astley, Sir Jacob, 1st Bt., 45, 102, 119, 210, 245

Atholl, John Murray, 1st Duke of, 276 n. 1

Atterbury, Francis, Bishop of Rochester, 198, 365

Augustus, King of Saxony, 284

Bacon, Sir Edmund, 6th Bt., 70

Bacon, Waller, MP, 210

Baker, Rev James, 69

Banbury, and corrupt practices, 371–3

Bank of England, 22, 23, 53; and

INDEX

Leeds, Thomas Osborne, 1st Duke of, xvi n. 1, 101, 120 n. 1
Le Gros, Major, 310
Leicester, 4, 59
Leicestershire, 18, 62
Leopold, Emperor, 94, 156
Letter from a Curate in Suffolk to a High Church Member covering the D. of M. and Mr W . . . . le (Anon), 183
Levant Company, 23
Leven, David Leslie-Melville, 3rd Earl of, 136
Lille, 145
Lincoln, Francis Fiennes-Clinton, 6th Earl of, 8
Lindsey, Robert Bertie, 3rd Earl of, 64
Littleton, Sir Thomas, 3rd Bt., 151
Liverpool, 51 n. 1
Local Government, 39, 42, 47, 49, 54, 71
Locke, John, philosopher, 38
Lombard, Peter, 311
London, 7, 23, 27, 31, 214; population, 3; life in, 8, 30; tory strength in, 32; government of, 50, 53-4; representation in Parliament, 56; and whig ministry, 169, 277; and peace with France, 158, 173, 186; and Jacobite riots in, 217; and Northern War, 233; and Quadruple Alliance, 266; and Spanish Alliance, 274; and Bank of England, 295; and John Law's success, 297; and Walpole, 331, 353, 367; and South Sea Company engraftment scheme, 336, 337; and South Sea Company settlement terms, 356
Londonderry, Thomas Pitt, 1st Earl of, 332
Looe (Cornwall), 56

Lord Justices, 76
Lord Lieutenants, 42-4
Lords, House of, cf. also Parliament, 74, 97, 301, 343, 368, 369, 370, 373; and bishops, 67-9; and whigs, 176, 177, 193, 244, 264, 276, 277, 342; creation of tory peers in, 178; and tory government, 193; and Schism Bill, 195; and condemned Jacobite leaders, 220; petitioned by Oxford, 254; and Oxford's trial, 255; and dissenters' bill, 268, 269; and Walpole, 274; and Peerage Bill, 278; and Civil list debt settlement, 288; and Bill against South Sea Company directors, 340; and Hutcheson's elections bill, 372
Lords of the Committee, 133
Louis XIV, of France, 37, 39, 98, 111; and War of the Spanish Succession, 94-5
Lynn, cf. King's Lynn

Madox, Thomas, historian, 50
Malplaquet, 145
Manchester, 50
Mann, Horace, 82
Mann, Robert, 178, 179 and n. 3, 180, 205, 208-9
Mar, John Erskine, 11th Earl of, 217-8
Marchmont, Patrick Hume, 1st Earl of, 276 n. 1
Marlborough, John Churchill, 1st Duke of, 7, 97, 98, 111, 129, 173, 295; and Walpole, 63, 131-4, 159, 166, 204, n. 1; and tories, 63, 168; and Sunderland, 114, 127, 156; and Queen Anne, 118, 141, 146, 151-2, 166, 175; victories of, 118, 127, 142, 145, 168; and Bolingbroke, 130; diffi-

397